PRIVATIZATION
IN THE ANCIENT NEAR EAST
AND CLASSICAL WORLD

PEABODY MUSEUM BULLETIN 5

PRIVATIZATION

IN THE ANCIENT NEAR EAST
AND CLASSICAL WORLD

■

VOLUME I
in a Series by The International Scholars
Conference on Ancient Near Eastern Economics

A Colloquium held at New York University
November 17-18, 1994

EDITED BY
Michael Hudson and Baruch A. Levine

Peabody Museum of Archaeology and Ethnology
Harvard University
Cambridge, MA 1996

TABLE OF CONTENTS

Acknowledgments

It is a reflection of this colloquium's path-breaking choice of topics that no ready-made terminology yet exists to describe the increasingly autonomous private control of land, handicraft workshops and credit from the Bronze Age through classical antiquity. An important feature of these meetings was therefore the interaction among the participants to develop a common vocabulary to clarify and indeed, debate the phenomena being discussed. Tapes of the discussion were made by Lynn Yost, who also designed this book and computerized its composition. Transcription of these tapes, replete as they were with terminology in seven ancient languages, was heroically accomplished by Anne Robertson, to whom I cannot acknowledge sufficient gratitude.

I also would like to thank the major participants for their interest in further pursuing the lines of investigation which this conference opened up. A Scholars Conference on Ancient Near Eastern Economies has been formed, comprising Baruch Levine (New York University), Carl Lamberg-Karlovsky (Harvard University), Muhammed Dandamayev (Institute of Oriental Studies, St. Petersburg) and myself. The group's biannual meetings will be split between New York and St. Petersburg, starting with a colloquium on "Urbanization and Land Use in the Ancient Near East" in 1996-97. Publication of these proceedings will inaugurate a new journal, *Ancient Economies.*

Many thanks are given to the Henry George School and New York University who helped host this inaugural meeting.

Michael Hudson

INTRODUCTION

Privatization:
A Survey of the Unresolved Controversies

The privatization of land, industry and finance over the past four thousand years is a topic that concerns nothing less than the direction of social evolution. Is private enterprise primordial, or does it represent the dissolution of originally public entrepreneurial practices? Is civilization moving toward increasing social control and public regulation, or away from it? Does privatization tend to go hand in hand with increasing economic inequality? If so, will this lead to more investment and more efficient resource use, or to less productive employment and ultimately, fiscal crisis and stagnation?

History provides a rich compendium of social experiments illustrating the private/public dynamic through the ages. Today's privatizations, for instance, are largely a response to public debt crises. Debt likewise was a major lever for privatizing communally held land in Bronze Age Babylonia, but in this case the obligations were personal agrarian arrears, not public debt. Agrarian debt played a similar role in transforming Roman land tenure, but here the large appropriators ended up creating a property-oriented law to secure their privatization of hitherto public land.

Rome's fight turned mainly on political tactics, not on the development of a market-oriented philosophy of privatization. Creditor-oriented jurists did not even begin to formulate a social-contract theory of property. Their objective was to legitimize the expropriation and enslavement of debtors or needy cultivators. The dominant Stoic philosophical school decried this hubristic greed and pined for a lost golden age, which they idealized as an age free of private property, an age in which men were guided by altruism and self-sacrifice rather than self-interest. Adam Smith's principle of an Invisible Hand steering private gain-seeking so as to create public benefits lay far in an unimagined future.

To prehistorians, the social sciences have all but closed their eyes to the archaeological record. Economists are notorious for taking private property for granted as being original and elemental in human history, and hence needing no historical explanation for its evolution. Public resource ownership and management are assumed to be symptoms of economic decadence, arising relatively late in civilization to stifle private enterprise and kill the goose that lays the golden eggs. It follows from this logic that the public enterprise found in early Mesopotamia was a false start whose inherent inefficiencies doomed it to be replaced by the less centralized private enterprise of classical Greece and Rome.

Everyone knows how inefficient and corrupt today's public bureaucracies are. Was this also the case in the Bronze Age with its "Oriental despotism"? Did not the flowering of primordial individualism in classical Greece and Rome liberate key elements of society? In the view of economic individualists we are dealing with two alternative modes of development.

What proves fatal to this foundation myth of free enterprise is the fact that it was Bronze Age Mesopotamia — specifically, Sumer in the fourth and third millennia BC — that developed the earliest entrepreneurial practices. Only in the second and first millennia did Indo-European speakers adapt these practices to a more individualistic, and indeed oligarchic context.

Greek history does not begin in the classical period of Solon and Pericles, but a millennium earlier, in the palaces of Mycenaean Greece. Here, as well as in Ugarit and Cyprus, we find a bridge between the Levant and Mediterranean lands. After the downfall of palace rule and a chaotic interregnum, Syrian and Phoenician merchants appear in the 8th century BC, bringing interest-bearing debt to Greece and Italy. This and related commercial practices shaped the classical takeoff, and also planted the seeds for the way in which it ultimately collapsed. For in the end, privatization of the land and usurious credit did not liberate antiquity, but led to widespread economic enslavement by promoting monopolization of the land — the amassing of properties into vast slave-stocked *latifundia*, which the ancients blamed for their economic decay.

For the past century, economic philosophers have rationalized private ownership as a universally valid and ultimately equitable principle. Yet anthropologically oriented historians have found something quite different in many epochs and regions: communal practices that discourage personal gain-seeking enterprise. Sustained investment and capital accumulation is first legitimized in the temple institutions of southern Mesopotamia (Sumer). It was these public institutions that acted as the prime catalyst for most of civilization's entrepreneurial practices, including the first regular land-rents, interest-bearing debt, bulk trade for profit, contractual formalities, account-keeping, its requisite measures and weights, and so forth.

What is equally remarkable about the Bronze Age Mesopotamian societies is that they managed to stave off the economic polarization that went hand in hand with privatization. Rulers regularly annulled their economy's debt burden so as to limit the privatizing of once-public resources. But ultimately, private wealth grew strong enough to undercut royal power. Privatization — and the emergence of private property as we know it today — became irreversible. Economic power was turned into political power, abolishing royal oversight and removing the richest properties from taxation. Oligarchies proceeded to expropriate poor cultivators and turned them into serflike dependents.

We all know what happened to the Roman Empire after its *latifundia* dynamic ran its course. It declined and fell. Is something similar in store for today's topheavy debtor economies? Will market forces again become swamped by a new growth in debt overhead? Will a new polarization enable the wealthiest classes once again to free themselves of taxes and other traditional obligations of ownership? Or will history be different this time around?

Was land originally held privately, or in communal/public hands?

Babylonian land tenure became a politically debated issue over a century ago, when Henry George ran for mayor here in New York City on the platform that land-rent should be publically collected by the city rather than privately appropriated by landlords. George claimed that throughout most of history, land-use and its rent had belonged to communities rather than to private landowners. He sought to restore older traditions by collecting land rent on behalf of the community at large — whose taxes and economic activity, after all, were paying for the improvements that gave a rising value to the land — leaving private holders to profit only from their investment in capital improvements to their real estate.

Many of George's followers were Irishmen who had emigrated to New York to escape the economic devastation of English landlordship and the famine it caused on the land. Others were Italian and central European immigrants. Given this constituency, it was inevitable that the Catholic Church would feel obliged to take a position in the land-tax controversy. Some bishops suggested treating George with silence, on the logic that to denounce him would merely draw more attention to his campaign. But as public controversy over the issue of land monopolization grew, the Church (and other establishment institutions) felt obliged to respond.

A German Jesuit group published a series of articles in the 1880s by the Swiss-born Father Victor Cathrein, *Stimmen aus Maria-Laach*, denouncing the theories of the French economist Emile de Laveleye as well as those of George.* Laveleye; *Primitive Property* (1878:xxxvii, xxvii) found ancient attitudes toward property governed by the idea of ensuring for all families the means of self-support on the land: "Whether in Europe, Asia and Africa, alike among Indians, Slavs and Germans, and even in modern Russia and Java, the soil was the joint property of the tribe, and was subject to periodical distribution among all the families, so that all might live by their labour, as nature has ordained." According to Laveleye, this practice was grounded in the classical ideal of equality as a precondition for liberty and democracy. Ancient lawmakers "had recourse to all kinds of expedients: inalienability of patrimonies, limitations on the right of succession, maintenance of collective ownership as applied to forests and pasturage, public banquets in which all took part . . ."

This primitive egalitarianism was the true "state of nature" in Laveleye's view, not John Locke's fantasy of private land ownership stemming from a primordial social contract. Surveying the fields of history and anthropology, Laveleye (1878:169) found private property in land to be a relatively late development, emerging only in Roman times. During 121-100 BC, Rome's large landowners destroyed the Gracchi and passed three agrarian laws "favoring the increase of large estates. The first . . . allowed everyone to sell the portion of land which he had received." This law unblocked the way for impoverished landholders to sell their shares to large estate-owners.

The new landlords occupied the *ager publicus* without any firm legal sanction, and were permitted to keep this appropriation by a second Roman law, which left this public land "in the hands of its present holders, a rent being paid by them, the amount of which was to be distributed among

---

* Andelson (1979:126) calls him "the most influential Continental European critic of Henry George." His *Moralphilosophie* and *Der Sozialismus* "went into twenty or more editions," making them the definitive representation of Roman Catholic economic thought. These articles were translated into French, Czech, and into English by upstate New York Jesuits at Canisus College in Buffalo, published in 1888 in the New York *Freeman's Journal*, and reissued the following year as a pamphlet *The Champions of Socialism: A Refutation of Emile de Laveleye and Henry George*. Cathrein elaborated his views in *Das Privatgrundeigentum und seine Gegner* (4th ed., 1909), and *Moralphilosophie*, II, Ch. 3 (1911:II, 257-94).

the citizens. . . . Finally, the third law abolished even the rent; so that nothing remained of the laws of the Gracchi but a single clause, favourable to the aristocracy, which gave a definite title to the possession of public land."

The result, concluded Laveleye, was that "A few sumptuous villas, and immense pasturages, replaced the varied cultivation, which had been carried on by small proprietors of Latin, Samnite, Etruscan or Campanian origin, and had maintained so many flourishing cities. To maintain the populace of Rome and to support the luxury of the great, it was necessary to pillage the conquered countries. Praetors, proconsuls, and public [tax] farmers, fell on the provinces like birds of prey, and ruined them to support the idleness of Rome." Economic polarization, having dried up the internal market by reducing cultivators to poverty and dependency, thus became the motive for Roman imperialism to seize from abroad what no longer was being produced at home. This dynamic inspired Pliny (*Nat. Hist.*, XVIII:7) to decry that *latifundia perdidere Italiam, jam vero et provincias*, "Latifundia have ruined Italy."

Underlying Rome's economic self-destruction was its property-oriented law. Land ownership was legitimized simply by virtue of possession, regardless of how the land was used or what the social consequences were. This was the ultimate in privatization. Considerations of public interest were set aside, and the status quo was blessed. This verdict on Roman law was popularized by Henry George in *Progress and Poverty* (1879), which became the best selling economic book of its epoch and triggered a worldwide land and tax reform movement.

"The steady progress of legal ideas drawn from the Roman law," George accused (1987:372, 382), "has been the great mine and storehouse of modern jurisprudence, [and] tended to level the natural distinction between property in land and property in other things." Roman law made individual proprietorship in land an "extension of personal liberty" for the appropriators rather than for the expropriated cultivators. Subsequent legal practice destroyed "all vestiges of the ancient tenure, and substitut[ed] the idea of Roman law, exclusive ownership." The ensuing struggle between the idea of equal rights to the soil and the tendency to monopolize it in individual possession "caused the internal conflicts of Greece and Rome; it was the check given to this tendency — in Greece by such institutions as those of Lycurgus and Solon, and in Rome by the Licinian Law and subsequent divisions of land — that gave to each their days of strength and glory; and it was the final triumph of this tendency that destroyed both."

This view of the consequences of privatization was attacked by the Jesuits, who drew upon the first fruits of the decipherment of cuneiform. At the heart of the controversy were the Babylonian property contracts that were just beginning to be translated in the 1880s. At the 1881 Congress of Orientalists in Berlin, Father Strassmaier translated the following contract from Larsa's ruler Rim-Sin (18th century BC): "A garden and house, real possession and property of Sini-Nana, property and inheritance (?) of the sons of Ubar-Sin, are assured by contract." The buyers are to pay 3½ mina of silver "as full price. . . . The name of his king he shall call upon (swear)." Father Cathrein (1889:71) concluded that this document made it "manifest with what scrupulous care private property, including the soil, was secured at so remote a period," long before Roman jurists were alleged to have invented private property in land.*

But the contract in question was not about the soil, at least not about subsistence shares in the land. Horticulturists specialized in cash crops. Today, a century after Strassmaier and Cathrein, cuneiformists know that Babylonian houses, orchards and gardens were treated as commercial investments. Unlike subsistence land allocations, these properties were immune from the royal renewals of economic order that restored the means of self-support to Babylonian citizens. These proclamations returned to family lineages the subsistence holdings they had been obliged to sell, pledge or forfeit under economic duress, as well as restoring the liberty of Babylonian citizens and their family members who had been reduced to debt bondage. (Not affected by the proclamations were investments over and above the minimum basic means of self-support, *e.g.* urban real estate, including gardens and fields, commercial silver-loans invested in trade ventures, and foreign slaves that had been bought outright. All these assets were firmly private.)

Also untouched by the royal restorations of order were temple and palace lands. As public property, these lands were set corporately apart from communally held land. Immunity from communal redistribution thus was granted initially to the public sector and its urban area, and only gradually was extended to the holdings of rural usurers. Surplus lands of lineages with shrinking membership probably were the first to pass into the market. Once sold, they became immune from royal restorations of order. Lands taken through debt forfeiture likewise became immune from communal and royal overrides, especially in periods when royal power became weak.

* This duly became official Church doctrine in Leo X's Encyclical *De cadit. opificum* (see Cathrein 1911: II, 276f.).

From at least 2400-1600 BC, subsistence lands seem to have been returned to their customary users when new rulers took the throne or, at a maximum, when kings celebrated their 30th anniversary of rule. The objective of these restorations of the *status quo ante* evidently was to enable cultivators to perform public duties that today are financed by the state: service in the armed forces, work on civic projects such as dike repair, and harvest work on royal lands. These levies were paid in labor services rather than in money to hire labor in the marketplace. (The labor market was too small in an epoch when laborers were not yet "free," *i.e.* not yet driven off the land.) Preserving subsistence land allocations in the hands of Babylonian cultivator families enabled them to use their land and its harvest to support these military and corvée services.

The result was that public sectors had little need either to hire military and public works labor or to levy taxes for this purpose. They also had no public debt. Indeed, temples and palaces were creditors, with the palace being owed corvée labor services and land rent. Bronze Age public sectors were self-supporting from the revenues of temple and royal lands, animal herds, workshops and money loans. Only after the land was privatized was this public self-support undercut.

Nineteenth-century writers had little knowledge of this broad social context of Mesopotamian land tenure, fiscal structuring and what often is called "divine kingship." It seemed reasonable to interpret Babylonian house-sale contracts as confirming the primordial existence of private property in land (as Fustel de Coulanges claimed in *The Ancient City*), in opposition to Laveleye's and George's belief that such property was a relatively late product of Roman law. George and other reformers were branded as utopianists for suggesting that land rents had once been collected by the community and might again be so taken.

In fact, most land in Bronze Age Mesopotamia seems to have been communally held. It did not yet have the earmarks of private property, if only because it was not aimed at producing a regular rent usufruct. Until a surplus could be generated, there was no incentive for absentee ownership save to amass as many clients as possible to build up one's status and power. Land tenure rights were still subject to heavy social obligations, and could not be permanently sold or otherwise alienated.

It appears that property in the modern sense, immune from communal and public overrides, made its first incursions on royal lands in southern Mesopotamia, followed by subsistence lands that had been rendered redundant by the shrinkage of the landholding community's member families. This surplus land seems to have passed into the market process as property "sold at the full price" voluntarily rather than as property relinquished under economic duress.

If this is indeed the case, then privatization of subsistence land, alienable irrevocably at the owner's personal discretion, is not something primordial as social contract advocates have argued, but developed relatively late in history. It thus is necessary to examine how privatization developed in each particular ancient society. How far did each society progress (or fail to progress) toward a Roman-style codification of owner rights? What common denominators emerge as the levers of privatization?

The precedence of public enterprise in the archaeological record

Underlying the problem of the evolution of property is the even more basic question of how landholdings were organized to produce a regular rental income in the first place. Anthropologists speculating on the origins of the state have approached this problem from the military perspective of alien warlords coercing an economic surplus in the form of tribute. Economists tend to view gain-seeking commerce as being inherent in the human spirit, not requiring unique historical conditions to emerge in place of "anthropological" gift exchange. A major question before this colloquium accordingly is whether public management was a necessary catalyst for the systematic taking of rent surpluses. A related question is whether this initially was done in a voluntary or coercive way, *e.g.* as prebend revenues to support temple hierarchies, or as military tribute.

A swing of the ideological pendulum away from social contract theories of private property occurred in the 1920s, when Anna Schneider and Father Anton Deimel put forth the view that the temples had owned *all* the land and enterprise in Early Bronze Age Sumer, or at least in Lagash. The implication was that an archaic system had existed, representing a distinct but geographically unique stage of economic development. But this Asiatic despotism (as Marx had called it) seemed to have been a blind alley with little relation to the Graeco-Roman continuum that fed into modern western civilization.

It is now clear that the temple-state idea was wrong. Southern Mesopotamia's temples did not control all the land but were more in the character of specialized public utilities, set corporately apart from the kinship-based communal sector in a symbiotic relationship to it. To be sure, most of the economic surplus was concentrated in the temples, as most families cultivated on the land on a near-subsistence basis. Personal wealth was obtained mainly by interfacing with the temples, civilization's first business corporations. It was the temples that first developed the practice of charging groundrent and interest, the twin foundations of modern *rentier* income.

In retrospect, we can see the logic in public enterprise appearing prior to private enterprise. The accumulation of capital requires a sustained generation of economic surpluses. These in turn require forward planning and account-keeping, and hence the design of standard weights and measures to form the basis for pricing and charging interest. In addition, land rent and interest presuppose the creation of contractual formalities and enforcement procedures. This seems to be why private gain-seeking emerged first and foremost at the center of society, in its public entrepreneurial institutions.

These preconditions for the subsequent privatization of entrepreneurial activity were developed in a particular time and place — Sumer in the third millennium BC — in a context of temple and palace enterprise. It was this public enterprise that generated (or squeezed out, depending on one's vantage point) civilization's first sustained and regular economic surpluses.

The account-keeping for which public bureaucracies have been notorious throughout history often is viewed as a costly overhead, yet it is a precondition for managing costs and budgeting resources to generate a profit. In this respect public accounting helped pave the way for private management to emerge. Without it, private enterprise would have had to start from scratch among the Indo-European speakers who settled the Aegean and Italy. For them, property was not primordial; it developed as a relatively late, symbiotic formation, catalyzed by innovations made by Bronze Age Sumer's temples and palaces. It thus emerged out of the womb of public enterprise, so to speak.

Maurice Lambert (1960) has described how accountability evolved into a veritable cost engineering under the scribe Enikgal in the Sumerian city of Lagash c. 2350 BC. The process has been traced back to the Uruk period a millennium earlier (Nissen *et al.* 1993). Throughout the Sumerian period, city-temples staffed their workshops, managed inventories and resource flows, rented out their lands and used the proceeds to undertake an expanding horizon of public investment.

When private control of workshops and rent-yielding properties first developed, it did so at the top of society. Ownership was asserted by palace rulers and their families, by leading members of the royal and temple bureaucracies, and by headmen of towns belonging to the imperial system. Personal *rentier* self-seeking proliferated especially among royal collectors and the *tamkaru* "merchants" who functioned as part of the public bureaucracy. To begin one's study of the history of commercial enterprise and private property only in classical antiquity is thus to miss the crucial first act of this great economic drama.

A generation ago, economic historians such as Mikhail Rostovtzeff and Fritz Heichelheim depicted "the state" as being antithetical to private property. Yet public investment by large institutions was undertaken long before the emergence of a private sector as our modern epoch knows it. Contemporary research by Assyriologists points to the state as the great catalyst of private enterprise. It was Sumerian public institutions that created usufruct-yielding lands and set them corporately apart from the periodically reallocated communal subsistence lands.

These public lands included temple lands cultivated directly by dependent personnel belonging to the public institutions; temple or palace lands cultivated by community members on a sharecropping basis; and prebend lands whose crop-rent was set aside for the temple administrators.

Royal property was administered at the ruler's discretion, and in this sense may be considered to be the first truly *private* property. This is just the opposite from the modern idea of progress as evolving from individualistic origins to increasingly large aggregations of wealth and, with it, an overbearing statism that ends up stifling enterprise. We see instead an economic "big bang" c. 3200 BC with the development of writing (first in conjunction with account-keeping), an elaboration of the temples into specialized workshops and other functions, seals and sealing apparatus for administrators, and the use of silver-money. What followed was a diffusion of these innovations from southern Mesopotamia to its trading periphery over the course of the Bronze Age.

Did water systems or trade dependency promote public resource ownership?

One problem still outstanding in the public/private debate concerns the extent to which the need for irrigation water led to public control over the land in Mesopotamia, Egypt, and the Indus and the Oxus river valleys. A number of academic theorists, influenced mainly by some briefly sketched suggestions of Marx, attribute the relative absence of private property in Bronze Age Mesopotamia and Egypt to ecological dynamics inherent in public irrigation systems. Control of the land was centralized in the hands of the ruler by virtue of his control over the water supply, without which crop yields could not be supported. Marx's idea of Asiatic despotism along these lines was picked up by the "hydraulic despotism" theorists Karl Wittfogel and Marvin Harris. But rather than trying to explain the priority of public enterprise in the Bronze Age Near East, their theories concentrate on the stifling impact of public power.

A forceful opponent of hydraulic despotism theories, Robert Adams (1981), has depicted Early Bronze Age irrigation in Mesopotamia as being mainly a local matter. He points out that by the time the Sumerian palaces got involved, it was mainly in the area of digging canals for commercial barge transport. In any event, irrigation was practiced in rainfed regions as well as arid ones.

The next most likely candidate for an economic determinist explanation of the priority of public enterprise in southern Mesopotamia is the region's natural resource dependency. Its rich alluvial soils lack metal ores, gems, and stone for building. As its population and handicraft industry grew, this raw-materials dependency required the organization of trade in unprecedented quantities. The question is, could gift exchange have been elaborated to handle raw-materials trade in bulk? Or did the Sumerians indeed need to trade in a way that went beyond the traditional gift exchange or segmentary trade that had long brought flint and amber to the region? Were its temples and palaces elaborated largely to take action to significantly increase the inward flow of stone and metal ores lacking in local alluvial soils? It is known that they became the coordinating institutions for mercantile disputes and upholders (indeed, sanctifiers) of contracts. And it was mainly temple workshops (and later those of the palaces) that provided the textiles exported in exchange for foreign raw materials.

Could private households have produced handicraft exports on a similar scale without the eventual concentration of production facilities in the hands of a few wealthy families? Did the desire to avoid such polarization motivate the Sumerians to concentrate their production facilities in public institutions? Or, were these institutions themselves controlled by headmen as means of power over their communities?

Who controlled Sumer's temples and benefited from their commercial activities?

Assyriologists continue to debate the extent to which temple administrators were the major beneficiaries of temple enterprise. The answer depends on how open opportunities for trade were, and how widespread the profits. The earliest temple positions may not have provided personal benefits beyond the prestige of holding hierarchic status, but as temples became production centers, opportunities must have grown for lucrative participation in their operations.

McGuiness (1981:54) certainly is right in suggesting that "we might now wish to move away from the attitude which supposed little connection between the economic system and the people who controlled it." However, the path by which individuals became *damgar* merchants and public collectors is not known, nor is the degree to which the earliest consignees of temple advances of goods and loans were akin to strictly private traders. How extensive were opportunities for administrative profiteering? And how much favoritism was shown to particular families in consigning temple textiles or silver?

We know that by the middle of the third millennium, temples left the task of running the scribal schools to leading scribal families, yet the basis on which admission to such schools was determined — or whether it entrenched a bureaucratic caste — is unknown. Particular families probably monopolized the control of temples as early as the fourth millennium BC, but the subsequent secularization of the economic order, and its geographic diffusion, certainly intensified the privatization dynamic.

A symbiosis evidently was at work. Bureaucratic opportunism no doubt increased as temples and palaces became commercial centers. Trade investments were lucrative, while the position of royal collector offered opportunities for petty usury and foreclosure on the assets of debtors in arrears. To the extent that these activities came under the control of just a few families, temple positions would have become important prizes.

It is well documented that by the 24th century BC in Lagash, rulers appointed their own family members to leading temple positions (discussed below, p. 15). This may be a relatively late development, as the palace succeeded the temples. But how far back does nepotism extend? And how do we reconcile the seeming strength of such family ties with the fact that temple administrators at least nominally relinquished their clan identities upon joining the temple brotherhoods? To what extent were their loyalties split?

Prosopography — tracing family connections and public positions through business and administrative archives — is a relatively recent area of research. Individuals can be identified and their careers analyzed via references to their names and patronyms in the surviving documents and inscriptions. From the well documented Third Dynasty of Ur (2112-2004 BC) through the Old Babylonian period, cuneiformists find nepotistic linkages and a worldly *Realpolitik* in the interface between the temple and communal sectors. Rulers and temple administrators are found managing public property virtually as their own, mixing their official correspondence with that of their family members and personal business. Throughout the Middle Bronze Age, observes Veenhof (1986:10), "private archives of some size normally belong to persons of substance. . . . Such persons usually had personal or business connection with the centers of administration, palace and temple . . . and not infrequently held offices." Indeed, our knowledge of many official phenomena, including royal *misharum* acts cancelling debts, derives largely from such private archives and their records of property litigation (Charpin 1980:28ff.).

Hallo (1972) and Zettler (1984/92) have shown that during the Third Dynasty of Ur, Nippur's governor belonged to the same family as did the chief administrators of the city's Inanna temple and perhaps the Enlil temple as well. This family conducted business through the temple for at least five generations, exhibiting a degree of control that seems all the more remarkable in view of Nippur's status as southern Mesopotamia's cult center. Zettler's study of the Inanna temple (1984:441ff.; see also 1992:209f.) elaborates how "the family archive of the chief administrator is mixed in with records of the temple's operations," so that "the distinction between private or family and temple is at best a nebulous one. . . . These texts indicate that members of the family, apparently without holding any official capacity in the organization, were involved in the affairs of the temple," with their own personal records forming "part of the larger temple archive."

Sumer's *damgar* merchants apparently had a landholding position in their communities alongside their public position, as did their Babylonian successors, the *tamkaru*. The earliest temples probably were established at least ostensibly to manage the economic surplus in the collective interest, not to channel it into the hands of particular families. Yet the temples' leasing of land, lending of money and consignment of merchandise for trade ended up increasing opportunities for commercial and financial gain on an unprecedented scale. If administrators and *damgar* collectors remained subject to strict accountability, it no doubt was more the result of each other's jealousy than from popular vigilance.

It seems to be no accident that the term *landlord* still recalls the idea of "lordship." As the first rent-collecting landlords, Sumer's temple and palace workshops (along with their lands and inventories) acted as catalysts for property managed economically to generate a net revenue. These public properties were organized as what modern management calls profit centers (perhaps "rent-center" would be a more appropriate term), yielding a scheduled income (prebend). The incomes from some properties were earmarked for the support of specified administrative offices. Temple prebend-holders thus became history's first documented *rentiers*, that is, individuals living off the proceeds of land worked by others.

The inheritability of prebend annuities within particular families is attested from the eve of the second millennium BC. Over the next four centuries they were bequeathed and subdivided, sold, auctioned off or otherwise transferred. Charpin (1986:260ff.) has shown that successive partitions of inherited prebend income occurred during this period (2050-1650 BC). Only in classical antiquity, however, did commercialization become a normal state of affairs for the landholdings of individuals outside of the public sector. And only in classical times did production and credit pass irrevocably into private hands.

Table 1 summarizes the arguments for and against the theory that individual families created the temples as trusts. The most extreme formulation is that of Zettler in his University of Chicago dissertation (1984: 443f., published as 1992:211), which seeks an analogy to Mesopotamia's temples in the Islamic *waqf*, that is, "real property set aside in perpetuity as a sort of endowment. The endowment must be for a purpose pleasing to God and two kinds are distinguished. *Waqf hairi* is an endowment patently religious and/or charitable in character; *waqf ahli* or family endowment is one whose proceeds go for the support of individuals specified by its founder, for example, his children or grandchildren. When the line of beneficiaries as specified dies out, the endowment falls under the term *waqf hairi* and its proceeds go for pious works and/or charity. The administration of endowments is in the hands of a person appointed by its founder and that person receives a salary. . . . Not infrequently the founder of the endowment acts as administrator. Establishing real property as *waqf* is one way of guaranteeing its integrity and keeping it from being confiscated." The threat in Sumerian times presumably would have been a communal redistribution of temple property.

This theory postulates private enterprise cloaked as public service, with family-oriented estates taking on a communal form as families died out. Zettler finds that when Shulgi rebuilt the Inanna temple, he turned its control over to Ur-Me-Me's family, who expended its income as if it represented "extended family-shares in the proceeds." He concludes that "the character of control held by the family of Ur-Me-Me over the temple of Inanna at Nippur is the result of that family's having given over, at whatever date, a block of its real property for the support of the temple. In this way the family could guarantee the integrity of its property and, presumably, its continued prosperity and prominence." Zettler assumes that family control of this property remained after it passed into temple hands, much like *naditu* heiresses managing their wealth through the temples.

Stone (1986) seems nearer the truth in viewing Ur-Me-Me as one of Amorite chieftains pressing into southern Mesopotamia from the western desert after about 2050 BC, and being bought off by the tribute-gift of prebends from what originally had been a communal institution. The Nippur temple's earliest foundations date back to Sumer's late Uruk period c. 3400 BC. There is no evidence that its founders belonged to a single family, or that any family remained in control through the Uruk, Jemdet Nasr and Early Dynastic periods (certainly no modern aristocracies can boast of such longevity). The greater likelihood is that each dynastic change opened the way for new arrangements to be made. Temples give every indication of having begun as communal trusts, ending up as family operations only in the wake of social upheavals or folk wanderings that weakened central authority in "intermediate periods." In this reading the Nippur temple most likely originated as a public entity and was appropriated during the Ur III regime by Ur-Me-Me's family in exchange for their delivering the city's important support to Ur's rulers.

It is easy to draw parallels between the privatization of temple wealth in the second and first millennia BC and the emergence of modern secular capitalism out of medieval Islamic and Christian forms of property. However, I think it is anachronistic to retroject modern forms of individualism back to the Bronze Age. The "family trust" theory of the origins of the Sumerian temples leaves too many loose threads. Did families other than the dominant one contribute resources? If so, how voluntary were their contributions? What did they get in return? What happened to the successive dominant families associated with Nippur's temple at one time or another after its fourth-millennium establishment?

The Marxist anthropologist Allen Zagarell (1986: 163, 170) believes that Sumer's temples always were controlled by family elders, if not by individual families. This view is plausible, but no evidence exists one way or another. A less cynical (and to me, more probable) logic of development would be an originally communal objective subverted to benefit particular families as wealth levels increased and economic relations began to polarize. Managerial families no doubt strove to minimize popular reaction by keeping up customary appearances, conforming to traditional communal expectations and developing a public rhetoric that evoked the common good. Such sanctimonious pretensions are found throughout history between rulers and subjects, masters and slaves, patrons and clients, and creditors and debtors. The question is, was there an original substance to this rhetoric?

Lagash rulers, as noted earlier, used the temples to build up their own patronage systems late in the Early Dynastic period, c. 2350 BC. But when Lugalanda directed the priests to turn over much of their income from performing burial and related ceremonial services to the palace, he was accused of encroaching on temple (and hence communal or "aristocratic"?) prerogatives, and temple administrators sponsored a coup. The new ruler, Urukagina, lowered the charges for priestly ceremonies, and probably also let the temples keep the proceeds for themselves, but retained firm palace control over public administration by placing his wife and children in charge of major temples.

No doubt temple administrators obtained more benefits as empire-building loosened local checks and balances. Temple offices often were inherited in Early Dynastic times, but there is no evidence of prebend incomes being passed down and subdivided within particular families independently of the actual performance of temple functions. If family control already was in place, it seems far from having evolved into a situation such as that of Ur-Me-Me's family in Nippur, to say nothing of classical antiquity's aristocracies.

The reality of how Sumerian temples were structured probably lies in between the "temple service" and "aristocratic" extremes, gradually evolving into vehicles for personal gain. It is plausible that early temple operations were administered by communal-sector families who, *ipso facto*, were in a position to turn their public office to some degree of personal advantage. But other families would have sought either to prevent undue profiteering or to join in it, pressing for an equitable distribution of temple power and proceeds.

My own view is that a catalytic institution was necessary to induce neolithic and other archaic communities to break the traditional social sanctions against gain-seeking trade and the accumulation of fixed capital investment. The traditional outlook was that wealth should serve the community. Temples were the line of least resistance in creating prestige export-handicraft workshops by pooling the community's resources, centralizing the economic surplus so that it did not pass into the hands of only a few families. Communalist values, including the desire for public acclaim for having served a higher social power, probably helped motivate early families to perform public functions. Even where individual families controlled the temples, the force of communalist values often would have deterred them from blatantly exploiting their position. But meanwhile, temple sponsorship of handicraft industry, trade and landlordship helped sanctify, and hence promote, commercial functions among the population at large.

One obvious question is why the temples kept accounts at all if they merely were fronts for individual families. Their cost accounting, associated with elaborate procedures of sealing storerooms and saving delivery receipts and allocation records, gives all appearances of developing as a means to check administrative abuses. Temple storerooms held communal grain, sesame and other food, as well as tools. Throughout history, accountability has been associated primarily with public administration and only secondarily with family affairs. Bronze Age temple officials were subservient to the ruler, and rulers are known to have visited temples from time to time to see that royal gifts remained intact.

Roth (1986) discusses an Ur III example in which the administrator of Nippur's Inanna temple was sued by his son (first unsuccessfully and then with success), but formal accounting is too important an innovation to have resulted simply from intrafamily squabbles. In any event, the standardizing of costs and product runs hardly could have resulted merely from informal family business procedures. It thus seems dubious to me that Sumerian families originally donated their property to the city-temple in tacit exchange for control of its operations and revenue.

Mycenae's position in the East/West public/private continuum

What intruded into the neat geographic and chronological dichotomy between Oriental and Western civilization was the anomaly of Bronze Age Greece, Crete and the Phoenician shore of the Levant. Greek history begins not with Athens and Sparta, but in the western periphery of the Late Bronze Age world, in Mycenae and other Late Bronze Age towns c. 1400-1200 BC. Here, Mesopotamian practices were transmuted into something new as the Mycenaean Greek palaces adopted syllabic record keeping (Linear B), sealing, and large workshop production — but not interest-bearing debt. The closest we come to debt, note Ventris and Chadwick (1956:118), is in Mycenaean tablets which "contain a total derived by simple addition from the separate items of the list, or a subtraction to show the amount 'missing' by comparison with the expected contribution."

Not only is debt missing, but money too: "Since the palace revenue is presumably derived from feudal dues and from foreign conquest, monetary or other media of exchange do not play any significant part in the

TABLE 1

WERE SUMER'S TEMPLES TRULY PUBLIC, OR MERELY FAMILY TRUSTS?

EVIDENCE FOR PUBLIC FUNCTIONS PRIOR TO 2100 BC	ARGUMENTS FOR TEMPLES SERVING AS FAMILY TRUSTS FROM 2100 BC

1. Locus of the economic surplus

Sumer's economic surplus had to be generated mainly by the temples and palaces, because traditional social sanctions blocked individualistic profiteering.	Self-interest is a primordial drive, although it often is obliged to protect itself by expending part of its profits to provide conspicuous social benefits.

2. Accountability

Accountability historically has been a characteristic of the public sector. Temples were strictly accountable so as to block administrative peculation by individuals in offices of trust.	In Ur III times, sons are found suing their fathers for misappropriating temple resources under family control.

3. Standardization of operations

The standardization of measures and weights, rations, prices and other public functions suggests centralized innovation.	Economic standards may have emerged simply from the logic of competition. Out of an original pluralism, one set of standards would have emerged preeminent in any event.

4. Corporate permanence of public institutions

Temples and palaces were endowed with land and working capital that were inalienable, indivisible, and not subject to communal redistribution, whereas family wealth (including temple prebends, once they passed into family control) was divided with each new generation.	Families used inheritable temple prebends as sinecures or trusts to support their heirs from one generation to the next, free of the threat of the family's wealth being returned to the communal pot through traditional property redistribution.

records. We have not yet been able to identifiy any payments in silver or gold for services rendered, such as at Alalakh" (*ibid.*:113). In lieu of money and the flexibility it affords for an efficient specialization of labor, the Mycenaeans denominated their levies in standardized "bundles" of commodities fixed in proportion. In the Pylos *Ma-* tablets, for instance, a number of townships are put down for contributions whose mutual proportions of six commodities remain constant at 7:7:2:3:1½:150.

No evidence of debt appears in Greece and Italy until it is introduced by Syrian and Phoenician merchants around the 8th century BC. Without intersectoral debt balances there was little need for rulers to cancel arrears as part of general restorations of order. Thus, the entire character of kingship became less commercially oriented (and less public).

The fact that centralized public property and traditions of royal oversight were weakest in Greece and Italy probably contributed to the fact that privatization developed most easily in these formerly peripheral regions after palace authority collapsed throughout the Mediterranean and Levant c. 1200 BC in the wake of a general social breakdown and drastic shrinkage of population and commercial activity.

The unsettled conditions of this period are reflected in the sudden elevation of the *basileus,* who had appeared in Mycenaean times as a local workshop overseer coordinating production and allocating rations on behalf of the palace, typically in subordinate towns and outlying regions. "The title *pa₂-si-re-u* is clearly to be connected with the Homeric *basileus,* who is not king, but a kind of feudal lord, master of his own territory but owing allegiance to the king," note Ventris and Chadwick (1956:121f.). Chester Starr (1961:130ff.) emphasizes that "One must always keep in mind the limited strength of the *basileus,* who dominated only a small area." After the collapse of palace authority, the *basileis* occupied the formerly royal estates, which became the "*temenos* assigned to them by the tribal community" or which they simply appropriated.

Records are missing for the Dark Age that lasted half a millennium. When the darkness lifts, c. 700 BC, the *basileus* is remembered as nothing less than a king. Evidently, after the dissolution of palace control in the 12th century BC, local managers consolidated their position as administrators of hitherto royal estates, keeping the usufruct for themselves.

Possession of these large economic households enabled the *basileus* to emerge as chieftain-king of his local community. However, he was less a ruler in the Mesopotamian tradition than a victor in the Dark Age war of all against all. Operating more unchecked than his Sumerian and Babylonian forebears, he did not issue New Year proclamations freeing debt bondsmen and restoring to customary holders the lands they had forfeited for debt or sold under economic duress. Just the opposite: He profiteered from the land's social distress by reducing its occupants to clientage to his own household. These were the kings who were overthrown and exiled by the 7th and 6th century tyrants.

By the 8th and 7th centuries BC the *basileis* were fading away, unable to "harness the main forces which might have aided them in assuming the central direction of society" (Starr, *loc. cit.*). The most important economic functions passed irreversibly into the hands of aristocratic wealth-holders, whose political power found itself unchecked by any central authority.

To private-enterprise oriented interpreters of history, observes Starr (1961:129 and 136f.), this decline of monarchy is a logical complement to the rise of the *polis*. Greek urbanization thus appears as a consequence of democratic privatization. Whereas medieval Europe's feudal lords "usually failed in efforts to curb the monarchs of England and France, the nobles of archaic Greece succeeded in dragging the *basileis* down to their level." Yet in Bronze Age Sumer and Babylonia, rulership and the *polis* emerged together. The earliest urban area was nearly coterminous with the public area and the complementary civil-sector buildings facing it. At the end of this process, Mesopotamia's rulers were unseated not by democratic movements from below, but by a royal delegation of authority by Hammurapi to local headmen in return for their military loyalty, and ultimately by alien chieftains and their bands occupying the land after 1595 BC.

It is with this militarized decentralization that classical antiquity proper begins, not as pristine youth as such, but in a state of breakdown of the old centralized social *dirigisme*. Paramount among the adoptions and adaptations was the privatization of land on a rent- and interest-paying basis by the emerging oligarchies. What occurred in classical antiquity's takeoff was thus not a new civilization brought by Indo-European speakers with distinctly individualistic economic traditions. Rather, antiquity privatized the catalytic Bronze Age "big bang" that had produced entrepreneurial institutions within a public framework that can be traced back to the Uruk expansion c. 3500 BC. This reading of history manages to incorporate Bronze Age Mesopotamia into the Western continuum. Instead of juxtaposing centralized and individualistic societies, this more historically comprehensive view sees both Bronze Age Mesopotamia and classical antiquity as "mixed economies" characterized by symbiotic relations between public and private life.

A modern parallel to what happened in Dark Age Greece can be seen in Russia's recent privatizations. As the Communists fell from power in the early 1990s, high-ranking Party officials — the top levels of the *nomenklatura* — registered state factories and other properties in their own names. They also seized for themselves a reported $13 billion in Russian foreign-exchange reserves, and formed a devil's alliance with the emerging forces of organized crime. Thus did the apparatchicks take the lead in privatizing Russian property.

Everyone got to keep the assets they occupied at the moment when communism was superseded by market turmoil. Families kept their apartments and dachas, farmers their lands and workers were given nominal equity in their factories. What followed was an economic polarization whereby the former bureaucrats emerged on top, and the old layers of society replicated themselves in what ostensibly was a "free market" atmosphere.

The British had long sponsored privatizations of a related variety in their colonies, as did France and other European powers. In Saudi Arabia the British authorities registered communal and subsoil wealth in the name of the ruling Saudi family. European powers did the same thing in Africa, often recognizing private ownership by chieftains only to have their own private businessmen quickly pry away this wealth through the debt lever or outright sale. This kind of development inspired by contact with a more commercialized society is just what Ugarit's public laws banned in the 13th century BC.

Classical Greek privatization presupposed an ability by the new *basilae* to protect their properties from interlopers seeking to become the land's new masters. The successful *basilae* mobilized their clientele and other dependent labor for military defense, and perhaps also to wage offensive campaigns against rival headmen.

This need to mobilize armed force evidently contributed to a democratization, at least as long as communities relied on their own *demos*-infantry and followed the time-honored practice of giving war veterans their own plots of hitherto public lands (often land that had been seized from defeated populations). Such grants enabled cultivators to outfit themselves for war according to their economic rank.

One finds a similar practice in Babylonian times, when Hammurapi settled members of the armed forces on royal lands. Many of these settlers fell into debt, above all to members of the royal bureaucracy who put their own interest claims on the land's crop yield ahead of royal claims. It was at this point that a conflict developed between the palace, private creditors (typically semi-public officials acting in their own personal capacity), and the local self-governing communities whose common law had not been designed to cope with these usury dynamics. (I will return to this point below, p. 28.)

Hammurapi and other rulers countered this privatization of credit and land tenure by periodically freeing Babylonia's populace from personal debt. However, the upheavals that culminated a thousand years later, in classical antiquity, saw the palaces lose power to aristocracies throughout most of the ancient world. With the evolution of these aristocracies into oligarchies, the Greek and Roman armies were disenfranchised, mainly through debt foreclosure. The epoch of privatization had arrived. The Roman tribune Tiberius Gracchus decried to the men of Rome, "You are called the lords of the world, yet have no right to a square foot of its soil. The wild beasts have their dens, but the soldiers of Italy have only water and air." Out of this privatization of the land a new social and economic ideology emerged: that of the imperial Roman law of property.

Mineral rights, from public to private

Public ownership of subsoil mineral rights is a tradition that has survived into the modern epoch in most parts of the world, although often by passing into the hands of monarchs these rights essentially became privatized. No doubt from neolithic times onward, key public gathering places and natural resources such as springs were sanctified and hence set apart from the control of any one family or group. In general, Bronze Age and ancient communities appear to have used their natural resources as public wealth rather than letting them be privately appropriated. In the 5th century BC, Athens derived a major portion of its revenues by leasing out its Laureon silver mines. Around the same time, salt mines in the Hallstatt culture's Alpine regions seem to have been managed in a similarly public manner. In medieval times, European rulers pledged — and forfeited — their mineral holdings to creditors, as when the Habsburgs lost their Spanish silver mines to the Fuggers.

Today, mineral resources not only are passing into private hands, but the oil and mining industries have turned their economic power into political power, obtaining tax-avoidance rights. Thanks to their depletion allowances and related tax-accounting loopholes, they now pay the lowest taxes of any sector. This is antithetical to the spirit in which ancient societies managed their mineral wealth.

Industrial workshops

The transition from subsistence handicraft production to public-sector production for sale and indeed, for export, is not fully understood. Households are found throughout history producing handicrafts for self-use. Metal-smithing hearths are found in what appear to be family households in Bronze Age Sumer. In Greece and Italy, handicraft production was concentrated in the *oikos* households from the outset, starting with the royal households in Mycenaean times.

What is important to recognize is how differently handicraft technology was organized in the large public institutions as compared to households producing for self-use. Public workshops produced for commercial sale in standardized batches. Accordingly, Sumer's industrial design and technology were set up to dovetail neatly into the temple and palace cost-accounting systems, along with standardized rations for dependent labor and standardized measures for raw-materials inputs so as to readily calculate production costs. Household production was less formalized, and had little need of detailed cost accounting.

What is not known is the extent to which temples and palaces earned their profits on marking up their industrial prices, as compared to land-rent and interest income. How were sales and purchase prices determined? Did interest accrue on inventories advanced to merchants? Non-economists tend to underestimate the importance of these questions, yet in our own modern society, large retail stores such as Macy's in New York earn the bulk of their profits not on their direct cash sales but via credit card transactions on which they charge monthly interest. General Motors Acceptance Corporation and General Electric likewise have used their production and sales systems largely as a means to promote their consumer debt operations. At first glance this may seem to be a case of the tail wagging the dog, but since the 1960s its profitability has been well known to retail planners and stock analysts.

There thus is good reason to ask whether the Sumerian temples and, in time, palace workshops also obtained a large part (or even most) of their gains by charging interest. It appears that the tradition of charging 1/60th per month (20% per year) on commercial balances originally was formalized by these public institutions. There is no documentation to tell us the character of temple and palace sales, however. Output presumably was turned over to merchants for subsequent sale abroad and at home. But on what terms was it sold, and why is such documentation lacking, given that the Sumerian and Babylonian economies were so extensively documented in other respects?

The absence of export documents suggests that trade in temple handicrafts and the monetary metals was conducted by merchants (otherwise, temple records would have survived). To what extent were these merchants acting privately and to what extent publically? Were temple goods (including raw materials for re-export, monetary gold and silver, tin and precious stones) advanced at interest calculated monthly, as is attested in private commercial contracts? Were the tablets broken when the obligations were paid off, something like burning the mortgage in modern times? (Merchants presumably would have been careful to repay debts to the temples and palace in order to maintain their privileged status.) It is necessary to ask these questions in order not only to estimate the profitability of the temple and palace enterprises, but to trace the course of their privatization.

Is it helpful to think of Sumer's temples as public utilities? Were certain industries considered public needs, much like water, to be provided at cost (or at a subsidized rate) rather than at a profit? Were they organized merely on a break-even basis to support their dependent labor, or was a profit generated?

In what ways did palace rulers benefit from temple activities? We know that classical Sparta's kings received the hides from meat sacrifices, presumably to use in their own leather workshops. If similar profits were provided in Bronze Age Mesopotamia, should they be considered to be public or private in character?

A related question concerns the character of Bronze Age professional guilds, which seem to have been organized as "company unions" run from the top down, not as self-promoting craft unions. (Hammurapi's laws regulated prices or wages for public professions.)

How much industry and professional labor was concentrated in the temples and palace relative to the household sector? Finally, with regard to private hearths and workshops, how much of their smithing and weaving output entered the market rather than being used simply to meet subsistence needs?

Commerce and merchants

The chief Bronze Age opportunities for private enterprise lay in mercantile trade. As noted above, Near Eastern merchants interfaced with the temples and palaces but traded on their own behalf. Indeed, when Alan Wace excavated the 13th century BC town of Mycenae, he found it reasonable to assume (in Bennett 1958:3) that it was organized much like a medieval English town. Outside the city wall he found some buildings with storerooms containing large numbers of jars, and designated these sites as "The Wine-Merchant's House" and "The Oil-Merchant's House" rather than as public magazines. After all, who else but private merchants would have been likely to store large amounts of expensive wine and oil?

There seemed little need to explain how enterprise and wealth came to be privatized, for it appeared natural for individuals to conduct commerce for profit and to charge interest on loans. Historians of antiquity found it natural for creditors to demand security for these loans in the best form of collateral available — the land — and to employ this land in the most profitable way, by replacing subsistence grain production with luxury-export crops such as olive oil and wine.

Ventris and Chadwick (1956:110) interpret the fact that tablets written in six different hands have been found in these Mycenaean houses as reflecting a relationship to the royal bureaucracy, for writing was a function restricted to royal scribes. The absence of private usage of Linear B is suggested by the archaeological fact that no styluses, pens or ink-pots have been unearthed in any Mycenaean site. Nor was Linear B used for descriptive texts, wall paintings or any monumental inscriptions as were the Egyptian hieroglyphs and other ancient scripts. It was limited to economic account-keeping. As Ventris and Chadwick conclude, "the almost identical sign-forms, spelling, phraseology and tablet shape and arrangement shown at Knossos, Pylos and Mycenae . . . may themselves show that writing was the preserve of specialists trained in a rigidly conservative scribal school."

Ventris and Chadwick conclude that the Greeks adopted Mesopotamian administrative practices in a thinner layer than occurred in the Levant. These borrowings were limited to the palaces, which probably evolved out of the households of chieftains. When royal control fell apart in the fighting after 1200 BC, writing and other centralized practices disappeared along with the rest of the bureaucratic systems.

None of this logic deterred Wace from sticking to his guns and anglicizing the ruins of Mycenae. Doubting that the storehouses outside the wall were appendages of the royal administration, he concluded that they were owned by "wealthy merchants or nobles" belonging to a Mycenaean "upper or middle class." This was an ethnocentric fantasy not unlike Tolkein's hobbits, for subsequent archaeological interpretation has confirmed that these houses were part of the public storage and warehousing network. Prosopographic analysis of the tablets found in them has shown that the oil was distributed to various palace professional workers, including woolmakers, seventeen bakers, a smith and potter, while other tablets "seem to be the record of clothes or cloths issued to members of a large household" (Ventris and Chadwick 1956:110, 322). Three prominent individuals named in these tablets belonged to the royal bureaucracy. Thus, the occupants of these structures were carrying out functions very different from those of an English guild merchant.

The belief that houses with large stores of inventories belonged to private merchants of *any* type might be more acceptable if it included a clear idea of the merchant's social position. Perhaps a less modern term than "merchant" should be used. One is tempted to revert to the Babylonian word *tamkarum*, the quasi-public individual acting on his own while having public status in the palace hierarchy, as Yoffee (1977) has shown. Acting within these public hierarchies, the *tamkaru* dealt on their own account as well as on behalf of the large temple and palace institutions (Oppenheim 1954). In Sumerian times they received temple rations and mules (Frankfort 1951). This mixture of public and private functions characterized most Bronze Age Near Eastern economies, but by Babylonian times many officials were acting largely on their own behalf, trading and lending money at interest and giving priority to their own loan collections in preference to palace claims on the rural usufruct.

From the Early Bronze Age to late classical antiquity, historians can trace society's economic dynamics (and the economic surplus) becoming more individualistic and free from central oversight. Individualism first emerges, culturally and economically, not from members of the "communal" (non-public) sector, but from palace rulers and their families. Even the Lagash reformer Urukagina, sponsored as ruler by the temples, is found with his family members administering the temple and palace estates virtually as personal domains just prior to Sargon's Akkadian epoch c. 2350 BC. This practice seems also to have characterized his predecessor Lugalanda.

Personal property in the modern sense developed originally in the palace sector. It was the ruler's own property that was the first to be made immune from communal-sector redistribution. Sargon's dynasty took over the temples to make the flow of surplus a one-sided tribute for vanquished cities to the new capital at Akkad. In this respect military conquest was a major catalyst of privatization. Palace warlords captured what originally had been public institutions, and transformed them into instruments of their personal economic power.

Mercantile trade became private in classical Athens and Rome, and indeed, dominated by foreigners. This tendency became even more pronounced in medieval Europe, whose paradigmatic outsiders were Jews and Levantines. At first glance these outsiders would seem to have been private merchants as in the modern sense, yet the Jews brought into England by William the Conqueror were the "king's serfs," wards of the crown, just as they were "servants of the chamber" under the German Emperor Frederick II (the "chamber" in this case being the counting room). The English kings established a special treasury, the Scaccorum Judaeum, to tax Jewish usury income. In this way the charging of usury and retail profiteering, condemned for the Christian population, became socially acceptable royal functions. This illustrates once again the public/private symbiosis which characterizes enterprise down to the present day.

Despite the customary ethic against profiteering from one's neighbors, classical and medieval rulers hardly could prohibit their subjects from charging interest and profits. But foreigners were prohibited from owning land in classical Athens, as in medieval England and France. Without this right, foreigners could not foreclose on land in settlement of debts. However, the traditional ethic of keeping land and natural resources in the control of local communities was undermined as domestic creditors came from near the top of the social pyramid — the leading families in classical Greece and Rome, and the medieval Lombard bankers linked to the Roman papacy.

Credit and interest

Interest-bearing debt became the prime lever of classical privatization, enabling wealthy family heads to pry away the land of smallholders. Elected officials in some Greek city-states pledged *not* to cancel debts or redistribute the land — just the opposite principle of Bronze Age rulership. Under these conditions the protected property was no longer that of the citizenry at large, but the large estates and fortunes of the few. Debt relations became even more polarized in Rome, where wealthy creditors turned what had been communally held subsistence landholdings into *latifundia* slave plantations.

It is curious that Assyriologists have not yet tried to explain how interest originated. Such a discussion now needs to be ventured in view of the fact that interest-bearing debt became the pivotal factor in the ancient economy, culminating in the collapse of the Roman Republic and Empire under an insupportable debt burden.

I therefore would like to suggest some issues that need to be resolved in order to place interest-bearing debt in its public/private context. An important hint regarding the character of early interest is the fact that it is first attested in Sumer at the interface between the public and communal sectors. Interest accrued on arrearages or other imbalances in the scheduled transfer of economic surpluses to the temples or palace by community members. Barley debts, for instance, represented financial claims arrears on sharecropping rents or related public fees. But no interest-bearing claims are found in the non-bifurcated economies of Mycenaean Greece, which only scheduled district contributions to the palace. (It is as if Mycenaean rulers either controlled all the land, or were empowered to tax it in a cone-shaped hierarchy.)

Why did interest-bearing debt originate in southern Mesopotamia, how did it spread, and what were its effects? With regard to commercial debts, I have suggested above that the temple workshops advanced goods at interest to merchants. This cannot be confirmed, yet I submit it as a working hypothesis until someone suggests a better explanation. *Some plausible scenario is needed*, and I hope that the participants in this conference will venture their thoughts.

Did interest-bearing credit indeed originate in southern Mesopotamia's large public institutions? Did it take the form of interest paid to the temples and palaces by individuals at large? And did commercial credit first evolve as payments by merchants to the temples for advances of commodities for trade? Or are other scenarios just as likely?

Taxes (and ultimately, fiscal crises) as a byproduct of privatization

As privatization increased — as industry and land passed into the hands of a proto-oligarchy — the state had to levy taxes in order to hire a mercenary army rather than continuing to provide domestic cultivators with land in exchange for military and other labor services. In classical Greece, money taxes on the land paid for public work, which was performed mainly by immigrants and other non-citizens, even slaves (a reflection of the demeaning status of public labor throughout antiquity) in place of the earlier levies of *corvée* labor.

The passing of rents, interest and profits into private hands (especially those of the wealthy) led to taxation of the commons for the benefit of large landowners. This was done in such a way as to aggravate the dispossession process. The state meanwhile reduced its role as public entrepreneur as its functions were taken over by private entrepreneurs. As Rostovtzeff has documented, the Roman state increasingly absorbed the costs or "externalities" associated with private wealth-seeking by the richest families (including the cost of defending the land against both domestic civil warfare and foreign enemies).

With privatization of the land, and the parallel shift of the handicraft export industries into private hands, came tax crises. The wealthiest families managed to avoid taxes, while pushing more and more of their own expenses onto the public budget. Instead of government reforming land tenure or taking over industry and socializing its revenues, economic control passed almost entirely into private hands. For all practical purposes, the wealthiest landowners became "the state," in alliance with barbarian war chieftains who seized land by military force.

Was Rostovtzeff right in holding that socialism strangled antiquity, or was privatization the culprit? The Stoics blamed Rome's decay on the *hubris* of wealth. Christians elaborated this idea by decrying society's inability to control personal egoism. Both groups idealized the Bronze Age as a mythical Golden Age in which individuals were guided by altruism rather than by economic selfishness of the type that clearly was destroying the Roman world.

Long before Pliny blamed the latifundia for ruining Italy, Judah's prophet Isaiah (5:8-9, c. 700 BC) had decried landholders "who add house to house and join field to field till no space is left" and the land became depopulated. One accordingly must ask if land monopolization spoiled Mesopotamian development too? Indeed, may the past four thousand years be viewed as a series of recoveries from repeated privatizations extending from Bronze Age Mesopotamia in the intermediate Dark Age periods of the second millennium BC to the Roman empire, culminating in the Byzantine experience in the 9th to 11th centuries of our era? Or is more helpful to view history as a steady advance toward the liberating force of private enterprise as it sheds the impeding constraints of public oversight?

The answer, of course, depends on one's political ideology. Assyriologists and prehistorians have spent a century trying to rid their disciplines of such ideological preconceptions. But social theorists across the broad political spectrum, ranging from private-enterprise advocates to Polanyi's substantivist followers, are not hesitant to use Bronze Age findings as an excuse to project modern ideas backward in time.

Matters are complicated by the fact that the documents do not really speak for themselves. They are too terse to explain the social structures and ideology at work. If this colloquium does not venture its informed opinions in the debates still outstanding with regard to the causes and consequences of privatization in antiquity, then others with less knowledge will do so.

As summarized below, the major debates concern how and when the land came to be privatized. How far did economies prior to Rome travel along the privatization path? Were the temples truly public institutions, or merely fronts for private administrators? To what extent did privatization result in economic inequality? Were its social consequences more beneficial than corrosive? And most importantly, what do we *mean* by privatization? Can we define the term in a manner that can be used cross-temporally and cross-culturally?

Ultimately, what was being privatized was the economic usufruct, but the entire productive system was transformed in the process. The generation of a surplus became associated with reductions in the wages and living standards for dependent personnel, and the transformation of free cultivators into debt-bondsmen or outright slaves, while the traditional communal claims on the land's surplus were forgotten. (The culmination of this process occurred in the nineteenth century with the development of the privately held limited-liability corporation, which no longer needs a royal charter or public purpose as a condition for its incorporation.)

Outright property ownership was the most direct way to expropriate the surplus in ancient times. It legally excluded all communal claims on the usufruct. In the case of land, the surplus consisted of rent, and in the case of credit it consisted of interest, while handicraft industry yielded profits. At a certain point the process became self-destructive. The productive system shrank rather than expanded. To what extent may this development have been planted in the early entrepreneurial organization of agriculture, handicrafts and credit in the Sumerian temples and palaces?

What has not achieved consensus are the causes of Sumer's economic "big bang." Did irrigation or some other powerful material factor stimulate its society to overcome the traditional sanctions against personal self-seeking? And was the subsequent privatization planned and in keeping with traditional social values, or unplanned and ultimately destructive of these values?

To frame these issues, Table 2 provides a provisional list of the virtues and shortcomings of privatization and public enterprise respectively. I hope the other participants in this colloquium will add to the list. If we are unable to reach consensus on all the controversies outlined above, perhaps at least we can establish what remains to be settled.

Michael Hudson

TABLE 2

VIRTUES OF PRIVATIZATION	VIRTUES OF PUBLIC ENTERPRISE
Avoids the inefficiencies of bureaucratic management.	Breaks down traditional communal sanctions against the accumulation of economic surpluses.
Restricts royal grandiosity and hubristic pride (*viz.* the Stoic myth of the Rape of Lucretia).	Restricts victimization of the landed population at large by managing property in the public interest.
Cuts unproductive "external" costs and overhead.	Provides socially necessary services at or below cost (Example: Britain's BBC).

SHORTCOMINGS OF PRIVATIZATION	SHORTCOMINGS OF PUBLIC ENTERPRISE
A petty market mentality seeks the "bottom line," not the interests of society as a whole.	An uneconomic public mentality is reluctant to run itself "efficiently."
Private enterprise limits itself to what is productive.	Public enterprise often is restricted to non-profitable welfare types of spending that subsidize inefficiency.
Leads to monopolization of the land and industry. Disenfranchisement of smallholders by expropriating their land through debt and other forms of economic duress.	Distributive equity is achieved at expense of economic efficiency. Example: The so-called "tragedy of the (unmanaged) commons."
Private operators cut expenses by throwing the external cleanup costs onto the public. (The idea of good government, in a privatized society, is to "socialize the losses.")	Public corruption and favoritism. No checks and balances preventing mega-engineering mistakes, *e.g.* pollution.
Interest-bearing debt claims tend to outrun the economy's capacity to pay, leading to mass bankruptcies and economic polarization.	Inflates the public debt to finance projects that benefit special interests, *e.g.* military contractors and war financiers.
More and more people in each community are excluded from rights to the commons, while the few remaining are obliged to bear the costs of supporting public infrastructure and the state.	A Procrustean bed of cost-plus price and profit supports, often politically, corruptly or otherwise non-economically motivated.

Summary of Issues

Major problems remain unresolved with regard to the transition from public to private patterns of land tenure, handicraft enterprise, mining, credit, and also of the arts, religion and culture. The most important problems concern:

- whether private, freely alienable ownership of the land (and hence its ability to be forfeited for debt arrears) was "original" or a relatively late and secondary development;

- whether the first breakthroughs in organizing the land and handicraft industry for profit, and to accumulate and systematically reinvest capital, were achieved by public institutions or by private households;

- whether the precedence of public enterprise in Sumer can be attributed to geographic factors such as irrigation needs or trade dependency on foreign raw materials;

- whether southern Mesopotamia's large temple and palace institutions were ever truly public, or were controlled from the outset by ruling families;

- the extent to which personal property and individualism emerged from the royal palace ("the state") rather than from the communal sector at large;

- the extent to which Bronze Age "merchants" held public or quasi-public status, and how their activities came to be privatized with the dissolution of centralized public authority;

- whether classical Graeco-Roman antiquity represents a new continuum based on inherent individualism, or whether its commercial practices are an offshoot of Bronze Age institutions developed prior to 1200 BC;

- the long-term historical consequences of privatization, such as the increasing dependence on state taxation of private wealth rather than on self-generation of public revenue through public enterprise

1.

The Dynamics of Privatization, From the Bronze Age to the Present

Michael Hudson
New York University

This paper traces the processes by which land tenure, credit and commercial handicraft workshops were privatized through the first two-thirds of documented history, from Sumer c. 3500 BC through the Roman Republic. During these millennia the privatization dynamic was complex, unplanned and often chaotic, but some common characteristics can be discerned:

(1) Corporate enterprise first developed in Sumer's city-temples, while personal landownership emanated mainly from the palace sector. This meant that privatization tended to begin at the top of the social pyramid, starting with the ruler and extending down through his administrative bureaucracy.

(2) A symbiosis existed between public and private enterprise, giving Bronze Age and early Iron Age economies a mixed character. Rulers and their bureaucracies behaved simultaneously in public and private ways. The tendency was for private self-seeking to overshadow public responsibility, which became increasingly nominal and merely rhetorical. Indeed, what enabled the earliest *commercants* to seek economic gain for themselves was precisely their public position. The perceived need to accumulate public surpluses (for export in exchange for needed raw materials) freed merchants from the customary pressures to conspicuously consume their gains.

(3) The paramount nonmilitary lever of privatizing the land was interest-bearing debt. Although public debts did not yet exist (temples and palaces typically were creditors), most private lenders were members of the royal bureaucracy and, in clas-

sical antiquity, the patrician elites. Communal land rights and personal liberty came to be pledged as collateral for debts by subsistence cultivators, and forfeited on an increasingly permanent, irreversible basis.

(4) Privatization of the land and other means of production ended up stripping away the traditional social obligations of wealth. Privatization thus went together with economic polarization and the debasement of the poor into permanent debt bondage.

(5) The fiscal stringency resulting from enterprise passing into private hands obliged governments to tax the less affluent classes more intensively, forcing them into debt. Economies became financially predatory, culminating in Rome. Its legal system redefined creditor rights, and their consequent property rights, along modern lines, by ending the Clean Slates that once had periodically annulled personal debts and redistributed the land.

(6) Culturally, privatization brought in its wake a tolerance for social polarization and what earlier societies had disparaged as *hubris,* the arrogance of wealth carried to the point of injuring the economically weak. As personal self-interest was freed from public oversight, economic balance was lost. Rather than striving to correct this situation (*e.g.,* with new Clean Slates), cultural and religious systems became other-worldly.

Underlying these dynamics were four major types of privatization. One form occurred when Sumerian rulers appropriated communal land and temple estates as their own personal property. Like the writing of poetry and possession of a personal god, this characteristic of individualism is first found in the royal household, from which it diffused downward via the royal bureaucracy to the rest of society.

A second type of privatization occurred when rulers gave property away to their relatives (often as dowries) or companions, or assigned control of these properties (or at least their prebend rents) as tribute to local chieftains. An example of this form of privatization is afforded by Nippur's temple of Inanna, which was turned over to Amorite headmen around 2000 BC.

A related type of privatization occurred as a byproduct of political decentralization, most notably when palace control collapsed. In such crises, royal managers or warlords tended to seize the royal lands and workshops. This occurred as Hammurapi's Babylonian empire fell apart, and after 1200 BC when Mycenaean Greece fell into a Dark Age.

A fourth type of privatization became the most prevalent: the transfer of communally held lands to creditors or other absentee buyers. Beginning in southern Mesopotamia, subsistence lands were appropriated by individuals from outside the local kinship-based groupings by royal collectors, creditors or merchants through debt foreclosure; outright purchase at distress prices; or, less frequently, at the "full market price."

The upshot of privatization was economic polarization between creditors and debtors, landlords and tenants, patricians and clients, while the private sector grew richer largely at the expense of the public sector. A major effect of the privatization of subsistence land, for instance, was a change in the economic uses to which the land's yield was put. Babylonia's subsistence cultivators had been obliged to provide corvée labor, serve in the army, and pay taxes or other fees to the palace in exchange for holding land. But the new private appropriators kept the land's usufruct for themselves rather than passing it on as taxes. The debtor's labor services, crops and, in time, title to his land were taken as interest and, ultimately, forfeited as collateral for debt. This often obliged the remaining community members to make up the individual debtor's fiscal shortfall; otherwise the net yield available to the palace was simply reduced.

A related consequence of privatization was a shift away from growing grains for the self-support of cultivators to more luxury-oriented and capital-intensive cash crops (olive trees and grape vines in the Mediterranean), increasingly on large estates which came to be stocked with slaves by the time of Rome's great *latifundia*.

Also privatized were numerous commercial practices that appear to have originated in the public sector. Bulk trade of goods sold in standardized lot sizes, at uniform prices, over long distances, with credit provided at uniform interest rates, seems to have been organized about five thousand years ago by the temples of southern Mesopotamia in a burst of entrepreneurial innovation that included the development of land-rent (as Sumerian temple prebends) and interest-bearing debt. These sources of *rentier* income became privatized as they spread from the temple and palace institutions to the population at large, and especially as they diffused from Sumer to less centralized societies in which commercial enterprise, rent and interest took root in family households, starting with those of chieftains and other headmen. Center-periphery relations thus played an important catalytic role as decentralization and privatization went together.

Privatization also occurred in the public industrial crafts (*viz.* the Greek *demiourgoi*), fine arts, drama and music. Culture evolved from a means of molding communal behavior to the production of luxury goods and services. In the sphere of religion, the economic laws that had formed the original core of Judaism were de-emphasized as being utopian and unrealistic. Christianity spiritualized the Jubilee Year's Clean Slate by turning it into the Day of Judgment, while making personal charity the measure of religious dedication. Judaism's own early focus on social right-eousness and periodic economic renewal was superseded by Hillel's *prôsbul*, accommodating religion to the new oligarchic state of affairs.

Privatization and the dissolution of economic order

For many centuries, the privatization of communal lands by public col-lectors or "merchants" acting as absentee landlords was reversed by royal proclamations restoring the land to its "original" citizen base. From the ruler's vantage point, the problem of privatization was that it led to a relinquishing of property (and hence, its usufructs) to wealthy appro-priators who took the crop surplus and harvest labor duties of the cultivators for themselves, at the expense of the palace.

Definitions and concepts are of critical importance in tracing these dynamics. Southern Mesopotamia's communally held land was not part of the *public* sector, yet neither was it *private* in the modern individualis-tic sense of the term. It belonged in principle to the community, and originally was not freely alienable, for an obvious reason: As long as taxes and a stipulated quota of corvée labor were paid by the community, the appropriation and withdrawal of land by private individuals would have thrown the fiscal and labor burdens onto the community's remaining members. Ultimately, of course, this economic polarization is just what occurred. The ensuing concentration of private economic power led to a loss of defaulting debtors' land and citizenship rights on a large scale, undercutting the army's strength and hollowing out the economy.

How public enterprise and land-rent preceded private enterprise

Sumer's great contribution to civilization was a complex of innovations that broke through the traditional "anthropological" or "soft" interper-sonal reciprocity of gift exchange to create the first known *economic* regime. The Sumerian innovations included bulk trade, standardized (hence, im-personal) money prices and lot sizes, sharecropping rents, wage-ration allotments, interest and contractual forms, and indeed the general system of weights and measures. All these innovations found their initial focus in the city-temples,* which were organized on the basis of a number of economic innovations that have shaped the entire world's subsequent evolution.

It would not be too much to call these temples history's first formal business corporations. Organizing an export trade to obtain foreign metals, stone, hardwood and other raw materials not found in the southern alluvium, Sumer's temples legitimized capital accumulation, that is, the reinvestment of surpluses *without reciprocity* to earn yet further gains. The objective of the new system was to expand the means of production and to build up monetary savings. Yet among all the Sumerian "firsts" that have been enumerated by Samuel Kramer and other popular historians, the above innovations scarcely have been mentioned.

Why did commercial gain-seeking originate in public institutions? The logical answer is that they must have been the line of least resistance to the social forces opposing major private gain-seeking. For although capital accumulation seems natural to modern eyes, it rarely develops spontaneously in low-surplus economies. Communal traditions discourage the pursuit of commerce beyond the level of gift exchange among chiefs and occasional barter by itinerant traders. It therefore is necessary to explain just how the commercial ethic first developed and spread, for it is not a universal and automatic phenomenon.

In Sumer, temples were organized to yield a *rentier* income in the form of prebends, that is, stipulated flows of rent earmarked to support administrative personnel. The various lands, workshops and herds were organized into what today would be called profit centers. Annual accounts were compiled of costs and expenses, attested by administrators' seals for each level of the bureaucratic hierarchy. The practice of sealing limited access to storerooms and certified transactions as being officially sanctioned. The ensuing record-keeping required the design of a system of standardized weights and measures, which paved the way for the development of forward planning.

Sumer's city-temples accumulated unprecedented amounts of capital. Indeed, it was probably only such public institutions that could have

---

* I adopt French usage (*cité-temple*) to preserve the sense of temples serving their *locality* rather than being denominational as in the competing churches found in modern cities. In the Bronze Age there is no indication of doctrinal clashes. The binding religious force was not exclusive theocratic teaching, but support for the community's welfare and, indeed, its economic survival.

placated the adherents of the archaic consumption-based ethic and generated surpluses in socially acceptable ways. Personal self-seekers could not easily have made the breakthrough on their own, for they would have been condemned as greedy. Thus, while the non-public sector (we cannot yet truly call it a *private* sector) long remained subsistence-based, the temples were able, as public institutions, to legitimize the accumulation of a surplus. It is in this capacity that they acted as a catalyst for a new entrepreneurial regime.

Organized to generate or squeeze out an economic surplus, public enterprise became more formalized and standardized in its production technology and specialization of labor than was the non-public "household" sector. Public rations, for instance, are carefully measured and proportioned, in contrast to the private family's *ad hoc* eating arrangements. Indeed, the public sector's guiding spirit traditionally has been one of standardization and schematic regulation, while the private sector is characterized by free-flowing spontaneity. Against the household sector's informal plasticity, the public sector manifests a symmetrical formality in its ceremonial art and architecture. With its carefully measured proportions and layouts, public architecture juxtaposes itself to the private sector's less formalized housing designs.

As early as the fourth millennium, careful measuring was essential for planning the production of an economic surplus. A usufruct in the form of land-rent and interest was calculated — indeed, stipulated — in advance. This scheduling required standardized ration levels within the administrative hierarchy, and a corresponding standardization of time to create symmetrical calendrical months. Members of every social rank were thereby rendered equal in the sense that they shared the same units of measurement. This nominal equality was expressed ceremonially and artistically, as well as legally and economically.

Prices were standardized, as were interest rates, which remained set for centuries on end. Most interest-bearing debts, for instance, reflected intersectoral balances owed by community members to the temples and palace. Settlement of these debts required a standardized means of payment, and two common denominators emerged to play this role: barley for agricultural obligations, silver for commercial ones. The main monetary unit of account was the silver shekel, whose value was set as equal to that of a "bushel" (*qa*) of barley. Both commodities were subdivided into 60ths, providing small enough increments to represent interest fractions on a monthly or annual basis (1/60th per month = 20% per year). (The Indus system of weights and measures hardly could be used for such a purpose, for it was simply a sequence of doublings, not a system based on calendrical fractions. A system of 1, 2, 4, 8, 16, 32, 64, etc. does not lend itself to calculations on a monthly basis; the closest approximation would be to calculate in terms of 32-day months and 64ths.)

Family households were much smaller than public institutions and enjoyed a higher degree of natural trust, and thus rarely needed the accounting oversight and the related financial checks found in public bureaucracies. Yet the distinction between public and private did not turn mainly on kinship relations. The palace was kinship-based, while many landholding bodies were not (*viz.* Mesopotamian and subsequent professional guilds and, in more modern times, the Russian *mir*). *The Sumerian distinction between public and private sectors turned on the decision to set apart the community's industrial enterprise — along with land, herds and money — to support its workers in a corporately distinct sector that belonged at least nominally to the city-community as a whole.*

If this public entrepreneurial initiative is difficult for many observers to acknowledge today, it is because the modern world has virtually inverted the relations of Bronze Age enterprise and finance. Profit-making investment is now left almost exclusively to the private sector. But this privatization took thousands of years to achieve. Today's public sectors no longer are creditors as in Bronze Age times; they are in debt, obliged to levy taxes to cover the cost of their operations rather than relying on their own enterprise.

As wealth has broken free of taxation, it has created a privatization of finance, via budget deficits that are funded by borrowing money at interest. This double concession to wealth — not taxing it fully, and paying interest to individual lenders to cover the government's shortfall — took even longer to develop, and was much more alien to the ancient mind than was the privatization of enterprise (as the stratagems cited in Book II of the pseudo-Aristotelean *Œconomica* illustrate).

The economic impact of war

War proved to be the great financial catalyst in the Bronze Age and classical antiquity, just as in today's world. But whereas war today forces national governments into debt, in antiquity the main financial victims were individual debtors, above all cultivators unable to pay public fees or otherwise make ends meet. The upshot was more polarized and centralized societies, economically as well as politically.

As warfare intensified among the Sumerian cities, the military dimension of rulership — *lugal*ship rather than *en*ship — became more important. By about 2800 BC the palaces had become separate functionally as well as architecturally from the temples. In addition, foreign conquest and tribute enabled victorious rulers to seize or purchase land from local corporate kinship or professional groupings, and to set up royal workshops modeled after those of the temples. (The Stele of Manishtushu in the 22nd century BC may reflect the forced sale of lands to rulers acting in a private capacity.)

As rulers turned into empire builders, they delegated authority and economic resources to local headmen in exchange for military support. These headmen became *de facto* proprietors when royal power weakened or collapsed, thus further shifting the locus of commercial enterprise, land tenure and the arts from a public to an individualistic context.

The public obligations of wealth

Ownership of wealth was long associated with an obligation to use it in the public interest. This is one reason why privatization of the land by absentee creditors or merchants at first was limited to only temporary duration, being repeatedly reversed by royal edict. Even in Rome, perpetual business corporations such as the *publicani* companies could be formed only to undertake public-interest projects whose scale was beyond the financial resources of individual families.

Historically, privatization sooner or later has stripped away the traditional social obligations of landholders. Medieval Europe's barons were required to use their fiefdoms to field military contingents in time of war and support the Crown fiscally out of the land's usufruct. Their holdings thus played much the same role as did royal lands in the second-millennium Near East on which armies were settled. However, privatization brought in its wake a casting off of the traditional obligations of wealth. This trend was especially strong when led rulers seeking to assemble empires had to rely on local satraps.

As land tenure and its associated citizenship rights became subject to alienation to creditors, obligations formerly attached to the land were replaced by many taxes on labor, *e.g.* poll taxes and other regressive levies. This intensified the centralization of land and money-capital in private hands, leaving governments indebted and all but powerless to deal with the new Leviathan of private-sector credit.

Public and private regimes each aimed at centralized control, but in their own ways, of course, and with differing sets of checks and balances. Royal political power sought economic dominance by charging for public services (often of a monopoly character), seizing foreign tribute, taxing populations, and buying domestic land, often at forced prices. A practical constraint on royal exploitation was the fact that while rulers based their power on a free army of cultivators willing to fight for their land, they also had to depend on an administrative bureaucracy whose members (whom modern writers typically call "merchants") sought to profiteer for themselves. The result often was a tug of war to obtain the community's economic surplus and, ultimately, the land.

Private wealth was consolidated by achieving political control, typically by replacing monarchies with oligarchic senates, the classical example being Rome. Private-sector strategies included taking property by force (easiest where royal overrides were weak), entrapping needy individuals in debt, circumventing the law by credit or making use of loopholes (*e.g.*, by arranging to inherit the land through "false adoptions" in which the borrower adopted the creditor as his heir in exchange for a money loan), and establishing petty monopolies charging extortionate prices.

In Babylonia, the power of the monied aristocracies was checked for many centuries by strong rulers. Instead of increasing taxes inexorably, Mesopotamian rulers *freed* families from creditors who had reduced them to debt bondage and taken their land. In time, however, the aristocracies grew strong enough to overthrow centralized royal power. As an independent class, they showed little interest in perpetuating the royal tradition of repeated debt cancellations. The indebted population lost its freedom for good.

The mixed character of ancient economies

There are no pure modes of production. All economic stages are "mixed." The economies under study at this conference are no exception: They were characterized by a symbiosis between public and private. From the Sumerian *damgar* and Babylonian *tamkarum* through the proprietors of the Mycenaean "merchant's houses" excavated by Wace, large traders are found interfacing with the royal bureaucracy, not acting on their own.

Today, the state is considered to be antithetical to private enterprise, yet industrial enterprise was first developed in Bronze Age times by rulers who operated through public institutions. In southern Mesopotamia, private profits were made by royal collectors and temple officers. The sector traditionally viewed as being most inherently private, that of merchants, played a symbiotic role throughout the period under discussion. Closely associated with the large public institutions, the merchants conducted trade in their private capacities even when they doubled as public collectors, and organized themselves into temple guilds to provide security of trade and (possibly) to qualify for temple consignments of export goods and loans.

The city-temples were the central organs through which the Sumerians mediated the economic surplus. Private household production existed alongside that of the temples, but seems to have been oriented more towards subsistence needs with only marginal production for the market. The products of the private households probably were less specialized and luxurious than those produced in the temple and palace workshops. However, inasmuch as these household commodities were produced "at the margin," their prices (and especially the price of barley, including that grown on public sharecropping lands) were free to rise and fall with changing supply and demand. Barley prices, for instance, rose dramatically in response to shortages stemming from the military disturbances that marked the transition from Ur III to the Isin-Larsa period.

One example of how public and private modalities can coexist is reflected in Sumer's elaboration of the calendar from a lunar one governing communal festivals to a solarized public-sector one. Neolithic and even paleolithic communities appear to have based their festivals on lunar rhythms, but lunar months vary in length and hence are unsuitable for allocating standardized rations. Sumer's temples and palaces needed to schedule large-scale flows of barley and other commodities on a regular basis, and therefore took the lead in introducing a 360-day public sector calendar composed of twelve equal 30-day months. This public solar calendar was adopted alongside the popular lunar calendar. (A similar dual calendrical system survives today for setting movable feasts such as Christian Easter, the Jewish New Year and Islamic Ramadan.)

The 360-day public year left an extra five days to balance out the true solar year, and an eleven-day excess of the solar over the lunar year. This interregnum — a "time out of time" — became the occasion for the New Year festivals that provided the occasions for new rulers to renew the social and economic cosmos by cancelling agrarian debts, freeing debt bondsmen and restoring the *status quo ante*, above all lands that had been forfeited to creditors.

Just as public and private calendars coexisted, so did public and private modes of production. Public commercial production stood in contrast to production on communal subsistence lands. Likewise, different rates of interest were adopted for the two spheres of economic activity: silver-denominated commercial debts accrued at 1/60th per month, while agrarian barley debts accrued at higher rates, typically $33\frac{1}{3}$% per year by the end of the third millennium. The result was a dual financial system operating as a bimonetary standard.

The impersonal economic formality of public institutions stands in contrast to the customary familial or neighborly informality. Throughout the Bronze Age, gift exchange continued among people of similar rank, while commercial exchange characterized relations among people of different status, or on opposing sides of the public/private divide, or from different communities. Debt obligations of the "anthropological" type among persons of similar status did not bear interest as late as the *eranos* loan clubs found among Athenian gentlemen, in contrast to loans from the rich to the poor or financial claims by public institutions on the citizenry at large.

Looking at the broad sweep of Mesopotamian development, we see privatized landownership gaining immunity from communal redistributions and royal overrides. At the end of this process, land titles became transferable at will. The resulting privatized land tenure stands at odds with the dynamics operating within the subsistence sector, where equity and balance remained the ideal if not always the rule.

Rulers were immune from this kind of balance, thanks to their *ex officio* claim to a crop usufruct to support their large public households. Thus, far from public and private being antithetical, private gain-seeking first emerged within the royal sector, with palace rulers playing a catalytic role in establishing personally disposable — and hence, truly private — property. Individualistic behavior in an economic sense may thus be said to have started with the ruler and worked its way down through the social pyramid via his family members, the royal bureaucracy, and the heads of families close to the ruler who were well on their way to becoming a hereditary oligarchy.

As to individuality in the cultural realm, Sargon's daughter Enhua-danna is the first named author of a literary composition (a hymn to Nanna). On the other hand, sculptural representations of rulers depicted them in highly schematized ways, as Winter (1989) has shown with regard to the Lagash ruler Gudea. Royal individuality thus was stereotyped as a public *persona*, at least as long as rulers were more public than private in their identities.

The distinction between Sumer's communal and public sectors

Privatization often is discussed in terms of a simplistic public/private dichotomy, but the dynamics of privatization have changed drastically over the millennia. A set of definitions specific to the Sumerian economy is therefore necessary, embracing the communal sector of self-supporting cultivators, the temples functioning as what one might call public utilities, and the palaces. Each of these three sectors had its own source of handicraft labor and its own form of land tenure, none of which originally were individualistic or "private" in character. It was the public sector that innovated the basic array of institutions needed for profit-making enterprise: corporate organization, writing and account keeping, contracts and their formalities, weights and measures, and interest-bearing debt. However, Sumerian public investment ultimately catalyzed the growth of a private-sector which ended up undermining temple and palace control. This was just the opposite of the Chicago School scenario whereby private self-seeking is primordial but repeatedly stifled by state activism and taxation.

Diakonoff (1982:25, 28, 32, 47, 59) has shown how Sumer's temples and palaces formed a corporately distinct sector within the larger body of society, which he calls the communal sector. And indeed, the term "communal" applies most aptly to this non-public sector, essentially a network of kinship-based and professional corporate communes which held land on a collective basis well into the second millennium. The land was redivided periodically or alienated as some families grew larger, others smaller, and new entrants joined the commune (these groupings often were open in character, *e.g.* as the later Irish gelfine). Families held tenure rights to cultivate this land, but were not "free" to transfer it as they chose — or, for that matter, to forfeit it permanently and thereby lose their economic freedom, citizenship rights and consequent obligations to serve in the army and to provide corvée labor. Land transfers among communal sector families did occur, but traditionally were limited to only temporary duration. (Little is known about these transfers, for scant documentation has survived concerning economic activities conducted outside of the public institutions prior to the second millennium.) The function of the communal land was to support its holders, not to yield a formal economic rent.

For these reasons what Zagarell (1986:418) calls the "public-communal mode of production" reflects a Marxist idealization in which public and communal are regarded as synonymous. In fact, in early Bronze Age Mesopotamia the public and the communal sectors were nearly antithetical. We therefore must reject references to the public sector as constituting "the collective property of primitive society" (Brentjes, comment on Zagarell 1986:420). Such modernisms do not demarcate a corporately distinct public sector, but suggest each family actually shared in the income of the temples and palaces, perhaps voting democratically in their administration. Yet by the time of the first surviving cuneiform records, public institutions already were being administered as corporately autonomous bodies, although (as Diakonoff emphasizes) their officials also belonged at the same time to the communal family groupings by virtue of their landholding status. To call Sumer's palaces and temples "communal" or "collective" is to gloss over their role in enabling their administrators to build up extraordinary family property, at least by the mid-third millennium BC.

Looking back from today's vantage point, when private enterprise is overwhelmingly dominant, we must ask why private forms of wealth did not take the lead from the outset. The simple explanation is that a private sector in the modern sense of the term did not yet exist in Bronze Age times. For a deeper answer it is necessary to review the anthropological record and the subsistence basis of most tribal economies. Almost everywhere they have been studied, such communities have displayed little interest in investing wealth to accumulate more wealth. Their tendency is to disparage personal wealth accumulation as being impolite, rude or miserly. Furthermore, the tribal communities known to modern anthropologists have little specialized administrative apparatus; their exchange of goods and services is conducted in an informal person-to-person fashion rather than a formally "economic" manner.

It would be anachronistic to call the cultivators who belonged to Sumer's landed groupings either a "private" *or* a "public" sector. They were not characterized by private property, for their subsistence landholdings were not theirs to freely sell or pledge for debt, at least not more than temporarily. Inasmuch as citizens held their allotments in exchange for an obligation to serve in the army and provide corvée labor duties, alienation of this land would have meant a loss of their citizenship status and its associated obligations. To prevent this public loss, communities imposed constraints on the alienation of land. The early documented land sales from communal groupings to the palace (collected in Gelb, Steinkeller and Whiting 1991) suggest that such transfers were irrevocable only when the purchasing party was the king. But a widening array of exceptions developed, enabling formal property to emerge.

Under normal conditions Sumerian and Babylonian families probably were able to produce a modest surplus over their minimum needs, but crop failures and military hostilities inevitably created economic imbalances. At such times ambitious wealth-seekers maneuvered to buy or foreclose on the lands of families in economic difficulty. Mesopotamian communities and their rulers, however, deemed the objective of ensuring widespread self-support for their infantrymen to be higher than that of upholding modern property rights. To preserve economic balance, they developed responses to the private concentration of wealth that were antithetical to the modern sanctity of property acquisition. Most notably, rulers acted to restore the *status quo ante* of widespread land tenure by freeing debt bondsmen and annulling the barley-debt overhang, although leaving intact most commercial debts, urban real estate and commercial gardens or orchards. In sum, the "private property system" emerged most strongly within Mesopotamia's surplus-creating sphere rather than in its subsistence sphere, which long remained communally based.

Debt's paramount role as an economic lever of privatization

The earliest attested market transfers of land took three forms. One was the purchase of land or its military appropriation by the palace. A second was the mercantile purchase of orchards, urban gardens and other lands that had passed out of the subsistence sector. Third, and ultimately the most critical (if unsettling) was the alienation of subsistence land on a temporary basis, often through forfeiture to creditors. In the latter case the tenured cultivators usually remained in place until such time as their land was redeemed by their relatives or neighbors, or restored to them by royal fiat. Personal property in land developed relatively late, at least in the modern sense of an asset owned irrevocably and disposable at will.

Land tenure by communal groupings may be deemed private in the sense that it is not public (*i.e.*, does not belong to the palace, temple or state agency), but it is not yet individualistic ownership. Nor is landownership *permanent* as long as it remains subject to communal redistribution, or as long as alienations are reversed by royal fiat to ensure that the land remains a widespread means of self-support for the citizen body. Modern property requires an end to such social overrides that block the land's irrevocable transfer.

A major lever breaking down the customary overrides was the attachment of financial claims to crop yields (and, in time, to property allotments themselves), turning them into collateral for loans. First emerging at the interface between the public institutions and individual members of the communal sector (either merchants or cultivators running up arrears), interest-bearing debts were a risky proposition for impoverished cultivators. The only resources these debtors could pledge (and subsequently forfeit) were their personal liberty (and that of their family members and dependents) and their right to the land. Insolvent debtors were obliged to turn over their means of livelihood to creditors — and became debt-bondsmen — until such time as the ruler intervened to reverse the social instability caused by this state of affairs.

The formal transfer of ownership was a logical conclusion to seizing the land's net usufruct. In the first stage of this development, public collectors claimed the land's crop and the labor of the cultivator-debtor as interest, often in competition with the palace ruler. Over time, such appropriation became less temporary, that is, more immune from communal reallocation.

In modern times a defining characteristic of property is the ability of its owner to transfer it free of social overrides. It is this personal security of disposition that constitutes the new "freedom" of property. For better or worse, the land may be pledged for debt and forfeited irrevocably. No longer must it be left to the owner's natural heirs, other relatives or neighbors. This "freeing" of the community's subsistence land from the traditional protective constraints transformed its character, bringing it into the economy of modern capitalism.

One cause of antiquity's endemic debt problem was setting interest rates in a noneconomic way, aiming mainly at ease of numerical calculation. There was no thought of market equilibrium creating equity by letting interest rates vary to reflect actual economic returns. Indeed, rates often exceeded the debtor's normal capacity to pay. Agrarian borrowing was undertaken not as a choice, not with an eye to making a profit on the borrowed funds, but out of dire need.

Rulers were well aware that the growing debt overhead caused economic polarization and adverse concentrations of land holding. Their solution was simple, but it was not a market-based one: They restored the *status quo ante* by annulling the debts and reversing the forfeitures of property and personal liberty that these debts had brought about since the last such annulment. The polarizing debt functions were then allowed to begin all over again.

Interest rates of up to $33^1/_3$% meant that a rising number of rural debtors were unable to meet their stipulated payment schedule. Natural disasters such as floods or droughts brought insolvency in their train, as did the military hostilities that called men away from their land and resulted in the capture, ransom, death or maiming of many. The financial consequence of such disturbances was a forfeiture of property to creditors — a rural tragedy that has repeated itself innumerable times over the past five millennia.

The problem is that financial claims, once established, grow at compound rates and attach themselves to every revenue-producing asset that can be collateralized. Creditors recycled their interest receipts into new lending, swelling the economy's debt burden at a geometric rate of increase. In the end, the attempt to service private and public debts fails. What remains are rich creditors at the top, and pauperized ex-peasants falling into bondage at the bottom.

Recalling the fate of Rome's *campania* following the Punic Wars with Carthage (see Arnold Toynbee, *Hannibal's Legacy,* 1975:II, 174ff.), today's privatizations in Latin America, Britain, the United States and elsewhere are largely a response to a bloated debt burden. But whereas in most ancient and modern cases it was war debts that transformed communal or public land into private, oligarchic, absentee-owned property, today's public debt burden is growing under its own force.

What is so remarkable about southern Mesopotamia is that despite the fact that it was the most commercialized and largest-scale economy of its day, its rulers countered economic polarization by proclaiming Clean Slates rather than resolving conflicts in favor of land appropriators and creditors. First attested by the Sumerian ruler Enmetena proclaiming *amargi* c. 2400 BC, and extending through the Babylonian and Assyrian rulers proclaiming *andurarum* and *misharum* in the Middle Bronze Age (2000-1600 BC), these restorations had the effect of minimizing many of the problems that subsequently came to be associated with debt foreclosure and absentee ownership. By freeing debt-bondsmen and restoring lands that had been forfeited to creditors, these royal restorations of order preserved basic minimum standards for the citizenry at large. They kept Mesopotamia's economic dynamics within more stable bounds than those of classical Greece and Rome, and find an echo in the biblical Jubilee Year of Leviticus 25. But in time, oligarchies dismantled the Bronze Age constraints on personal self-aggrandizement.

It was in the periphery rather than in the core (especially in the Mediterranean lands) that the privatization of public or quasi-public enterprise led to the most pronounced economic inequality. In tribally organized communities, chieftains enriched themselves by adopting the commercial and interest-bearing debt practices pioneered in Sumer, but often did not adopt Sumer's system of communal constraints on privatization. The classical oligarchies in particular dispossessed much of the population from the land.

This "progressive" development of concentration of economic property and power in private hands rather than those of centralized public institutions was promoted by creating a new body of law to make land transfers irreversible. What had been the hallmark of sacred rulership in

Bronze Age Mesopotamia — royal restorations of "straight" economic order, equity and liberty — was replaced by government as a naked tool of a wealthy landowning class. The epoch of mortgage debt, land monopolization and widespread personal bondage and slavery had arrived.

Private land appropriators were still far from asserting a Lockian justification for their privatization. No ancient Milton Friedman appeared to say that all this was the best. Just the opposite: Stoic writers in the Hellenistic and Roman eras blamed the economic strangulation of their world on the tyranny of debt and the self-centeredness of the wealthy. They pined for a return to the golden age of Saturn, in effect an idealized Bronze Age in which moderation rather than economic acquisitiveness was the personal behavioral ideal.

Yet the Greeks and Romans had lost all memory of ideas of the debt Jubilee and related cancellation of agrarian consumer debts. The classical idea of progress implied just the opposite: an irreversible arrow of time. The tradition of economic renewal came to be replaced by an endorsement of personal alms-giving to the poor, not a broad financial restructuring. Only after debt had wreaked its damage did the new Church condemn usury outright.

The diffusion and decontextualization of enterprise

Privatization in antiquity is best understood as part of a process of *decontextualization*, that is, the transplanting of holistic institutions originally developed in one context (typically a highly integrated one) piecemeal into a smaller-scale, peripheral context. The new way of doing things often lacks the checks and balances found in the core. And as the creation and appropriation of an economic surplus becomes less centralized, the tendency is toward miniaturization of the industrial production units. By the time the Mediterranean lands embarked on their classical takeoff, the production of high-income cash crops, the organization of industrial workshops and the charging of interest on debts was undertaken mainly by chiefs in their own personal *oikos* households and those of other headmen or well-to-do patricians, not via a corporately distinct public sector.

Economic self-seeking typically was introduced in peripheral lands by merchants from the core, *e.g.*, by the Sumerians and Assyrians in Anatolia and Syria in the third millennium, and by the Phoenician and Greek merchants establishing the trade entrepot on the island of Pithekoussai (Ischia) in the 8th century BC. The fact that no interest-bearing debt is documented in Mycenaean Greece, or even in the Hittite economy, seems to me to suggest that such debts arose mainly at the interface between the core's temple or palaces and the communal sector, which included merchants as well as cultivators who owed arrears on sharecropping rents or other public fees. But inasmuch as the Mediterranean was composed more of private households from the outset, debts were owed largely to local chieftains and "big-men," including family heads of the sort overthrown by Greek tyrants in the 7th century BC.

So far-reaching has been the subsequent disembedding from their ancient context of most of our surviving economic and contractual formalities that many observers have overlooked how civilization's commercial practices initially were developed as parts of an overall social complex. The diffusion of these practices from Sumer to less centralized (and less public-sector oriented) economies resulted in the loss of many elements of the initial Mesopotamian synthesis. Interest-bearing debts and consumer usury, for instance, were transplanted to the Mediterranean lands in the 9th or 8th century BC (Hudson 1992) without the practice of restoring widespread land tenure via royal cancellations of the agrarian debt overhead. When Solon was appointed *archon* to resolve the Athenian debt crisis in 594 BC, his one-time emergency measure, the *seisach-theia*, was the limit of what his propertied aristocratic peers would accept.

Given this basic context for the evolution of enterprise and capital accumulation from public to more private and individualistic modes, we may now return to the questions posed earlier. Why didn't neolithic and Bronze Age communities evolve directly into classical Greek and Roman aristocratic and oligarchic societies? Why was a catalyst needed, in the form of the entrepreneurial lead taken by Mesopotamia's public temples and palaces? And why was financial and economic balance better preserved more in Mesopotamia's Enterprise Revolution than in that of classical antiquity?

It seems natural enough that holistic social constructs should be strongest at the inception of a civilization's commercial takeoff, as in Bronze Age Sumer. It is in the nature of systems to be developed initially as parts of a single related complex. It also is natural for the diffusion of these practices into new and less centralized contexts to result in the loss of many of the early checks and balances. This is what occurred in the cases of interest-bearing debt, the charging of rent and related entrepreneurial practices. One indeed might say that what constituted privatization in Greek and Roman society was precisely the stripping away of the original safeguards, that is, of the Sumerian social armoring.

So thoroughly did this stripping-away process succeed that scarcely any memory survived of the initial public-sector context for interest-bearing debt, land tenure and the Clean Slates that kept the early dynamics of privatization in line. The Sumerologist Samuel Kramer confused matters a generation ago by anachronistically calling these Clean Slates "tax reductions," and depicting them as stimulating rather than curbing the emerging private sector. Indeed, on the day President Ronald Reagan was inaugurated in February 1981, a letter by Kramer in the New York *Times* urged the president to emulate Urukagina's example c. 2350 BC and cut taxes. This reading of Bronze Age debt cancellations was made at a time when America's own debt overhead had pushed commercial interest rates to the 20% level where they had stood in Mesopotamian times.

A decade ago, only a few cuneiformists read the Clean Slate proclamations for what they really were. Even the Biblical Jubilee Year and related first-millennium debt ameliorations were viewed as utopian religious statements, not as practical programs. Placing such debt cancellations in the context of civilization's privatization dynamic now enables us to see just what economic safeguards have been lost.

Privatization of craft labor

Craft labor in the Late Bronze Age seems still to have been public labor. This usually connoted dependent workers with a low social status, often slaves, foreigners, and various classes of unfree domestic dependents. The low status of craft labor in this era was a result of two factors. First, craftsmen often lacked land of their own; this is why they had to work at a craft as their means of self-support. "In the Mesopotamian temple-state economy of the third millennium BC the craftsmen were bondmen controlled and fed by the palace, and this relationship is still reflected in the low status of the smith as a *mushkenu* in the Code of Hammurapi (§274)," note Ventris and Chadwick (1956:133). "The Ur tablets list the activities of eight palace workshops, those of the sculptors, goldsmiths, lapidaries, carpenters, smiths, fullers and tanners, tailors, and caulkers (bitumen workers)."

These craftsmen doubtless worked on their own for individual clients in addition to performing their public work. And when their royal clients dropped from the scene, their sole remaining market was the non-state sector of individual wealth-holders. The privatization of craft labor thus involved a supercession of royal and temple workshops by those of landed aristocrats. Meanwhile, more and more craftsmen became self-employed or emigrated from their native towns as journeymen.

Political philosophy and the enterprise revolution

The thesis of public-sector precedence suggests that economic individualism is not the "original and natural" way of doing things, but rather a product of the dissolution of the Bronze Age social cosmos. Free-market economists, political theorists and historians tend to shy away from tracing the genesis of modern practices back to the preclassical breakdown of Mesopotamian institutions originating as public utilities embedded in broad, socially holistic complexes. To examine these Bronze Age roots of commercial practices would undermine the mythology of free enterprise.

It also would stand at odds with nearly all popular theories of private property and the state. Constitutional theorists tend to pick up the history of the state only at the relatively late point where it becomes synonymous with government as such, making and enforcing laws, waging wars, and taxing private property holders. The modern state is defined as the protector of private property, including the security of debt-claims.

Compared to Mesopotamia's temples and palaces, today's governments have both broader and narrower powers. Their role is broader in enacting laws binding on all society, taxing the property and income of all residents, and accruing debts to private-sector creditors — debts that governments no longer can cancel at will. On the other hand, modern states no longer control religion, nor do they undertake commercial enterprise for profit. In contrast to Sumer's temples, they studiously avoid such enterprise, and indeed are now busy privatizing the public utilities that remain the last reflections of government responsibility to undertake enterprise in the public interest.

A thorough study of the prehistory of the state would address how enterprise and lawmaking existed *before* the land, industry and government came to be privatized. It would examine how the scope of palace legislation was limited to the palace's own public-sector operations and their interface with the non-public sector; and also the extent to which the communities at large continued to govern themselves by oral common law traditions.

If John Locke's natural-law views were universally valid, Sumer's archaeological sites would reveal private rather than temple and palace estates and workshops. And if market equilibrium theorists were correct, no Bronze Age overrides on private wealth-seeking, credit, land foreclosure and monopolization would have been needed to guarantee liberty and economic self-sufficiency to the population at large. A vested oligarchy increasing its financial riches would be deemed a step forward in capital formation, not a corrosive development ultimately stifling civilization's first commercial takeoff. Classical antiquity's accumulation of personal wealth would have raised society's economic horizons, not deprived populations of their economic self-sufficiency via land expropriations, disenfranchisement and the spread of slavery. Security of property ownership (at least for the well-to-do, if not for needy debtors) and the associated principle that possession is nine-tenths of the law are supposed to have helped cement society, not rend it apart as occurred in the Roman Republic and Empire.

Mesopotamian rulers viewed the privatization of enterprise from a different perspective than that of today's political philosophers. Modern governments are charged with the duty of defending creditor claims against debtors' rights to their own economic freedom and means of livelihood. But Bronze Age rulers protected debtors against creditors. In doing this, they had a simple implicit answer to a problem that Locke and subsequent theorists of private property have failed to address: To what extent does the buildup of interest-bearing debts and the rich man's appropriation of land connote an expropriation of the assets needed by poorer families to meet their basic needs, forcing them into dependency relationships? To what extent does their loss connote a loss to the public sector and *its* needs? Mesopotamia's public institutions coped with this problem of economic inequity and private patronage by countering the arrogance that tended to be inherently associated with wealth.

Like Locke, modern socialist writers presuppose the primacy of private property in the emergence of enterprise, but invert Locke's logic to reason that if the state's role from the outset was indeed to protect private property, then it is *ipso facto* an instrument of class warfare. Engels' *Origin of the Family, Private Property and the State* is the classic statement of this position, followed by Lenin's *State and Revolution*. This idea leaves little room for the notion that rather than being formed to protect private property, the Sumerian temples (and in the north, the palaces) brought the first corporate economic property into being. Indeed, Mesopotamia's public sector also may be said to have brought into being the first documented economic classes, in the form of bureaucratic hierarchies and their dependent labor.

In sum, the large Sumerian institutions created entrepreneurial structures on a large and comprehensive scale. Economic balance was imposed by rulers from outide this system, not by self-adjusting market stabilizers. Temples were the first "lords" to establish absentee landlordship and collect groundrent, which — as in the case with interest — was emulated by private landlords only later. And when this later individualism developed, on a smaller scale, it was because the larger institutions had created a basic context. But no new economic stabilizers were developed such as the earlier Clean Slates. Economies accordingly polarized. And this polarization became a key characteristic of privatization.

To be sure, exploitation was part of the Bronze Age commercial systems. A surplus was squeezed out of propertyless labor, but this process was not based on economic classes in the modern sense of the term. The temple labor force was composed of widows and orphans, the aged and infirm, and war prisoners whose dependency was an accident of physical disability, the loss of their husbands or fathers through warfare, or of military subjugation. What prevented them from supporting themselves on the land was these personal circumstances, not their belonging to a landless class as such. Taken out of their family context, they were placed in temples charged with caring for their needs while mobilizing their labor to produce textiles and other export handicrafts.

At the turn of the Late Bronze Age, southern Mesopotamia's palaces were taken over first by Kassite and then Chaldean warlords, much as Mycenaean Greece was conquered after 1200 BC. The ensuing periods of social and demographic breakdown widespread saw the personal appropriation of hitherto public or communal property and power. It was in these periods of decentralization that a new class of appropriators privatized communal land, extended their control over the temples, and increasingly produced industrial handicrafts in their own workshops.

As economic life became more decontextualized and privatized, the character of rulership changed accordingly. Public officials, warlords, military aristocrats and wealthy landholders and handicraft producers emerged as counterparts to a landless pauperized dependent class. If the wealthy supported the needy as clients, it was on their own estates so as to use them as a political lever. The presence of these clients in the army no longer was as necessary as before, for the army was being privatized. The peasant-infantrymen of old were replaced by mercenaries recruited largely from hill tribes — from outside rather than from within society.

The privatization of law, religion and culture

Modern criminal law has become increasingly public and formally binding on society at large. Whereas archaic and tribal communities down to the present century left the enforcement of laws to the injured parties, modern law makes hitherto civil offenses criminal in character, *e.g.* by considering them to "break the king's peace." Accordingly, fines are paid to the state; victims must recover through separate civil actions.

On the other hand, civil law has become more private. Nowhere is this more pronounced than in the evolution of the legal power to create corporate bodies. Individuals now can form limited liability corporations at will, whereas until the mid-19th century it took an act of Parliament to create a corporation. Such acts could be passed only after the incorporators had demonstrated that their company served the royal interest. Today this legal innovation of limited liability companies, far from serving the public interest, protects individuals from legal recourse by society at large. The effect is to shift today's locus of social planning from public control to private companies gaining increasing immunity from public oversight.

Also increasingly immune from public sponsorship (censorship?) has been culture. Yet one may ask whether it is entirely natural for society to let drama, myth, poetry and even sport become mere instruments for profit-making. Is culture one of those sectors whose "external economies" outweigh its direct market costs and profits, and hence cannot well be brought within the measuring rod of money? Should television be essentially a vehicle for commercial advertising, for instance, or should it become part of a process of uplifting individuals and expanding their understanding of the world's horizons?

This question can be posed as a historical rather than philosophical one by asking what changes have occurred as a result of privatizing culture and drawing it within the market sphere. For one thing, the content of culture has shifted. A major theme of Greek drama (and also its early poetry; see Nagy 1985) was *hubris*, the unchecked arrogance of wealth becoming power-mad and insatiable, to the point of injuring others. Many Stoics and other social philosophers of imperial Rome (*viz.* Plutarch, Livy, Seneca, and before them Blossius and Poseidonus) described their society as being rent apart by the economic *hubris* that tended to accompany oligarchic privatization. Yet no one in antiquity recommended the option of productive debt and investment. This idea is as uniquely modern as is that of an equilibrating market-price process. It was left to Adam Smith to put forth the idea of an Invisible Hand of self-interest spurring progress for society at large. Subsequent economists have elevated the personality trait of self-interest to the motive force of economic progress. One thus might say that the objective of modern economic education is to rationalize economic *hubris,* and to define alternative personal motives and social systems as unnatural. This is the ultimate cultural consequence of privatization.

How today's privatizations go beyond those of antiquity

Modern economics assumes that market forces, if left alone, will produce the best of all possible equilibria. Wealthy individuals will use their wealth to build up society's productive powers, and imbalances or inequities will be self-correcting rather than leading to further economic polarization.

These assumptions do not well describe ancient society. Chieftains, headmen or traders in tribal communities were expected to maintain their position by using their resources to keep dependent families afloat. The alternative was for their communities to suffer attrition — or else simply to unseat the chiefs. It was with the emergence of oligarchic regimes that economic behavior grew more narrowly self-serving.

One result of our modern world evolving out of Rome's collapse rather than directly from the Mesopotamian upswing is that our legal traditions sanctify debt obligations rather than providing for their cancellation when they grow too topheavy. Modern industry is financed with borrowed money via mortgages, bonds and bank loans. Even our governments are debtors, not creditors as in the Bronze Age. Indeed, in an attempt to service these public debts, governments throughout the world are privatizing natural resources and public utilities long considered to be part of the national patrimony.

A century ago the Austrian free-enterprise economist Anton von Menger used the word *Verfügung* ("disposition") to describe the decision-making process of modern investors. This also is the word Fritz Kraus (1984) used to describe Mesopotamia's royal Clean Slate proclamations. The major Bronze Age policy option concerned just when rulers would relieve the destabilizing forces of debt, privatization of the land, and personal debt bondage. Today's major economic decisions concern just the reverse: how to extract interest from economies by turning governments into agents to oversee the transfer of *rentier* incomes to private creditors.

Epilogue

Looking over the course of medieval European development, we see a replay of privatization. Early capitalism was, to a large extent, planned by royal advisors as a means of obtaining more taxes for the Crown. Following the Norman Conquest, for instance, England's land was turned over to barons to enable them to supply troops for the king's army, and also to squeeze out rent to pay the taxes needed to finance royal military campaigns. (The Domesday Book was compiled for this purpose, stating each area's potential usufruct-yield.) Jews were brought into England and France as "royal serfs" to lend the population the money needed to meet these obligations, and Jewish usury income was then heavily taxed by the Crown, making it the ultimate usurer.

Industry — and hence, immigration of skilled craftsmen — likewise was promoted as a means of strengthening the royal fiscal position. Later, Crown Corporations such as the East India Company were chartered to pay off the national war debt by earning private corporate profits (*viz.* the Bank of England in 1694, and the South Sea Company in 1708).

However, as the surplus controlled by individuals grew, the wealthier mercantile classes managed to break free of public control. This counterdynamic is seen in the Magna Carta, the Revolt of the Barons, and the 1688 Glorious Revolution. Finally, in the 19th century, the limited liability joint-stock corporation emerged as a fully free mode of private-sector corporate organization.

The privatization of wealth and power has produced a drive for dismantling the public regulatory state. The ultimate objective of the privatizers, today as in antiquity, is to gain control of the public sector to serve their own economic interests.

So far, this has been achieved mainly by the debt lever rather than by equity investment. The most fertile field for *rentier* income — and also the most risk-free field — is public debt, followed by real-estate debt. Today, it is international creditors that use governments (most conspicuously in third world countries) to extract money from the private sector. A growing proportion of this money is channeled through offshore banking centers which serve as tax-free zones, contributing to the chronic fiscal crisis of recent decades. In this fiscal crisis our epoch is being brought into line with the major privatizations that ended up engulfing past societies from Babylonia through Rome and Byzantium.

DISCUSSION

Edzard: When you define types of rulers, you said there was a real *ruler* in the south, whereas in northern Mesopotamia you rather had what you called chieftains. Did I correctly understand you?

Hudson: Yes, I believe there is a difference between the south and the north.

Edzard: As far back as we can trace our historical sources, we had of course rulers' titles, but they do not connote what I would call "chieftains." One term is LUGAL, which signifies the big man *par excellence*, from LÚ, "person," and GAL "big," literally the "big one." (I don't think he is the big householder, but that is another question.) Then there is the *šarrum*, "king." The title's literary correspondence is to *rubā'um*, "the big one" again. We have titles in Ebla, but we cannot firmly read the Eblaite logograms LUGAL and EN. If LUGAL is like a *šarrum*, I would be at a loss to find the word for "chieftain."

Hudson: That is my point. I am contrasting the royal personal households and those of the public organizations, that is, the private and public contexts. Of course you have in every society people on top of an economic and social pyramid. I think that a "big man" implies someone much like you find in anthropology — one who is in control. But such a man is different from a *ruler*, which implies the idea of *rule*, measurement with a view towards ensuring equity. This association is confirmed by the ceremonial iconography of Sumerian rulers. Their attributes are the rod and ring, that is, the measuring rod and the coiled measuring rope. This idea of measurement connotes a public institutional bifurcation of society. As far as I know, you don't find this anywhere near as much in the north, in the Mediterranean, or anywhere else outside southern Mesopotamia.

I am told, for instance, that nowhere in the Ebla texts are references to interest-bearing debts found. The first appearance of such debt seems to be at the interface between the public institutions and the communal sector. In a society such as Ebla, or the Hittites, or the Mycenaen Greeks lacking interest-bearing debt, I think that the reason it is lacking is because they did not have the bifurcation or trifurcation found in southern Mesopotamia. There was no ruler of a distinctly public sector set corporately apart from the community, providing surplus-creating economic resources on which payments accrued.

Edzard: The reason you don't have interest in either Ebla or the Hittite society is, in my opinion, we do not have private contracts for either of these societies from contexts where interest would be liable to turn up in loans. Or, their words for interest simply may not have been found. In the south we have interest, at least in historical inscriptions. The word *hubulla* refers to loans with interest. In Hittite there are many state documents, but no private ones as far as I know. We thus could not say anything about whether the Hittites had interest or not. I know nothing about the Mycenaeans.

Mitchell: You do have the example of the *wanax* and the *basileus* in the Greek world, namely the appearance of an overriding authority (*wanax*) at a time when there were also so-called kings (*basileis*) who in reality were princes who will then emerge out of the dark ages as *basileis* or kings in the Greek world.

We know of obligations to the *wanax*, as far as I can determine (my lack of expertise in Linear B is rather dramatic). I think you have what I would call obligations, and I would like to offer one modification of a question Michael asked, namely, whether the whole idea of privatization can be expanded somewhat to include the privatization of obligations. If I have read my Max Gluckman correctly, in Africa you don't have clear-cut designations of property. You have obligations between people, and these obligations are inherited. It would be just as unthinkable for the ruler to break an obligation to his subject as for the subject to break an obligation to the ruler.

Such a condition has nothing to do with boundary stones, but you know what your boundaries are. They go to the river, the tree, or wherever. These obligations are so fundamentally important that in classical law you can make an argument that the obligation resulting from loans can easily slide into theft, and hence into crime. You thus get enslavement for debt because the debtor has broken a kind of moral requirement and thereby breached the agreement and failed to fulfill his obligation. I'd thus like to offer obligations as another way of looking at privatization.

Hudson: I think that while the Mycenaen documents do have obligations, these are more in the character of deliveries that are made or are due to the palace, or the failure to have met a scheduled delivery. There is no interest or penalty connected with this; it is only an accounting record saying "Here is what is scheduled, and here is the shortfall." This is quite different than the loans and debts that you find in Mesopotamia.

Lamberg-Karlovsky: I am going to comment on Dietz's inability to find a terminological distinction on the presence of chiefs, because that is an aspect which I very much touch on. The way in which you distinguish a *chief* from a *king* is contextual, based on the social organization, the social order and the community. A chief is apparently not hereditary; kings are hereditary. In that context I would question whether the texts convey enough information to distinguish between chiefs and kings. One's preference to use one word or another is, in effect, an arbitrary choice. Hawaiian chiefs sometimes are called chiefs and sometimes kings. The Dhome and the Ashanti are sometimes called kings and sometimes called chiefs, depending upon the criteria which wants to use in the distinction. Criteria are almost always social, political, etc. I don't think that in the third millennium you are going to have the texts to make that kind of distinctive social coherence that would allow you to say one is or is not. Your ability to eliminate the presence of chieftainship is because of your arbitrary designation of LUGAL as king.

Maidman: I would also like to take up an issue that Dietz raised, and that is the matter of documentation. I'd like to stress as an axiom that I cannot go beyond the issues that the documents touch on. The question may be excellent, but if there are no data that pertain to the question, then I'm in no position to respond to it except as speculation or theory. Specifically, you mentioned that you don't believe there is aboriginal private property. I would suggest that if there were aboriginal private property, there would be no need for documentation, let alone documentation being preserved to attest to that fact. Consequently, I'm less than confident about that observation.

Beyond the absence versus the presence of documents, there is another issue that arises from your observation on how the idea of interest comes into being, how does rent come into being. Again, the answer is beyond the capacity of our sources to answer. There are too many unanswerable questions regarding the origins of institutions. That is why we have the book of Genesis, because there are no sources, and so people develop wonderful explanatory models or myths.

In addition to the lack of documentation, not all documents are created equal, yet we tend to lump all documents together in terms of their verisimilitude, in terms of their accuracy. I'm not speaking of lumping royal inscriptions together with laundry lists, but even within the realm of laundry lists we too often ignore the possibility, not necessarily of deliberate falsification, but of economic formulas as literary *topoi*.

Consequently, we tend to take things literally and let our guard down when we are dealing with allegedly objective documentation. In Nuzi, for example, it is a standard penalty clause in real estate transactions that he who violates the stipulations of the contract shall pay two minas of silver, two minas of gold, or sometimes more. But it is an economic impossibility to pay even the lower amount. Consequently, the clause means "don't do it, you will be fined, you will be punished." You interpret at great risk if you take literally the amounts that are being described. I would urge, along with Dietz, a sensitivity to textual nuance no less than to archaeological nuance.

Heltzer: There has been quite enough spoken about the sources, but nobody has reacted to the comment about weights and measures. Weights and measures naturally are very important to standardization, and even more important for international trade or trade between various countries, communities and areas. Zaccagnini (1986) shows that there are at least four weight systems in use all over the Mediterranean, including Sicily and Sardinia. This was the only way to find a common weight system for international trade, which was achieved in the ancient Near East in the middle of the second millennium.

Von Dassow: When you point out the rod and ring iconography of kingship as supporting your thesis, are you aware that this has been interpreted (*e.g.* by commentors on Agnes Spycket's paper, "The Rod and the Ring," at the recent A.O.S. meeting at Chapel Hill, North Carolina) as a stick of chastisement and a lead-rope with a nose ring on the end, by which the god or his delegate the king, controls the people?

Hudson: That interpretation seems to me to be inspired more by modern anthropological tribal practice. In fact, it highlights the contrast between Mesopotamia's public-type rulers and the big-man type found in tribal communities. I hold to the older interpretation of Mesopotamian rulership as guarantor of distributive justice and economic equity.

Von Dassow: Even though kings and gods are frequently depicted with such a lead rope and a nose ring?

Hudson: I think they became that in time. The question is, were they that initially? Certainly by Roman times, lictors had clubs. But did these batons really begin as clubs? Already in the Ice Age, Marshack has described the inscribed calendrical batons apparently held by leaders. Was there initially a public persona different from that of rule by force, or was it coercive from the beginning? It is possible that this was frequently the case, but I think there was something in Mesopotamia's public-sector rulership that was non-coercive and voluntary.

von Dassow: But it seems you are going back and forth between supporting your interpretation of rulership by reference to the iconography, and supporting this interpretation of the iconography by reference to your theory of rulership.

Hudson: Well, it wasn't originally my interpretation. I think the idea that you put forth, as you point out, is the new idea here — and I think it comes more from anthropology than from the Assyriologists.

von Dassow: Your own approach seems in many ways modernist, in the sense that you use modern categories and seem to be seeking a uniform process. Most of us probably would agree that our fields of scholarship face the danger of sliding into marginality if we do not relate them properly to the study of history, and indeed to the history of law, economics and science. The danger, of course, is that we burden the subjects of our research with terms and interpretive models that more properly belong to the modern conceptual frameworks and categories that underlie today's social sciences.

We may be dealing more with modern logical categories than actual evidence. I sense that many of the papers at this conference use the terms "private," "privatization" and "ownership" in their own particular ways. It is necessary to establish what these terms mean, and to establish criteria for determining whether property was privately owned, and whether a process of privatization took place. The notion of progressive privatization of property, for instance, evaporates along with the postulate of "original" communal ownership.

It seems to me that your programmatic statements describe a fairly uniform historical process spreading from Mesopotamia westward, operating on a fairly uniform substratum involving "communal" ownership of real estate. But at the 1994 Rencontre Assyriologique Internationale in Berlin, Reinhard Bernbeck delivered a paper emphasizing the differences in social structure in Hassunan and Samarran sites in the sixth millennium in Mesopotamia. He found that whereas Hassunan sites exhibit features suggesting communal social structure, Samarran excavations reveal what seems to be a society organized into private extended-family households with little sign of communal organization.

This suggests that prehistorical Mesopotamian society was not uniform in terms of the relevant socio-economic characteristics. It therefore is unlikely that socioeconomic and political development proceeded according to a uniform paradigm in the historical period; unless, perhaps, such a paradigm were imposed on diverse substrata by a controlling authority.

Hudson: I agree, of course, that nearly every region developed its own ways of coping. But Prof. Edzard has just criticized me for making this very point. The real point, of course, is that among the variations, the privatization phenomenon had numerous common tendencies spanning these regions. These general tendencies are summarized in the charts at the end of my paper. First of all, I find a weakening of communal traditions and sanctions restricting the sale of land to only temporary duration (that is, subject to Clean Slates), restricting land use to support its tenants, and attaching obligations to land tenure to ensure that it be used for public purposes, including the support of its holders in order to enable them to supply corvée labor, serve in the military draft, and pay various types of taxes or fees.

I hope that I have not left a wrong impression in trying to sift out the common denominators that I find to be at work through the ages. No doubt as an economist I am especially prone to use modern categories. But instead of reducing history to a series of abstract, uniform "stages of development" as Polanyi did, I try to find common denominators as characteristic phenomena and processes. I pinpoint some sources of instability, such as debt and land monopolization that spread throughout the ancient world, and a direction of change in the types of response over time, *e.g.* from Clean Slates to Roman property-based law.

Although commercial practices became uniform, "privatization" as such occurred in a different way in nearly every region. No doubt the substrata probably were indeed different, for many variables were at work and it became almost a mark of strong leaders to make each society distinct (Sparta and Athens are examples). Yet common denominators and tendencies are found at work throughout such variability. Ultimately there was a convergence, imposed externally by Roman force. What was imposed from above by imperial Rome was not a "public sector," of course, but just the opposite: a regime of private property. Throughout most of the world ever since, such property forms have had to be imposed by force, for they break up what went before, often to the benefit of foreigners. Of course, "what went before" differed widely as between the Near East, Eastern Asia, Africa, South America and so forth.

Dandamayev: You mentioned taxes several times. Do we have any explicit documentary evidence regarding taxes for these early periods? If we have, what were these taxes?

Hudson: I try to avoid the word "tax" for the early period, because I don't think there were taxes as such. The word is indeed anachronistic. I think taxes develop only as privatization develops. Once enterprise passes into the private sector, the public institutions no longer are self supporting, but must tax society's privately generated surplus for their support. My view is that setting up enterprise in the temples and palaces meant that these institutions did not have to tax the population initially. Each sector was, in principle, self-supporting. This is why I try to avoid using the word taxes in the third millennium, and even the second millennium.

Hallo: As one Assyriologist who has promoted the rod and ring interpretation as signifying the goad of an ox, I tried to persuade Dr. Porada of that in her last article, which she invited me to co-author with her. I was unsuccessful, but appended a note that I would discuss the subject elsewhere.* But to get back to your main point, I was much taken by your raising of the question of the origin of interest, because I am busy finishing a book on origins, and I hadn't thought about interest at all. Now you've started me thinking, and one line of investigation that you didn't use was the etymological one. One area not touched on was that of animal husbandry. I wonder whether I can sneak past Professor Edzard the notion that the Sumerian word for interest, *máš*, has anything to do with the Sumerian word for goat, and whether in fact the whole process began not with agriculture, but with animal husbandry. Some of our earliest intelligible economic texts deal with herds presumably entrusted to a herdsman, with the increase in these herds presumably being divided between him and their owner. That famous article by Gelb on the growth of a herd (which is now generally re-interpreted as some kind of school exercise of ideal proportions) shows the importance of the natural increase of

---

* Edith Porada, "Cylinder of Kurigalzu I?" (Additional notes by W. W. Hallo), in *Beiträge zur Altorientalischen Archaeologie und Altertumskunde: Festschrift für Barthel Hrouda . . .*, ed. by Peter Calmeyer *et al.* (Wiesbaden, Harrassowitz: 1994):234.

herds and the responsibilities of herdsmen in reporting on it. But it later was extended to agriculture, and here again etymology may help. Generally speaking, seed grain was loaned at seeding time, when the cultivators were without the means to provide it themselves, but it was due back with interest at harvest time. Typically, the word used, at least in Akkadian, was *šibšu,* which I relate to Sumerian *ŠU.PEŠ,* which means to do something for the third time, to divide into thirds.* This provides an older etymological basis for the one-third interest you describe as being normal by Ur III times.

In connection with slave release, I discovered in the Babylonian collection at Yale a sliver of text that proves that the Edict of Samsuiluna, the first of Hammurapi's successors — and the first of those edicts — was, I now think, designed to undo some of the idealistic provisions of the laws of Hammurapi, without quite seeming to. Whereas the laws of Hammurapi (whether or not they would have been enforced is not the issue at this point), provided for triennial release, the new evidence suggests that this was reformed in the later Old Babylonian edicts so that a more practical arrangement was used. Only when the king pronounced a release of all debt-slaves was there such a release, implying that the automatic releases that the laws envisioned through the years were impractical. They probably dried up the sources of credit, so that a reform was needed.

Hudson: I have just completed an article on the early words for interest, and I do not believe that interest has a pastoral origin. I think that the word *máš,* although it indeed means "kid or young goat," is corollary in idea to the same idea in Latin *fenus* and Greek *tokos.* I think what is meant is not a young animal literally, but the idea of birth. The idea of birth connotes the birth of interest with each new moon. Literally the increment, the 1/60th, is "born" each month along with the new moon. You have this very clearly in Greek *tokos.* And in classical Greek times, silver-interest still accrues or "is born" on the new moon. We see this in Aristophanes' *The Clouds.* The word *máš,* not to be taken literally.

Buccellati: I think it is difficult to address just one paper, when Michael addresses the questions that all the others are dealing with. But I find a greater similarity between the south, the north and the west in the third millennium. The term we are using more often now is Syro-Mesopotamia, because it tends to stress this type of commonality. To some extent

* W. W. Hallo, "Choice in Sumerian," JANES 5 (1973):169.

the archaeological evidence for places like Ebla, Mozan, Brak, Leilan, which are much closer, if not identical to the great cities in the south, and different from the small towns in the north. This implies that there is in fact a great structural similarity in this political system.

Of course, we cannot work without documentation, and we should be ready to be sober and prudent. Still, I think the discussion that has already developed shows the usefulness of having overarching questions about systemic issues, to which we try to give answers and then look back at the texts once more. This issue of the origins of debt is an example.

von Dassow: One final point regarding your views on these origins. As I understand your paper, you are arguing against the "communal" model of primitive society. You point to ethnographic documentation for rights of ownership over land even among nomadic peoples, and among settled peoples you observe the presence of separate storage facilities associated with individual family dwellings, in neolithic sites such as Çayonu. This suggests private ownership, at least on the family level; certainly neither "communal" nor "public."

Hudson: I want to ward off a possible misunderstanding concerning just where the "family" fits into the public/private taxonomy. Where families appear to be the organizational unit, we usually find *groups* of families. When traditions prevent land from being sold, forfeited for debt arrears (permanently) or otherwise alienated out of the family under distress conditions, I have classified this as a "communal override" because it spans these families. Such property is not yet private. If it is not the "community" as a whole that is the basic unit, then perhaps we need a third, intermediate category for family-based units sharing common modes of land tenure. I prefer simply to define the community in terms of kinship-based landed units, but the important point is not so much one of terminology as it is of the dynamic processes at work.

Cleveland: Even the most primitive societies have some varieties of private property in land. For example, tribal elders may allocate grazing and watering rights among families. Such rights are limited, loosely-defined and temporary. The more formal and secure property rights become, the more it costs to define and enforce them. "Advanced" property rights in land, as in Nuzi and finally, Rome, will be found only where population density is high enough that the benefits of private propety exceed tis costs. From this perspective, the story of privatization in the ancient Near East is not one of change from "communal" to "private" property; it is rather the story of the transformation of vague and insecure property rights into "advanced" property rights as population grew and technology improved. The transformation may have been gradual and incremental, or abrupt as in the English enclosures.

Hudson: I can only agree that this entire subject is fraught with dangers of confusion stemming from the terminology we use. Anthropologists have tangled over the idea of communal property in terms of what Garrett Hardin (1968) called the "tragedy of the commons," representing the commons of feudal England (and other regions) as being, allegedly, open to everybody. His essay has become one of the most widely reprinted ones in the anthropological literature, appearing over seventy times. Yet historians were quick to point out that the commons are almost never open to all, but are managed under certain well-understood conditions, spelling out the specific rights of each family. These criticisms prompted Hardin to write a follow-up paper in 1991 qualifying his earlier views by acknowledging that only the "unmanaged" commons are a tragedy! (Unfortunately, this paper is not appended to the frequent reprinting of his earlier essay.)

In my view, such "unmanagement" tends to be a form of privatization, in the sense that it is a free-for-all of each user acting in his own interests, with no communal traditions to steer land use in an orderly manner. So I think you are right in the sense that we need a common terminology. Otherwise, we may be in agreement over the phenomena we are describing, but not exactly what to call it.

Levine: I just want to conclude by saying that the hidden agenda here is the hidden agenda of the humanities and the social sciences generally these days: the relative roles of theoretical models versus the given data, the actual evidence of one sort or another. There is always the danger that the model will overtake the evidence and become a procrustean bed into which we stuff the evidence to make it conform. But there is also the opposite danger of going about our business without an agenda. The model gives us the questions that need to be answered. As the old philosopher said, "The question is, What is the question?" Here, we are trying to improve the quality of our questions.

NOTES

1. **Processes that became public in antiquity as the state's three defining modern chracteristics:**

   Law. Today's criminal law punishes lawbreakers for "breaking the king's peace." Punishment is carried out by the public sector rather than being left to the victims to enforce. However, the public sector rarely makes restitution (that must be pursued in a separate civil action). Thus, civil and criminal law have become separated.

   The monopoly of force and military power.

   Taxes (mainly to finance the costs of war). Tax obligations traditionally go with wealth. Yet wealth at the top has largely freed itself from these obligations through tax loopholes, offshore banking, and the general de-taxation of land and natural resources.

   The public sector no longer is a net saver but a debtor. It also no longer undertakes corporate commercial enterprise, but leaves this to the private sector (to be taxed). Only in Stalinist Russia and Maoist China have modern states engaged in large-scale industry and collective farming — and these attempts are widely recognized as failures.

   Could history have taken a different path? Could more public constraints have been maintained to shape the context of private enterprise so as to avoid the extreme polarization found in Roman times and again today?

   Why was it that the most polarized economy — Rome — emerged as the dominant one in its epoch? Does its victory show that privatization ultimately is the most efficient mode of social organization? Or does the way in which Rome collapsed suggest that all polarized societies are doomed to self-destruction?

2. **Processes that have become privatized:**

   Today's state has turned over profit-seeking activity to the private sector. It runs its operations at a loss, and finances them by levying taxes on the private-sector surplus.

   Rent originally evolved as prebend income to support temple hierarchies. The securitizing of rent is first found in Nippur's Inanna temple prebends. As for *subsistence land tenure*, the land — along with subsoil wealth — has become increasingly alienable to individual holders on a permanent basis. The objective of this land is to yield rents, often by inducing public investment in the "externalities" (transport, provision of water and other infrastructure).

Interest originally was owed to the public sector to "even out" the well-to-do debtor's self-seeking gains from delaying payment. As such, it evolved from a penalty into a time-preference discounting the future relative to the present.

Public utilities: The temples were essentially utilities, organized as the first business corporations. Modern utilities include transport, air lines, power, and communications.

The ability to form corporations: Originally, the act of incorporation had to be deemed in the public or national interest. But today, the limited-liability corporation represents a protective shell insulating private investors from public recourse for civil wrongs.

Industrial profits: Were there indeed such profits in Bronze Age Mesopotamia?

Culture: Communal by definition, it promoted acceptance of the ancient world-view and its social cosmology. Modern culture no longer warns against economic *hubris*, that is, obsessive-compulsive wealth-seeking.

Sport: From religious games to consumer entertainment for profit.

The family: From the communalist unit to the autonomous and self-seeking individual household.

3. **Hypotheses to be tested:**

If the above economic dynamics began as public, were they promoted or were they stifled by being privatized?

If they began as private enterprise, were they stifled by "creeping socialism"?

REFERENCES

Adams, Robert M. (1981), *Heartland of Cities* (Chicago).

Andelson, Robert V. (1979), "Cathrein's Careless Clerical Critique," in Andelson, ed., *Critics of Henry George: A Centenary Appraisal of Their Strictures on Progress and Poverty* (Rutherford, N.J.: Fairleigh Dickinson University Press):126-136.

Bennett, Emmett L., Jr. (1958), *The Mycenae Tablets II* (= *Transactions of the American Philosophical Society*, n.s. 48, Philadelphia).

Cathrein, Rev. Victor S. J. (1889), *The Champions of Agrarian Socialism: A Refutation of Emile de Laveleye and Henry George* (tr. J. U. Heinzle, Buffalo).

— (1911), *Moralphilosophie* (2 vols., Freiburg im Breisgau).

Charpin, Dominique (1980), *Archives familiales et propriete privee in Babylonie ancienne* (Geneva-Paris)

— (1986), *Le Clerge d'Ur au siecle d'Hammurapi* (Geneva-Paris).

Coulanges, Numa Denis(1980 [1864]), *The Ancient City: A Study on the Religion, Laws, and Institutions of Greece and Rome* (Baltimore).

Deimel, Anton (1931), *Sumerische Tempelwirtschaft den Zeit Urukaginas und seiner Vorgänger* (Rome).

Diakonoff, Igor. M. (1982), "The Structure of Near Eastern Society before the Middle of the 2nd Millennium BC," *Oikumene* 3:7-100.

Edzard, Dietz Otto (1957), *Die zweite Zwischenzeit Babyloniens* (Wiesbaden).

Frankfurt, Henri (1951), *Kingship and the Gods* (Chicago).

Gelb, Ignace J.; Steinkeller, Piotr; and Whiting, Robert M. Jr. (1989-91), *Earliest Land Tenure Systems in the Near East: Ancient Kudurrus* (2 vols., Chicago=OIP Vol. 104).

George, Henry (1987), *Progress and Poverty* (New York [1879]).

Hallo, William (1972), "The House of Ur-Meme," JNES 31:87-95."

Hardin, Garrett (1991), "The Tragedy of the *Unmanaged* Commons: population and the disguises of Providence," in Robert V. Andelson, ed., *Commons Without Tragedy: Protecting the Environment from Overpopulation — a New Approach* (London and Savage, Md.):162-185.

Hudson, Michael (1992), "Did the Phoenecians Introduce the Idea of Interest to Greece and Italy — And If So, When?" in Günther Kopcke and Isabelle Tokumaru, *Greece Between East and West: 10th-8th Centuries BC* (Mainz):128-143.

— (1994), Land Monopolization, Fiscal Crises and Clean Slate 'Jubilee' Proclamations in Antiquity," in Hudson, G. C. Miller & Kris Feder, *A Philosophy for a Fair Society* (London).

Kramer, Samuel (1959), *History Begins at Sumer* (New York).

— (1963), *The Sumerians: Their History, Culture, and Character* (Chicago)

Kraus, Fritz (1984), *Königliche Verfügungen in altbabylonischer Zeit* (Leiden=SD 11).

Lambert, Maurice (1960), "La naissance de la bureaucratie," *Review Historique* 224:1-26.

Leveleye, Emile de (1878), *Primitive Property* (tr. G. R. L. Marriott, London).

Nagy, Gregory (1985), "Theognis and Megara: A Poet's Vision of his City," in Thomas J. Figueira and G. Nagy, eds., *Theognis of Megara: Poetry and the Polis* (Baltimore and London).

Nissen, Hans J., Peter Damerow and Robert K. Englund (1993), *Archaic Bookkeeping: Early Writing and Techniques of Economic Administration in the Ancient Near East* (Chicago [1990]).

Oppert, Julius (1877), *Documents juridiques de l'Assyrie et de la Chaldée* (Paris).

Roth, Martha (1984), "Appendix to Zettler, 'The Genealogy of the House of Ur-Me-Me: A Second Look,'" *Archiv für Orientforschung* 31:9-14.

Schneider, Anna (1921), *Die Anfänge der Kulturwirtschaft: Die sumerische Tempelstadt* (Essen).

Scott, William Robert (1912), *The Constitution and Finance of English, Scottish and Irish Joint-Stock Companies to 1720* (Cambridge, 3 vols.).

Smith, George (1875), *Ancient History from the Monuments. Assyria from the earliest times to the fall of Nineveh* (London).

Starr, Chester G. (1961), "The Decline of the Early Greek Kings," *Historia* 10:129-38.

Stone, Elizabeth (1987), *Nippur Neighborhoods* (Chicago).

Toynbee, Arnold (1965), *Hannibal's Legacy* (2 vols., Oxford).

Veenhof, Klaus R. (1986), *Cuneiform Archives and Libraries* (=CRRIA 30:1983)a (Istanbul).

Ventris, Michael, and Chadwick, John, *Documents in Mycenaean Greek* (Cambridge: 1956).

Winter, Irene (1989), "The Body of the Able Ruler: Toward an Understanding of the Statues of Gudea," in Herman Behrens, Darline Loding and Martha

T. Roth, eds., *Dum-E$_2$-Dub-ba-a: Studies in Honor of Ake W. Sjoberg* (Philadelphia):573-83.

Wittfogel, Karl (1981), *Oriental Despotism: A Comparative Study of Total Power* (2nd ed., New York).

Yoffee, Norman (1977), *The Economic Role of the Crown in the Old Babylonian Period* (Malibu).

Zaccagnini, Carlo (1986), "Aspects of Copper Trade in the Eastern Mediterranean during the Late Bronze Age," *Traffici Micenei nel Mediterraneo.*

Zagarell, Allen (1986), "Trade, Women, Class, and Society in Ancient Western Asia," *Current Anthropology* 27:415-30.

Zettler, Richard (1992), *The Ur III Temple of Inanna at Nippur Mediterraneo. Berliner Beiträge zum Vorderen Orient,* 11.

2.

The Archaeological Evidence for International Commerce: Public and/or Private Enterprise in Mesopotamia?

C. C. Lamberg-Karlovsky
Peabody Museum, Harvard University

The character of the ancient economy has long been the subject of debate. Johannes Renger (1995) recently has reviewed the different positions with respect to ancient Mesopotamia, and shown how the arguments hinge on the extent to which the ancient economy resembles that of the modern world. To what extent did open markets characterize antiquity? What was the extent, if any, of the development of private capital? Did mechanisms of supply and demand affect prices, wages, etc., or was the ancient economy characterized by categories alien to the modern economy, such as reciprocity, redistribution, gift-giving, and extensive communal and/or state control over the means of production (Polanyi, Arensberg and Pearson 1957)?

Two and a half centuries ago, Jean-Jacques Rousseau identified the emergence of private property as the primary evil that lured us from paradise and its state of innocence. Since then philosophers, economists, anthropologists and historians have debated the nature and significance surrounding the emergence of private property. Finally, in the twentieth century the Soviets introduced an effort to abolish all private property in order to re-enter that lost Eden — that stage in human history when private property did not exist.

But was there ever a stage in human history in which private property did not exist? A careful study of the earliest texts in Mesopotamia suggest that private possession of land already was extant (Gelb, Steinkeller, Whiting 1991). Thus, we are left to conclude that private land ownership already was a prehistoric phenomenon.

The manner in which the political economy is embedded forms the material foundation for any complex society. Furthermore, the specific structure which this political economy takes will establish the distinctive mechanisms used by elites to maintain their power and legitimate their role. Institutions of domination and integration formed the post and beam of state formation. In southern Mesopotamia these institutions of state were first the temple, later the palace, and later still, a self-conscious antagonism between temple and palace.

T. N. D'Altroy and T. K. Earle (1985) have distinguished two forms of political finance: staple finance and wealth finance. These authors suggest that the large-scale centralized storage of goods represents "staple finance," available for paying personnel who render services to the elite. Hunt (1987) makes a similar point, emphasizing the role of elite authorities in collecting surplus grain and storing it in centralized and bureaucratically managed facilities. In southern Mesopotamia staple finance involved taxation, gathered in the form of quotas for staples such as cereals, livestock, and finished commodities. Characteristically, the state — taking the form of its dominant institution, such as the temples in third-millennium southern Mesopotamia — owned improved lands, controlled irrigation systems, and maintained an almost exclusive control over long-distance trade. In return for the right to cultivate institutionally owned state land, individual households provided labor and goods to the owner.

Staple finance is simple and direct. The central management of staple production permits the state and/or institution to mobilize goods needed to support state personnel (priests, scribes, administrators, soldiers, artisans, *et al.*). In the absence of extensive markets and standardized currencies, staple finance was the direct means of supporting the state's operation. It required the central management of production, storage and distribution.

The problems of transport, communication and processing of necessary information must have made staple finance a logistical nightmare. To diminish this nightmare Renfrew (1975) has suggested that staple finance can be effective only in small city-states in which territorial boundaries do not exceed 50 km. Actually, however, staple finance can function in more extensive states by dispersing public functions. When a multiplicity of institutions compete with the state, as did private households, temple estates, and the royal estate in the second half of the third millennium (in southern Mesopotamia), tensions emerged in the control and establishment of centralized authority.

In contrast to staple finance, wealth finance uses currency, primitive money, or finally just valuable commodities as a means of payment or barter. These proto-monetary objects may function as personal ornaments and status symbols, or they may be emblematic of esoteric knowledge, whose production involves some privileged or sacred knowledge. The objects are made highly desirable by their rarity, skillful production, sacredness, and/or foreign origin (Helms 1988). Control over these products forms the foundation for institutional finance, and derives largely from control over exchange and/or production.

In both southern and northern Mesopotamia, wealth finance was in the hands of individuals who were able to directly control the manufacture of proto-monetary commodities. But who were they? The answer to this question has been the subject of a long, frequently acrimonious debate. Mesopotamian texts suggest that the personnel involved with the production of wealth-objects were controlled by state institutions. Frequently the production of these objects, from gold to stone bowls, involved rare foreign resources that either were manufactured in the households of the administrative elite or in the institutional settings of the temples and palaces.

In order to reduce theft and pilferage, artisans were carefully monitored with respect to the amount of raw materials given for the production of finished goods. Ores were weighed, and then related to the weight of the finished product, suggesting that overseers understood the difference in the ratios between raw materials and the losses engendered in manufacturing the final product. Throughout Mesopotamia local staples were redistributed by the state, and/or its institutions, in order to support the artisans devoted to the production of wealth. Highly valued objects belonged to the central authority and were strategically moved about in order to retain an integrated control over the political economy.

Such is the view to be derived from the texts. But is this an accurate perspective? Do the texts in fact capture the totality of the political economy of third-millennium Mesopotamia?

Craft production and the case of the potters

Michael Hudson, in his studies of the ancient Near East, emphasizes the positive results to be derived from state control of economic surpluses through the establishment of a public utility dedicated to serving the public weal. His perspective is informed, and appears to be supported by the documentary record. This perspective subordinates private enterprise and household production — at least as far as the permanent accumulation of economic surpluses is concerned — to the authoritative command of state-controlled labor, production, and the monitoring of consumption. Does this public structure capture the totality of the complexity of the Mesopotamian political economy?

Most writers have emphasized the nature of state control over craft production. There is, however, ample evidence to suggest that craft production also was undertaken in the context of a private market economy. Although pottery is the most common artifact recovered in an archaeological context, it is only recently that archaeologists and philologists have turned their attention to the social and economic context in which this pottery was produced (Wattenmaker 1994; Steinkeller 1994; Blackman and Stein 1993; Weiss 1992; Waetzoldt 1971). These studies have emphasized both the public *and* private contexts of pottery production. A potter was involved with a staple finance commodity when producing ceramics for the state authority, but he (or she) could and did produce pottery for a market economy, thus involving the production of wealth finance. A single producer could be (and the texts indicate that they indeed were) involved with both public and private domains of production.

Based on his studies in and around the site of Leilan in northern Syria, Gil Stein (1994:16) has emphasized the important distinction between the organization of agriculture and craft production. The regional economy of the Leilan area required a tributary system for procuring the cereals necessary to support increased urban demand, while "ceramic production took place more or less independently at every level of the settlement hierarchy — centers, secondary centers, and villages."

Steinkeller's recent (1994) review of texts pertaining to the production of pottery indicates that among the potters of Pre-Sargonid Lagash c. 2500 BC, "rather than working permanently for the state, [the potters] owed to it only a specific contributory service." Implicitly, one must assume that they were free the rest of the time to produce for their personal benefit.

In the later Ur III period, c. 2100 BC, the texts indicate the existence of three categories of potters: (1) potters under the control of the local governor (*énsi*), (2) potters under the control of the royal/crown organizations (*báhar lugal*) and (3) "potters of the countryside" (*báhar ma-da*). Potters working full time were given six *iku* of land, while those working half-time were allotted half the amount of prebend land. In addition, full time potters obtained 60 liters of barley and five liters of oil per month, as well as four pounds of wool per year. The texts also indicate that potters could own their own seals, were called upon for *corvée* service, and had their sons follow them in the craft. Pottery produced in the provinces of Umma were considered part of the *bala* duty, *i.e.* the annual contribution (tax or levy) of commodities and resources produced in specific provinces for delivery to the central government. The number of pots delivered, typically to Umma's state-owned breweries, could be very high. The potter Lukala produced 2,573 pots during the sixth year of the reign of Amar-Sin, 2,588 in Amar-Sin's seventh year, and 2,478 in Amar-Sin's ninth year.

Waetzoldt's pioneering study (1971) of the Ur III potters at Umma is of special significance with regard to the private operation of the potters. Six liters a day were designated as *á báhar hun-gá*, "wages of the hired potters." This indicates that potters could hire themselves out for "wages"; for 6 liters a day or three times the regular "state" allotment. In a review of the status of potters in the Ur III period the summary view of Steinkeller (1994) is directly relevant to this symposium:

> . . . these facts suggest to me that, in the Ur III period Babylonia, pottery industry was a home-based activity, which was carried out in individual, family-owned and family-operated workshops. Although the potters were members of particular institutions, and as such owed services to those institutions, they apparently worked at home, in their own workshops, rather than in the facilities belonging to and directly managed by such institutions. . . . it will not be unreasonable to assume that, during the time that they were not working for the state, they were free to produce pots and other clay artifacts to satisfy the needs of the general population.

This conclusion receives support from the archaeological record. At Ur, Nippur, Uruk, Abu Salabikh, Tepe Gawra, and the sites of the Diyala, virtually every excavated site in which a substantial horizontal exposure was uncovered, archaeologists have exposed activity areas of pottery, stone, and metal manufacture within a *domestic* context (see Woolley and Moorey's [1982] discussion of the neighborhoods of Ur; Stone [1987] for Nippur; and Delougaz, *et al.* [1967] for the Diyala).

The archaeological evidence for a domestic context of production is as true for the Ubaid of the fifth millennium as for the later Hellenistic period. The archaeological record, however, does suggest a difference in context between the production of rare resources and that of more common resources. Far more pottery kilns have been recovered from domestic contexts than have kilns indicating the production of metal. A statistical analysis of the context of production would differentiate, I suspect, between utilitarian crafts produced from available resources in domestic contexts, and luxury crafts manufactured from rare resources in "state"-owned institutional contexts. To the doemstic category would belong pottery production, reed-working, carpentry, and at times, to be sure, the limited production of metals and textiles. Gold, silver, semi-precious stones (lapis, carnelian, *et al.*), the large-scale production of metals and textiles, and even beer, were produced under "state" authority, while exotic feathers, animals and plants were derived through the intermediary of a state agent involved in long-distance trade.

The production of elite goods was closely integrated into the "great organizations" of state. The workshops of these "great organizations" were devoted largely to the manufacture of strategically important status items: elaborate garments, jewelry, ornate furniture, wagons, weapons, boats, etc. We read in the texts of the production and control of these items, while in the archaeological record we read of the production of less "strategic" goods in domestic contexts. At Ebla, for instance, there is an abundance of pottery in Palace G (Mazzoni 1988), but it is not the pottery that is discussed in the texts, it is their contents: oil and wine. These two commodities represent important assets of staple finance, and as such were monitored by the state. Pottery production, produced in domestic contexts, was all but ignored by the political elite (Archi 1982:212-218).

With regard to the crafts and craft production, I believe that the texts offer a biased perspective, particularly within the context of the ration lists. The texts, after all, represent the perspective of the urban managerial elite. In the ration lists craftsmen are listed collectively, suggesting that they formed communes of production, organized into work-groups that worked in a specific location. Yet the archaeological record simply does not support this contention. There is not a single archaeological site of the fourth to first millennium that has recovered a large-scale "industrial" activity area, one in which the recorded large-scale production suggested by the texts could take place. When workshops are uncovered — and they are pitifully few — they consist at most of a kiln or three, regardless of whether they are recovered from the context of a "great organization" or a domestic context.

In sum, although the texts suggest large-scale industrial production controlled by the state, the archaeological record suggests that most craft production took place outside of the physical context of a centralized state bureaucracy. This is most clearly evident in the case of pottery. Specific attention has been given to the archaeological context of pottery production in a number of recent excavations dated to the third millennium: Leilan (Stein 1993), Kurban Höyük (Wattenmaker 1994) and Lidar Höyük (Hauptmann 1983:95). The character of production at these sites is well summarized by Patricia Wattenmaker (1994:115): "ceramics were produced in multiple workshops and . . . ceramic production was not administered by the political elite." In this regard Steinkeller's (1994) conclusion seems in harmony with the archaeological record:

> . . . the central and enduring feature of the early Babylonian crafts was that they were home-based, and that they operated on a family level. This provided craftsmen with a considerable degree of independence from the state. Depending upon the period, the margin of economic freedom enjoyed by craftsmen differed considerably, of course. In the periods of increased centralization, they would be more closely integrated into the state structures. When the central government weakened, they would be practically independent.

There is one point on which we must rely on inference alone, as neither the texts nor the archaeological record shed light on the question: How did the community's ordinary population obtain their everyday articles: shoes, pottery, reed mats, wooden and stone tools (of which there are a goodly number, *e.g.* sickle blades, arrow points, etc., typically left unreported by archaeologists dealing with Bronze Age Mesopotamia), baskets, wooden tools, cordage, bricks, simple furniture, *et al*? There is no evidence in the texts that the "great organizations" ever got involved in the distribution of these mundane commodities to the general population.

One hardly can avoid the conclusion that the distribution of these commodities was not directed by state bureaucrats from centralized warehouses. These everyday essential goods were obtained from private craftsmen who produced them for purchase or barter within a market economy. No doubt, as in the case of potters, they also produced specific quotas for delivery to state institutions. In Afghanistan there are itinerant communities consisting of artisan guilds devoted to the production of specific items (*i.e.* sieves, pottery, metallurgy) or specialized in specific types of skilled labor (*i.e.* threshers). In the anthropological literature these itinerant groups are referred to as "peripatetic" or "commercial nomads" (Rao 1987; Olefin 1994). "Peripateticism" denotes a strategy, a mode of subsistence that combines spatial mobility, non-subsistence commerce, and group endogamy. Where the basic elements of pastoralism are labor, pastures and livestock, those of the peripatetics are labor, customers, and skills/goods. We are entirely ignorant of the existence of such peripateticism in the Mesopotamian economy, yet in the ethnographic literature they remain a global phenomenon of importance to their communities for making available specific crafts and skilled labor. Invariably where the peripatetics exist, they do so as private entrepreneurs engaged in the sale or barter of their goods and/or labor.

Mesopotamian texts suggest that craftsmen and farmers, in fact all primary producers, were responsible for producing a *specific* amount of their products for delivery to the state authority. I believe that the documentary evidence allows for the following interpretation: *all* primary producers were responsible for delivering to the state *a set quota*, a specific amount of their manufactured product. Thus, the staple and wealth finance in the hands of the state institutions came in the form of specific quotas derived from the primary producers. When the primary producer filled his/her/their quota, the remainder of time and labor was their own. This is what the third-millennium texts elaborate upon when discussing the office concerned with the *bala*, meaning "to turn over." That which they "turn over" is their quota. The texts clearly indicate that primary producers were responsible for "turning over" quotas, the *bala* to the state.

There is no reason to disbelieve that once these quotas were achieved, the laborer was able to profit from his/her/their own private production. Everything produced beyond the quota could be freely disposed of in an open market of barter exchange. It is difficult to conceive of what other mechanism would have existed for satisfying the growing population's everyday needs.

The archaeological context of production

There are a number of sites in greater Mesopotamia that contain a specific type of architecture that is central to the question of private vs. public production. At Tell-es Sawaan, Kheit Qasim III, Eridu, Tell Abada and Madhhur (a sampling of representative structures of different date and geographical distribution) archaeologists have uncovered buildings referred to as "T-shaped" (figs. 1-3). Initially these T-shaped structures, occurring some two millennia before their Uruk and Early Dynastic temple descendants, contained the "household" or *oikos* — the social foundation for the formation of the Mesopotamian temple. Maisels (1990:160) succinctly puts forth the argument: "I therefore suggest that such large, multi-family, T-form houses are characteristic of the demands imposed by the concentration of resources and storage where rainfed agriculture is not viable or highly risky," *i.e.* southern Mesopotamia. This suggests that the temple community already was extant in the early Ubaid. Further-more, a few of the buildings uncovered at Tell-es Sawaan share the same architectural attributes, suggesting that the T-shaped structures — and presumably their affiliated social structures — reach back into the Hassuna/Samarran of the mid-sixth millennium.

Needless to say, this hypothesis can be sustained only if one believes that the similarity of architectural form, the T-shaped building, is di-rectly ancestral to the Early Dynastic temple, and that the consistent form of architectural type signifies a commonly shared structure of social organization. Archaeological evidence supports both contentions. J. D. Forest (1984) has recently excavated the entirety of such a structure at Kheit Qasim III (Fig. 2). He believes that the 10-room T-shaped struc-ture "is clearly a 'private dwelling,' indicated both by the facilities (bins, fireplaces), and by the artifacts (pottery, flint, animal bones)." The au-thor offers sound archaeological evidence for suggesting that the structure represents a stratified private household containing several generations.

The existence of these extended households, the *oikiai,* can be traced right to the heart of the southern Mesopotamian alluvium. Excavations on the West Mound of Abu Salabikh, possibly ancient Eresh, uncovered "four contemporary enclosures or compounds occupying the major part of the site during the Early Dynastic I period" (Postgate and Moon 1984: 731). In discussing these T-shaped "compounds," the authors continue,

> one is forced to the conclusion that each compound housed a single "private" establishment and if we seek to interpret our plan in human terms, we must visualize a city composed architectur-ally of large enclosures and socially of corresponding groups of persons, presumably extended families.

This form of extended household, averaging 30-40 persons, struc-tured around a dominant family surrounded by their relations and non-kin dependents, was deduced from the textual record over a decade ago by I. J. Gelb (1979) and I. M. Diakonoff (1982). Diakonoff held the view that these extended households owned their own agricultural lands.

The extent of cultural and economic complexity that characterized late sixth millennium(!) communities is best exemplified by the recent excavation of Sabi Abyad, in the Balikh Valley of northern Syria. Review-ing the evidence, the authors (Akkermans and Verhoeven 1995:99f.) state:

> The abundant occurrence of sealings at Sabi Abyad and their careful storage in "archives" suggest that these objects were part

of a widely accepted, standardized system of administration and recognition involving well-developed concepts of ownership and the presence of bureaucratic means to control it. . . . the present distribution of sealings is part of a more extensive, community-wide pattern, implying that access to the trade network was not restricted to a few individuals only but was open to the community at Sabi Abyad as a whole. In other words, receipt of the sealed goods or objects at Sabi Abyad seems not to have been centrally organized but, on the contrary, was in the hands of many people.

It is clear that the earliest *oikiai,* such as those at Sabi Abyad, were not merely residential groupings but were economic entities — ones involved in private commerce. Maurizio Tosi (1984) has argued that on the Iranian Plateau, archaeologists have recovered the small-scale production of a variety of crafts in domestic contexts. He believes the evidence from a number of sites supports the existence of private craft specialization throughout the third millennium, *i.e.,* of pottery, metals, bead working, stone bowl production, et al.

From an analysis of Mesopotamian Sargonid texts, B. R. Foster (1982: 17) distinguishes three types of archive: "family or private, household, and great household." Furthermore, the "great household" archives are in many respects similar to the "household" archives, the difference being only one of degree.

The difference between the "household" and the "great household" indicate more than a doubling of personnel managers and food production, and something beyond a tripling of industrial production and legal-commercial concerns. There is little reason to believe that from the Ubaid period (perhaps earlier) and throughout the third millennium the extended family was not a primary and self-sufficient unit of production. Over 35 years ago Thorkild Jacobsen (1957) argued that *lugal* originally denoted the large householder, large because he commanded the "great house," the *é-gal, ekallum.* This consisted of an extended family, "his personal servants, and retainers bound to him by exceptionally strong ties of dominance and obedience." Later, Diakonoff (1969) added his voice in support of the existence of "extended patriarchal families or family communes" involved in primary production. Additionally, Diakonoff (1982) argued for the existence of "territorial communities," directed by a council of elders composed of the patriarchs of the significant "family communes." Archaeological evidence would support the contention that

GASUR ARCHIVE

Subject Including	% of Subjects Counted	
	"Household"	"Great Household"
Grain	43	6
Food	12	29
Beer, oils and fats, legumes, flour brewing ingredients		
Land	10	19
Personnel Management	9	22
Livestock	9	9
Sheep, goats, cattle, pigs, hides, sinews		
Industrial Products	4.5	13
Pottery, textiles, wood, metal		
Legal, Commercial	4.5	16
Learner's exercises	4	
Letters, Bullae	4	

already in the Ubaid period there were private households as well as temples; that is, both private and public enterprises.

From Hassuna/Samarra times (that is from 5500 BC) to the end of the Ubaid (c. 3800 BC) a process of political centralization involved increasing bureaucratic dealings that structured the relations of power between (1) the leading patriarchs of lineages and family communes, (2) temples, and (3) councils representing territorial communities. The *political* process involved the interaction of these distinctive social units, providing the primary cells for the emergence of a state sector, so clearly evident in both the archaeological and textual record by Uruk times (3500 BC).

Recently Reviv (1989) has traced the political importance of the role played by the council of "Elders" in pre-monarchic Israel and correctly, I believe, suggested (a) that this body formed the basic political unit throughout the ancient Near East and (b) was one of its most enduring political bodies. The "family communes," "territorial communities," "council of elders," and what Jacobsen(1943) referred to as "primitive democracy" were increasingly absorbed into the powerful patronage of the temple economies and the "houses" of the ruling elite — which may have consisted of the same constituency.

To view the temple as a benign public utility, dedicated to the public interest, overlooks the struggle for power that involved each of the above segments of society. The process of political evolution saw the temple become increasingly subordinate to the private households:

> The struggle for the control over the temples was also a struggle for reserve and export grain funds (and, consequently, for imported raw materials); for supremacy in matters of communal irrigation; and finally, for ideological prestige ensuing from the temple's role of intermediary between the community and the deity, held to be responsible for the former's well-being or its ruin. (Diakonoff 1982:64ff.)

The above quote captures the essence of the process involved in the struggle for power that almost certainly began in the Ubaid period, in the mid-fifth millennium. Control over the temples permitted their heads to increasingly subordinate the private households. By the 25th-24th century the temple estates increasingly fell under the control of a specific ruler and his family, becoming *de facto* their private property.

Within the long Ubaid period there is ample archaeological evidence both for the existence of temples and for private households involved in production. By the Uruk period (3500 BC) the temples had gained the upper hand. In subordinating the dominance of the private household, the temple became the uncontested institution of state, involved in the monitoring of labor, production, and consumption.

The search for evolutionary stages, in which the state and its "great organizations," the temples and the palaces, initially functioned as benign "public utilities" beneficially serving the general weal, followed by a subsequent stage in which the communal nature of the "great organizations" is replaced by a capricious "privatization," oversimplifies a complex and contradictory pattern involving processes of both economic *and* political development.

Conceptualizing the past in terms of a series of successive stages is an evolutionary perspective inherited from the nineteenth century. Such a perspective both simplifies and falsifies. One of the most influential models of evolutionary stages was introduced by Lewis Henry Morgan in his *Ancient Society* (1877). He portrayed the evolution of society as characterized by a series of technological stages termed "Savagery," "Barbarism" and "Civilization." This perspective attained canonical status with its adoption by Karl Marx (see Hobsbawm 1965 and Friedrich Engels 1902). The fact that evolutionary stages still characterize the anthropological literature is evident in the influential works of Service (1975) and Fried (1967). Recent literature has replaced the three stages of "savagery," "barbarism," and "civilization" with the less objectionable terminology of "band," "chiefdom" and the "state." The evolutionary perspective of the earlier terminology emphasized technological and materialist concerns; the recent terms emphasize the evolution of political systems.

The ethnographic record amply demonstrates the co-existence of public and private property. Among hunters and gatherers the ownership of land is communal, belonging to all, at least to all members of a specific tribe, lineage, etc. Tools, on the other hand, are reckoned as private property. And even in this instance one must note that the communally owned land of one group, be it a family and/or tribe, is perceived of as distinctive from the communal lands claimed by another group. In this regard the communally held lands of each group are regarded by that group as their private property. Similarly among nomads, grazing lands are held as tribal property and seen as distinctive from the grazing lands "owned" by other tribes. And while the grazing land is communally owned, the animals remain the private possession of individuals.

The search for "pristine stages" and/or "pure systems" in which one stage of cultural evolution is followed by another is an 18th century conception — typical of the later writings of Marx, and a 19th-century delusion. Vico, Condorcet, Marx, and Comte are among the many theorists that shared the view that humanity (1) has a common destiny, (2) is subject to a single law of development, and (3) will be redeemed in the final stage. This implicitly Christian doctrine of fall, alienation and redemption is perhaps most explicit in Hegel's view of history.

Today an appeal to developmental stages, concluding with a revolutionary redemption, has lost its centuries long certainty. History has fallen back into the hands of the Epicureans — wherein historical movements are seen as largely directed by chance. An appreciation for contradiction, complexity, tension, asymmetry, subtlety, and a reflexive concern for rooting out ideological bias, characterize modern approaches to understanding a more richly varied past — one in which, from the Neolithic to the present, tensions between public and private have been an omnipresent concern. At different times, and for different reasons, the fulcrum that differentiated the private from the public was set at different points — at times weighing in favor of the public against the private, and at other times the reverse.

The asymmetry of trade

In considering long-distance trade one is struck by an asymmetry in the evidence between the texts and the archaeological record. The texts indicate that by the second half of the third millennium both state personnel and private agents were involved in long-distance trade (Adams 1974). Extensive trade was carried out between Dilmun, Magan, and Meluhha, geographic points typically identified as the islands and eastern shores of the Persian Gulf, Oman, and the Indus Civilization. A few scholars, rather unconvincingly, have attempted to reconstruct "World Systems" of commerce that united these distant regions (Kohl 1978; Frank 1993). Edens (1992) has even characterized the relationship of these regions as involving aspects of dependency theory, that is, the "development of underdevelopment," *i.e.* Dilmun was a subservient client of Mesopotamia, allegedly because of its dependence upon Mesopotamian surplus grain.

Today, as opposed to 20 years ago, I believe these claims to be exceedingly dubious. In the early 1970s, while excavating the levels at Tepe Yahya involved in the extensive manufacture of chlorite bowls, I first suggested that Mesopotamia dumped its surplus grain on its neighbors in order to exploit and even control its access to distant resources; invoking the epic tale of "Enmerkar and the Lord of Arrata" as supporting evidence (Lamberg-Karlovsky and Tosi 1973; Lamberg-Karlovsky 1975). Couched in the terms of "interaction spheres" the above concepts were given new life by the adoption of a new terminology: "world systems" and "core-periphery" relations. There is, however, absolutely no reason to believe that the communities on the Iranian Plateau, or for that matter in Dilmun, were not entirely self sufficient in agricultural production.

The texts indicate that there was a considerable amount of long-distance trade, but the *archaeological* evidence in support of this view is *exceedingly* limited. Let me clarify. It is clear that metal, lapis, carnelian, turquoise, certain types of wood, etc. were brought into Mesopotamia by trade. Mesopotamia lacks a whole suite of animal, vegetable, and mineral resources, and the texts clearly indicate that each of these categories was brought into Mesopotamia. Furthermore, the texts indicate that the agents of commerce were exclusively *Mesopotamian* merchants. Why is there no mention of foreign merchants? Was trade controlled only by the merchants from Mesopotamia?

The texts suggest that the principal commodities exported from Mesopotamia were grain and textiles. Except for the latter product, there appears to be no "market" for Mesopotamian finished products; the export of finished products is neither mentioned in the texts, nor have the archaeologists recovered them beyond Mesopotamia. Is the perception correct that the texts detail imports more accurately than exports? In considering each of these questions what is of interest is the asymmetrical evidence that characterizes the *archaeological* and the *documentary* evidence for the trade that brought the Gulf, the Indus Valley, Mesopotamia and the Iranian Plateau into contact. The descriptive nature and extent of this trade has been recently reviewed by Christopher Edens (1992, 1993). The archaeological evidence suggests the following asymmetries of evidence:

1. Artifacts of the Indus Civilization are found in considerable number in both Mesopotamia and the Gulf, *e.g.* Indus seals, etched carnelian beads, and ceramics, yet:

2. Not a single Mesopotamian artifact has been recovered from the Indus, and only one seal from the Gulf (Dilmun) has been discovered in Indus context.

3. Mesopotamian texts indicate a considerable trade with Magan, identified as modern-day Oman. This trade involved the export of copper (and onions) from Magan to Mesopotamia. Yet not a single Mesopotamian artifact has been recovered in Oman, and save for the export of ingots from Magan, no object or category of Magan product has been recovered in Mesopotamia. Analysis of copper objects in Mesopotamia supports the contention that ores from Oman (Magan) were utilized for the production of Mesopotamian artifacts (Berthoud 1979).

4. On the Iranian Plateau (excluding Khuzistan [Susiana]): (a) save for a few isolated etched carnelian beads, on a handful of sites, and a single sealing at Tepe Yahya there are no manufactured objects that can be traced to the Indus Civilization; (b) there are virtually no finished objects to be found of Dilmun (Gulf) or Magan (Oman) type on the Iranian Plateau; (c) products of the Iranian Plateau are found in the Gulf, *i.e.* black-on-gray ware ceramics (Wright 1984), but are exceedingly rare in Mesopotamia, and are all but absent in the Indus Valley.

What can be deduced from such asymmetric patterns of exchange? The archaeological record offers little in the way of a methodological approach that would permit us to distinguish the shifting patterns that directed the activities of merchants. Nevertheless, certain observations can be made. Perhaps the first is the well-established fact that there is little *archaeological* evidence for long distance trade in *manufactured* commodities. Excavated evidence suggests that raw resources were transshipped, *i.e.* metal ore, semi-precious stone, etc. which was manufactured at the point of destination. The principal Mesopotamian exports, grain and textiles, are not preserved in the archaeological record.

The texts point to trade as an important economic component in the hands of both public and private institutions, *i.e.* the temples, state (palace) administration, and private entrepreneurial undertakings (Larsen 1976, Foster 1976, 1986). There is a certain predisposition to believe, initially at least, that foreign commerce was a state monopoly. This I very much doubt.

The Mesopotamian state did *not* control the regions from which the texts indicate they obtained copper ore (Magan), lapis (Afghanistan), silver (Anatolia), or for that matter any other distant region from which they derived their raw resources. In fact, if one were dependent only upon the archaeological evidence, it would be impossible to attest that the cultures characteristic of these distant points were even aware of the existence of each other, let alone that they were in commercial contact. Mesopotamian texts of the third millennium are biased in detailing trade that was directed by their own state agents. There is virtually *no* mention of the involvement of foreign merchants in Mesopotamian trade. In fact, the Mesopotamian texts are almost entirely mute concerning the foreigners from whom they obtained their raw resources. There is every reason to believe that foreigners were involved in long-distance trade, and that they were beyond the control of both the Mesopotamian state and their own indigenous state — if indeed a state even existed on the distant periphery, *i.e.* Oman (Magan), or on the distant reaches of the Iranian Plateau.

Two cases may suffice in driving home the point. In the highlands of Oman at the site of Maysar, archaeologists have discovered metallurgical installations containing kilns and copper ingots. An analysis of the ingots, the local copper ore and finished objects from Mesopotamia strongly suggest that Mesopotamia procured at least some of its copper ore from this region (Weisgerber 1980; Hauptmann 1985). However, the archaeology at Maysar and its surrounding settlement pattern does not indicate the existence of a state polity. Thus, metallurgical production at Maysar was not undertaken under the auspices of a state authority, and there is *no* evidence for a Mesopotamian presence at Maysar. The archaeological record suggests that the production and trade of the metal ingots was in the hands of local, private households. These private households involved in the production of ingots took the first step in a *series* of exchanges terminating in the hands of the *alik tilmun*, the merchants of Dilmun, who passed them on to Mesopotamia. Similarly, at Tepe Yahya the production of chlorite bowls was most certainly not under the control of a centralized state. Amiet (1988) has even suggested that this commodity was manufactured and distributed by nomads who temporarily resided at Tepe Yahya. From physico-chemical analysis (Kohl, Harbottle and Sayre 1979) we know that the "Intercultural Style" carved chlorite bowl was very widely distributed; the products of Yahya may have even reached Mari. To interpret Mesopotamian commerce, and specifically long-distance trade, as an undertaking controlled by the merchants of that state is to overlook the entirety of the non-Mesopotamian world.

Relying exclusively on Mesopotamian texts to construct a world view of the ancient Near East offers a peculiarly distorted Mesopotamocentric perspective, but this can be moderated and redressed by the archaeological evidence from both inside and outside Mesopotamia. In doing so, the archaeological evidence from Palestine, Anatolia, the Arabian Peninsula and the Iranian Plateau strongly supports the notion that trade and exchange, both local and long-distance, was principally in the hands of non-state authorities.

Significantly, the archaeological record does not support the notion that long-distance commerce was involved in the wholesale transport of bulk commodities. Within Mesopotamia there are *limited* numbers of foreign resources manufactured into local commodities. When these are discovered they invariably are recovered from an elite context: tombs, temples or palaces. One looks in vain for a single item of lapis in the private houses of the Diyala; predictably, when recovered they were found in the Temple Oval. The presence of imports in elite contexts, emphatically the target of past excavations, distorts the picture by suggesting a more expansive commerce than probably existed.

Finally, neither the texts nor the archaeological evidence indicate the status of the merchant. Students of the ancient economy (Weber, Pirenne, Jones, Polanyi, Finley, Hasebroek, etc.) have long argued that merchants were men of little social consequence. Whether during classical or medieval times, it is believed that men "left the commercial origins of their wealth behind when they purchased landed estates, the only socially acceptable form of wealth, and moved into the municipal or governing class" (see Raschke 1978 for an important discussion and references pertaining to the role of the "The Middlemen" in antiquity). What was true for classical antiquity is true among the Afghan merchants today who echo the above comment: "Trade is most profitable, but if they get enough money, they will buy land — it is like your roots; while trade is like a hat — it can blow away" (Olesen 1994:181).

The Uruk Expansion

From at least the end of the Neolithic a centralized and institutionalized inequality characterized Mesopotamia (Kohl and Wright 1977). Trends toward the development of increasing storage facilities, community agglomeration, public architecture, and "urban" architectural densities already can be seen c. 5000 BC on such sites as Tell-es Sawaan, Umm Dabaghiyah, Yarim Tepe, and later, Eridu and Tepe Gawra. Even allowing for the above, it is principally in the Uruk period, around 3500 BC, that the fundamental form of the Mesopotamian city-state emerged.

The Uruk period gave definition to the physical layout of the city by constructing walls around the perimeter of the settlement; by elaborating upon the construction of temples within a "sacred" precinct; and by developing new systems of social control through the invention of writing, cylinder seals, and standardized units of measurement. The above constitute the development — a relatively *rapid* invention over two to three centuries — of a social technology. This technology had a clearly defined function: the control and coercion of the community's population by an administrative elite. Walls encircling the city, monumental architecture taking the form of temples, and the construction of extensive irrigation canals all suggest a centralized control over the community's labor force. Each of the above three attributes — walls, temples, and canals — create new boundaries and establish new social dimensions that distinguish between internal and external space.

Whether it is the invention of writing or the cylinder seal, the circumvallation of the city, or the construction of a substantial irrigation canal (to mention but a few items that appear for the first time in the Uruk period), it is apparent that all signify a new socioeconomic and political landscape. They are visible symbols of a new social order that emphasizes the power of the elites and their newfound ability to manipulate both labor and production — while legitimizing their authority through centralization of religious belief and ritual. What Marfoe

(1979:16) has written for southern Syria appears to hold for Mesopotamia: Initially, "the accumulation of political power would have lain not in the conquest and aggregation of land, but in the control of people."

The emergence of the city-state is the paramount achievement in the second half of the fourth millennium. Its development went hand-in-hand with the phenomenon known as the "Uruk Expansion." The archaeological evidence for the Uruk Expansion, characterized by the emigration of thousands of people from southern Mesopotamia to distant regions, has been well summarized by Guillermo Algaze (1993). A near consensus of archaeological interpretation suggests that the establishment of Uruk colonies in Iran, northern Syria and Anatolia were entrenched in order to control the trade routes and exploit the local resources that Mesopotamia lacked. In a word, the expansionism of the Sumerian "core" was directed toward the economic exploitation and colonization of the distant "periphery."

Although the Uruk Expansion has been the focus of numerous studies it should be noted that an earlier, and less understood, expansionist movement characterized the earlier Ubaid period. The Ubaid expansion was directed, on the one hand, toward the south, where numerous sites from the United Arab Emirates and Qatar are identifiably Ubaid, and on the other hand, toward northern Mesopotamia and southeastern Turkey.

I believe the consensus view — namely, that these expansionist tendencies were motivated by commercial interests — to be misdirected. It suffers from one of the two syndromes affecting virtually all archaeological "explanations" that attempt to grapple with culture change: namely (1) environmental and/or climatic change, and (2) changes in the economic order, invariably are seen as "causal," the directive agents of all social change. In the instance of the "Uruk Expansion" the relationship between the "core" and the "periphery" has counterintuitive aspects. These should be considered as well as the well-worn rhetoric of "empire," "imperialism," "colonialism" *et al* attributed as motivating forces fueling the Uruk Expansion. Several observations may be made: (1) There is *no* archaeological evidence in any of the foreign Uruk colonies for large-scale production, storage, or distribution of any local resources being directed to the Sumerian homeland. (2) Although no statistical analyses have been undertaken, there is little archaeological evidence to support the arrival of new resources, or their dramatic increase, in southern Mesopotamia during the episode of the Uruk Expansion. (3) There is little, if any, direct evidence that can be interpreted within the context of the Uruk Expansion for conflict, warfare, etc. between the Uruk colonists and the indigenous populations. (4) Recent excavations at the rural site of Hacinebi, in Turkey, illuminate our understanding of the relationship of a distant Uruk village site within a network of local Uruk sites in southeastern Turkey. The sites appear to have maintained an economic self-sufficiency within a political hierarchy of integration.

Surprisingly, the process of thousands of Middle (Late?) Uruk (ca. 3500 or 3300 BC) immigrants colonizing the periphery is wholly ignored in both the contemporary and later documentary records. Attempts to understand the "Uruk Expansion" have fingered economic determinants to the exclusion of any alternative hypotheses. Political and ideological factors have been entirely subordinated to processes involving economic causality and materialist concerns. In fact, there is little evidence in the archaeological record to link the Uruk Expansion with either an increase in, or a control of, commerce.

It also is unlikely that the Uruk Expansion succeeded in an enterprise that hardly engaged the Roman Empire — the control of commerce in foreign lands. As put by Raschke (1978:647): "The financial interests in commerce of the politically powerful, ruling landed aristocracy does not, however, necessarily indicate that commercial motives were important in Roman foreign policy under the Empire." The author offers a convincing argument that not only Roman expansionism, but that of the Han Empire to the Western Regions was directed by political rather than economic interests (Raschke 1978:616). It therefore is to the political and the ideological that I now turn, for within these categories rest the sociopolitical processes that fueled the engine of the "Uruk Expansion" and gave later definition to the "Great Traditions" of the Mesopotamian city-states.

Adams (1972, 1981), Wright and Johnson (1975), and Johnson (1973) have all detected that shifts in settlement and demographic patterns characterized the region of southern Mesopotamia and Susiana during the Uruk period. There is little reason to believe that these shifts in settlement patterns were undertaken to maximize an economic advantage. There is every reason to believe that settlement and demographic shifts were occurring within a context of a changing political geography, increasing centralization, conflict and territorial control. It was during the Uruk period that the settlements of Uruk and Susa, to mention but two communities, *rapidly* evolved into cities that politically dominated the surrounding countryside.

Adams (1981) refers to this period as one of rapid settlement increase, one characterized by what he calls "hyperurbanization." It seems reasonable to assume that a rapid increase in urban population requires an intensification of agriculture. This in turn can be brought about by increased production derived from territorial expansion and/or an intensification of production dependent upon new technologies. The former instance is readily apparent in Sassanian Mesopotamia. The necessity of intensified agricultural productivity, brought about by a rapidly increasing urban population, compelled the Sassanians to exploit new territories that were increasingly distant from the centers (Christensen 1993).

Although the archaeological evidence which recognizes the importance of colonization and territorial expansion is relatively recent the relationship between increased agricultural production, territorial expansion, and the emergence of the *earliest* state polities was recognized almost 30 years ago by Robert Adams (1966: 46f.):

> Trends toward territorial aggrandizement, political unification, and population concentration within the political unit accordingly can be interpreted not merely as expressions of the outcome of the Urban Revolution but as functionally interrelated processes that are central to it. . . . Extensions of territorial control, new forms of political superordination, and a multiplicity of technological advances all may have had as much effect on the size of the surplus as improvements in immediate agricultural "efficiency" while the deployment of the surplus, however it was formed, obviously had important effects on these factors.

When Adams wrote the above, there was no archaeological recognition of the Uruk Expansion. Nevertheless, he appears to have anticipated the phenomenon by identifying three components which characterize its nature: (1) "extensions of territorial control," (2) "new forms of political superordination," and (3) "technological advances," *i.e.* the invention of what I call a technology of social control, namely, writing, seals, and standard units of measurement.

Joining the phenomenon of the Uruk Expansion are the recently discovered "colonies" of (1) the Egyptians in southern Palestine (Oren 1989), (2) the Harappan in northern Afghanistan (Francfort 1989) and, (3) the Oxus on the Iranian Plateau (Hiebert and Lamberg-Karlovsky 1992). In the New World comparable expansion and colonization has been documented for the Chimu of Peru (Keatinge and Day 1973) and Teotihuacan in Mexico (Santley and Alexander 1992). It would appear that territorial expansion, and the establishment of colonies in distant areas, is characteristic of the formative processes involved in state formation.

Stanley Diamond (1974) may not be far off the mark when he comments that the appearance of class-stratified state-based societies began with "conquest abroad and repression at home." Greg Johnson (1988/89), writing at the time when the Berlin Wall was being torn down and thousands were fleeing to the West, has offered a highly original perspective on the Uruk Expansion: thousands of people were escaping from southern Mesopotamia because of the oppression experienced in the newly founded city-states. However, it is difficult to imagine why those fleeing this oppression would carry with them the new tools and the new class of administrators able to dominate their labor, production and consumption. The tools of dominance invented in southern Mesopotamia — writing, cylinder seals, and standard units of measurement — are also found in most of the Uruk colonies.

The emergent political organization was characterized by a system of ranking in which the newfound elite controlled exchange, resources and labor. Control over agricultural labor was essential for extracting the surplus that sustained the state bureaucracy. Equally significant was the control over resources, particularly foreign goods (metal, semi-precious stone, furniture, exotic animals, etc.). Access to these exotic goods, and their conspicuous display, served further to establish the rank and power of the ruling elites. Access to metal, whether initially copper and later silver, served to accelerate the process of social stratification by providing a "currency" or "standard" for which emerging polities could compete — both within and between distinctive communities.

The Uruk period's expansionism and colonialism served to direct and intensify the sociopolitical changes occurring in society. As indicated above, there is no quantitative evidence during the "Uruk Expansion" for an increase in either trade-goods or the production of new materials from distant resources. Nor is there direct archaeological evidence for conquest or military conflict. Yet the construction of city walls, and scenes of conflict depicted on seals, certainly suggest increased hostilities. The key to understanding the "Uruk Expansion" rests not in the economic sphere, but in the political: the establishment of a stratified elite which legitimized itself by a religious ideology and reserved for itself the right to monitor and control the economic productivity of its subordinated population.

We noted above that expansionism appears to be a universal element in the emergence of early state systems. Expansionism characterized not only Mesopotamia, but also the earliest states in Egypt, the Indus Valley, China and the Oxus, as well as Teotihuacan and Chimu in the New

World (Lamberg-Karlovsky 1982; Algaze 1993, 1995; Hiebert and Lamberg-Karlovsky 1992). Recently, Alexander Joffe (1993:57) has written with great insight regarding Egyptian expansionism an idea that also would pertain to Sumerian motivations for expansion:

> . . . to exercise control by Egyptians over *Egyptians* through the act of sending them great distances to the southern Levant in order to set up a small system which imitated the larger polity and its administrative and bureaucratic forms. This was accomplished through settlement creation and administration, and reinforced through the hierarchical organization of the settlement system, by such means as rationing and labor management.

Certainly many of the Uruk colonies appear as mirror images of their parent communities in southern Mesopotamia. They are walled, contain temples, and indicate the full presence of the technology of social control: tablets, seals, bevil-rimmed bowls, *et al* (Strommenger 1980). Mary Helms (1988) has shown that knowledge of foreign places and access to distant resources are frequently the prerogatives of politico-religious elites that form important avenues of prestige enhancement and legitimation. Geographic places, resources and people all could be manipulated, and knowledge of them differentially distributed. Knowledge of the above reinforced patterns of administration and alliances — both within and between distinctive communities. All of the above served to reinforce hierarchy, establish dominance, and assure the role of the state as provider to the community.

For over a century, archaeological research has concentrated upon "core" civilizations, *i.e.* Mesopotamia, Egypt, China, Mesoamerica, Greece, Rome, the Inka *et. al.* In comparison, the "periphery" has been all but ignored. Thus, it is only in the past two decades that the Bronze Age of the Arabian Peninsula has been given definition (Tosi 1986) and the Central Asian Oxus Civilization discovered (Sarianidi 1986, Ligabue and Salvatori 1989). Moreover, what had previously been considered a single "core," namely Mesopotamia, is now coming to be viewed as two distinctive culture areas, a northern and a southern (Steinkeller 1994). A singular concern for "cores" has diminished our appreciation of the diversity of past societies. Generalizations derived from an understanding of a "core" region may have little to do with understanding a "periphery," and certainly add little, if anything, to an understanding of their interrelationship. Interaction between the "cores" — which typically are large-scale societies — and the "periphery," small-scale societies, were critical to the evolution of cultural complexity in *both* areas (Eisenstadt and Shachar 1987).

In recent years, archaeologists have come to appreciate the tensions that exist both within and among distinctive social forms such as urban, village, and nomad. All three of these categories are complementary, interdependent, and socially permeable. Within the archaeological context it is difficult to conceive of one without the other. Typological thinking in the form of neo-evolutionary stages of development such as band, tribe and state have given way to a more subtle appreciation of complementarity, contradiction, and indeterminacy. Tensions between social categories, whether "village" or "nomad," "sacred" or "secular," or "private" and "public," are to be seen along the lines of a continuum rather then as categories in opposition, *e.g.* "sacred" vs. "secular," or "private" vs. "public." The analysis of these categories when seen as pristine realities, or independent variables, simply falsifies. There could not be, and never has been, one of these attributes without the other. Concerns for focusing upon indeterminacy, complementarity, and contradiction form the dialogue that emphasizes the cyclicality of what archaeologists refer to as the rise and fall of cultural complexity. The idea of privileging a single social form (*e.g.* patriarchy), institution (temple), or economic attribute (private property) in the evolution of cultural complexity is a curious form of 19th-century Lamarckian evolution.

Throughout the long history of Mesopotamia, few generalizations can be sustained over the millennia. One generalization, however, seems to prevail. When government was powerful, it maximized its extractive, tributary nature. During times of a strong centralized authority, the center extracted from the subordinated villages cereal and livestock; dominated in the control of long-distance commerce; and monopolized the production of elite commodities. When the central government was weak, it was less able to achieve its extractive ambitions. Throughout Mesopotamian history the economy of the urban centers depended upon the extraction of tribute, set in terms of quotas of specific commodities, *i.e.* cereals, livestock, pottery, *et al*, delivered to the state. It is not unreasonable to assume that under the circumstances of these asymmetric, urban-rural, tribute-based economies, the subordinated villages attempted to maintain a degree of independence and resilience.

The texts shed little light on the nature of the shifting political and economic relations that integrated centers, and tied these in turn to their subordinated countrysides. Only rarely, if at all, do the texts indicate the *inability* of urban centers to extract tribute from the countryside. When this did happen, and happen it did, there must have been significant shifts from the specialized production and extraction of surplus to the more general subsistence economy of the individual community and household (*e.g.* Adams 1978). Changing modes of regional organization that involve shifting political boundaries become fundamental to an understanding of Mesopotamia from at least the Uruk period. For analytical purposes the study of continuous variables, such as regional organization and scale, rather than upon categorical differences such as rural/urban and private/public may prove to be more profitable for gaining an understanding of the Mesopotamian world.

Conclusion

Both the archaeological and documentary evidence point to the fact that private property existed in conjunction with property controlled by the state. In a word, both private and public property co-existed from the earliest times in the ancient Near East in an uneasy tension, much as it does today. During times of a powerful state, *i.e.* Ur III, the state attempted to monopolize all property and establish all production by state command; when the state was weak, *i.e.* Kassite Babylonia, property and production fell into the hands of private families and individuals. In the final analysis property forms, whether private or public, are not independent variables, they are linked to a complex suite of interdependent variables that need to be identified and put into a specific historic context. We are all indebted to Michael Hudson for having begun to isolate those attributes which at different times and for different reasons gave primacy to either the public and/or the private.

DISCUSSION

Edzard: I am extremely grateful that someone now said that there is a private sector of the economy for all sorts of households, because I always wondered whether dependent persons went to the palace to get the tablet entitling them to a bimonthly haircut at the barber.

Lamberg-Karlovsky: I think that is exactly the point. Everything could not have been so structured by the state.

Edzard: Do we really have no evidence for foreign merchants being present? We have Sargon's inscription about the boats of Magan and Meluhha boats mooring at the quai of Akkad; the seal of a "Meluhha interpreter" (*emi-bal me-luh-ha^{ki}*). Of course, wherever merchants go, they need interpreters. The seal owner may have been some "Mesopotamian" who had picked up some bits of "Meluhhese."

Lamberg-Karlovsky: There is no doubt. Certainly when Sargon is boasting about who is coming to dock up there, they must be foreigners. Certainly the translator sitting on the lap of this individual was an interpreter. What I am saying is that we don't know the social structure they are representing. Are they private, individual merchants? Are they representing some configuration of the outside world? How do they relate as foreign merchants to the internal merchants, to the state agents who are merchants, maybe private, maybe state? That is what the text doesn't tell us.

Edzard: I never sided with those who imagined that there had been loyal civil servant-like state merchants to whom personal profit was anathema. Coming from a north German Hanseatic town, I always think of merchants as being devoted to something private. Successful merchants have an urge to buy something much cheaper than they sell it for — and not without a very nice profit.

Lamberg-Karlovsky: I should not disagree.

Mitchell: I want to go back to your introductory remarks and see if I can tie a question to the observations you made about the artificiality of the ages of savagery and similar characterizations. Weber noticed a long time ago — and his conclusions recently have been reinforced by classical scholars such as Bourriot, Roussel and Starr — that the typical description of archaic classical societies as ones divided into tribes, *curiae*, brotherhoods and similar associations, presents a problem because these units or groups are absent from the tribal societies that precede urbanization. They first appear during the period of urbanization. One of the arguments about these groups — tribes, *curiae*, phratries and so forth — is that when they appear as part of the structure of Greek and Roman states they have an artificial quality. They consist of units of three, six, ten, twelve, sixty, hundred, or some other "artificial" number. Because they appear artificial it has been frequently argued that they must therefore be fabricated by our sources of information. But of course they are artificial because they were imposed on societies in the very earliest stage of urbanization, and they remained a consistent and constant characteristic of those societies.

Some scholars have offered that this entire system is imposed at a particular point in the urbanization process by a Solon, Cleisthenes, Romulus, Servius Tullius or some other founding father similar to the individual who succeeded to the T-shaped structure and imposed an artificial system. Because no demographic information existed, the system had to be artificial and arbitrary. It has tens, it has quarters and many other artificial, mainly decimal, numbers. Such an arbitrary numerical feature also helps explain the artificiality of the responsibilities and obligations placed upon individuals, who may be required to pay a sixth or a tenth, or a fine or repayment expressed as a decimal percentage of the original loan.

I am reminded that the Etruscans were very important creators of the Roman system, although Romans tended to denigrate them and their contributions to the greatness of Rome. But even the Romans admitted that virtually their entire political system and institutional structure, its symbols and characteristic features, were Etruscan in origin and that the method of creating the system was contained in ritual books that described how to set up tribes, *curiae* and centuries — all the components of the Roman public system. I am not even going to touch on — *non dicam* as Cicero would say — the fact that the Etruscans, according to one source, came from the east. But I wonder whether or not you would agree that this system looks arbitrary and artificial because it was imposed, as distinct from its having been fabricated by our sources who lacked specific information about the earliest system.

Lamberg-Karlovsky: I would agree. Of course, there is a fundamental problem in terms of the classificatory devices as to what are ours and what are theirs. Let me give you an example. From my understanding of the texts, in Sumerian there is no distinction of the kind of terminology that we use, cities, towns and villages. *URU* is a place. There is no hierarchical distinction. There is just one term for place, as opposed to the way in which we would term a hierarchy of settlement, cities, towns, villages — this is our classification, not theirs. Out of that classification we derive a whole series of assumptions. There is a political hierarchy ranking cities, villages and towns. There is a political structure representing some aspect of state formation, etc. These are our classifications. When it comes to talking about the internal structure of a society based on the texts, we find that lineages, clans, moieties and phratries are not there.

Wright: I have a couple of comments I'd like to make, going back to Michael's paper. I thought Carl might touch on some of it, so I didn't want to bring it up earlier. First, I am unfamiliar with this dichotomy that you make between anthropology and economy in discussing informality vs. formality, coercion vs. measuring. What you really are talking about is what anthropologists call a substantivist view of economics vs. a formalist view of economics. This issue has been part and parcel of discussions in anthropology about different kinds of economy. I'm afraid that when you make that kind of dichotomy, you unconsciously imply a sort of evolutionary development — there was an anthropological time, and now you have this economic time. As an anthropologist, I just wanted to defend my position, which you and I have talked about before, but I wanted to do it in public.

The second thing about anthropology (and I think Carl was implying this, but I'm not sure that you were) is the so-called chiefdom model. First of all, there isn't any chiefdom that we know about that hasn't been touched by western civilization. In fact, in the recording of it, all of them by the time anthropologists began recording with the only templates that the anthropologists had available to them going back to somebody's theories that Carl mentioned, Vico etc., all of those things influenced the way they were recorded, in fact what they had become. So the only evidence we would have of anything we could call a chiefdom would be archaeological evidence, where there wasn't the influence of the west. Of course, it is very hard to interpret that.

I also want to mention that I am surprised no one has mentioned (and I know this is a controversial interpretation): Denise Schmandt-Besseret's ideas about tokens and bullae. That would seem to me to be evidence of privatization (and again, I may not understand this term the way that you do). Also, stamp seals seem to me to be evidence of early privatization. They might represent the genesis of ideas about private property, that they began very early. We might say we have the archaeological evidence for it.

I want to talk about what Carl discussed, because I am interested in pottery. I think you are right, and not only with this evidence. In an ethnographic context it is clear that a lot of product, even the production of things that contribute to states, is done by small groups in domestic contexts. Speaking of the imposition of western concepts even on third world forms of production, we always ask, "Who is the potter?" One man steps forward, but pottery production is really carried out by families, and these anciliary people are not recorded. When you go into a potter's workshop, you see lots of people contributing to production. The women are out back painting, or they may be doing something else. The old grandfather is collecting the clay. So these are family productions.

One place where I would want to modify what you said, Carl, is that just because we can only document the 2,500 pots that eventually went to the state, it doesn't necessarily mean that the person was engaged in private sale, although I think intuitively that you probably are right. Most potters are indeed barbers or something else, and they do pottery at certain times of the year. The potter might have a two-chambered kiln, but he only uses it at certain times of the year, during seasons when there isn't a harvest or planting or something like that.

Turning to the question of the asymmetry of trade, I think we also can talk about the asymmetry of archaeological evidence. You taught me that we can't argue from negative evidence, but I will bring it up. There are various kinds of things that could be exported that don't preserve well. I want to mention some that you missed, commodities that were finished products in Mesopotamia. We have the long-barreled carnelian beads that definitely are an Indus product, as well as etched carnelian beads. You did use a caveat not documented, and I think you refer to scientific evidence. We do have in the Indus this knobbed ware, whatever it is, so that could be Mesopotamian.

Lamberg-Karlovsky: It's all over the Iranian plateau too.

Wright: One product I did mention that you didn't cite in your talk is textiles. Are you willing to use the same model here? I agree that there was private production of textiles. We know this because people brought the cloth into the temple. The large scale of production is the difference . . .

Lamberg-Karlovsky: It is state, I agree. There may or there may not be a fundamental difference between the way Michael and I perceive this question. It rests on the following premise. If Michael believes there was a pristine period of time in which the world was communal, then we have a fundamental disagreement. [*Professor Hudson shakes his head no throughout this statement.*] I believe that private and public are a polarity embedded in each other. One gives definition to the other, and it has always been there, even in the context of the paleolithic, when the individual person was making the tool. Whoever made that tool probably had some rights and obligations over it. In this particular context right and left, sacred and secular, private and public are in a context in which the very definition of the one is given meaning by understanding the other. I believe the pristine model, if Michael believes in that, is fundamentally wrong ethnographically.

Hudson: Regarding Rita Wright's comment on tokens, from the ninth to the fourth millennium they are taken as signs of mercantile obligations to deliver what the courier had been given. Denise Schmandt-Besserat's idea is that he is given a consignment and a pack of tokens. He is consigned a shipment, and sealed tokens show what he has been given. He seems to be an agent, not an independent possessor. If the goods were his own, he wouldn't need tokens for what he had. At the end of his journey the recipients (buyers? gift-receiving chiefs?) compare the tokens to the consignment, to make sure that the merchant has delivered what he was supposed to. But for whom is the consignment intended? And on what terms? How formal was all this?

Lamberg-Karlovsky: Michael, let's stop there. It is pure speculation. From the ninth to the fourth millennium, these tokens lack anything even approximately like a context. There are no bullae, there are only tokens. They are simply tokens. They are not necessarily geometric tokens. It is pure speculation.

Hudson: All right.

Lamberg-Karlovsky: Denise may be as right as she could be, or one hundred percent wrong.

Hudson: I think she is right.

Lamberg-Karlovsky: That is your preference. No problem.

REFERENCES

Adams, R. McC. (1966), *The Evolution of Urban Society: Early Mesopotamia and Prehispanic Mexico* (Chicago: Aldine Press).

— (1974), "Anthropological Perspectives on Ancient Trade," *Current Anthropology* 15:239-258.

— (1978), "Strategies of Maximization, Stability, and Resilience in Mesopotamian Society, Settlement, and Agriculture," *Proceedings of the American Philosophical Society* 122:29-335.

— (1981), *Heartland of Cities, Surveys of Ancient Settlement and Land Use on the Central Floodplain of the Euphrates* (Chicago: University of Chicago Press).

— (1988), "Contexts of Civilizational Collapse: A Mesopotamian View," in *The Collapse of States and Ancient Civilizations*, ed. Norman Yoffee and George L. Cowgill (Tucson: University of Arizona Press): 20-42.

Adams, R. M. and H. J. Nissen (1974), *The Uruk Countryside, The Natural Setting of Urban Societies* (Chicago: University of Chicago Press).

Akkermans, Peter M. M. G. and Marc Verhoeven (1955), "An Image of Complexity: The Burnt Village of Late Neolithic Sabi Abyad, Syria," *American Journal of Archaeology* 99:5-32.

Algaze, G. (1993), *The Uruk World System The Dynamics of Expansion in Early Mesopotamian Civilization* (Chicago: University of Chicago Press).

— (1995), "Expansionary Dynamics of Some Early Pristine States," *American Anthropologist* 95:304-333.

Amiet, P. (1988), "Elam and Bactria," in *Bactria: An Ancient Oasis Civilization from the Sands of Afghanistan*, ed. Giancarlo Ligabue and Sandro Salvatore (Rome: Erizzo Press).

Archi, A. (1992), "About the Organization of the Eblaitic State," *Studi Eblaiti* 5:201-220.

Berthoud, Thierry, *Etude l'analyse de Traces st la Modelisation de la Filiatio entre Mineral de Cuivre et Objets Archeologiques.* Thesis presented to L'universite Pierre et Marie Curie, Paris, VI.

Blackman, J. and Gil J. Stein (1993), "The Organizational Context of Specialized Craft Production in Early Mesopotamian States," in *Research in Economic Anthropology* 44:29-59.

Christensen, Peter (1993), *The Decline of Iranshahr* (University of Copenhagen: Museum Tusculum Press).

D'Altroy, T. N. and T. K. Earle (1985), "Staple Finance, Wealth Finance, and Storage in the Inka Political Economy," *Current Anthropology* 26:187-206.

Diakonoff, I. M. (1969), "The Rise of the Despotic State in Ancient Mesopotamia," in *Ancient Mesopotamia: A Socio-Economic History. A Collection of Studies by Soviet Scholars* (Moscow: Nauka.)

— (1982), "The Structure of Near Eastern Society Before the Middle of the 2nd millennium B.C." *Oikumene* 3:1-100.

Diamond, Stanley (1974), *In Search of the Primitive A Critique of Civilization* (New York: E.P. Dutton).

Delougaz, P., H. D. Hill, and S. Lloyd (1967), *Private Houses and Graves in the Diyala Region* (Chicago: Oriental Institute Publications 88).

Edens, Christopher (1992), "Dynamics of Trade in Ancient Mesopotamian 'World Systems,'" *American Anthropologist* 94:118-139.

— (1993), "Indus-Arabian Interaction During the Bronze Age: A Review of Evidence" in *Harappan Civilization*, ed. Gregory Possehl, second edition (Oxford: IBH Publishing Co.).

Eisenstadt, S., and A. Shachar (1987), *Society, Culture and Urbanization* (Newbury Park: Sage Publications).

Earle, Timothy (1994), "Wealth and Finance in the Inka Empire: Evidence from the Calchaqui Valley, Argentina," *American Antiquity* 59:443-60.

Earle, Timothy, and Terence D'Altroy (1982), "Storage Facilities and State Finance in the Upper Mantaro Valley, Peru. In *Contexts of Prehistoric Exchange*, edited by J.E. Ericson and T.K. Earle (New York: Academic Press).

Engels, Frederick, (1902), *The Origin of the Family, Private Property, and the State* (Chicago: Charles H. Kerr).

Forest, J. D., "Kheit Qasim III: an Obeid Settlement," *Sumer* 40:Nos. 1-2.

Foster, B. R. (1986), *Administration and Use of Institutional Land in Sargonid Sumer* (Copenhagen: Mesopotamia 9).

— (1982), "Archives and Record-keeping in Sargonid Mesopotamia," *Zeitschrift für Assyriologie* 72:1-27.

— (1976), "Commercial Activity in Sargonid Mesopotamia," *Iraq* 29:23-30.

Francfort, H. (1989), *Fouilles de Shortugai; recherches sur l'Asia centrale proto historique* (Paris: de Boccard).

Frank, Gunder (1993), "Bronze Age World System Cycles," *Current Anthropology* 34:338-340.

Gelb, I. J. (1988), "Household and Family in Early Mesopotamia" In E. Lipinski, ed. *State and Temple Economy in the Ancient Near East* (Belgium: Katolieke Universiteit te Leuven):1-97.

Gelb, I. J., Piotr Steinkeller, Robert M. Whiting (1991), *Earliest Land Tenure Systems in the Near East: Ancient Kudurrus* (Chicago: University of Chicago Press).

Hauptmann, A. (1983), *5000 Jahre Kupfer in Oman* (*Der Anschnitt*, Vol. 4, 1985).

Hauptmann, Harald, "Lidar Höyük, 1981," *Türk Arkeoloji Dergisi* 26.

Helms, M. (1988), *Ulysses Sail* (Princeton: Princeton University Press).

Hiebert, F. T. and C. C. Lamberg-Karlovsky (1992), "Central Asia and the Indo-Iranian Borderlands," *Iran* 30:1-17.

Hobsbawm, E. J. (editor), (1965), *Pre-Capitalist Economic Formations* by Karl Marx (New York: International Publishers).

Jacobsen, T. (1943), "Primitive Democracy in Ancient Mesopotamia," *Journal of Near Eastern Studies* 2:159-172.

— (1957), "Early Political Development in Mesopotamia," *Zeitschrift für Assyriologie* 18:91-140.

Joffe, A. H. (1993), *Settlement and Society in the Early Bronze I & II Southern Levant* (Sheffield Academic Press).

Johnson, G. A. (1973), *Local Exchange and Early State Development in Southwestern Iran*, Anthropological Papers 51 (Ann Arbor: Museum of Anthropology).

— (1988/89), "Late Uruk in Greater Mesopotamia: Expansion or Collapse," *Origini* 14:595-613.

Johnson, A. W., and T. K. Earle (1987), *The Evolution of Human Societies* (Stanford, California: Stanford University Press).

Keatinge, Richard, and K. C. Day (1973), "Socio-Economic Organization of the Moche Valley, Peru, during the Chimu Occupation of Chan Chan," *Journal of Anthropological Research* 29:275-295.

Kohl, P. (1978), "The Balance of Trade in Southwestern Asia in the Third Millennium B.C.," *Current Anthropology* 19:463-492.

Kohl, P., G. Harbottle and E.V. Sayre (1979), "Physical and Chemical Analyses of Soft Stone Vessels from Southwest Asia," *Archaeometry* 21:131-159.

Kohl, P., and R. Wright (1977), "Stateless Cities: The Differentiation of Societies in the Near Eastern Neolithic," *Dialectical Anthropology* 2:271-283.

Lamberg-Karlovsky, C. C. (1975), "Third Millennium Modes of Exchange and Modes of Production," in *Ancient Civilizations and Trade*, ed. by J. A. Sabloff and C. C. Lamberg-Karlovsky (Albuquerque: University of New Mexico Press).

— (1982), "Sumer, Elam and the Indus: Three Urban Processes Equal One Structure," in *Harappan Civilization*, ed. by Gregory Possehl (New Delhi: Oxford and IBH Publishing).

Lamberg-Karlovsky, C. C. (1973), and Maurizio Tosi, "Shahr-i Sokhta and Tepe Yahya: Tracks on the Earliest History of the Iranian Plateau," *East and West* 23:21-53.

Larsen, M. T. (1975), *The Old Assyrian City-State and its Colonies* (Copenhagen: Mesopotamia 4).

Ligabue, G., and S. Salvatore (1989), *Bactria: An Ancient Oasis Civilization from the Sands of Afghanistan* (Venice: Erizzo Press).

Maisels, Charles Keith (1990), *The Emergence of Civilization* (New York: Routledge).

Marfoe, L. (1979), "The Integrative Transformation: Patterns of Socio-political Organization in Southern Syria," *Bulletin of the American Schools of Oriental Research* 234:1-42.

Mazzoni, Stefania (1988), "Economic Features of the Pottery Equipment of Palace G" in *Wirtschaft unr Gesellschaft von Ebla*, edited by H. Hauptmann and H. Waetzoldt, Heidelberger Studien zum Alten Orient 2:81-105 (Heidelberg: Heidelberger Orientverlag).

Olesen, Asta (1994), *Afghan Craftsmen* (London: Thames and Hudson).

Oren, E. (1989), "Early Bronze Settlement in North Sinai: A Model for Egypto-Canaanite Interconnectons," in *L'urbanisation de la Palestine. Actes du Colloque d'Emmaüs* (Oxford: British Archaeological Reports).

Polanyi, Karl, Conrad M. Arensberg, and Harry W. Pearson, (eds), (1957), *Trade and Market in the Early Empires* (New York: Free Press).

Postgate, N., and J. A. Moon, "Excavations at Abu Salabikh — A Sumerian City," *National Geographic Reports* 17:721-743.

Rao, A. (1987), *The Other Nomads* (Cologne: Bshlau Verlag).

Raschke, Manfred G. (1978), "New Studies in Roman Commerce with the East," in *Aufsteig und Niedergang der Rsmischen Welt*, II, edited by Hildegard Temporini and Wolfgang Haase (Berlin: Walter de Gruyter).

Renfrew, C. (1975), "Trade as Action at a Distance: Questions of Integration and Communication," in *Ancient Civilizations and Trade*, ed. J. A. Sabloff and C. C. Lamberg-Karlovsky, 3-39 (Albuquerque: University of New Mexico Press).

Renger, Johannes (1995), "On Economic Structures in Ancient Mesopotamia," *Orientalia* 63:157-208.

Reviv, H., *The Elders in Ancient Israel* (Jerusalem: Manes Press).

Santley, Robert S., and Rani T. Alexander (1992), "The Political Economy of Core-Periphery Systems," in *Resources, Power, and Interregional Interaction*, edited by E. M. Shortman and P. A. Urban (New York: Plenum Press):23-49.

Sarianidi, V. (1986), *Die Kunst des Alten Afghanistan* (Leipzig: E.A. Seemans Verlag).

Stein, G. (1993), "The Organized Context of Specialized Craft Production in Early Mesopotamian States," *Research In Economic Anthropology* 14:29-59.

Steinkeller, Piotr (1994), "The Organization of Crafts in Third Millennium Babylonia: The Case of Potters," Paper delivered at the Eleventh International Congress of Economic History, Milan, Italy.

— (1994), "Early Political Development in Mesopotamia and the Origins of the Akkadian Empire," in *Akkad: The World's First Empire*, ed. by M. Liverani (Padua).

Stone, E. (1987), *Nippur Neighborhoods* (Chicago: University of Chicago, Studies in Ancient Oriental Civilization 44).

Strommenger, E. (1980), *Habuba Khabira: eine Stadt vor 5000 Jahren* (Mainz).

Tosi, M. (1984), "The Notion of Craft Specialization and its Representation in the Archaeological Record of Early States in the Turanian Basin," in *Marxist Perspectives in Archaeology*, ed. by Matthew Spriggs (Cambridge: Cambridge University Press).

— (1986), "The Emerging Picture of Prehistoric Arabia," in *Annual Reviews in Anthropology* 15:461-490.

Waetzoldt, H. (1971), "Zwei unveröffentlich Ur III Texte Über die Herstellung von Tongefüssen," *Die Welt des Orients* 6:7-41.

Waines, David (1977), "The Third Century Crises of the Abbasids," *Journal of Economic and Social History of the Orient* 20:282-306.

Wattenmaker, Patricia (1994), "State Formation and the Organization of Domestic Craft Production at Third Millennium B.C. Kurban Hüyük, Southeast Turkey," in *Archaeological Views from the Countryside*, ed. by Glenn M. Schwartz and Steven E. Falconer (Washington, D.C.: Smithsonian Press):109-120.

Weisgerber, G. (1981), "Mehr als Kupfer in Oman. . . .", *Der Anschnitt* 35:174-263.

Weiss, H. (1992), "Tell Leilan 'sila bowls' and the Akkadian Reorganization of Subarian Agricultural Production," *Orient-Express* 2.

Woolley, L., and P. R. S. Moorey (1982), *Ur' of the Chaldees* (London: Routledge).

Wright, H., and G. A. Johnson (1975), "Population, Exchange, and Early State Formation in Southwestern Iran," *American Anthropologist* 77:267-289.

Wright, Rita (1984), "Technology and Style in Ancient Ceramics," in *Ancient Technology to Modern Science*, edited by W. D. Kingery (Columbus, Ohio: The American Ceramic Society).

Yoffee, Norman (1988), "The Collapse of Ancient Mesopotamian States and Civilizations," pp. 44-68, in *The Collapse of Ancient States and Civilizations*, edited by Norman Yoffee and George L. Cowgill (Tuscon, Arizona: University of Arizona Press).

3.

Private Land Ownership and its Relation to "God" and the "State" in Sumer and Akkad

Dietz Otto Edzard
Universität München

This paper presents some general considerations on landed property in early Mesopotamia, with special emphasis on the privatization of royal land under Hammurabi of Babylon.[1]

Ownership is an idea that must have found *audible* linguistic expression from the very beginning, but we have no way of knowing just when the idea formally came into being. Languages have different ways of expressing ownership. Possessive pronouns or their semantic equivalent at first were probably restricted to inalienables, such as parts of the body, relatives, kin and clan members.[2] We may rightly speak of ownership as soon as a possession indicator could be applied to something alienable.

In time, the idea of ownership found *visible* expression by means of symbols. The oldest examples known to us are the stamp seals from Mesopotamia and adjacent regions of the ancient Near East. This type of seal is older than the cylinder seal.[3] The impression of such a seal, left permanently on soft material such as clay and attached to an object (or a string holding an object), created a relationship between an individual (or group of individuals) and the object in question. It connoted responsibility for that object, an obligation to report on it, or ownership. Of course, there may have been still older methods of indicating such a relation by means of colored strings or other perishable materials.

In addition to implying alienability at the holder's discretion, ownership entails the idea of possible loss or misappropriation. It therefore also entails the right of restitution or indemnification if a third party is liable — at least if a powerful institution grants and protects ownership titles. But it is impossible to find the origin of ownership in the written sources of any civilization. The idea may have arisen some ten thousand years or so ago. By the time the oldest written sources appear in Mesopotamia toward the end of the fourth millennium BC, we are well along in the flow of history,

Whereas movable property can be lost or stolen as well as possessed, immovables stay in place, as the word literally indicates. They can disappear or be damaged only by *force majeure*. Strictly speaking, ownership of landed property cannot "pass" to a new owner; that person will have to come to it. In this fact lies the most important difference between giving, selling or exchanging real estate as compared to movable property.

Of course, changes in the ownership of movable property no doubt occurred via gift or exchange long before our oldest written sources appear. But where landed property is concerned, we are unable to make any binding and incontrovertible statements.

The oldest cuneiform documents dealing with real estate transfers are made "for eternity," even more definitively than would be the case with tablets of baked clay. The media are stone, often real tablets and often of unusual format, occasionally showing human individuals along with the script, such as the Blau Stones[4] or the *Figure aux plumes*.[5] The late I. J. Gelb called these most ancient documents *kudurrus*, borrowing a Middle Babylonian term.[6] Many of these oldest contracts have been edited in an appendix to my *Rechtsurkunden des III. Jahrtausends aus der Zeit vor der III. Dynastie von Ur* (1968),[7] and have been treated in a new, more detailed and enlarged edition in 1991 by Gelb, P. Steinkeller, and R. M. Whiting.[8] C. Wilcke, in his review of Gelb *et al.*, doubts whether all these documents actually represent deeds of purchase.[9] In some cases he prefers the idea of enfeoffment instead of sale.

The reason for classifying the oldest *kudurrus* as land contracts (of whatever category) is essentially the presence of four elements, not all of which occur simultaneously: 1) the sign for "field" combined with a sign (or signs) for surface area measure, 2) the sign SA_{10}(NINDA ŠE) which, later, we associate with the idea of purchase, 3) signs for precious metal or commodities combined with signs for measures of weight or capacity, and 4) personal names.

Around the middle of the third millennium BC, transactions reflecting changes in the ownership of landed property are attested on clay tablets. I strongly prefer to refer to these texts as documents of sale and purchase, not of exchange, and to translate the Sumerian verb sa_{10} as meaning "to buy," and the noun *sam* as "purchase" or "purchase price." (For the sake of brevity I refer the reader to J. Krecher's article "Kauf," in the *Reallexikon der Assyriologie*, where he explains his reasons for this reading.[10])

It has been noted that the sellers in these documents rarely act alone and exclusively on their own behalf. Third parties — members of the seller's family, as far as they can be identified — join in. They are called "those who have eaten (*i.e.,* who have had the usufruct of) the purchase price." The transaction customarily takes place before witnesses, but we know nothing about the origins and antiquity of this institution.[11]

Krecher, in his RlA article, supposed that originally the purchaser had to be adopted into a position comparable to a host, a son-in-law, or some other kind of relative so that the deed virtually would have been concluded within the basic or extended family. This is, of course, difficult to prove, but in some surviving communities, such as the Pueblo Indians, land is still owned collectively and no portion of it may be sold to an outsider.[12]

Be that as it may, by the middle of the third millennium BC we find real estate owned by private individuals, or groups of individuals, who do not form part of a royal household or temple. In other words, they stood in no special relation to the "God" or "the State." They had the right to cede ownership titles by sale. Unfortunately, we have no idea just how much arable land in given territories or "city-states" was privately owned. Neither do we know whether we would be justified in drawing generalizations from one city-state to another. (Personally, I carefully adhere to the statement pronounced by F. R. Kraus in 1951, when he warned us not to synthesize the disparate evidence of different sites and maybe of different centuries, into a seemingly coherent picture which we would claim to represent "history."[13])

Apart from private citizens, members of the royal families, including the ruler in his own personal capacity, were active in third millennium land transactions.[14] It is extremely important to note that they subjected themselves, at least formally, to the same legal procedures as did private citizens. Their contracts thus follow the same form as contracts concluded among private individuals. We may conclude that rulers on such such occasions acted as private citizens, bound to the same (albeit unwritten) law. One pre-Sargonic deed the contract of Lu-pa(da), land registrar of Umma, specifies the location of fields by naming the fields' neighbors; one neighbor is a smith, another a "leather worker." This deed incidentally provides evidence for not just one single privately owned field, but for groups or clusters of such fields.[15]

There are various theories of how Mesopotamian kingship originated, and speculation about the possible priority of archaic priesthood over kingship, but real evidence is lacking. Thorkild Jacobsen held that a *lugal* "king" (lit. "big person") was originally some kind of warlord. Toward the end of the fourth millennium we can reconstruct the architectural outlines of enormous temples, but we really have no idea about how these complexes were organized. We interpret a "ruler," regardless of whether or not he was sacred, to have been an archaic person feeding domestic animals, receiving offerings or proceding in a boat,[16] yet we know nothing about his title, status, and functions. We are left only to make guesses or inferences based on later "historical" periods. It goes without saying that there must have existed some important power to direct canal work and building activities. Viewing ancient Near Eastern history as a whole, we would rather suppose a ruling individual than a collective body behind such power. But our theorizing must end there.

In historical times we have rulers' titles such as *en, ensi, lugal* in complementary distribution over Sumerian (and later over Sumerian and Akkadian) city-states or larger territorial units.[17] But we still have no idea of how much land individual temples or the palace owned, and how their titles of ownership came into being. What we lack is the Sumerian or even pre-Sumerian equivalent of a "*landnama bok*" or Domesday Book, either divine or secular in character. We do not even have a clear idea of the origin of the "Big House," *é-gal*, where the "Big Person," *lugal*, resided.[18]

At the risk of forcing open doors, I would like to refer briefly to two cuneiform texts from the 24th century BC that have become known as the "Reform Texts" of Irikagina (formerly read Urukagina or Uruinimgina).[19] This ruler, in a patently apologetic way, and probably in order to veil the tenuous status of his own legitimacy, maintained that the (unnamed) predecessors on his throne had usurped vital rights of the temples. I will not quote extensively from his texts, which are among the most familiar in all Sumerian literature. Irikagina asserts to have re-instituted as field owners (*lugal*) the divine triad Ningirsu-Bau-Sulsagana, thereby expressing that formerly temple property had been unlawfully occupied by the Palace — or more exactly, by the ruler, his wife, and the crown prince of the city-state of Girsu-Lagash. Plow-oxen of the gods had been taken for the ruler's vegetable gardens. The passages in question, along with others, have often been quoted to establish and defend the theory of a (or *the*) Temple City.[20]

The alleged Temple City has been considered to have been a political unit whose arable land was owned, at least theoretically, by the city deity as his (or her) family. The ruler in theory would be a viceroy instituted to represent the the deity. Private ownership of fields would be (at least theoretically) excluded.

If someone today were to act as a devil's advocate for this position, he might find one argument in favor of this theory which, as far as I know, has not yet been brought forward: the fact that the territory of the political city-state unit was called, in Sumerian, the "field of god So-and-so," *i.e.*, the city-deity, in the case of Girsu-Lagash the "field of Ningirsu." In Ur-Nammu's land register text (Ur III), a region defined as the Northern, Southern, Eastern, and Western limits is called "the borders (*ki-sur-ra*) of god NN of city NN."[21] To be sure, we now know that neither this nor any of the other arguments advanced in favor of a Sumerian "temple-city" holds up. The theory accordingly has lost popularity over the last thirty years, having been disproved by the existence of acts of land purchase.

Even today, out discussion may indulge in unwarranted schematizing if we postulate too clear-cut a contrast or dichotomy between temple and palace. At least from the Sargonic period onward there is ample evidence for rulers' children serving as high priests or priestesses of a city deity.[22] The formal procedure was oracular, based on liver omens, but we may be certain that rulers could exert enormous influence in such matters. Given the family ties between the palace and particular temples, strict border-lines were of course obscured. Besides, the temples and palace partly served the same goal in promoting the welfare of the population. Once a year, some city deities proceded to Nippur, Sumer's cult center to find the "firm promise" (*nam-tar*, usually translated as "decision of fate").[23] Pronounced by the supreme god Enlil, it granted everything that was needed for the welfare of the State: an abundant harvest, growth of its herds, punctual arrival of the river flood for irrigation, and much more. The final grant was "long life in the Palace."[24]

In discussions of the alleged Sumerian Temple City during the fifties and early sixties it sometimes was argued that there may have been different views among Sumerians and Semitic Akkadians with regard to private ownership of land. Were the Akkadians unrestricted (or at least, less restricted) by religious ideas? Today we would speak of possible differences in "mentality."[25] We would therefore enter the debate (which is far from being closed) about possible differences, and even a certain antagonism between Sumerians and Akkadians. This would lead us far away from our topic, and for the present I see no possibility to focus the debate on the question of private landholdings.[26]

So far I have dealt with the ownership of fields. It has been established that both the temples and the palace disposed of fields, gardens, orchards, meadows, and perhaps pasture land (although it is uncertain whether any pasture land was owned by individuals. Nothing is known about pasturing rights reserved for special groups of herd owners). A third sector represented private ownership of fields by individuals or families, but the extent is unknown. There is no reason to disbelieve that these three sectors existed since Early Dynastic times and even earlier. Let me add here a reference to a literary text, the *Instructions of a Farmer Given to his Son*, recently re-edited by M. Civil.[27] Like many other Sumerian literary texts, the *Instructions* probably had their origin in the third millennium. In my opinion they can only be understood as representing conditions of private field ownership.

Where then does "privatization" come in? The word is not contained in the title of my paper, a fact which reflects my uncertainty, at least with regard to large-scale occurrence of this phenomenon. We first of all need a strict definition. I define as "privatization" only the transition of field ownership either from the temple or the palace into private hands. Although as we have seen above, the ruler sometimes acted as a private person when concluding a land purchase, we will not count such cases among privatization. Nor will we consider as such the real (or alleged) expropriation of temple land by a ruler. The misappropriations of which Irikagina accused his predecessors will not be viewed as privatization for the simple reason that under normal circumstances the palace was not regarded as a private institution on a par with other citizens. Immediate privatization of temple land probably has been rare, and restricted to times of disturbance. Under such hypothetical circumstances we hardly would expect to find official sale or foreclosure transactions and documents. Allocation of temple land by way of rental was of course a different matter, but did not constitute privatization.[28]

A conspicuous case of palace property finding its way into private hands was part of the *ilkum* system of Old Babylonian times, mainly known to us from the reign of King Hammurabi of Babylon. If a house with orchard and field, at first granted by the king to persons in his service, stayed in the hands of a family for two or more generations, it could be defined as a case of privatization *par excellence*.

We should not forget to state at this juncture that it is totally impossible to reconstruct the topographical situation in or around any of the cities known to us from our sources. We simply cannot know where the fields owned by one of the three sectors — the temple, palace or private owners — actually lay. There is an incredible wealth of Old Babylonian field names and *Flurnamen*, and many of them can safely be related to a given city. But we do not have precise locations, partly because we cannot reconstruct the networks of irrigation canals and ditches derived from the rivers, river arms and large canals. Hence, even if occasionally a topographical mark on a field is mentioned in a text, it does not enable us to locate it.

Let us then turn to *ilkum* as an important starting point for the privatization of landed property. The most extensive treatment of the *ilkum* institution to date is that by B. Kienast in the *Reallexikon der Assyriologie* (1976),[29] but the subject has by no means been exhausted. It is difficult to render *ilkum* by a modern expression. On the one hand it connotes a house with a garden and a plot of field, *i.e.*, something specific allotted to a person in state service in lieu of a regular "salary" (the latter usually being an income measured in grain). On the other hand, ilkum also denoted the service performed in compensation for the allotment. The word has often been translated by "fief," *Lehen* in Assyriology, but the translation has been criticized because of its misleading associations with medieval European institutions.[30]

Our information on *ilkum* essentially stems from two kinds of documents: the Code of Hammurabi §§(26):27-31 and 36-41, and the correspondence of Hammurabi with his governor Shamash-hazir at Larsa.[31] We do not have a unified compilation of references century by century or even decade by decade. Instead, much has to be inferred from an archive covering only a short time. This is the situation often found by scholars of cuneiform studies, and we have mentioned above (fn.13) that inferences and arguments by analogy are dangerous ways of procedure in Mesopotamian history.

The Code of Hammurabi mainly refers to *ilkum* allotted to two categories of soldiers, *redûm* and *ba'irum*.[32] Their *ilkum* as well as *ša naši biltim* "of someone subject to paying rent," was not allowed to be sold or bequeathed. Apparently such regulations served to enforce a rule that already had started to be loosened. I will only talk of the *ilkum* here, and not of a possible predecessor and relative, the *a-sa suku* (KUR$_6$), the "subsistence field" as it is normally translated.[33]

The Code of Hammurabi (§40) allows some special kind of *ilkum*, to be sold, but the obligation to be available for royal service remains linked to it. In other words, the former owner or holder had to see to it that the palace was granted the right to further enjoyment of the obligations, whatever they were. Despite the holder's right to sell this land, we cannot speak of privatization in the strict sense, for the *ilkum* remained tied to the crown.

If an *ilkum* could not be sold "in the free market," it might nevertheless pass from father to son. This probably was not achieved by a will, but was tolerated by the palace. In fact, if an *ilkum* were managed efficiently and there was a good chance that such management would continue from one generation to the next, it was much easier for the crown, for there was much less "clay work," so to speak, in leaving the *ilkum* in this way than to withdraw it and re-allot it for another period of time, possibly to the heir of the former holder. With this in mind we easily understand that in Hammurabi's corrrespondence, *ilkum* holders speak repeatedly of *bit abiya* or *bit abini*, "my (or our) paternal estate," literally "the house of my/our father."[34] We read this, *e.g.*, in cases where the far too eager Shamash-hazir had, by his personal decision, cancelled someone's *ilkum* title and re-allotted the *ilkum* to a third party.[35] Strictly speaking, the *ilkum* that had remained within a family for two or more generations was not yet private property, for the *ilkum* holder did not own it. But we can easily see that there was a chance for an *ilkum* ultimately to become privatized.

Apart from the *ilkum*, there is another type of land tenure often on the edge of being privatized: the A.ŠA GU(.UN), *eqel biltim*, a field for which rent had to be paid. Whereas the *ilkum* was rent-free (but a service had to be performed in lieu of rent), the *eqel biltim* was service-free (an annual amount of grain or silver was due, but no royal service). The tenant of such a field was called *iššakkum*.[36] Holding titles of *iššakkus'* fields apparently could get obscured with the passage of time, for one of Hammurabi's letters (AbB 4 no, 39, end) says that two *iššakkus* lay claim to each other's fields (*bitquru*, stative Gt of *baqarum*).

Here is a more extensive citation from Kraus, AbB 4 no. 40. Hammurabi at first quotes from a complaint he received from a person called Ibbi-Adad:

> The field of my paternal house which we have been holding (*sabtanu*) for a long time (*ištu umi madutim*) Š., son of A., claimed against me. Thereupon, Shamash-hazir convened the city and the elders. They looked into the matter of that field and found proof that A. (the father of Š.) did not take possession of it, so that the field in question was our holding (*sibitnima*). They gave me a tablet on that matter. By the way, in the tablet which they gave me, A., the father of Š., appears as a witness. Just now, however, Š., son of A., laid claim against me with regard to my field and, on top of it all, he keeps watch on (*i.e.*, withholds) my barley.

Hammurabi states that if the complaint of Ibbi-Adad was justified, they are to return the field and the barley. If, on the other hand, the complaint was not made on clear grounds, if Shamash-hazir has not been able to clarify the title to the field and has not yet given it (back) to Ibbi-Adad, the "weapon of the god" would have to come down on the field in question (*i.e.*, a court procedure was to take place in the presence of the divine emblem). Then, Shamash-hazir, the city and the elders would have to find proof before the god and "give it (imperative plural) ana *durišu*." Kraus translated the last sentence as "give the field to its intended designee" ("*führt das Feld seiner eigentlichen Bestimmung zu*"). I would prefer "give the field as a permanent holding of his" (*i.e.*, of the person favored by the jury); *duru*, "duration, permanence," is also found elsewhere in that meaning.

Matters of *ilkum* and related categories of holding thus could become quite complicated. This hardly is surprising, inasmuch as much time had elapsed and the political situation was as unstable as it had become during the middle of the Old Babylonian period.

There is an incredible wealth of information in these Hammurabi letters, from which we have quoted only one example.

It is difficult to sum up the discussion because reference was made to sources covering an entire millennium, a period which experienced far-reaching political changes and turbulence. During this time Sumerian culture, along with its living spoken language, started to become a culture of the past, an heritage. I have been unable to find proof of large-scale privatization of landed property owned either by temples or by the "state" as represented by the palace. On the other hand, I believe that there always existed a private sector of agricultural land alongside that of the temples and the palace ruler.

DISCUSSION

Hudson: Your paper clearly draws the distinction between property and social responsibility for its use. When you get into property in the form of land, there no doubt were families who farmed the same land through many generations. But was this land property in the modern sense? Over the past five thousand years there has been a progressive dissociation between property ownership and the public obligations for property. I would describe modern property in an economic sense as being free of reciprocal responsibilities to the community. What you are describing is a time when property and responsibility went together. What interests me is how this property came to be separated from its archaic responsibilities.

Edzard: As a philologist, the linguistic expression is for me the first criterion. I always try to find out how you say "we" or "our" with regard to property. So the first question is, what did people say? The answer depends on how we interpret *ilkum, sibtum,* and how we express the idea of possession (in Semitic languages by means of possessive pronouns).

Buccellati: If I heard you right, you said that the sale of property from the state or the king, from the *ekallu* or from the temple to a private person, would be considered an example of privatization.

Edzard: Over time, a field given by the state became property. That would be privatization. *Ilkum* and the like would become private by customary tenure and habit, not by force.

Buccellati: It seems to me that it would be better to retain the term privatization for some kind of deliberate policy or a massive transfer of property. As long as we have just a few contracts like the ones Maynard will be citing from Nuzi in his paper, it seems to me that we have simply the transfer of property by one particular owner, who happens to be the king or the temple, to another. But it is not a real phenomenon of privatization, which is why your mention of the *ilku* particularly interested me, because that is a larger-scale example.

I look for something that recurs as a pattern, not that just happens once or twice. Regarding the *ilku* pattern, I think it is indispensable to remember that the letters Shamash-Hazir send back to Hammurapi of Babylonia, deal with a conquered territory. Land that Babylon has conquered presumably is redistributed to some extent to its soldiers, who thus benefit from the conquest. What happens is simply that private property that belonged to somebody passes to some other private owner. This is not really an example of privatization.

In addition, I think the *ilku* and *sibtu* are different types of institution. The *ilku* refers only to land that remains in the ownership of the palace. The term refers to the public responsibility the purchaser takes on. *Biltu* signifies a set amount, whereas *ilku* refers to the responsibility to maintain. It's almost like field maintenance, a general term referring in many cases to just the responsibility to carry out obligations of whatever sort. In the case of a field, the *ilku* duty is to cultivate the field. In the case of tablets, it is to write tablets and maintain an archive. Land which is defined as *ilku* remains the property of the palace. If somebody appropriates it, whether by mistake or theft or whatever, the transfer is annulled.

Sibtu is instead the *bit abiya*, the homestead as I call it, the family property that remains inalienable. It is different from the *ilku* in that it is the land that has remained with the family. The reason why Hammurapi defends the property of the Larsa homesteader against his own governor, Shamash-Hazir, is that he treats these homesteaders as privileged even against his own soldiers. Land rights for the conquering soldiers or royal administration does not override those of homesteaders. Those rights are sacred even outside of Babylon. The only lands being redistributed are those that were not *sibtu*, not the homesteads of individuals. They might have been *ilku* for the king of Larsa. Therefore, I don't see that one can use the *ilku* as an example of privatization, although it is the only real example of privatization.

Edzard: I did not mean to throw together *ilku* and *siptu*. I meant that *ilku* could, after some generations, become *sibtu*.

Buccellati: Yes, squatters' rights, OK.

Mitchell: Romans drew a distinction between *possessio* and *occupatio*. You could *possess* private property, but could only *occupy* other property, usually public in character. The occupied public land, when records were lost, tended to turn into private property, and that is one of the complaints the Romans made about their system in the late Republic. The occupation of that public land involved the payment of a modest rent or tax, presumably collected in kind originally.

I wanted to interject at the end of the last paper that the Roman word for money is *pecunia*, and that one was permitted to graze a certain number of large and small animals on public land for a percentage payment made to the state. Our major difficulty in understanding *possessio* is that of all the property generally characterized as *ager Romanis*, we know the least about what percentage private property was of the total. Most of our information and all the debate about the use and misuse of lands focuses on *ager publicus*. When the Romans defeated an enemy they took some of the conquered land and made it *ager publicus*, usually a third or half the lands were converted to Roman public lands and therefore subject to occupation. However, frequently an unknown amount of land was taken and converted to private ownership — *possessio* — when it was awarded to soldiers, as colonists, and their commanders.

You mentioned the homestead. We have no idea about the amount of land in private hands, but we do know its possessors did not pay taxes on it. When it comes to private possessions in Roman law, I disagree with many legal historians who maintain that the Romans were so litigious that they had wills from the time of Romulus. I believe that intestate succession was normal, and that those whom the deceased wanted to inherit did so automatically. The *sui*, the children, were the direct agnate heirs who received the property automatically. We are not told much about the common practices, we are better informed about unusual or exceptional cases. This is one of the major difficulties with legal evidence. Law and legal materials and discussions frequently address the atypical. It was important to record the unusual because it was so unusual because it had to be mandated or controlled in some sense. The body of information that survives may not reflect the quality and quantity of the no longer extant material. But certainly intestate succession must have been the rule as long as normal traditions and family practices obtained.

Levine: I want to tell everyone not to look to me for sympathy about the limitations of written evidence, because as a Biblical scholar I work under more severe limitations than any of you!

Maidman: First, in relation to one of Michael's comments, if I understand correctly, private property entails *no* obligation?

Hudson: In the modern economic sense, I think what you're talking about is a form of tenure more than the concept of property as free of social overrides as it has become today.

Maidman: Do you consider holding title to a house on which real estate taxes are due to be private property?

Hudson: In today's sense, yes.

Maidman: Well then, there is public obligation attached to such property.

Hudson: But by no means as much obligation as we find back in the Bronze Age.

Levine: I was going to say the same thing. I don't think you ever, even today, get to the point of property that is entirely free of obligation. You're talking about taxes here, but I am talking about the social status of the property.

Maidman: That is very different.

Hudson: Yes, it is.

Maidman: My second point addresses Dietz's talk. Regarding the progressive privatization of *ilku* land, as opposed to Giorgio's concept that *ilku* remains linked to the palace, I have some weak support. I say weak because when we talk about Nuzi, we are talking about a later period, and one which is different geographically and I would be loath to see an evolutionary connection. *Ilku* obligation at Nuzi is attached to land and is transferable with that land. When land goes from A to B, so does the *ilku*. As far as I can tell, it is nothing more or less than a real estate tax, payable in labor annually.

Buccellati: I think that the *ilku* is not a tax, and was also not equal from one time to another. I give a field provided that you keep farming it. That would be an *ilku*. It simply means "responsibility." It is a "service" in the sense of an encumbrance on the field.

Maidman: It consists of obligations as well as the right to alienate the land.

Buccellati: That is a different matter. You may or may not have a field you can alienate. You may alienate a field that has free title, or even with an encumbered title . . .

Mitchell: A servitude in Roman law is not something that is negotiable. It does not end with sale. The sale included the private servitude, that is, the third party's right to a road or water or to anything else that is a natural or customary part of the object sold.

Edzard: The main difference I see between *ilkum* and *biltum* or *naši biltim* (literally "who bears a load," *i.e.,* "who owns a field for which he has to pay rent/tax/tribute") is that *ilkum* is a recompence for service performed. The service you do is what you pay for *ilku*. But *biltum* has to be paid for a field received. You first get the field, and then you pay tax on it.

Buccellati: Correct, except that I wouldn't say you get the *ilku*. You get the field. I think it is not quite correct to say that the *ilku* is the complete thing. I think it always refers just to the service which is attached. This service is an encumbrance. It is not a field, it is not a complete thing. In fact, you find it referring to all sorts of things that are not just fields. So to speak of the *ilku* as connoting just a field is kind of a extrapolation from the laws of Hammurapi where this is mentioned prominently.

Maidman: The point is that it is alienable. There is no connection between title to property (or to the use of property) and attachment to the state authority. *Ilku* becomes detached from the state in the sense of the state having a permanent interest in regard to the land's disposition.

Hudson: What happens when a creditor forecloses on *ilku* lands? Who bears this tax?

Maidman: The creditor.

Hudson: You are talking about Nuzi, but I am asking Dietz about Babylonia. Is the situation the same?

Edzard: Can you elaborate what you mean by "foreclose."

Hudson: To take property as collateral or security when debts are not paid. My question is, when a creditor takes possession of lands that have been pledged and forfeited for debt arrears, do the remaining community members (as Diakanoff describes matters) have to bear this obligation? Is the situation the same as in Nuzi, or is it different?

Edzard: I would say that in principle the ruler is not allowed to pledge royal lands. If he does, he already has privatized these, and they are his own lands, not those he holds *ex officio*, so to speak.

Dandamayev: We have some explicit documentary evidence on the status and obligations of the owners of *ilku* lands from Achaemenid Babylonia. Royal soldiers were settled on state land and granted fiefs that were transferred by inheritance along the male line. These soldiers had to perform their military service, as well as pay taxes in silver and in kind. During campaigns, they had to set forth with their own equipment. In fulfilling these obligations, they frequently had to resort to the assistance of creditors to pay monetary taxes, and were forced to pawn their lands — and, naturally, were not always in a position to redeem them. In theory their lands were not alienable, and creditors could take only the harvest as an equivalent of the debt. But under the guise of adoption, creditors could become the *de facto* owners of the mortgaged fiefs. In such cases the military service was performed by the soldiers themselves, to whom the creditors gave arms, a horse with equipment, and money for subsistence during the periods of military campaigns.

Levine: In my area of inquiry I must consider both semantic transactions and legal transactions. The Hebrew term *'aḥuzzāh* is similar to Akkadian *sibtu*, since both derive from roots meaning "to seize." Through applied usage, both came to designate properties acquired through purchase, or lease. Although the etymology of Hebrew *naḥalāh* is not quite as clear, in its usage *naḥalāh* may designate something possessed by conquest as well as property acquired through grant and inheritance. Thus, Jacob's daughter, when they felt they had been disenfranchised, complained that they were no longer part of their father's *naḥalāh*. Similarly, David, when in flight, complained that he had been driven off God's *naḥalāh*. This is, of course, applied usage, showing that there is a great deal of drift in the meaning of legal terminology in biblical literature.

Regarding the developmental aspect of institutions relevant to land ownership, I think the Bible comes at the chronological end of a long historical process. Biblical literature is a coda. When you look at the contents of the Bible this way, you become aware of all the confusion, the blending of different genres of texts that weren't intended primarily to record information of this sort. When you trace terms of reference you see how much has changed in their usage.

Here is a good example. In Ezra the charge is voiced against the Judeans that if they complete construction of the temple in Jerusalem, the Persian treasury will no longer receive from them: *mindāh* (Akkadian *mandattu*), *belô* (*biltu*), *wahalak* (*ilku*), the three best known taxes. I doubt that whoever wrote these words in Aramaic knew of the legal technicalities involved in these three terms. He simply meant to say that the Persian authorities would never get a penny from Judea if ever Jerusalem was restored.

There are often tremendous gaps in historical attestatin. You may pick up a Biblical reference to a practice undocumented for hundreds of years, and be left wondering how the Biblical writer knew about it in the first place. We therefore must be very discrete in our usage.

Mitchell: Are we working on two kinds of assumption? One is that if there is such a thing as possession of private property, it must be maintained because of the fundamental importance of the family (sounds like Dan Quayle); or (number two) since the family plays such an important role in the transmission of property, the state takes an interest in the family, because the state wants to maintain the family's obligations. I don't think you would find much in the way of written evidence if the state was only involved with reinforcing obligations that automatically were going to occur as a consequence of inheritance patterns designed to protect the family. In Roman law, if you want to disinherit your son, you have to specifically name him in the will. He has to be disinherited by name, because it was assumed he would inherit. He naturally would inherit the obligation to the state.

NOTES

1. For much of the following discussion the reader is referred to *Das Grundeigentum in Mesopotamien* (ed. B. Brentjes), with the contributions by P. Steinkeller (pp. 11-27: "Grundeigentum in Babylonien von Uruk IV bis zur frühdynastischen Periode II"), H. Neumann (pp. 29-48: "Zum Problem des privaten Bodeneigentums in Mesopotamien, 3. Jt. v.u.Z."), and J. Renger (pp. 49-67: "Das Privateigentum an der Feldflur in der altbabylonischen Zeit").

2. Some kind of archaism seems to be reflected in the Sumerian lexical series dealing with parts of the human body, *Ugumu* (ed. By B. Landsberger and M. Civil, MSL 9, 1967:51-73), combines each entry with the suffixed possessive pronoun *-gu$_{10}$*, "my".

3. A useful introduction to stamp and cylinder seals is offered by D. Collon, *Near Eastern Seals* (Interpreting the Past, London 1990); see also her *First Impressions* (1987), with extensive bibliography.

4. See most recently, I. J. Gelb, P. Steinkeller, and R. M. Whiting, *Earliest Land Tenure Systems in the Near East: Ancient Kudurrus* (= OIP 104, 1991) 39-43.

5. Gelb *et al* (as fn. 4) 66f.

6. *Kudurru* is, strictly speaking, a misnomer when applied to archaic documents. For the Middle Babylonian term see J.A. Brinkman and U. Seidl, RlA 6 (1980/83):267-277. A *kudurru* was the monumental "edition" of a royal grant of immunity as applied to landed property.

7. To be used together with the extensive review article by J. Krecher, ZA 63 (1973):145-271.

8. See fn.4.

9. Forthcoming in ZA 86 (1996).

10. Kauf, A. I., "Nach sumerischen Quellen vor der Zeit der III. Dynastie von Ur," RlA 5 (1976/80) 490*f* 498, and specially p. 490; also Krecher (as in fn.7):151-160. Krecher defines "purchase" as "*Austausch ungleichartiger Güter*" ("exchange of dissimilar goods").

11. For witnesses see Krecher (as fn. 7) 160f.; A. Falkenstein, *Neusumerische Gerichtsurkunden I* (1956):54-58, 72f. (quoting older literature).

12. *Cf., e.g.,* R.D. Cooter and W. Fikentscher, *Is there Indian Common Law? The Role of Custom in American Indian Tribal Courts* (= John M. Olin Working Paper Series. Olin Working Paper No. 92-3, Law School, Univ. of California at Berkeley, 1992) esp. pp. 31-45.

13. JCS 3 (1951) 1.

14. *E.g.*, Eannatum of Lagash, Edzard, *Rechtsurkunden* (see above fn. 7) no. 14 (the object is a garden); En-entarzi of Lagash, Edzard, *ibid.* no. 31 (house); Lumma-TUR, son of Enannatum I of Lagash, Edzard, *ibid.* no. 117 (field); R.D. Biggs, *Bibiotheca Mesopotamica* 3 no. 10 (field).

15. See Edzard, *Rechtsurkunden* (as above, fn. 7) no. 115.

16. *Cf.* the cylinder seals of the Uruk IV stratum in D. Collon, *First Impressions*, fig. 2; E. Frankfort, *Cylinder Seals* (1939, reprint 1965) pl. III e.

17. For ancient Mesopotamian royal titles *cf.*, *e.g.*, W. W. Hallo, *Early Mesopotamian Royal Titles* (= AOS 45, 1957); D. O. Edzard, "Problemes de la royaute dans la periode predynastique," in *Le Palais et la Royaute* (= *XIX Rencontre assyriologique internationale* 1971 ([1974]):141-149. Jacobsen had first interpreted *lugal* as a "warlord" (ZA 52, 1957:103f.) and later as "great householder"; see most recently his "Notes on the Word lu," in *R. Kutscher Memorial Vol.* (= Tel Aviv Occasional Publ. 1, 1993) 69-79: "Person in charge of others," "head of a household" with ref. to Edzard's interpretation as "Person," "*jemand*" (JAOS 110, 1990, 121). Also W. Heimpel, "Königtum und Herrentum im vor- und frühgeschichtlichen Alten Orient," ZA 82 (1992):4-21.

18. In historical times, *é-gal* was the royal residence in a narrower sense, and it included all royal property as well as the residences of local officials who depended on a given ruler, in its more extended meaning.

19. The reading Irikagina (as against Urukagina, Uruinimgina or, more cautiously, Uru-KA-gina) was proposed by Edzard in *Aula Orientalis* 9 (1991):77-79. W.G.Lambert tried to defend his reading Uruinimgina in *Aula Orientalis* 10 (1992):256f. For the texts see H. Steible, *Altsumerische Bau- und Weihinschrifte* = FAOS 5/1, 1982: 288-324 and FAOS 5/2, 1982: 143-166.

20. Note the "classical" essay by A. Falkenstein, "La cité-temple sumerienne," *Cahiers d'histoire mondiale* 1/4, (1954) 784-814; = *The Sumerian Temple City* (= Monographs in History: Ancient Near East 1/1, 1974, transl. by M. deJ. Ellis). His title is indebted to Anna Schneider, *Die Anfänge der Kulturwirtschaft: Die sumerische Tempelstadt* (1920). Note also A. Deimel in the recapitulation of his extensive studies of the pre-Sargonic Girsu archives: *Sumerische Tempelwirtschaft* ... (= *Analecta Orientalia* 2, 1931).

21. See F. R. Kraus, "Provinzen des neusumerischen Reiches von Ur," ZA 51 (1955):45-75.

22. E. Sollberger, AfO 17 (1954/56):23-29: *les grandes-prêtresses de Nanna*.

23. But note Th. Jacobsen, ZA 52 (1957):101 with fn. 15, "to command with absolute authority and effectivity."

24. See A. J. Ferrara, *Nanna-Suen's Journey to Nippur* (= Studia Pohl Series Maior 2, 1973).

25. In 1939, Jacobsen reacted to the predominant interpretation of early Mesopotamian history as one of racial contrast and conflict between Sumerians and Semites when he published his programmatic article, "The Assumed Conflict between the Sumerians and Semites" (JAOS 59:485-495). Since then, possible differences in attitude and religious custom of the Sumerians and Akkadians have been discussed, but the idea of an outspoken Sumero-Akkadian ethnic conflict has lost ground.

For "mentality" *cf.* (ed. U. Raulff) *Mentalitäten-Geschichte* (Berlin 1987) with contributions by A. Burguiere, P. Burke, R. Chartier, J. Le Goff, P. Hutton, Chr. Meier, R. Sprandel, and M. Vovelle.

26. It goes without saying that if there had actually been a Sumerian temple-city, the idea of a sector of agricultural land privately owned might have been in conflict with the idea of the "god" owning all the land.

27. *The Farmer's Instructions. A Sumerian Agricultural Manual* (= *Aula Orientalis*, Supplementa 5, 1994).

28. For *asa₅ apin-la* "field leased (by temple or 'state')" see Steinkeller and Neumann (as in fn. 1).

29. RlA 5 (1976/80):52-259.

30. See the definitions proposed in CAD I p. 70.

31. See essentially F. R. Kraus, *Altbabylonische Briefe* 4 (1968).

33. No convincing translations can be offered for *redum* and *ba'rum*. The literal translations of *redum* as "someone who goes behind, follows, or accompanies," and of *ba'rum* as "catcher" (fisherman), do not reflect the specifically military functions of the two categories of soldiers.

34. See Steinkeller and Neumann (as in fn. 1).

34. See, *e.g.*, Kraus (as in fn. 31) nos. 16:8, 24:16, 40:7, 43:5', 9'-10', 51:20-21, etc.

35. *E.g.*, Kraus (as in fn. 31) nos. 16:8-9, 24:13, etc.

36. The word is a loan from Sumerian *ensi(-k)*. It first denoted an independent ruler of a Sumerian city-state. The word's etymology has not yet been established. In the Akkad and Ur III empires the ensi tended to become the semi-independent governor of a province. Within only two

centuries after the fall of Ur III the word occurs in a still more devolved meaning, "tenant farmer." The latter is, so to speak, the holder of an atomized "province," a field (of whichever size).

4.

The Role of Socio-Political Factors in the Emergence of "Public" and "Private" Domains in Early Mesopotamia*

Giorgio Buccellati
University of California
Teologia di Lugano

Conceptual domains

Irreverently, let me begin the way *Pinocchio* does.
"Once upon a time, there was . . .
— A king! — so would my young readers say right away.
— No, kids, you got it wrong.
Once upon a time there was a piece of wood."
Listen now to the *Enūma Elish:*
"When, high above, the heavens were not identified as yet
and, down below, firm ground was yet without a name, . . . "
Given our modern expectations, we would be tempted to continue:
"then it was that the divine world took shape above,
and then it was that *man* was created down below . . . "

---

* The text of this paper retains the style of the original oral presentation. In keeping with its programmatic scope, I do not provide detailed documentation or bibliographical references. I will only note here that the argument I advance about *kudurru* and *sikkatu* as elements used for boundary definition has now appeared under the title "The Kudurrus as Monuments," in *Cinquante-deux réflexions sur le Proche-Orient ancien offertes en hommage à Leon de Meyer* (Mesopotamian History and Environment. Occasional Publications, Vol. 2. Louvain: Peeters, 1994):283-291.

I also wish to note in this regard that my student Stephen M. Hughey is writing a major doctoral dissertation on the techniques of surveying in ancient Mesopotamia and its pragmatic ramifications in terms of material culture. He has served as the chief surveyor on our archaeological expeditions to Terqa and Mozan, and I am indebted to him for stimulating my sensitivity for the theoretical as well as practical implications of surveying.

But no, the emphasis in the ancient text is instead in quite a different direction. The creation of man is in fact almost incidental in the *Enūma Elish* (vi 33f). It is instead the city, in its specific cultural embodiment as Babylon, that emerges as the object of major attention and concern (v; vi 56-78).

It is the same theological locus we find in the Sumerian *King List*: the descent of kingship from heaven, and its transfer as a tangible good from one territorial urban seat of power to another. What is being transferred transcends the individual kings even as it lists them as concrete representatives of the institution itself. It reflects a perception that places rank and function ahead of the individual. Or think again of Atram-hasis. Mankind is created to assume, as a social group, the collective task of serving the gods, to replace what a lesser class of gods had done previously. What is remarkable is that the accent is not on the individual but on the group, in its social, economic and political configuration.

We may speculate whether perhaps there could be here a reflection of the changes brought about by the urban revolution. The answer must remain speculative, but it seems reasonable to assume that such a revolution (as indeed it was) did not exhaust itself in the creation of new structures of power, new technologies of manufacturing and new systems of communication. It also affected the perceptual world of the people involved. The increased size of settlements created a critical mass whereby face-to-face association no longer was possible among each member of the social group. And yet, remarkably, the group retained an internal solidarity that gave it a strong identity and permanence. Individuals belonged together because of ties that were not inscribed in personal relationships, but rather were mapped within the boundaries of a shared territorial organization. We thus may infer that the city loomed large as a psychological dimension, an overarching reality that acted as a living organism, through whose tensional pull many individuals recognized themselves as parts of a larger whole.

It seems reasonable to assume is that no such picture would have obtained in pre-urban times. Within a pre-urban village (as distinct from the para-urban villages discussed below) face-to-face association was the bond of solidarity. Personal acquaintance preceded group solidarity, serving as its foundation. Such solidarity also was tested in identifying people outside the group. The foreigner was anyone who could not personally be recognized.

In such a perspective the group itself — and this brings us closer to our topic — was private. It had commonality of interests (which is what made it a group), but this commonality rested on the reciprocal personal awareness of those who shared whatever they had in common.

If this is correct, then the dichotomy between public and private is coterminous with the origin of the city. In this sense the city may be defined as a public group, one whose internal solidarity derives from factors other than the reciprocal private knowledge of its individual members.

Alternatively, it stands to reason that the very distinction between "public" and "private" was inoperative in pre-urban times. To speak of pre-urban villages as private groups means in effect that they had not yet developed in such a way as to aquire an institutional reality *vis-à-vis* their members. Of course, groups had their own symbols, internal articulations, and even their separate identities; otherwise they would not have been groups. But they remained entities perceptually identical with the sum of their members. For this reason I see in the breaking of the barrier of face-to-face association the origin not so much of a *distinction* between public and private, as if one derived from the other, but rather the origin of the opposition itself. If by "public" I mean not just the group of individuals I already know, but the group as the source *through* which I can identify individuals as my associates, then by "private" I must mean not just an individual I already know as individual, but the individual in his *opposition* to the group. In linguistic terms the two poles of the opposition can only be marked once the opposition obtains, not independently apart from it.

All the factors we associate with the urban revolution support this conclusion. The sharper articulation of (1) political controls provided an administrative infrastructure and an ideological suprastructure. Through the administration we see the life of this public organism take shape; through the ideology we see the perceptual apprehension of the social group's unity affirm itself.

The dramatic advances in (2) manufacturing technology, monumental architecture, irrigation works and metallurgical production, along with the complex development of long distance trade, put the individual before the finished products. Such products were far removed from nature, and also no longer universally understood in terms of their genesis. They were public, in the sense that they required chains of transformation transcending the perceptual range of any given individual. The production process was a system of steps that entailed a non-contiguity between at least some of these steps (*e.g.*, a metal weapon could be acquired without the user having witnessed each and every step in the chain from mining ores to transshipping ingots, smelting and casting). It is in this sense that we can properly speak of an "industrial" production.

As a new (3) system of communication, writing served to standardize discourse and flatten personal idiosyncrasies. As an external extension of logical brain functions, it gave these functions an existence that could be inspected at any time by any one technically prepared. This gave a public mode of visibility and verifiability that countered the privacy of individual domains.

(4) The differentiation of social ranks and specialization of occupational crafts created a new perspective in the way humans looked at each other. They came to play functional roles within impersonal systems. As such, many easily stood to lose their own personal identities — witness especially the introduction of slavery (if we can associate that too with the city), the most extreme functionalization of human individuals.

Finally, (5) law emerged as something different from custom. Uniform standards were applied to resolve conflicts. These standards acquired a hypostasis of their own as an independent reality, regardless of contingent circumstances.

These considerations suggest a perceptual framework in which the notion of a public domain may have developed in Mesopotamia. True, it did not acquire a lexical identity; at least I do not know of Sumerian or Akkadian lexical terms that cover the semantic range of our words "public" and "private." However, the emphasis on the communal or social dimension of human life, and the implications inherent in the urban revolution, suggest a structural contrast between the individual and the community. The community acted not only as a group of individuals, but *as an individual itself.* In other words, individuals interacted not only among themselves (singly or as groups), but also with a distinct entity that we may identify as "public." The king was not just a more powerful private individual, he embodied a distinct organism. We do not just have kingdoms as the domains of private individuals more powerful than their subjects; we have, properly, states.

I submit that these distinctions are not anachronistic, irrelevant or inconsequential to our topic. It is important to know whether by privatization we mean the fight toward equalization of individuals (in which case "public" would refer simply to stronger individuals, whose power others wanted to erode), or whether we mean a structural transformation in the relationships between the individuals and their community as an individual *sui generis.* I believe we can make a case for the latter alternative, and that the concept of "public" was really applicable to specific aspects of political power, economic expansion, legal categorization, social intercourse and technological development.

In what follows I will suggest certain practical implementations of the dichotomy between "public" and "private," and how the process took place between one and the other, with particular reference to the direction privileged by this privatization symposium. I will first ask how the concept of "boundary" may have been significant in defining very specifically an area of control, and — just as important — also the point of origin from which control was exercised. By "control" I mean the placing of limits on the ability to alienate a parcel of land defined by specific boundaries.

In some cases, we see the community acting as a legal person, *i.e.*, in such a way that it exercises control in its own name. The tensional factors that hold together ever larger human groups are particularly apparent in the political domain, where group integrity and coherence is fostered by (and contributes to) effective administrative mechanisms. Control thus becomes institutionalized. Hence political institutions should be considered as powerful factors in affirming the reality of the public sphere.

It is in juxtaposition to this emerging public sphere that the role of the private sphere acquires its identity. Concretely, "private" refers to the individual and his (or, to a more limited extent, her) immediate range of action and control. For instance, certain types of land become inalienable (*nasbu*) in order to protect the economic base of individual families (*muškēnum*).

Beyond that, antagonistic tendencies also develop. A notable example is the way in which control over herds on the Middle Euphrates (Mari) remains in the hands of private rural families, in contrast with the development of state herds in southern Mesopotamia and in Ebla. This evolves into new political and economic ("public") structures, *i.e.*, the tribal institutions of pastoral nomadism.

In conclusion, I suggest we consider the ideological component. Public religious structures provided an essential scaffolding for private piety. Do not omina and incantations cater to private needs? Increasingly, perhaps, but with some exceptions. The Amorite agro-pastoralists of the Middle Euphrates developed what may be termed a para-urban religion representing a form of ideological privatization.

Control mechanisms: the technology in the service of the institution

I will use the concept of boundary as a concrete example to show how the public and private realms were closely intertwined. This can be seen in how each utilized mechanisms that affirmed the necessity of the public while serving the needs of the private.

Boundaries define not only adjacencies, but also ranges of control inside and outside of the domain they encompass. The care exercised in defining and recording them represents an index of awareness of the practical limits within which control could be exercised. The complexity of the mechanisms employed, and the safeguards brought to bear on guaranteeing their results, suggests clearly that public standards were developed, followed and advocated to protect very concrete interests. In examining this issue I will propose a new interpretation of some relevant data, and refer to the impact these mechanisms had on consolidating a "public" conceptual domain.

The two major Mesopotamian items we should consider are the *kudurrum* and the *sikkatum*. The first is generally understood as a boundary stone, with the attendant question left unresolved as to whether the monuments that can be so labelled were placed in the fields or were only commemorative objects kept in a temple. I suggest that the *kudurrum* was not a boundary stone as such, but rather a surveyor's benchmark. The generally pointed tip of the stone monuments would be particularly well suited to mark the point from which distances could have been measured. The very term *kudurrum* may refer etymologically to a single underlying root meaning "to be crest-like" (physically like a rooster, a kudurrnum, or perhaps psychologically in the sense of being overbearing). The logogram NIG$_2$.DU may be understood as the "thing of walking" or "pacing," *i.e.*, the point from which the "father of the rope" (*abi aslim*, the Akkadian term for "chain-man" or surveyor) would have stretched the rope for measuring. Note that NIG$_2$.DU is also a term for a measure of distance (almost 6 meters), which may have been the standardized length of the surveyor's chain.

The *kudurrum* may have been not only of stone, but also of wood with a metal pin. The description sculpted on the Votive Boulder of Puzur-Insushinak found in Susa may represent just such a benchmark, to which the text inscribed on it would refer in speaking of "a copper and cedar nail." The deity shown in a kneeling position and holding this presumed benchmark in his hands would then be sighting along the top of the nail, much as a surveyor would. The text further says that the ruler opened a canal and set up a statue near the city gate. This may be understood as referring to the need of sighting elevations from the gate, so that the new canal's water would not overflow into the gate itself.

A commemorative dimension came to be associated with these benchmarks in two ways. First, an inscribed version of an actual benchmark in stone would be placed in a public place to identify the details associated with the surveying operation itself, and with the events that accompanied the change of ownership. Second, a miniature version would be included with the items placed in foundation deposits to indicate that title to the property had been formally established through proper techniques. In either case the *kudurru*s came to provide a parallel perceptual embodiment for the field as a distinct physical reality, which was now identifiable as a precisely measured entity.

The *sikkatum*, on the other hand, would be the (temporary) marker or control point to which the distance was measured, starting from the benchmark itself, *i.e.*, from the *kudurrum*. For actual surveying operations it might have been of metal or wood, but the clay version is the one we know best because it is the one used as a symbol of ownership.

For a number of reasons which cannot be detailed here, I assume that the proper display setting of these clay nails was within the frame of perforated plaques of stones that would have been embedded in a wall. It is conceivable that such display would have obtained not only in the building whose title of ownership was being declared in the document, but also in communal spaces such the temple or a public square.

What is common to both the *kudurrum* "benchmark" and the *sikkatum* "control point," in terms of their monumental utilization for display purposes, is the metonymic value attached to them. The symbols of specialized surveying tools represent (a) the formality of the operation as a guarantee that proper technical standards had been employed, and (b) the integrity of property measured and its ensuing title of ownership. They thus stand for both the surveying and the surveyed, the bounding and the bounded, the boundary as action and as result.

The implications for our topic of privatization are significant. In a way we may say that surveying is the conceptual equivalent of coinage. By placing a public guarantee on an operation and its result, it provides a safeguard for public or private use. While coins guarantee movable wealth, benchmarks guarantee real estate. This is clearly linked to the significance the public dimension had come to acquire, and to the awareness for it that must have developed as something above and beyond the private sphere. It is not only the technical complexity of the operation that escaped the ken of normal private individuals; it is especially that the efficacy of its results, and the limits it placed on private interaction, was established through channels that necessarily were, and could only be, public. Not only was the public sphere present and operative, it was absolutely required if private relationships (affecting in this specific case title to property) were to remain stable.

What I have attempted to show is that the distinction between public and the private spheres was not just a blurred perception of something that vaguely transcended the reach of the single individual. It was rooted in the recognition of specific ranges of control that were dependent on technical standards known only to the practitioners, but guaranteed by the state. By "range of control" I mean in this case that alienation of real estate could take place only by following such technical standards. The surveyed boundaries defined the parcel's integrity, and therefore the applicability of the owner's control.

A reason why I attach great significance to this particular aspect of ownership derives from the need to define more specifically what we mean by private ownership. It goes without saying that individuals and groups would have felt and expressed, from early prehistory, a proprietory disposition toward tangible goods. We may also well expect that there would have been conflicts in relating to goods, when more than one individual or group claimed the same good as their own. But properly speaking we should restrict the beginning of the notion of private property to the moment when the concept of alienation is introduced. Only when the control of a given good can be handed over according to recognized mechanisms does ownership become more than temporary exclusive use. To be valid and binding, such mechanisms must be public. Once again, the idea of a private dimension makes sense only if it can be seen in its polar opposition to the public domain. We will now look more closely at the role of the state as the main institutional embodiment of this domain.

Focus of control: the institution as legal person

I have already referred to the lack of Mesopotamian words for "public" or "private," but I have tried to show how these domains were present as operative principles, if not as explicit semantic categories. Analogously, we do not find a term that would be equivalent to "state" or even "kingdom." Yet the identity of the public institution is clear, in both its legal and its political implications.

The 23rd article of the Code of Hammurapi states that if the victim of a robbery cannot be reimbursed for his losses because the robber has not been found, then "the city and the city-mayor (*âlum u rabîânum*) in whose territory and jurisdiction the robbery took place" will recompense the victim for his loss. In the 32nd article it is stated that if a prisoner is ransomed in a foreign country by a merchant, the individual will be responsible for defraying the merchant's costs. Should he be unable to do so, the funds will come from the treasury of the city temple (*bît il âlišu*). If that too is depleted, the royal treasury (*ekallum*) will pay. In both instances the city appears as a legal and economic entity, which is represented administratively by the mayor in one case and the temple in the other. The responsibility is guaranteed by a higher authority, the state, embodied by the king. On the one hand he includes these statements in his "decisions of righteousness" (*dînat mîšarim* , CH xlvii 1-2), as he calls his laws; on the other, he adds the palace as a final source of funding when all other avenues have been exhausted.

There is an interesting extension to the sphere of international law of the principle envisaged in the first situation. It is found in a letter sent by a Kassite king, Burnaburiash, to the Egyptian pharaoh Amenhotep IV (EA 8). Complaining about the murder of some of his merchants and the theft of their goods, Burnaburiash asks that the local kings of Canaan, where the events had taken place, be held responsible and punished accordingly, with the goods being returned to Babylon. He appeals to a general principle: "Canaan is your land, and its kings are your servants. In your land I have been offended. Get to the wrongdoers and return my silver to me" (24-26). The kings of Canaan and their cities are considered as equivalent to the mayor and his city in the *Code*, and Pharaoh is considered as ultimately responsible in his role as the overlord to whom the vassal kings owe their allegiance.

Conversely, we may consider those instances (*e.g.*, in Ugarit) where a breach of private contracts results in the payment of fines to the palace. It is as if the state were collecting a fee for the service provided in guaranteeing the integrity of the contract.

We see in these examples a link between legal principles and the state in such a way that the state (or its component elements, such as a provincial city or a vassal kingdom) acts properly as a legal person. But the constitutive moment of this entity is not so much legal as political. In my view it is the factor of power and its administration that brings about the coalescing of the human group and establishes a "public" entity in the proper sense of the term. The sense of self-identity of a community is correlative to the effectiveness of political power. It is established as soon as we go beyond the level of the non-urban village.

We should now look at alternative types of such power structures and how they reflect the variety of historical embodiments of the "public" domain.

(1) I mentioned earlier the need to distinguish between a pre-urban (or non-urban) and a para-urban village. Although they might be analogous in terms of general settlement size, and possibly also in terms of the size and nature of their individual buildings, the two types of villages are markedly different. In a para-urban village the population presupposes the city. It is a component of a hinterland that gravitates around the city, and presupposes the services of the city at the same time that the city presupposes the services of the village. Whether it is the availability in the village of material goods coming only from the city, or the presupposition of an institutional framework within which the village is integrated (*e.g.*, the legal system as administered by courts and judges), or the background presence of significant institutions otherwise physically absent in the village (such as the great religious festivals, or even simply the existence of a city temple to which the village also relates, if from a distance), all these factors imply a different perception of the community for a para-urban village than for a non-urban village. They also imply the apprehension of a public dimension lacking in the non-urban village understood as a private group.

These considerations about diverse village communities may help us appreciate the variety of political realities in Mesopotamia in terms of a progressive expansion of structural complexity. As I mentioned earlier, the public domain of (2) the early city-state, with its hinterland of villages, is based on breaking the barrier of face-to-face association, yet it retains a link between the perceptual awareness of the territory on the part of the community's members and the effective range of political control on the part of the state. To put it simply, at some point or another the individual members of the group would have seen with their own eyes, or at least would easily have had the possibility of seeing, all the territory that defined the boundary of their group as a public entity. The city-state is a *territorial* state in the sense that territorial congruence is the defining factor for group solidarity; but it is a *city*-state in that such congruence is physically subsumed within the perception of each of its individual members. In many cases the top of a temple tower provides a physical point from which the boundaries of the state can be encompassed within the horizon actually visible to human eye from that artificial height.

The following moments in the political growth of ancient Syro-Mesopotamia read almost like stages in a normative sequence: the boundaries that define the public domain widen in progressively concentric circles, but the cement that holds the resulting organisms together never seems to weaken.

(3) The expanded territorial state goes beyond the perceptual confines just described for the city-state, in that only a few of the community's members are acquainted with the physical layout of the overall territory, whether it is geographically homogeneous (which we may term regional, *e.g.*, Eshnunna) or macro-regional (*e.g.*, Mari).

There remains in the second millennium a fundamental unity of culture within the political group, but even this barrier is broken in the first millennium with the establishment of (4) the first true empires. Here territorial contiguity remains the basis for the internal congruence of the political group, but the component parts are separated by broad differences in language, ethnic affiliation, local traditions and so on. That we can properly speak of a single type of "state" from the beginning reflects the uniform way in which public institutions remain anchored in the administration of power along territorial lines.

If the territorial state is the first and major socio-political construct in ancient Syro-Mesopotamia, we also witness here the origin and growth of a different construct, where public domain is not rooted in territorial congruence: (5) the tribe. Originating, as I see it, in the progressive detachment of rural classes of the middle Euphrates from their territorial allegiance to the central city, the clustering in tribal units developed new bonds of solidarity resting on the perception of common kinship ties. This process was the converse of what had happened in the village and city. While every (post-urban) village presupposes the city and is properly para-urban, the tribe presupposes the family and is properly para-familial. Family trees (genealogies) may well be fictitious, and enlarged family traditions may reflect historical developments in manners quite different from scribal historiography. But what matters most for our purpose is that the perception of a para-familial, *i.e.*, tribal bond served as a powerful political factor establishing a kind of public domain very much alternative to that based on territorial contiguity.

From public to private: the individual behind the institution

As indicated in Section 1, it seems plausible to assume that the dichotomy between "public" and "private" *originates* as an opposition. Once the urban institution (and then, by derivation, the state) is marked as "public," its individual members are marked as "private." In this sense "privatization" is a process that goes hand in hand with the development of the public sphere. It can be (1) a way in which private individuals take advantage of the public domain for their own advantage. Or, it may serve (2) as a means whereby certain private privileges are protected systemically, not necessarily out of a developed social conscience but because of the benefit this provides for the public domain. It can also develop into (3) a conflictual position where individuals oppose the public institution, and may lead to the establishment of alternative public institutions. We will look at these three points in turn.

(1) Leadership within the new public group enabled select group of individuals to turn public political institutions to their private gain. By their nature, public institutions were complex systems resting on a delicate balance among their component parts. The construction of massive urban defense systems around the beginning of the third millennium is a case in point. First, their engineering expertise was considerable. Though not comparable to that required in roofing large spaces, for instance, they required the calculation of proper foundations, joints and buttresses, the horizontal leveling over long distances, and the proper layout of the moat in relation to the wall. Second, management of the operation had to follow what can only be called industrial patterns, in the sense of a segmented chain of production. A large number of individual work crews would work at different tasks over a very long period of time, without necessarily being aware of how their individual contribution fit into the larger scheme of things. Third, the motivation to build the wall required strong persuasion and enforcement. A partial wall was of no use whatsoever, and nothing but a fully completed ring would have served its purpose, without the smallest gap. Finally, the economic means had to be made available over an extended period of time, managed in such a way as not to have (at any given time) either excess or lack of funds. All the planning that would have gone into such an operation gives us a measure of how complex the system was to erect such structures. None of that planning, coordination and execution could have been managed without effective central leadership.

Leadership thus served as the public institution's nerve center. And yet the concrete position of leadership, its function and interests, were private and remained so. Section 6 below will describe how an ideology was developed that represented the king almost as a public servant. If this was the image projected, it was because there was an audience for it, that is, because a certain public need (ideological if nothing else) was being served. But as a matter of course, the king used leadership for his own private gain.

The range of control over the public domain was essentially his, and "personally" his. Hence, the first form of "privatization" may be considered to be the exploitation of controls made newly available by the public domain.

The converse is also true: The public domain probably would not have come into existence without the impulse provided by the prospect of private gain. This is how social stratification and economic differentiation made a quantum leap in the wake of the urban revolution. Control of the public domain became a launching platform that catapulted a few individuals rapidly to socially stratospheric heights.

It also plunged others into abysmal lows. I referred earlier to slavery, which I assume to have begun (at least in a systematic way) as a consequence of the development of public domains. In this respect the growth of slavery may be seen as a counterpart to the growth of leadership. The leader is the individual who most directly manipulates the public domain. But the public domain consists ultimately not so much in the natural wealth of a territory as in the human resources themselves, the individuals who make up the group. If the human group is considered as a group that can be handled, so can its component members. The religious dimension that came to be embedded in kingship (about which more later, in Section 6) provided an elegant rationalization for this conceptual development. It left fundamental private freedoms intact, while proposing an almost emotional fulfillment in the acceptance of one's status as a subject. Slavery, on the other hand, is a much more brutal, certainly less elegant *reductio ad absurdum* of the same principle. As a pure and simple functional slot within the system of a public institution, the slave loses in principle "its" private dimension. "It" is the minimal (human) unit of the public sector.

I do not mean to speak here of a distinction between slaves belonging to the palace or the temple as public slaves in contrast with slaves belonging to individuals as private slaves. I mean that the very notion of slavery is mapped into the public domain. Slavery is not an occasional, frequent or even regular abuse of an individual by an another (of which we may well assume many cases in pre-urban times). It is part and parcel of the depersonalization process intrinsic to the public domain's development. The public dimension of the city, of the state, developed in opposition to the private sphere precisely because it grew so large as to cross the threshold of groups based on face-to-face association, *i.e.*, on mutual personal acquaintance. In the city, personal recognition among members of the group rested on their jointly belonging to an overarching impersonal institution. As a result, human beings began to relate to each other not necessarily (and not only) as persons, but also as functional actors in a well-coordinated system. A potter would serve my functional needs whether known to me personally or not. He would serve as a functional slot which I would expect to find without hesitation in any well-ordered system, in any city. Such functionalization of human relationships may be seen as the conceptual precondition that made it possible to accept slavery as normal.

(2) Between these two extremes of the king and the slave stood the vast majority of individuals. They were simultaneously "servants" of their king and "sons" of their city, subjects and citizens at the same time. Certain mechanisms were soon developed to correct imbalances — not with a humanitarian goal in mind, to be sure, but simply to maintain the fine homeostatic equilibrium that ultimately made possible the system's survival.

One such mechanism aimed at protecting the subsistence basis of private individuals. This was done by setting aside certain parcels of real estate as inalienable property. This acquired a very concrete institutional manifestation, so that there are (at least in my understanding) specific Mesopotamian terms used to describe it. As I see it, the term *muškēnum* referred specifically to an individual so protected, a "homesteader" as we may say in English. His "homestead" (*eqel muškēnum*) could be alienated, but not permanently, because it would revert to him or his family at certain points in time and under certain conditions. The (temporary) purchase of such property would not be a good investment, hence its value would be proportionately lower.

We know from the Khana contracts that other parcels were privileged, and their having a clear title was clearly spelled out. They are called *nasbum,* which I understand to mean "allodial, *i.e.*, with a clear title unencumbered by liens, including homesteading rights." They are qualified as *lâ bāqârim u lâ andurârim,* "for which no repossession right may be recognized, whether as a result of private or state intervention."

Ironically, protection of the homesteader may be viewed as resulting more from a concern for the public domain than as a phenomenon of privatization. The economic efficiency of the state was better served by virtue of having a class of homesteaders able to maintain themselves. Their homestead was protected not so much against encroachments by the state, as against purchases by private capital holders intent on increasing their investment. It appears that even in conquered territories (at least in Larsa after its conquest by Hammurapi) the rights of local homesteaders were protected, at the very moment when other types of real estate were being distributed to Babylonian newcomers.

(3) In ancient Syro-Mesopotamia there was hardly a trace of institutional opposition to such private exploitation of the public good. Political changes were always changes of political fortune, not of structure. The concept of dynastic succession was accepted, and indeed used as a yardstick of legitimacy for the transfer of power. This phenomenon must not be underestimated. Political stability of the public domain was predicated on the most private of relationships, biological descent.

We may sum this up by saying that the state was essentially monarchic, and monarchy essentially dynastic. I say there was *hardly* a trace, but nevertheless a trace. What little can be found is particularly interesting in view of its structural contrast with the established norm, as the following section will make clear.

Private against public: the fight for privileges

As a rule, opposition came in the form of attempts to retain or obtain privileges on the part of certain individuals or certain sectors of the private sphere. (1) An example can be found in the management of animal herds on the middle Euphrates. While in the south and west (Ebla) the great herds were mostly under the direct control of the state, in Mari they remained in the hands of private groups. These groups comprised the rural classes originally at home in the valley floor, progressively swelling into the steppe. Known to us under the common label of "Amorites," they developed a strong sense of ethnic identity and an alternative political system, the tribe. (This at any rate is my understanding of what otherwise is generally seen as nomadic movements *from* the steppe.) There is no indication that the state administration ever attempted to take over a direct control of these herds. A likely reason is that the size of the herds, as well as the nature of the terrain where they grazed, made it impossible for the state to do so. But the state was very keen on imposing military service and levying tribute on these groups. In this it was only partly successful.

(2) Along similar lines, but with a more direct effort to obtain legally binding exemptions, certain territorial enclaves within the expanded territorial states sought relief from taxation. This involved entire cities or what the literature has designated as "feudal" lands, *i.e.*, districts whose local rulers retained a degree of economic independence from the central government. This formula is found particularly in Babylonia in the late second millennium, for instance with individuals such as a certain Ritti-

Marduk, to whom Nebuchadnezzar I granted considerable autonomy from taxation and conscription and the exercise of judicial functions.

An analogy may be seen with a phenomenon dating from the same period, but which is admittedly different in other respects, namely the relationship of Syrian vassal states to their Hittite and Egyptian overlords. The release from royal jurisdiction in internal affairs granted to Ritti-Marduk of Bt-Karziabku is in many ways analogous to the conditions of vassalship accepted by an Ammistamru of Ugarit. We should not be too nominalistically impressed by the use of the term "king" used for the latter. One may not think at first of Ugarit or Byblos as evincing a type of privatization, if for no other reason than for their rulers having the title "king." But in terms of broader implications, these rulers may be considered as landlords who pay a fee for the use and exploitation of their territory (their "kingdom"). In so doing, they provide a "private" alternative to the incorporation of their territory as a province within a fully integrated empire.

(3) On a different level is the movement of individuals who, in various ways, escape from a given state's normal territorial jurisdiction and live either as small bands or as isolated individuals. Political treaties of the late second millennium dealt at great length with these fugitives (*munnabtûtu*) to gain an international level of supervision that could extend where internal state controls had failed. It is as if these individuals had found a zone of private escape by falling through the cracks of the great territorial public organizations of the cosmopolitan Late Bronze Age. Handling their status through recourse to international law is indicative of the ever widening range of the public domain. A related earlier phenomenon is attested with the *'âbirû*, whom I understand as the individuals who evaded the control of the territorial state to join a *'ibrum*, i.e., a small clan within the developing system of agro-pastoralist tribes.

(4) The latter, i.e., the tribal system ethnically identifiable with the Amorites, was the only type of public domain which emerged in Syro-Mesopotamia as a real alternative to the city and the territorial state (see briefly above, Section 3). In its structure and final outcome, the tribal domain is not so much to be understood as a contrast between private and public, but as the contrast of one type of public system against another. In its origins, however — as shown, among other things, by the resistance of private herders to state controls in Mari, and by the isolated but significant phenomenon of the *'âbirû* — tribalism seems to have been rooted in an effort to assert private interests against the urban territorial state's overriding influence.

As a corollary, it may be worth mentioning two other anomalous political structures that seem to have developed in later periods, deriving in different ways from the tribal public domain. (5) The first is the kingdom of Amurru. This was not, in my view, a state like the others in the Syro-Palestinian world of the late second millennium, *i.e.*, a city-state with expanded hinterland. It was rather the first real *steppe* kingdom. It originated, in my view, from the collapse of the kingdom of Khana. It was the first territorial state that had, and retained, its center in the steppe, and continued to show some measure of its dependence on the tribal background from which it derived.

(6) The other anomalous political structure was the national state of a slightly later period. Ancient Israel is the best known example, and the only one that retained a scribal memory of its past. It is particularly interesting that within Israel, and through its perception of its national past, we find the only articulate record of a proper anti-urban and anti-monarchic ideology. From the patriarchal rejection of the Mesopotamian city (Abraham) to the prophetic warnings against establishing a royal government (Samuel), this tradition makes an argument like no other in the ancient Near East in favor of private resistance to the otherwise inexorable sweep of the public urban domain.

The ideological balance

The pivotal role of private leadership lent a personal dimension to what was otherwise an impersonal construct, the state. This development was in the nature of things, but it also was in the awareness of the individuals involved. The transposition of this personal awareness into an ideological construct went hand in hand with establishment of the institution. Such a transposition occurred along two major lines: (1) metaphorical and (2) religious. An important byproduct was (3), the development of ceremonial circumstances that catered in a special way to the presentation and fruition of this ideological superstructure. Let us review these three points in turn.

(1) There was obviously a vested interest on the part of leaders to develop ideological canons that would uphold their public character and function. Instead of being seen merely as exercising coercive power, the leader would want to project, in his military functions, the image of the shepherd who protects his flock, and who extends his capable help in defending the community against threats to its integrity and interests. Instead of being seen as merely amassing wealth for his personal profit,

the leader would want to project, in undertaking public works, the image of a father building up his household and bringing about the economic growth of his family. Instead of being seen as merely a self-serving master setting up rules for his own advantage, the leader would want to project, in maintaining the legal order, the image of a caring judge upholding the rights of even the weak and oppressed. This is not to say that these images, and others, were wholly fictitious. However cynical these leaders might have been in exercising their power (and however cynical we may choose to be in our analysis), it seems plausible to assume that the cliché behind the image reflected some kind of goal toward which they would in fact strive in establishing and implementing policies. It is even possible that some sense of human fairness might have been present in some at least of these rulers. But even a simple sense of administrative pride would have justified their striving to implement the canons that encouraged the system's stability.

Whatever the motives behind this ideology, it is meaningful to note the function it served. It balanced the harshness of the public institution as an impersonal entity by emphasizing the private character of its leadership. Community members were "private" precisely because of their structural (not necessarily political) opposition to the community as "public." Their relationship to this new entity was mediated through the private nature of its leadership. Whether or not the image of the ruler as shepherd, father or judge matched the reality of things, and regardless of how much the ruler might manipulate these images through the skillful rhetoric of political propaganda, the fact remains that the metaphorical mechanisms were effective in promoting a sense of solidarity for private individuals *vis-à-vis* the public institution.

(2) We need not assume a nominal correlation between royal leadership and secular ideology on the one hand, and on the other, priestly leadership and religious power. Whether royal or priestly, leadership was political and its ideology was both secular and religious. The religious ideology was political in that it served similar purposes to those I have labelled metaphoric. Here, too, we should not let an overly cynical attitude steer our analysis. It need not surprise us that religious beliefs should have been used to serve political means, for there is no period in history when this did not occur. But the converse need not surprise us either. There was indeed room for some authentic religious beliefs. The articulation of religious systems gave public shape and form to private perceptions of the divine and its affecting presence. Whatever private response there might have been to the divine, it was channeled through a public conduit: the identification of specific divine beings (mythology), the decoding

of their particular means of self-manifestation (divination), the vehicles for structured human response (cult and magic) were all elements of a shared religious culture that provided the interface between important private and public realms.

So, a first understanding of the interrelationship between private and public in religion is that as religious culture became more public in its complexity, it continued to address genuine private needs. A second dimension concerns the use of religion for political aims. The gods as well as the king served as a hinge between public and private. As religious culture was elaborated into a complex public system, its range of applicability overlapped with that of the state. The pinnacle of the system, the gods, affected the private individuals in ways similar to how they were affected by their political leader. Just as private individuals related not so much to the state as to the leader, so private worshipers related not so much to religion as to the gods. And inasmuch as the highest gods stood in a special and particular relation to the political leader, peoples' access to the gods was facilitated through their access to the leader. This was the major political dimension of religious ideology.

I have referred to all this as ideological balance because I view the effects of ideology as the most articulate and coherent attempt to bridge the gap between the two newly emerging domains of the public and the private. Ideology proposed a rationalization. It also proposed (3) new mechanisms for the fruition of the superstructure it had been offering. I refer to the great religious ceremonies and festivals with which the temple came to punctuate the rhythm of daily urban life. Without undue cynicism, we may view this activity of the temple as serving, next to others, the same purpose that the entertainment industry serves today. These temple activities were urban and public. In their function as a "show," the great festivals gave a public display for private fruition. The different layers of sacrality involved — space, time, persons — were given a perceptual embodiment that brought the public institution within private reach. The sacralized version of urban culture was thus visible and palpable to all. The kerygma was clear: the climax of creation had been the city.

Levine: We own a home in Connecticut. The municipality privatized tax collection, so that checks for the bi-annual property taxes are made out to a certain Joseph X, not in the name of the township.

What you have projected is, therefore, very interesting: With respect to a larger political unit, the smaller unit is private. The City of New York is not presently a "corporate person," because so much of what it does is subject to the approval of the State of New York. But, if the City of New York could manage all of its taxes, that is, pay a certain amount to the State and to Washington, and for the rest, decide exactly how to organize its schools, its police, and the like, it would constitute a legal, corporate person relative to the larger political authority. What I am hearing from you is that there is something relative about the notion of "private."

The free cities of the ancient Near East, with all of their privileges, controlled most of their activities. Because of this degree of independence and control over their own resources, they may have functioned less as public, and more as private organisms.

We ought not to fall into the trap of defining the unit we call private solely in quantitative terms. Is a clan private? Does a family cease to be private when it grows to large proportions?

Mitchell: The private entrepreneurs who conducted Rome's business were called publicans. They bid on taxes as private individuals. They had their own businesses, but they are *publicani* because they collect the public taxes and work in the public sector.

Levine: May I follow up about the guilds we were discussing this morning? I once was criticized for calling something a guild. I was told that they were involved in three aspects of the economy: production, very often marketing, but also recruiting and training, the educational side of manufacturing. This morning it was intimated that this function tends to remain in the family through the generations. For various logical reasons, the major factor in transmitting these crafts was likely to remain in families, but not always so. With regard to this domestic production you were talking about, is this just apparently passing this on from father to son and so on and so forth or wife, or are there outside people. What role does the educational side of this play? It seems to figure somehow in what you are talking about.

Buccellati: It is true about technical skills, such as surveying.

Hudson: Speaking of guilds, one of their important roles was to establish corporate responsibility for their members to parties whom their members injured economically. This points up the importance of defining social units in terms of their responsibility, in contrast to their autonomous property rights. A continuity can be traced from the laws of Hammurapi holding the city responsible for injuries to travelers, down through medieval Europe where, if a merchant was robbed, not only was the city responsible but letters of mark could be issued against any citizen of that city, enabling the injured party to take recourse. While personal responsibility for social costs and injuries has been reduced over the millennia, property's immunity from responsibility has increased. The process reached a watershed a century ago, when the limited liability corporation was innovated to insulate private legal bodies from social recourse against their owners. Throughout most of history, people have had economic recourse against the corporate bodies responsible for causing them injury or damage. But now you have corporations being formed as corporate shells to protect their individual owners from such recourse. This is why New York has so many law suits. So you have a steady narrowing of the legal scope of responsibility down to the individual, even to transient corporate shells, a stripping away of responsibility. This is just the opposite from what you find in Sumer's temple bodies.

Lamberg-Karlovsky: There are many different places one could choose to intersect on your wide-ranging paper. A point I want to bring up — I think that you mentioned it, and Dietz too — that we are dealing with something that exists already as a mature configuration when we find it in the third millennium. You were sort of cogitating on the perceptions of those who first undertook the urbanization process, and you pointed to its agricultural origins. I want to go back to this remote period of agricultural origins, because here rests some fundamental aspects of private versus public in the archaeological context of just who commands the surplus. Where is the surplus stored? Who controls access to it? Who distributes it?

There has been a fundamentally important transformation in our understanding of the neolithic in the past several years. It turns on the idea best advanced by Ofer Bar-Yosef, that the neolithic's agricultural origins were confined to a smaller geographical area than previously believed, and took place within a much more rapid schedule. It took place somewhere around 8000 BC in the southern Levant. I want to skip to the period of 6500 BC. If you look at the Pre-Pottery Neolithic B sites, what is becoming increasingly apparent is that the context where things are stored is in the domestic house, not centralized storage facilities. Adjacent to it are clearly storage facilities. Someone is bringing up the emmer and the barley and such. It is highly probable, I would argue, that the individuals who lived in those houses commanded that surplus, and that they owned it privately. It is also not unreasonable to assume that at least 20% (and maybe as much as 30%) of the harvest had to be stored as seed corn. The germinating aspect of the early seed types were not so robust. That amount of the harvest represents a substantial amount of labor, once again probably undertaken by the householder and stored in the house. That is private property.

Just for the fun of it, let's reverse the aspect from privatization and consider the possibility that what you are dealing with is, in effect, a process of communalisation. Suppose the initial conditions of the neolithic were autonomous household communities, villages that were basically self-sufficient. Suppose that they somehow were directed by headmen, by senior members of lineages etc. That is entirely speculative, but the dominant aspect that would suggest that the surplus is in the hands of domestic households and owned privately. This is capital, if you will. What then happens in the context of urbanization is that the emerging administrative authorities are going to extractively command your private surplus into what now becomes the corporate surplus of the city.

What we might be dealing with here is quite the opposite of the process of privatization from the neolithic to the urban epoch. A large amount of productive capital, labor, craft, etc. was undertaken in the domestic community. What happened with the urban process from this aspect? Was the institutionalized form of this capital surplus — whatever form it took, palace, temple or whatever — one of a corporate elite extracting from all these individuals, centralizing and coercing a surplus?

With regard to writing I often think of it as permanent memory. But Giorgio, regarding what you are dealing with in the earliest texts, I do not see them as what you suggested they were. Perhaps this happened later, but aren't the earliest records intended for very temporary usage, not for long periods of time? They are effectively monitoring production, consumption, etc. They indeed make up a permanent record, but the memory is very short. In time, they become more permanent in the context of memory.

I am not playing the devil's advocate by reversing the arrow from privatization, but I think there is substantial speculative, archaeologically derived argumentation which has substantive evidence behind it.

Buccellati: What I mean is that to have two days of work written up allows you to compare those two days in a way that human memory does not allow. It creates a form of memory that even para-urban villages develop, even if they do not have writing themselves.

Going back to your other point, I agree with your suggestion that there may be communalisation. I agree if you would call "private" whatever comes before. I don't think the villages of the Halaf type had "public" buildings or structures, because the group is too small. I like to see the growth of the group as the standard whereby the public becomes truly public. In that sense, yes, there is communalisation, because "public" begins only when there is a city.

Wealth differentiation is limited in the agricultural state. It is at that point that there is communalisation. But as soon as you get public, you also get private. I really don't see much to this idea that there is a real distinction between the pockets of the king and the public sectors; even the Assyrian Empire was an extended personal palace of the king.

5.

"Privatization" and Private Property at Nuzi: The Limits of Evidence

Maynard P. Maidman
University of Toronto

In Memory of Jonas Greenfield

In exploring privatization of the economy at Nuzi, I wish first of all to define and to limit certain key concepts central to this exercise.[1] The first concept is that of privatization, by which I mean the permanent transfer of property (and specifically, real estate) to individuals, whose economies represent either their own interests or those of their nuclear or extended families. In using this concept of privatization I do not imply any intent or policy by any segment of Nuzi society to effect a transfer of property to the private sphere. Not only do I fail to detect any such impulse, I do not find any lexical evidence reflecting native awareness of complementary concepts of state and private sectors, although the imposition of taxes on private property and apparent tax exemption of state property implies a contrast between the two different spheres.

Next, I wish to define ownership in terms of the legal right of a possessor to alienate his property. By property in the case of Nuzi I mean once again, real estate. Tracing the privatization of mobilia is elusive and ambiguous, by dint of the transitory nature of such property and the largely absent textual record. I also believe such property to be inconsequential as compared to the transfer of real estate.

Finally, if we talk of the privatization of property *to* the private sphere, I think it best to avoid the notion that it is alienated *from* the so-called "public" sphere. By "public," I sense the notion of the commonweal, the collective interests of a local society. I do not sense a clear consciousness of this concept among the Nuzians, although defence and canal maintenance services rendered to the community are certainly attested. The appropriate Nuzi contrast to the private sector is the state, or, perhaps even better, the government inasmuch as the identity of the state in the person of the king is a shifting concept in the Nuzi texts. As for the temple sector, it is to be dismissed entirely as an independent entity. The temples appear to have lacked any economic independence at all. They were supported by the government. Neither need we bother with any possible institution of extended family communes. They appear sporadically at best and were of no perceptible significance, despite occasional assertions to the contrary by Soviet Assyriologists in the past.[2]

The corpus of material with which we are dealing is impressive for such a small town, a town numbering probably fewer than 2,000 inhabitants in the core and suburbs at any given time. The number of recovered documents totals between 6,500 and 7,000 texts. Most of these stem from various government bureaucracies in the main settlement, while perhaps 3,000 documents were excavated from over two dozen private family archives. Those archives were located throughout Nuzi, in every neighborhood of the walled town as well as in the suburbs.

Three institutions are represented both in the architecture of Nuzi and in its documents: the government, the temples, and the private sector represented by individuals and families. As I already have noted, the temples have no independent economic identity. They generated no documentation, and government records strongly suggest total ecclesiastical dependence on the state. Private parties engage in the full gamut of economic activity, ranging from plutocratic landlords and manufacturers on down to peasants barely able to eke out their subsistence, and even to chattel slaves.

Whereas delineation of the temples and the private populace are simply defined, the government is less so. Nuzi was subject to three levels of government. The municipal government was headed by a mayor, that is, a *hazannu*, responsible for local administration, local economic redistribution, and defense. Nuzi was, however, part of the local kingdom of Arrapha, led by a king, *šarru*, whose chief residence was the city of Arrapha. This kingdom in turn was a dependency — the usual term in the scholarly literature is "vassal" — of the kingdom of Mittanni, whose leader also was called king, *šarru*. The large governmental architectural complex on the main mound of Nuzi gives every indication of having been the seat of the local municipal government led by the mayor. Now this complex and the institution which it housed is called in the texts, *ekallu*, conventionally translated "palace." But here we are not dealing with royalty at all, and so the English "palace" obfuscates rather than enlightens. I have elsewhere called this complex and associated institution "government house."[3]

Real estate in the Nuzi texts often is described as belonging to the *ekallu*, most frequently in contexts providing no precision regarding the identity of the three possible *ekallu*s: government house, the kingdom of Arrapha, or the kingdom of Mittanni. This leaves us with a dilemma as to which level of government is meant in any given case where so-called "palace" real estate is mentioned. But there is no such ambiguity when it comes to defining which *ekallu* can alienate real estate. Where there are precise data, the alienating party is either the king of Arrapha or the king of Mittanni, never the mayor or *ekallu* of Nuzi. Inasmuch as neither the kingdom of Arrapha nor the kingdom of Mittanni had local offices in Nuzi, it is not surprising that very few documents deal with privatization of land, and that most of those that do deal with this subject derive from private rather than government archives.

What were the real estate holdings of the government — or governments? The great government-house complex at Nuzi was obviously local government real estate. And Nuzi texts from all over the site regularly define plots of land as bordering other real estate, including that of the *ekallu*. Such so-called "palace" real estate is located in many cities, towns and villages.[4]

Neither the list of towns nor the texts cited is exhaustive. The real estate included agricultural land plain and simple,[5] (barley being the chief crop), pastoral tracts,[6] threshing floors,[7] canals,[8] dikes,[9] orchard plots[10] and other specialized plots,[11] various urban holdings,[12] and perhaps even a village.[13] Such real estate and its facilities generated income in the form of agricultural and other food items, finished textiles and other manufactured goods. Part of this income was exchanged for imports of various other goods from all directions. Such imports included manufactured goods, skilled labor and luxury items.

One might mention in this context that the government derived income from a series of taxes, at least some of which were based on title to real estate. Thus, the *ilku* is a labor tax based on ownership of real estate,[14] and was owed to the local authority, the *hazannu*.[15] This corvée was employed for civilian projects and is not to be confused with periodic military service, which constituted a separate impost and was not linked to ownership of land. Individual landowners also paid an *iškaru* tax to the local government, usually consisting of finished goods.[16] Land on which such taxes were due must be deemed private, not state property, and this could be freely alienated.

There is no evidence to suggest that government attempted in the least to wrest ownership of real estate from the private sector. Indeed, for the most part the government did not intervene in the operation of the private sector. Such non-interference in the private sector's real estate dynamic must be considered a hallmark of Nuzi society.

Private real estate holdings are ubiquitous in the Nuzi texts. The variety attested is impressive indeed. Holdings in and near dozens of towns and villages are noted, vast rural estates as well as tiny urban plots. Attestations of agricultural land are supplemented by mention of specialized plots for growing fruits and vegetables, in urban and rural environments alike. Houses, threshing floors, dikes, wells, towers, as well as built up and unbuilt urban plots and rights-of-way all appear in the Nuzi real estate texts. However, the private archival records represent a skewed picture of economic activity. Documents pertaining to ownership and possession of real estate, in contrast to texts dealing with mobilia, were deliberately preserved. Nevertheless, the evidence of dozens of private archives leaves one with an unmistakable impression of considerable and variegated real estate activity by a host of private parties.

Against this background, the documentation derived from Nuzi, the nature of its institutions, and the outline of who owned what real estate where, we may now turn to the dynamics of real estate transfer. How is title to real estate established? In theory, one may posit several means by which this process is accomplished. Original settlement is one such way but, however one may imagine this phenomenon, it is undocumented in the records we have, and so must be set aside. The same holds true for settlement by means of conquest. Whether the victorious state allocated land to its warriors or individuals appropriated land following conflict, neither is attested. Neither, therefore, can be discussed other than speculatively. At Nuzi, we do not really know if there even was sudden conquest, let alone by whom or against whom.

There is clear documentation for real estate being obtained by inheritance. Similarly, the texts reveal multiple instances of alienation of title to effect payment of debt. However, though well attested, these categories of land transfer really beg the question we are interested in. The shift of title to property from one private party to another evades the issue of how such property came to rest with private parties in the first place.

Other attested means of obtaining property suffer from the same difficulty. Squatting and perhaps other means of illegal distraint are frequently described and constitute a chronic problem in the agrarian regime of Nuzi. Purchase in its variegated forms is ubiquitously described. These forms include outright purchase, complementary purchase which we call "exchange," purchase of land by means of contracts employing the terminology of adoption,[17] and other forms. None touches on the problem of privatization.

Nor do royal proclamations regarding periodic debt remission, called *šudutu*s in the Nuzi texts, help in our investigation of privatization of real property. *Šudutu*s are issued by the king, almost certainly by the local Arraphan king. The best known of these deals with commercial transactions in human beings rather than with real estate.[18] Yet allusions are made in various real estate conveyences to the sudutu or to the "new" *šudutu*.[19] And so, one or more royal proclamations regulating real estate transfer may well have been issued. We do not have explicit knowledge of the complete contents of such proclamations — no real estate *šudutu*s survive — but it is reasonable to assume that they were intended somehow to regulate alienation of land, perhaps to limit the flow of such property from the peasantry to an increasingly powerful landlord class. The model for this assumption is the Old Babylonian *kittum u mišarum*.[20] It is noteworthy that such proclamations are attested only in the last generations represented by the Nuzi texts.

Incidentally, there is no reason to believe that such proclamations were effective. That a *šudutu* was issued, and then a "new" *šudutu* perhaps points in this direction. But even more telling, we know of these *šudutu*s because of their appearance in texts where real estate is alienated, the very phenomenon the *šudutu* was allegedly designed to discourage.[21]

Even if the *šudutu* were meant to redress economic imbalance, and even if it could have been effective, then the most we could posit is a sporadic, feeble, and apparently inconsequential royal attempt to regulate the balance between various segments of the private sector, not to shift ownership from one institution to another. This regulatory function represents state interest much the same as taxation of property redounded to the benefit of the state. It cannot represent any fundamental struggle between government and private spheres. However, the existence of the *sudutu* may well indicate that, within the private sector, there took place an ongoing shift of real property from the small peasantry to a class of large landlords.[22]

Only one means of real estate transfer attested at Nuzi addresses the central question of how real estate shifts from government to private ownership. And that is by royal grant. But of all the attested means by which real estate is transferred in this community, royal grant must surely be the most poorly documented. Of the six to seven thousand Nuzi texts at our disposal, *perhaps* nine pertain to the crown's disposal of land, alluding to actual ways by which alienation takes place.[23] A very few other documents may be relevant to our investigation but are too poorly preserved to be useful.[24] The nine texts may divided into three groups.

The first category are those instances where the government transfers real estate to members of its own establishment. Three documents describe or allude to the cession of property to such individuals.[25] In one,[26] a plaintiff in a court case claims that the king has given him some land — a claim that apparently is now disputed by another individual. Usually in these contexts the individual is identified by personal name and patronymic, but here he is called "Tarmiya, miller of the 'palace' of the town of Silliya." He is thus clearly a government dependent and his claim to have received a donation from the state most likely is linked to that state of dependency. At least one other text[27] — and possibly a second[28] — lists discrete donations of some sort consisting of "houses" (that is, structures) to males and females. These persons bear personal names but no patronymics. In the less ambiguous of the two texts, they are designated as "palace" slaves.

Whatever the nature of these donations, they emanate from the government. Privatization does not come into play here. Rather, we are dealing with a shifting of resources within an institutional framework. There is no textual evidence of these properties later turning up in other, private, contexts. Circumstantial evidence strongly suggests that the government in these cases is that of the vassal kingdom of Arrapha, not Mittanni.

The second category of royal grant comprises instances where the king transfers real estate to members of his own family. Two documents describe or allude to this kind of cession of property.[29] In the first,[30] the king of Arrapha donates land, in this case a valuable urban vegetable garden, to the household of his son or his son's wife. The document and its special sealing establish that donation. The second instance occurs in perhaps the single most famous of the Nuzi texts, the royal letter from a king of Mittanni.[31]

This document is of sufficient moment that a rehearsal of its contents is in order here. The letter is addressed by an unnamed king[32] — a king of Mittanni, it is clear — to one Ithiya, who may safely be identified as the king of Arrapha. The king of Mittanni announces that he has given a local settlement, an *âlu*, to a particular man, one Uke. This settlement bordered on, or was part of, another settlement which the same king of Mittanni had previously given to a woman named Ammin-naya. It is all but certain that Ammin-naya is the daughter-in-law of the king of Arrapha to whom the letter is addressed.[33] That is one of the reasons the local king receives this letter in the first place. The king of Mittanni then states that he has sent an official to establish the common border so that neither Uke nor Ammin-naya might encroach upon the property of the other, and that the integrity of Ammin-naya's property, in particular, be maintained. Finally, the king of Mittanni assigns yet another settlement, this time belonging to the king of Arrapha, to Ammin-naya.

Three royal grants of land may be traced in this text. First, the king of Mittanni originally gave an estate to Ammin-naya, daughter-in-law of the king of Arrapha. Second, he subsequently granted land to Uke, possibly from Ammin-naya's original estate. Finally, he transfers land from the king of Arrapha to Ammin-naya, possibly by way of compensation for her loss of land to Uke, that is, if she lost land at all. This last donation strongly suggests that that same land had previously been given to the king of Arrapha by the king of Mittanni and that title still rested with the overlord who now reassigns this property. It is a complicated series of relationships. And there is significance in these transfers for the topic of privatization.

The donation of real estate from king to king is perhaps least troublesome, though the nuances of the transfer elude us. Donation of land by the ruler of Mittanni in this case clearly is not an example of privatization. It may be considered either a shift of possession from one branch of a government establishment to another or, better, a transfer of property from one member of a private *oikos*, a special *oikos*, to be sure, to another. But in neither case does the land go from one type of establishment to another. Also, it is clear that title to property, that is, the ability to dispose of the real estate, continued to rest with the original donor even after he had given it to the king of Arrapha.

The case of Ammin-naya is more complicated. She receives two pieces of real estate, one from the king of Mittanni and, as announced in this letter, one from her father-in-law at the direction of the king of Mittanni. What is the king of Mittanni doing giving land to a member of a provincial royal family? This question is tied up with the larger one of the legal and social relationship of the two monarchies, in which the king of Mittanni is clearly in a position of superiority. This is demonstrated by the fact that he can take land away from the local king. Furthermore, his superiority is implied in the epistolary style of this particular letter. He addresses the king of Arrapha by personal name only (a hypocoristicon, at that) while announcing himself simply as *šarru*, "the king." That he takes such direct and favorable interest in the daughter-in-law of the local king suggests that Ammin-naya might in fact be a daughter of his. If this is so, then one might deduce that the linkage of local dynasties to the ruling house of Mittanni was effected through a system of royal marriages. At any rate, if Ammin-naya were a daughter of the king of Mittanni, this would efficiently explain the involvement by the Mittannian overlord, including transfer of real property, in the local world described in the Nuzi texts. One must always remember, however, that just because an explanation is efficient does not make it correct. Whatever the relationship of the donor and recipient may have been, the fact that the woman is an important member — a future queen, in fact — of the local dynasty indicates that these real estate transfers, like the one from the king of Mittanni to the king of Arrapha, fall outside the realm of privatization.[34]

The transfer of land from the king of Mittanni to Uke is described minimally. We don't know who this individual is. He could have been a private individual but this might be surprising given the family connections established elsewhere in this text. Also, Uke lacks a patronymic, indicating either inferiority — unlikely here — or, better, intimacy vis-à-vis the sender or recipient of this letter. It is more plausible that Uke, like Ammin-naya, has some connection to one or another royal household. In any case, one may not use such a laconically described transfer as evidence for privatization.

In short, though much property changes hands in this royal letter, such transfer of property is most reasonably explained as redistribution within a single *oikos*, albeit a uniquely powerful *oikos*. In these cases, as in the first category, we are not dealing with privatization. Whereas in the first instance, the property was simply reassigned within the framework of the government, here we are plausibly dealing with a special case of transfer of property within the sphere of the *private oikos*. The king transfers title to property — his own property, not that of the state — to other members of his family. In the case of the first text, the *oikos* is that of the king of Arrapha while in the second it is the household property of the Mittanni king which, *de jure, might* include the household of the king of Arrapha. These transfers are achieved on a larger scale, no doubt, than is the case for other nuclear families and their holdings, but in principle we see here simply another case of manipulation of property in the families of the large landlords of the Nuzi region.

Thus the first two categories of royal real estate grant take place either within the institution of the *ekallu* or within royal houses conceived as private households. In neither case may we consider privatization to have taken place.

The third category are those instances where the government more or less clearly transfers real estate to private individuals. Four documents describe or allude to three cases of cession of property from the state to such individuals.[35]

The first case involves a prominent private family of the town of Arrapha.[36] In a testamentary document, property to be bequeathed is described. In a somewhat broken context — what else should we have expected? — mention is made of fields of a member of the family which had been given to him from the *ekallu*. Information regarding the context of that donation is probably contained in the crucial lacuna. The point is, though, that this land is heritable and so title must have been received from the government. In short, state land was privatized.

The second case is even clearer.[37] In a courtroom dispute over title to land, one party contends that the land had been bequeathed to him by his father who had himself obtained the property by means of purchase. An individual supporting the opposing party contends that the disputed land had been obtained by his own father from the king. A second tablet seems to allude to the same contention.[38] The claim of a royal donation was ultimately dismissed by the court, but that is quite irrelevant. What is telling is the verisimilitude of the claim: such agricultural land *could* have been obtained by royal grant. Such a contention seems to have been reasonable and had to be taken seriously.

The third case is also a real estate dispute[39] and its significance also lies in the verisimilitude of the claim rather than its truth. A group is accused of illegal distraint of real property. They counter that the property they are occupying belongs — or once belonged — to the palace and that their occupation is based on that status. The claim is further raised that some members of this group seem subsequently to have sold this property. If this understanding of the text is correct, then the claim basically implies that land was obtained from the palace and subsequently alienated. In other words, privatization has taken place. The sense of the text is not quite clear but enough is clear to place this document with the others in this category.[40]

What, then, is the extent of privatization of real property at Nuzi? We may discount entirely that category of evidence which describes the shifting of land within the governmental economy, and also royal grants of real estate to members of the royal family. Such recipients would include the Arraphan king Ithiya, and his daughter-in-law, the future queen, Ammin-naya.

But apart from particular textual evidence, what of more generalized archival phenomena? Does the existence of a certain type of private archive itself point to privatization? A case in point is the archive of Ammin-naya's son, Šilwa-tešup. It is clear from his texts that this individual supervised a flourishing economy from his extensive villa in Nuzi's suburbs. His activities included real estate, agriculture, domestic manufacture, and trade, and were undertaken with a variety of private parties. All these activities have the characteristics of Nuzi private enterprise. This is reflected in his house as well, which was situated in a neighborhood otherwise occupied by private parties. Is his inherited largesse, acquired from, not one, but two palaces — that is, Mittanni and Arrapha — testimony to privatization of state property? Not necessarily, and not even probably. As intimated above, it seems preferable to depict his patrimony as stemming from the private property of kings. This distinction between state property administered by kings and the king's own property is a feature of Mesopotamian monarchy from third-millennium Agade[41] to first-millennium Assyria.[42] Analogy argues for the plausibility of that system at Nuzi as well.

This conclusion is to be preferred because the only remaining evidence — the only clearly valid evidence — for privatization consists of four texts alluding to three cases. Thus, as we have seen, the unambiguous evidence for privatization at Nuzi — or even the ambiguous evidence, for that matter — is extremely limited. That extreme rarity is telling, especially given the large number of private archives identified at Nuzi and their function. One of the chief purposes of these private archives is to preserve real estate texts for use in future land claims litigation. Thus, records of royal land grants certainly would have been preserved.[43]

The fact that real estate is a major focus of these archives, combined with the large number of archives containing thousands of texts and the absolute paucity of evidence for privatization of land, leads one to conclude that privatization existed but was a minor, insignificant phenomenon at most. It certainly never benefited those elements of the private community which emerged as the large landowning class. It may even have been limited to some former dependents of one *ekallu* or another.

By and large, state and private sectors remained distinct and separate in an ongoing, stable relationship. Most real estate activity appears to have taken place within the private sphere. Stated in terms relating to the theme of this conference, private acquisition of property stemmed in practically all attested cases from private, not state sources: inheritance from earlier generations of the nuclear family, purchase from private parties, dowries, and so on. This impression is supported by the dozens of private archives in the suburbs and all over the main mound attesting to transfer of real property.

Internal evidence of the texts supports this impression of vigorous private real estate activity in other ways as well. Wherever the archives yield the history of plots of land, going back sometimes four or five generations to the earliest attested period of Late Bronze Age Nuzi, such land stays within the families of private individuals or is obtained by them from other private individuals. There are no known connections between royal donations and later private transactions. It may be difficult to determine whether the dominant form of property-holding at Nuzi was private or governmental, but the role of the private sector, conceived as either individuals or nuclear families rather than as extended families, was at least very prominent. Such private parties represented an emerging landlord class and, secondarily, a free peasantry.

So there was probably no ongoing, structured process of privatization. That such structures could have existed is demonstrated by the ongoing institution of (multiple) *šudutu*s whereby the state appears to have tried to maintain the vigor of the private sector. Whatever privatization there may have been would therefore have been sporadic and unimportant. Whatever dynamic shifts took place in property relationships at Nuzi took place within the private sphere where the landlord class seems gradually and inexorably to have broken a free peasantry of its legal title to the soil.[44]

DISCUSSION

Hudson: If we do not use the word "privatization" for what happened in Nuzi, then we need some other word for a large absentee-landlord appropriation of land, *e.g.*, when a military leader such as Tehip-Tilla appropriates Nuzian land.

Maidman: First of all, Tehip-Tilla was not a military leader.

Hudson: I stand corrected on that point. But you have given clear reasons for not using the word "privatization" for the Nuzian experience in the sense that Diakonoff and his Russian colleagues call the non-public sector a *communal* sector, and speak of privatization of formerly *communally* held lands. Fair enough, I'm willing to accept that, but what word will you choose to signify the monopolization that occurs *within* this non-public sector, whether we call it "private sector with traditional safeguards," or "communal sector," or whatever? The concentration of landownership forms an important dimension of the privatization phenomenon.

I think one statement you made does not necessarily follow from the facts you described. You point to the repeated *šudutu* proclamations as evidence that they are ineffective. But their intent was not to ban usury or prevent new debt arrears from accruing at interest. They did not anticipate the Bible on this point. They let the process take place again, and then to some extent restored the *status quo ante*. Their mentality was not that of effecting a permanent cure. If you claim there was no permanent effect, you're quite right, the proclamations only restored a clean slate, and then the economic polarization process started up again. This is why their view of time was cyclical and renewable, not one of linear progress. It seems to me that their clean slates succeeded in what they were intended to do, which was to get rid of the debt overhead when it got too top-heavy, and to annul the property alienations that had occurred as a result of agrarian debts.

When you say that you don't find a tension between the ruler and the large land owners over this issue of absentee landownership, the closest analogy I can think of is Byzantium. Byzantine emperors repeatedly abolished the economic power of the large landowners. But between the 9th and the 11th centuries, they couldn't devise a way to field an army without strengthening the local landlords, who were also the warlords, so they stopped fielding an army. We all know what happened to the Byzantines after that, which is why these are the last texts of the Byzantine empire, just as these texts are the last of the Nuzian proclamations.

Maidman: First, in terms of the effectiveness of the *šudutu*, it is speculative, because we don't know what the *šudutu*s said, so it is hard to say whether or not they were effective.

Hudson: Assuming you're right, say the *mišarum* or *šudutu* . . .

Maidman: Well, I am less sanguine. But regardless, we have no evidence that they meant to re-establish a *status quo ante*. If they did, they were conspicuously unsuccessful, on the basis of the following circumstantial evidence. These proclamations had absolutely no perceptible effect on any landlord economy, not even temporarily. We find real estate alienated before the *šudutu*, and listed in the catalogue of properties of the same landlord's family after the *šudutu*, so there is clearly no effect. It also is a misapprehension to believe that there were continual *šudutu*. At most we have attested possibly two, and these did not take place in the generations during which most real estate transfers occurred, but afterwards.

Heltzer: I have a small question. You mentioned a list of persons without patronymics?

Maidman: Yes.

Heltzer: Do you consider these persons to be dependents of the royal court or . . .

Maidman: In one of the two relevant texts, they are called slaves of the palace, ÌR.MEŠ *ù* GEME$_2$.MEŠ *ša* É.GAL (HSS, xv, 287:23).

Heltzer: The lack of a patronymic is not always the sign that people are not free or are slaves.

Mitchell: I want to offer a possible legal characterization of at least part of what you talked about when you said that royal edicts did not represent privatization. From Festus, and also from information from law books, we know that there was such a thing as precarious tenure. An individual who had property gave it to someone, and that property was immune from any kind of claim from a third party but not from the original owner. The one who bestowed it could always take it away.

Regarding slaves with or without patronymics, in Latin we have them both. Slaves usually take the patronymic and association of their manumitter. A slave who could (and they frequently did) get land by precarious tenure or some other means could not bequeath it, could not marry, and therefore could not have a legitimate offspring unless his patron agreed, that is, his ex-master agreed. Hence the latter had a kind of continuous control over that slave (now a freedman), and over his property and its growth, unless he agreed to sign off and allow the slave to own this property in some other manner.

Maidman: I welcome your observation regarding precarious tenure. Obviously, my knowledge is not nuanced enough in that particular area. But I don't see any trace in Nuzian society of the kind of client relationship that you are describing.

Mitchell: I'd be remiss if I tried to suggest that all states are alike; they are not. That is always the danger, when we get people talking about similar phenomena from quite different periods. What I meant to suggest was that there is evidence of a system whereby slaves can hold property but not have title. They can hold it forever as long as the patron doesn't want to do anything about it.

I would like to offer one more observation about evidence. If we only had Diocletian's Edict, we would think that a helluva lot happened in the third century, and it didn't. We know that this edict was a dead letter from the day it was passed. Property, prices, and everything went through the ceiling thereafter. So if we only had that information, we would be led to believe that certain kinds of social and economic activity were curtailed at a particular point in time, when just the reverse was the case.

Buccellati: Regarding the *šudutu*, did you say that the same property was involved in more than one event?

Maidman: The same one.

Buccellati: Fields, or property, or owners?

Maidman: What I was saying was that a given field is attested in the economy of the Tehip-Tilla family a generation before the issuance of a *šudutu*, and also afterwards. In other words, there is no reversion of this property as a result of that hypothetical edict.

Cleveland: Is that royal land?

Maidman: Oh no, it is private land held by an individual, and it is attested both before and after the edict.

Buccellati: But how do you know the *šudutu* applies to the field, to that property?

Maidman: I don't. I don't think *šudutu* edicts applied to property, that is my point. It may have in theory, but as far as I can tell, it had no practical effect whatever.

Buccellati: So what do you think it applied to? Debts of various kinds?

Maidman: The only evidence that I have for the content of *šudutu* is that in one text (JEN 195) we are told that a merchant who ransoms a hostage from the land of Lullubum may command a price of no more than thirty shekels in the land of Arraphe, no more. You can ransom a hostage, but you can't expect to receive more than a certain amount for the erstwhile hostage.

Buccellati: But what has that got to do with the *šudutu*?

Maidman: That is the only kind of *šudutu* about whose contents we have any inkling.

Buccellati: You would equate ransom with *šudutu*?

Maidman: No.

Levine: It's a notification.

Maidman: In other words, the term *šudutu* doesn't apply at all to real estate. It is a royal proclamation. The contents of these proclamations remain indeterminate, except in this one case dealing with hostages.

Hudson: *Simdat* in Babylonian came to be almost a connotation of debt cancellation. Isn't it the same thing here?

Maidman: *Simdat šarri* is certainly not the same thing.

Dandamayev: You said that in addition to royal property there existed also state or government property different from royal property. Have you come to such a conclusion from some internal evidence, or do you have some precise terms for this?

Maidman: There is no terminological difference, but we have certain properties called *ša ekalli*. As a matter of fact, in the instances that I described, the alienated king's property is not called *ša ekalli*. That is a weak argument in support of this dichotomy, but an argument nevertheless. Basically, it's context; it's just there are two categories of property.

Buccellati: You said that there is a general distinction between the property of the king and that of the palace?

Maidman: I didn't say general, I said it is attested from Old Akkadian to Neo-Assyrian times.

Buccellati: How is it, though? Just because something is called *ša ekalli*, would you say that it belongs to the state, and that there is a different monitoring system for something that is called *ša ekalli* from the private property of the king?

Maidman: In terms of a bureaucratic apparatus, I don't know. To judge from some of the middle Assyrian archives, I would suspect that there was a shared bureaucracy, dealing at least in part with a royal economy and the economy of the king personally.

Hallo: You mentioned in passing the fictive adoptions, which I always thought were rather characteristic of land sales at Nuzi. I wonder whether they have any light to throw on the relative rarity of either privatization or the opposite, taking private land for public use. It occurred to me as you talked that perhaps it had something to do with the *šudutu* as a means of circumventing that. We do know about the *šudutu*, don't we (correct me if I am wrong), that it was proclaimed by the herald with a horn-blowing. Aaron Shaffer's article in the Oppenheim Festschrift comes to mind, which would be a parallel with the Old Babylonian *anduraru*, proclaimed by raising the golden torch.* At any rate, whatever the *šudutu* was, what is the rationale behind this insistence on maintaining, at least fictitiously, land in one and the same family?

Maidman: I persist in treating the *marûtû* in terms of its attested function rather than in terms of what it originally may have been. I don't know what it may have represented in terms of the inalienability of real estate outside the family in the period before the Nuzi texts. All that is pure speculation, because as far back as we can take it the *marûtû* is clearly (and even the scribes themselves realized this) a device for the permanent alienation of land, usually in exchange for something else — in other words, sale. In one passage (JEN 159:18-22) the *quid pro quo* for land received through adoption is called *šîmu*, "price," where *qîštu*, "gift" would be expected. For this and other examples, see Zaccagnini, "Land Tenure," 82-84. Clearly there is no fiction involved. There may be a frozen formal terminology, but nobody is trying to get around the law. We have not only the exquisite evidence of the *qîštu* being called the *šîmu* but we also have the very common institution of the real-estate exchange, which is nothing if not a mutual alienation of land.

Hallo: Getting around it and hiding it are two different things. I am not saying that nobody was wise to this technique. But surely no person would be adopted by twenty-five different "fathers" under normal circumstances.

Maidman: Why not?

Hallo: What adoptors wanted was to be provided for in their old age.

Maidman: But that is not the *quid pro quo* in real estate adoptions; cash is.

Hallo: It is still not a rational explanation for the popularity of this scheme of alienation.

Maidman: Inertia. Absolutely. Enough kinds of contract exist where alienation is clearly the object for us to assume that, just as we use the word mortgage to this day, precious few of us know exactly what it means and

---

* A. Shaffer, "*kitru/kiterru*: New documentation for a Nuzi legal term," in *Studies Presented to A. Leo Oppenheim* (Oriental Institute of the University of Chicago: 1964):189f.; *cf. idem*, "Hurrian *kirezzi*, West-Semitic *krz*," *Orientalia* 34 (1965):32-4.

what its origins are. Most of us who have mortgages don't think in terms of their historical origins. We think simply in terms of monthly payments, and in a similar way I think of real estate (*marûtû*) as of virtually no significance in the society in which it is employed as a contractual device.

Cleveland: I am interested by your comments on the concentration of land-ownership. Over what period did it happen, and do we have any estimate of it?

Maidman: To answer the second question first, no estimate has been made. The evidence we have for the increasing concentration of land extends to close to a hundred and fifty years, roughly 1500-1350 BC.

Cleveland: What happened to the people who were displaced?

Maidman: As far as I can tell (and there is some circumstantial evidence), they remained on the land as tenants.

Mitchell: In Roman political life, with all the donneybrooks between patricians and plebeians, between oligarchs and the *populares*, periodically a *concordia* was proclaimed: "We are going to have *concordia*," and they publish it. It doesn't last. Can the *šudutu* proclamations be that kind of text? Is there a reference in the material to show that canceling debts is really happening?

Maidman: Look, it could be anything. As long as you don't have any evidence . . .

Mitchell: Well, you don't have any evidence for *concordia* either, that is not my point. My point is that sometimes "evidence" has no basis in reality.

Levine: It's now time to take a break and then go on to the next paper.

NOTES*

1. I am indebted to Michael Hudson and Baruch Levine for providing such a stimulating and convivial atmosphere in which to explore the topic of privatization in the ancient world. I also thank them and the other participants in this conference for their thoughtful remarks. My understanding of this issue has been materially advanced as a result.

   This article is dedicated to the memory of Jonas Greenfield. He was a brilliant scholar with a fine wit and catholic interests — even including Nuzi studies (see his "'Le Bain des brebis', Another Example and a Query," Or NS 29 [1960:98-102]). We met for what was to be the last time at the New York University conference on privatization — yet another sweet memory of those days, though tinged now by sadness.

2. For example, N. B. Jankowska, "Communal Self-Government and the King of the State of Arrapha," JESHO 12 (1969):233-282; *idem*, "The Role of the Extended Family in the Economic Life of the Kingdom of Arraphe," *Oikumene* 5 (1986):33-42; I. M. Diakonoff and N. B. Jankowska, review of Gernot Wilhelm, *Grundzüge der Geschichte und Kultur der Hurriter*, BiOr 42 (1985):147-153, esp. cols. 150-152. Contrast for example C. Zaccagnini, "Land Tenure and Transfer of Land at Nuzi (XV-XIV Century B.C.)," in Tarif Khalidi, ed. *Land Tenure and Social Transformation in the Middle East* (Beirut: American University of Beirut, 1984):79-94, esp. pp. 85-86.

3. "Nuzi: Portrait of a Provincial Town," in Jack M. Sasson, ed. *Civilizations of the Ancient Near East* (New York: Charles Scribner's Sons, in press).

4. Al-ilani (JEN 619), Hulumeni (JEN 43), Karanna (JEN 28), Nuzi (JEN 484), Sinina (JEN 74?), Tilpaste (JEN 17), Tursa (JEN 525 ¶670).

5. JEN 28, 43.

6. JEN 750?

7. JEN 336.

8. JEN 257.

9. JEN 243.

---

* Abbreviations follow Erica Reiner, ed., *The Assyrian Dictionary of the University of Chicago*, vol. 17: S, Part II (Chicago: The Oriental Institute, 1992):ix-xxvi, with the following additions: G = Tablets published by C. J. Gadd, "Tablets from Kirkuk," RA 23 (1926), 49-161; Yale = Tablets published by Ernest R. Lacheman and David I. Owen, "Texts from Arrapha and from Nuzi in the Yale Babylonian Collection," in Lacheman AV:377-432.

10. JEN 74.

11. JEN 525 (*di, 750 dimtu*-tower).

12. JEN 619.

13. JEN 325.

14. The sequence of events described in JEN 467 and 699 demonstrate this proposition. This is but one example of such a demonstration.

15. For mayoral misappropriation of of such labor, see AASOR, XVI, text no. 1.

   AASOR, XVI, nos. 1-14 attest to the malfeasance of Mayor Kussi-harpe of Nuzi. To that corpus of texts, the following documents may be added: AASOR, XVI, no. 91 (= HSS, XIII, "446," see *ibid.*, p. xiv, a; but this text stems from a different room than the other texts in this corpus; see also further below, this note); HSS, XIII, 286, 430?; EN, 9/1, 470. For the identification of the first two of these texts, see G. Wilhelm, "Parrattarna, Saustatar und die absolute Datierung der Nuzi-Tafeln," *Acta Antiqua* 24 (1976):153; and E. Cassin, "Heur et malheur du hazannu (Nuzi)," in *Pouvoirs locaux*, 112 (Cassin incorrectly describes HSS, XIII, "446" as coming from room C2). For the last text, see the preliminary edition of Roy Edmund Hayden, "Court Procedure at Nuzu" (Ph.D. diss., Brandeis, 1962):176-177. *Cf.* G. Wilhelm, "Hurritisch *e/irana/i* 'Geschenk'," in H. Otten, *et al.*, eds., *Hittite and Other . . . Studies in Honour of Sedat Alp* (Ankara: Türk Tarih Kurumu Basimevi, 1992):504.

16. For example, garments (HSS, XIV, 7:24-26; *i.e.*, the last three lines — the line numbering in the publication is incorrect) and helmets (HSS, XV, 24). The assertion of CAD, I/J, 248a, that the *iškaru* as a tax is confined to the Neo-Assyrian Period is incorrect.

17. There is no evidence that the real estate *marûtû* documents have anything to do with adoption into family, clan, or any other group. It is an otiose, probably archaic contract form with no contemporary significance whether for privatization or anything else.

18. AASOR, XVI, no. 51; JEN 195. On the significance of JEN 195 and other *sudutu*s, see M. P. Maidman, review of J. D. Hawkins, ed., *Trade in the Ancient Near East*, BiOr 37 (1980):188f.; *idem*, "Some Late Bronze Age Legal Tablets from the British Museum: Problems of Context and Meaning," in B. Halpern and D. Hobson, eds., *Law, Politics and Society in the Ancient Mediterranean World* (Sheffield: Sheffield Academic Press, 1993):45f.

19. JEN 116:11-12; and EN, 9/1, 4:35-36 actually gloss "new" *šudutu* by "royal decree," *qibiti sa šarri* .

20. See Maidman, review of *Trade*, 188. The presence of parallels to Old Babylonian type *mišaru* edicts at Nuzi is denied by Carlo Zaccagnini, "On Prices and Wages at Nuzi," AoF 15 (1988):49.

21. A circumstantial but still strong case can be made for the ineffectiveness of any alleged real estate *šudutu* based on the following data. The *šudutu* is first attested in the generation of Enna-mati son of Tehip-tilla. For the literature on this point, see Maynard Paul Maidman, "A Socio-economic Analysis of a Nuzi Family Archive" (Ph.D. diss. University of Pennsylvania, 1976):335f., n. 205. Yet property acquired prior to this time is still attested as remaining within the same family after the generation of Enna-mati. In other words, family title to purchased real estate, or real estate obtained by exchange, was unaffected by the *šudutu*. Attestations of this phenomenon are easy to muster.

    Thus JEN 144 and 662 describe Tehip-tilla's acquisition of land by exchange. That land eventually passes to his grandsons, the children of Šurki-tilla, a younger brother of Enna-mati. The court affirms the legality of the land's remaining in the family for those three generations.

    JEN 799 and 399 (*cf.* JEN 668 with the latter text) attest that Tehip-tilla obtained land by exchange and that the same land was eventually inherited by a great-grandson of Tehip-tilla, a grandson of Enna-mati. Title once again is confirmed by the court.

    G 59 together with JEN 126 depict a similar situation, Tehip-tilla on this occasion having purchased the land outright.

    See JEN 345 and 473 for two further examples of the apparent meaninglessness of the *šudutu* proclamation.

22. *Cf.* Gernot Wilhelm, *The Hurrians*, trans. Jennifer Barnes (Warminster: Aris & Phillips, 1989):48.

23. HSS, IX, 1; XIV, 2, 31; XV, 287, 288; JEN 325, 365, 651; Yale 6.

24. HSS, XIV, 1, 3, 4, 5; JEN 754.

25. HSS, XIV, 31; XV, 287, 288.

26. HSS, XIV, 31. The text is edited by Carlo Zaccagnini, *The Rural Landscape of the Land of Arraphe* (Rome: Università di Roma — Istituto di Studi del Vicino Oriente, 1979):79. *Cf.* Gudrun Dosch, *Zur Struktur der Gesellschaft des Königreichs Arraphe* (Heidelberg: Heidelberger Orient-verlag, 1993):69.

27. HSS, XV, 287. *Cf.* Dosch, *Struktur*, 69.

28. HSS, XV, 288. *Cf.* Dosch, *Struktur*, 69.

29. HSS, IX, 1; XIV, 2.

30. HSS, XIV, 2. This text has been partially edited by Zaccagnini, *Rural Landscape*, 130f. This tablet and three others from Nuzi bear impressions from a single Arraphan royal seal whose function relates to the status of real estate. See M.P. Maidman, *RIM: Assyrian Periods*, vol. 1, p. 335, no. 21; Diana L. Stein, "A Reappraisal of the 'Sauštatar Letter' from Nuzi," *ZA* 79 (1989):47-49; and *idem, Das Archiv des Šilwa-Teššup* Heft 9: *The Seal Impressions (Catalogue)* (Wiesbaden: Harrassowitz Verlag, 1993):498-500, no. 659.

    Other royal seals are attested and one of these at least (the impression on HSS, IX, 1) is associated with a real estate transaction. See Maidman, RIM, pp. 333-335, esp. 333, no. 1; Stein, "Reappraisal," 36-39, 46-47, esp. the former; and *idem, Seal Impressions*, 528f., no. 711. In addition to those seals, there is now a possible additional royal real estate seal. See M. P. Maidman, *SCCNH*, 6:292-293. Unfortunately, none of these special seals or their legends seems to address directly issues treated in this paper.

31. HSS, IX, 1. This text has been noted numerous times in the literature. See Borger, HKL, Bd. I, 385 (esp. "Rez."; add to "n 1....O'Callaghan Aram Naharaim" p. 59, n. 1); Bd. II, 223. In addition, the text was first edited by E. A. Speiser, "A Letter of Saushshatar and the Date of the Kirkuk Tablets," JAOS 49 (1929):269-275. See also the treatments and assorted comments of I. M. Diakonoff and N. B. Jankowska, review of G. Wilhelm, *Grundzüge der Geschichte und Kultur der Hurriter, BiOr* 42 (1985):151, n. 5; Paul Koschaker, review of JEN, vol. 6 and of E. R. Lacheman, "Nuziana II," RA 36 (1939):113-219, OLZ 47 (1944):104; E.R. Lacheman, "Le Palais et la royauté de la ville de Nuzi," CRRA XIX, 362-364; M. P. Maidman, "The Office of *halsuhlu* in the Nuzi Texts," Lacheman AV, 236; Martha A. Morrison, "The Family of Šilwa-tešub, *mâr šarri*," JCS 31 (1979):15; Wilhelm, "Parrattarna," 155; and Carlo Zaccagnini, "Les Rapports entre Nuzi et Hanigalbat," *Aššur*, 2/1 (1979):18, n. 73.

32. The king is Sauštatar according to the seal legend. However, which king actually commissioned this document has recently been disputed. See Stein, "Reappraisal":36-60, esp. 45, 58-60.

33. For details, see the literature cited above, n. 31, especially the comments of Wilhelm and Zaccagnini.

34. The text itself, incidentally, was found in room A34 of the suburban Nuzi estate of Ammin-naya's son, Šilwa-tešup, identified in the Nuzi texts as "son of the king."

35. JEN 325, 365 with 651; Yale 6.

36. Yale 6. On this text, see Katarzyna Grosz, "Daughters Adopted as Sons at Nuzi and Emar," in CRRA XXX, 30; *idem, The Archive of the Wullu Family* (Copenhagen: Museum Tusculanum Press, 1988):49-51, 267f. (see also the review of this volume by Meir Malul, BiOr 47 [1990]:421); and Jonathan Paradise, "Daughters as 'Sons' at Nuzi," *SCCNH* 2:203-213.

   The family is that of Wullu son of Puhi-šenni (not to be confused with the family of Tehip-tilla son of [another] Puhi-šenni).

37. JEN 365.

38. *Cf.* the broken JEN 651:48-50 with the clear JEN 365:16-18. For the restoration of JEN 651:48-50, see Abdulillah Fadhil, *Studien zur Topo-graphie und Prosopographie der Provinzstädte des Königreichs Arraphe* (Mainz am Rhein: Verlag Philipp von Zabern, 1983):307b. *Cf.* Dosch, *Struktur*, 69.

39. JEN 325. This text was first edited by Hildegard Lewy, "The Nuzian Feudal System," Or NS, 11 (1942):339-341. See also Hayden, "Court Procedure," 126f. This document is part of a series of seven interrelated texts. I hypothesize their sequence to be as follows. JEN 644 is background to JEN 325 and/or 388 (if both, then probably in that order). In the next generation, JEN 184 is a deposition for JEN 321. JEN 512 and 135 were depositions not submitted since they were not sufficiently unambiguous. *Cf.* the reconstructions of Lewy, "Nuzian Feudal System," 326-334 (JEN 644, 325, 388, 135, 184, 512, 321); and Hayden, "Court Procedure," 119-130 (JEN 321, 135, 184, 512, 325, 644, 388).

40. Note should be taken here of JEN 336, if only to dismiss its relevance to the issue of privatization. This text has been edited by Noel Kenneth Weeks, "The Real Estate Interests of a Nuzi Family" (Ph.D. diss., Brandeis, 1971):277f. This trial revolves around real estate abutting land of the palace of Turša. The king despatched a real estate official (*i.e.*, a *halsuhlu*) to survey the land, which was then awarded to one of the contesting parties (ll. 5-9). Lewy, "Nuzian Feudal System," 8 with note 4, contends that this passage demonstrates royal ownership of land and, furthermore, that such land was allotted by the crown.

   Aside from the fact that Lewy's "feudal system" whereby the king assigned fiefs to his subjects is insupportable on the evidence, her reading of the passage is moot. A more likely interpretation of these lines is that the crown is responsible for despatching a lands officer to determine which of the two parties has a prior legitimate claim on the land, not that the crown itself dispenses that land. Indeed, the *halsuhlu* official exercises a similar function in HSS , IX, 1. See Maidman, "Office," 235-236. If these lines really were describing a royal donation, the services of a *halsuhlu* would not have been needed.

41. Benjamin R. Foster, "An Agricultural Archive from Sargonic Akkad," *Acta Sumerologica* 4 (1982):7-51, esp. 36-38.

42. J. N. Postgate, "The Ownership and Exploitation of Land in Assyria in the 1st Millennium B.C.," in M. Lebeau and P. Talon, eds., *Reflets des deux fleuves: Volume. . . . Finet* (Leuven: Peeters, 1989):146, 148.

43. In addition, one may not dismiss prestige as a factor favoring preservation of records of royal land grants. Note the remarkable, if still incompletely understood, bronze tablet, HSS, XIV, 1.

44. The small fraternity of scholars who focus on the Nuzi texts often hold divergent views on broad issues of Nuzi's social and economic history and structure. Yet the perspective presented here on the relations of the state to the private sector as reflected in the Nuzi texts would not, I believe, inspire serious exception on the part of these colleagues. This belief is based, for example, on Wilhelm, *The Hurrians*, 44-48; and Carlo Zaccagnini, "Transfer of Movable Property in Nuzi Private Transaction," in Alfonso Archi, ed., *Circulation of Goods in Non-Palatial Context in the Ancient Near East* (Rome: Edizioni del'Ataneo, 1984), 139-140; *idem*, "Land Tenure," 86.

A somewhat different view has been taken recently by Dosch, *Struktur*, 69-71. I hope to address her assertions elsewhere in the near future.

6.

The Symbiosis of Public and Private Sectors in Ugarit, Phoenicia, and Palestine

Michael Heltzer
University of Haifa

This paper deals with the economies of the "West" from the mid-second millennium down to the advent of Hellenism. I concentrate on the best documented western land: Ugarit. Despite the fact that it was an important international center of trade, records are lacking in anywhere near the detail found in Mesopotamia. Hence, we can piece together only limited answers to the major questions posed by this colloquium.

Private property in Ugarit

At Ugarit we encounter a royal redistributive system operating in a kingdom covering about 3,000 square kilometers. An ubiquitous royal control and personal dependency on the royal establishment limited the private sector down to the beginning of the 12th century, when the country and its thriving commercial economy were destroyed. During 1400-1200 BC, almost a third of the population consisted of royal dependents (*ardē šarri*, in Akkadian, *bnš mlk* in Ugaritic), organized into professional groups supervised by royally appointed *rbm* "managers" or "headmen," who often were allotted land as *ex officio* conditional holdings. We thus are obliged to make plausible inferences.

Elsewhere, I have discussed these and other features of Ugarit's economy, including conscription into the army of originally non-military dependents and their transfer from one sector to another.[1] Foreign trade was a royal monopoly,[2] operating alongside a rural community of peasant landowners.[3] We must assume that artisans produced certain necessary items for this peasant economy — pottery and utensils manufactured in their homes — although unfortunately we do not possess any information about these artisans.

One indication of a relatively well-developed private sector flourishing alongside the royal economy and village communities is the real-estate tax known as *unṯ/unuššu*. Scattered information has survived about private land tenure, including the alienation of rural land, which was subject to strict control by palace administrators. Cultivators who failed to pay their taxes or submit to conscription as laborers or soldiers were declared *nayyālu*, and their land was confiscated by the king.[4]

Wealth evidently had come to be based on private ownership of land. We possess at least 37 documents pertaining to the sale and purchase of land at Ugarit. Although we know the size of the parcels only in six cases, the surviving records indicate an average price of about 37.5 shekels of silver per *ikû* of land (=0.35 hectare). The properties in question consisted of orchards, olive groves, vineyards and fields. Perhaps this helps explain why their price was three to ten times higher than in other Near Eastern countries of the epoch, including irrigated lands. The lands were well developed and productive, not used for subsistence.

At least two cases of private owners mortgaging land are attested, for 80 and 400 shekels of silver respectively. These are at least what Ugarit's citizens paid to redeem their lands from mortgage liens. Evidently individuals were able to acquire money by mortgaging their land.[5]

We also have information concerning house purchases. According to PRU III 15.159 from the reign of king Niqmepa of Ugarit, a certain Yaheŝar, son of Mussi, purchased a house for 110+x shekels. PRU III 6.202 informs us that the *sākinu* "vizier" of Ugarit, Ŝaitenu, bought a house for more than 200 shekels. PRU III 16.283 relates how king Niqmepa received 200 shekels of silver for a house which he transferred to a certain Abdimilku. In *Ugaritica* V.5 (=RS 17.22) we read of the purchase for cultic use of a small plot of land between 34 and 36 square meters for 30 shekels of silver. According to KTU 4.755 (RS 31.80) a certain *Yrmn* bought various houses for 250, 66, 44, 30, 20 and 10 shekels of silver, and in KTU 4.750 (=RS 29.94) we read that various persons possessed three, four and even fourteen houses in various locations in Ugarit.[6]

However, holding land was often legally restricted, and burdened by obligations to perform or provide various services for the king. There is also evidence that owners of plots of land, held as private property, were required to pay "the *unṯ (unuššu)* of their houses." It is not clear just what this tax consisted of,[7] but we find land confiscated from holders who failed to perform their obligations by paying the taxes due. In all the recorded cases, the king received specific amounts of silver.[8] This was compatible with private land holding, of course, as taxes and transfer payments are due in today's world as well.

The king's role in land transactions

The kings of Ugarit, like those of neighboring lands, also engaged in commercial property relations with private foreigners (*Ugaritica* V.53 [RS.21.15; PRU IV, 17.129]). In such transactions they acted as equals, that is, as private persons themselves.

Also connected with the palace as royal traders were Ugarit's *tamkāru* merchants. Some obtained the privilege of collecting the royal land taxes, accumulating uncoined silver. The chief royal *tamkāru*, Sinarunu, son of Siginu, paid the king thousands of shekels for fields in various locations. (At the time, a Ugaritic shekel weighed 9.4 grams.)[9] One text records large land transactions by Sinaranu, but it is not clear which of his transactions were undertaken as private business, and which were undertaken in his role as royal *tamkāru* "merchant" (PRU III, 15.109).

Private property also was created by the exchange of "gifts" among high-ranking officials of Ugarit and neighboring countries (see Zaccagnini).[10] A major document containing information about property ownership in a royal context comes from PRU IV, 17.129: "Ammistamru, king of Ugarit, went to court with Amaraddu. Amaraddu lifts his hand (*i.e.*, renounces his claims) from 2 talents of silver." The king of Ugarit must declare that:

> Amaraddu renounced his claim to the house (in the village) Aru and the *sākinu* (governor) of the village (or vizier of the country) will take 5,000 shekels of silver, and will not give them to him (namely, Amaraddu).

> The king gives his pledge to Amaraddu, concerning 4000 shekels of silver, and bronze objects containing 3 talents of copper, 80 cows, 16 work oxen, 250 sheep, 7 slaves, 6 female slaves, 5 tables of boxwood, 3 beds, 20 chairs, 20 footstools, 6 donkeys — all these things belonging to the house of (the woman) Tewa. Also his orchard, his olive grove, his vineyard and everything that he owned. Concerning Enuwa — his daughter in law — he (the king) ordered him (Amaraddu) to take an oath in this case.

Enuwa acknowledged all these items of property, and Amaraddu may not contest this action. All these actions are to remain with Amaraddu. He shall have no claim against the king of Ugarit in the matter of the 3 talents and 2,000 shekels of silver. To any who may have claims, this tablet is to be shown.

Private land tenure

Evidence of private land ownership includes the following cases. In PRU 16.174, a certain Typpiyanu bought land for 125 silver shekels. In PRU III,16.147 we find Ariradu, son of Abdinergal, bought houses for 200 silver shekels during the reign of King Niqmepa. In a text composed in an earlier reign, a certain Ḫuttenu, son of Aḫamaranu, gave 3 *ikû* of his fields, together with its *dimtu*-building to Yapašarru, son of Sinaru. Yapašarru gave 3 *ikû* of arable land in the fields of Harsatu and 500 (shekels) of silver to Ḫuttenu in exchange for his fields (PRU III, 16.246). This text records a free exchange between two persons, involving large sums of money. One of the partners added 500 shekels of silver, perhaps because the lands he received were of higher quality.

This document shows that relatively large sums of money, as well as commodities valued in silver, were in the hands of private persons. It also suggests that land could be exchanged between parties as private transactions. The high price of land in Ugarit reflected purchases by well-to-do individuals, although these often seem to be public personages, to be sure. The realm's commercial prosperity — reflected in the population density normal in commercial port areas — also contributed to high land prices, especially as it stimulated intensive agricultural development. References to olive groves, vineyards and orchards in virtually all recorded land transactions suggest that landowners attempted to enhance the value of lands in their possession.

Several ways existed for individuals to obtain the money to buy real estate. Large estates could be obtained through royal grants, or by royal sale. Land also was obtained through foreclosure on debts collateralized by the land (and its crops), *i.e.*, "mortgage debts." In such cases, the debts seem to be unpaid balances owed by small individual landowners.

However, foreigners were not allowed to own land in Ugarit. According to PRU IV, 7.130, *tamkāru* merchants from the Hittite Empire's seaport, Ura, enslaved their debtors and their families, and even might have sold them into slavery abroad, but the debtors' lands remained the property of the king of Ugarit — or at least, the king took over lands that otherwise would be forfeited for debt arrears, and dealt directly with the foreign creditor.[11]

The role of women

A third feature of the documents is that in at least seven cases (PRU III, 16.135; 16.154; 16.343; 16.131; 16.253; 16.261, U.V.6 = RS 17.149)[12] women appear as sellers or buyers of real estate, sometimes as co-owners. It seems that they acted independently and held legal rights as land holders equal to those of their male counterparts. Perhaps their husbands were royal agents, and held land conditionally at the king's disposal. Men might have been compelled to conceal privately purchased land under the names of co-proprietors, who in reality were often their wives.

A more likely explanation may be that women were perhaps not subject to the royal service and conscription duties which constituted the major public obligations associated with property holding in Ugarit. Some texts relating to land transactions do not mention any royal service or tax, but some allude specifically to such levies by stipulating that they are *not* in force for the properties being bought and sold.

This does not contradict the fact that *unuššu/unt* would be imposed as a tax on these properties. In a document written in the presence of King Ammistamru II (PRU III, 16.154), a woman named Unmiḫibi buys fields from two brothers for 870 silver shekels. The properties include a field, vineyard, olive grove and *dimtu*-building belonging to Abdimilku, son of Dinniya, near the waterway Naḫraya for 740 silver shekels, and that Abdimilku and Pilsu also delivered 2½ *ikû* of arable land, together with the olive groves between the fields of this same waterway to Unmiḫibi for a further 130 shekels. The contract stipulates that "she must perform the *pilku* service of her house" (*pil-ki bîti-ša ú-ba-al*). She is not a royal servant, and we may infer that the *pilku* was equivalent to what elsewhere is called "the *unuššu* obligation of the house."

Regarding such service obligations and taxes, some texts relating to land transactions do not mention any royal service or tax, but in some cases they specify that such obligations are not in force for the lands in question. This does not contradict the fact that *unuššu/unt* would be imposed as a tax on these properties. The *pilku*-service associated with a house might have been equivalent to the *unuššu* of the house. The two kind of texts thus would be reporting on the same type of legal arrangement.

Another document written in the presence of king Ammistamru II (PRU III, 16.131) states that "Ṣadeyanu, son of Muluzi gave 4 *ikû* of arable land in the fields of Sa'u for 270 (shekels) of silver to Išmišarri. Further, the fields of the (woman) Binḫatiyana in the fields of Raḫbanu are given as a guarantee to Išmišarri, and the fields of Kišena in the fields of Kulkuli are given in exchange for the fields of (the woman) Binḫatiyana as guarantee to Yatarmu, son of Ḫaliyanu." This text actually records two private transactions: Išmišarri purchases lands belonging to persons, one of them the woman Binḫatiyana, and these are then mortgaged by Išmišarri and Ḫaliyanu.

In another fragmentary text composed in the presence of Ammistamru II, a woman Ammuya receives land (PRU III, 16.253). And yet another text written in the presence of Ammistamru II states that "The woman Laeya and Addumislam and (the woman) Batsidqi — her children purchase the field of Yaplanu and of Hismmiyanu and Uzzinu and Subammu, sons of Sasiyana, together with its *dimtu*-building, together with its olive groves, vineyards and everything they contained, 2,200 [+ x] (shekels) silver. There is no *pilku* service for these fields" (PRU III, 16.261). In this case the transaction was enacted between two groups of people. It is important that the four brothers involved received at least 2,200 shekels from three persons: mother, daughter and son. Once again we see the important role of women in such transactions.

In another Ugaritic text (*Ugaritica* V, 6 (RS 17.149) we read: "Munahimu, the scribe: As of this day, in the presence of witnesses, Rasapabu and his wife Pidda purchased 4 *ikû* of arable lands with their olive groves, slaves and trees in the fields of Sa'u from Yarimanu, son of Huzamu for 400 (shekels) of silver. Further, these fields belonged to one Izalda, the father of Pidda and now the field returns to Pidda and her sons(?)." This is yet another land transaction which was associated with family property, this time that of a wife and her father, once again indicating the rights and privileges of women to possess land.

Certain acts of adoption were concealed appropriations of property in settlement of debts of the type reflecting earlier Near Eastern usage, *e.g.* at Nuzi (*e.g.* PRU III,16.200 and 16.344). As in other Syrian centers of the period, most adoption contracts that have survived are evidently fictitious, being in fact property transfers. What is striking is the dominant role played by women in these cases.

The cataclysm of c. 1200 BC and handicraft professions

The great cataclysm at the end of the 13th and at the beginning of the 12th century BC brought about a barbarization and tribalization of

Levantine society, as it did in Anatolia and in Mycenaean Greece. The urban culture of small states and kingdoms was destroyed, although the coastal towns of Phoenicia seem to have survived.[13]

In the wake of this devastation we see small village craft centers emerging, served by craftsmen who seem to be the Levantine counterparts of the Greek *demiouergoi* alluded to by Homer. These artisans worked for the village and received their livelihood from it. This situation is attested in at least three locales in Israel (Canaan) during the period of the Judges (1200-1100 BC), and there is archaeological evidence of this phenomenon from Khirbet at-Talal in the Galilee, Raddana in central Canaan, and Tel Masos in the Negev. This correlates with the biblical record of Judges 17:1-4 and I Sam. 13:19-22. Local metal craftsmen apparently supplied the needs of their villages.[14]

There is also evidence of private land ownership, at least in the upper strata of society, primarily by royal families. Kish, father of King Saul, was a large landowner (1 Sam. 9); likewise, a certain Nabal owned much land and had 3,000 sheep (1 Sam. 25).

A symbiosis of private and royal economies developed. Even if the famous anti-monarchic speech attributed to the prophet Samuel (1 Sam. 8), denouncing the royal establishment as compelling the people to serve the monarch's economic and political interests,[15] was written at a later date, it reflects how the Canaanite city-state conducted its business in an erlier period. A service network organized in a manner similar to the Canaanite redistributive system operated in the royal economy of David at the beginning of the first millennium. According to the Bible, David introduced modifications into the administrative system of dividing between production and storage. He also instituted royal supervision of herding, both of camels and mules, which constituted major means of transportation.[16]

It appears that the accumulation of private wealth was greater in the coastal Phoenician cities, where seafaring produced considerable revenues, as did piracy at the beginning of the first millennium. A good example of this is the tale told by Eumenes (*Odyssey*, XV) about how he was kidnapped by the Phoenicians, together with other people and goods.

This period saw important economic developments whose effects would be felt in subsequent centuries. Biblical narrative relates that at the middle of the 10th century the Canaanite system of the second millennium was still in operation. Thus, Solomon paid King Hiram of Tyre for construction work accomplished by the "servants of Hiram" (I Kings 5). In contrast, by the 9th century, Yoash, king of Judah, paid the craftsmen individually for renovating his temple in Jerusalem. They were paid according to their particular skills (1 Kings 12:11-16; 2 Chron. 2). The same system is reflected in 2 Kings 22, which records renovations undertaken by Josiah toward the end of the 7th century BC. Even later, in the post-exilic period, masons and carpenters from the Phoenician towns who worked in Jerusalem were paid out of the Persian treasury (Ezra 3). Nehemiah 3 records that various artisans resided on special streets within the rebuilt Jerusalem during the Persian period. Clearly, there persisted a class of free artisans, a fact also supported by archaeological and epigraphic evidence.

Among the Greeks, one of the most important signs of the independence of artisans was the inscription of an artifact with the maker's name, and with the legend "I am made by (PN)." The same features appear in the Phoenician cities at least from the 7th century BC, possibly also at Ashdod, where a potter so inscribed his product. The 7th-century finds from the Ophel in Jerusalem bear the names as well as the marks of potters. The fact that ceramic workshops in Sarepta (near Sidon) and in Carthage were modest may attest to individual artisan work.[17]

It is possible to document the spread of free, private work among ivory carvers, mainly a Phoenician profession. In their campaigns in the west, the Assyrians carried off large numbers of such craftsmen to work on the ornamentation of their palaces. We also find Phoenicians migrating westward voluntarily, as fugitives from the Assyrians, from the 9th to the 7th centuries BC. This was analogous to the later, westward flight of Greek artisans after Persia's occupation of Ionia. Ivory carving subsequently emerged in the western Phoenician colonies, where local imitations soon entered the market.[18]

From Phoenician and Punic inscriptions and inscribed objects we can see how crafts were organized in the Phoenician-Punic regions on a private basis apparently independent of the government. We encounter generations of metalworkers within the same families in the Phoenician cities, as well as in Cyprus and Carthage from the 7th to 5th centuries BC.[19] (See table of professions on page 186.)

The above sources enable us to trace at least four generations of metal casters and two generations of surgeons in the same families. Scribes, builders and craftsmen called *ḥršm* worked under "masters" called *rb* or *bʿl*,[20] but we do not know the source of their authority. Were they appointed, rated by professional skill, or did they accede to their positions simply by order of seniority? In any case, we see the beginnings of professional organizations, whose members seem to be working solely for their own interest and compensation as free artisans, associated with the marketplace through the production of commodities.

The classical Greek ethos viewed artisans as "unesteemed" persons (*banausoi*). Several contemporary inscriptions from Phoenician-Punic society indicate their status to be that of metics. The first example appears on the tomb of a potter from Ibiza in the 5th century BC. One of the ceramic *arkoi* bears the inscription '*bdmlqrt gr*, "Abdmelqart the *gēr*," that is, the *metic*.[21] A later inscription, incised on an amphora jar before baking, comes from Paphos on Cyprus, and is dated to the 4th century BC. It reads '*bd/n.gr nsk*, "belonging to 'Abdon, the *gēr* (metic), the metal caster.'"[22]

Some Phoenician artisans were *gērîm*-metics who had not been granted citizenship or political rights, but others enjoyed a higher status. An inscription from Carthage (CIS I.5447) dated to the 4th/3rd centuries BC and devoted to the goddess Tinnit and the god Baal Hammon refers to "Shsft, daughter of 'Abdmelqart, the carpenter who is of the *mḥšbm* magistrates." The *mḥšbm* were a college of Carthaginian magistrates, possibly elected, who dealt with current financial affairs of the state, probably much like the Roman *edili*.[23] The fact that a carpenter could be accepted into an important council of magistrates implies that Phoenician artisans might have enjoyed a high social position. Archaeological evidence indicates that Phoenician artisans in this period were mostly individual producers, operating without any significant auxiliary labor force.

In the pre-Hellenistic era of the first millennium the town of Sarepta (near Sidon) had an industrial area of at least 800 square meters. It contained potters' kilns, small metal workships, and small textile tying shops. The workshops were so small that they might have belonged to individual artisans.[24] The excavated industrial areas of Punic Carthage at Byrsa, and also at Phoenician Motya in Sicily and other areas, reveal the same general features.[25]

When it comes to large-scale workshops, we simply have no way of knowing if they were public or private. The discovery of the Carthaginian ship at Marsala, investigated by H. Frost,[26] shows that at least some Carthaginian warships were assembled from pre-fabricated sections (Bartoloni 1988:276). This would have required an organized force of craftsmen working under the direction and technical supervision of skilled specialists, perhaps someone like the *b'l ḥrš*, "chief worker," attested at Sardinia (*Sardinia* 36, IFPCO).

For special projects, or at times of urgent need, guilds of artisans were mobilized in an extraordinary fashion. An inscription from Carthage

Figure 1

CRAFTS DESCRIBED IN PHOENECIAN AND PUNIC INSCRIPTIONS

WORD	PROFESSIONS TRANSLATION	EAST	WEST
'pm	bakers	Kition Cyprus	-
'rg	weavers	-	Carthage
bn'	construction worker	Kition Byblos 5	Carthage Sardinia 32 & 36
'br	engraver (?)	-	Carthage
glb	barber	Kition	-
hrm	producer of fishing nets	Egypt	Carthage
hrš	workman (producer of non-metalic items)	Akko Kition	Carthage
hrt	vase painter or engraver	-	Carthage
tbh	cook or butcher	-	Carthage
yṣr	potter	Byblos 17	Sicily 3
mmlh	fish salter or salt mine worker	-	Carthage Sardinia 9
ngr	carpenter	-	Carthage

(Mahjoubi and Fantar 1966), perhaps dating from early in the 3rd century BC, begins as follows: "The street was opened and built up to the place of the New Gate (*šcr ḥdš*) which is at the wall." This inscription relates to the reconstruction of Carthaginian defences, possibly at the time of the sudden invasion of Agathocles in 305 BC. After listing the magistrates, it mentions *pls Yhw'ln*, "the architect is Yehaw'alon," who directed the works. Further on we read that "The merchant ship, the porters, tailors who are in the *'mq qrt* (name of part of the city), the silver weighers (money changers) who . . . Gold-jewelers and makers of vases and oven builders and sandal makers together with . . ."

The text concludes with an order that persons absent from work will be fined 1,000 pieces of silver by the *mḥšbm*,[27] suggesting that guilds of skilled workers were mobilized in emergency situations according to the needs of the state. The situation may be compared with the biblical record of Nehemiah's construction of Jerusalem's city walls in 445 BC (Neh. 3).

WORD	PROFESSIONS TRANSLATION	EAST	WEST
nsk	metal caster or smith*	Achzib Kition Paphos (Cyprus)	Carthage
nsk ḥrṣ	gold casters or jewellers	-	Carthage
nsk brzl	iron smiths	Kition	Carthage
nsk nḥšt	copper (bronze) smith	-	Carthage
nsk hnskt	caster of molten (metal)	-	Sardinia 5
bn nsk	member of metal guild	Pontecagnano, Italy	-
sfr	scribe	Carmel Kition	Carthage -
pls	architect	Amrit Kition	Sardinia 12 Carthage
pʿl	worker, producer	Kition	Carthage
mqdh	driller (wood or stone)	-	Carthage
qlʿ	sling maker	Cyprus	-
rfʾ	surgeon	-	Carthage
rqḥ	drug mixer or perfumer	Abydos	Carthage
rqm	brocade weaver	-	Carthage
šql	weight producer	-	Carthage

Achaemenid borrowings and adaptations

In the Achaemenid period we see a symbiosis of public and private networks for the handicrafts. Private craftsmanship certainly does not fully replace ancient Near Eastern royal economies in the crafts, or even in agriculture. Indeed, backtracking to Judah in the pre-exilic period enables us to trace the persistence of the royal economy under shifting poitical circumstances. The ostracon from Mesad Hashavyahu records a reaper's complaint c. 620 BC. Its contents indicate that after the collapse of Assyrian rule in Palestine's coastal region, the Judean king retook this

* The Akko text speaks about *bn ḥrš* "sons" (i.e. members of the guild of *ḥršm*); the texts of Carthage give *ḥrš ʾrnt* (sarcophagi producer) and *ḥrš glt* (cartwright). Texts from Sardinia and Carthage and Spain record *ʾb ḥršm* "lord, or elder of the *ḥršm*" and *rb ḥrš* "master of *ḥršm*" is known from Kition.

area and instituted a royal estate under the supervision of royal officials. The reapers belonged to the staff of workers.[28]

The *lmlk* ("Belonging to the king") stamps on standard jar handles date from the time of Hezekiah (end of the 7th century BC), as demonstrated by D. Ussishkin and N. Na'aman.[29] Below the word *lmlk* these stamps also recorded place names: Hebron, Sif, Sokho, and *Mmsht*. On at least one of the four jar handles there was also a private stamp bearing a person's name and that of his father. This was the stamp of an official guaranteeing the jar's volume. The four place names designate royal depots for processing wine and oil, where the jars were filled and then distributed to Judaean fortresses. These stamps were discovered at the destinations. Neutron activation tests show that all the jars were produced with material taken from the same clay pit,[30] showing that in southern Judah, large ceramic workshops were in operation under the supervision of royal officials.[31]

This pattern continued into Achaemenid times. The Achaemenid Empire had at its disposal an enormous work force, in addition to private undertakings. The Persepolis Fortification and Treasury tablets provide the best evidence for this, and indicate the occasional use of forced labor. By the time we reach the Hellenistic period in the Near East, we observe greater diversity in everyday life. General development became more dynamic, and the profit motive played a major role. An important change catalyzing free commerce was the appearance of local coinage at the beginning of the 5th century BC in Phoenicia, and in the 4th century in the Judean province.[32]

DISCUSSION

von Dassow: Your general thesis of privatization of artisan production in the Iron Age echoed Carlo Zaccagnini's article of about ten or twelve years ago: "Patterns of Mobility among Ancient Near Eastern Craftsmen" (JNES 42 [1983]: 245-64). That study dealt in part with whether artisan production was controlled by the state or was under their own control. Although this privatization of production does seem to be a general trend, based on the types of documentation you have mentioned, I would submit that especially in the earlier periods, artisan production that was not controlled by the state might not have been documented in a way we can trace.

Heltzer: You can certainly say that in Ugarit it was fully controlled, and also in Alalakh.

Maidman: If it was not controlled, how would we know it? What kind of evidence would it leave?

von Dassow: In Alalakh, to be sure, we don't have private documents. One of the points of agreement among Assyriologists is that sales of *mobilia* were characteristically cash transactions. Such sales do not need to be documented. This doesn't mean they did not take place. It is just another example of an argument from silence. If there were privately owned and operated shops at Alalakh or Ugarit (and I am not saying that there were, but *if* there were), why would we expect to have their receipts and evidence for their production? We might, but the fact that we don't does not necessarily mean privately owned shops did not exist.

Heltzer: I suppose that they had material for writing. Clay was in abundance.

von Dassow: What if they had no need to write? What if they had no need to document? If the products are sold on the spot, and it is a cash transaction, which is essentially how most transactions in the ancient Near East were made, then why should they preserve a record of what they had sold, or what they had produced?

Heltzer: Really, I can only agree with you. We have no data about the social organization in this sphere. I tried to find out how, at that moment in time, these things were organized socially. But where we have no texts, no data, it is very difficult to say.

Maidman: I have a question regarding the jars and the common clay used to make them. There are two ways I can interpret the process. Either they took the raw clay to the potters' or oil- or wine-makers' places and made the jars, or they made the jars locally and shipped empty jars to these places and then stamped them.

Heltzer: No, all the stamps are made before firing.

Maidman: So they shipped finished jars?

Heltzer: Yes.

Cleveland: I thought they were stamped *after* they were filled. You said the stamp was to guarantee the contents.

Heltzer: No, what was stamped was the volume, not the contents — how much cubic capacity or liters the jars held.

Maidman: Without questioning your conclusions, I am concerned about the way you use Biblical texts. For example, in citing the anti-monarchical speech in I Samuel 8, there are good reasons for suggesting that it is exilic or post-Exilic.

Whether or not this is so, I am saying that we have to be conscious of the dates of the documents, as distinct from what is being described in them. You say, regarding I Samuel, that although it may be post-Exilic, it reflects the economic relations of the earlier period. If you are going to say that, then you cannot argue in the next paragraph that the Eumenes episode, and the kidnapping should be taken as evidence for the Iron Age. Using a consistent methodology, you have to say this is genuinely Late Bronze Age. You can't have it both ways. Either you take it as evidence for the date of composition, or evidence for the date of the reference itself.

Heltzer: Concerning I Samuel 8, we have Isaac Mendelsohn's classic article, "Samuel's Denunciation of Kingship in the Light of the Akkadian Documents from Ugarit," *BASOR* 143 (1956:17-22), and today we can develop things much more than he did. One thing is clear: Samuel shows the economic relations of the pre-exilic period, not of the Persian period. The situation was similar to the Canaanite times of the early monarchy, especially in Ugarit.

Maidman: So what do you do with the evidence of Homer's *Odyssey*, the evidence of Eumenes and the kidnapping? Are you saying that evidence should be taken in the context of the Iron Age during which the *Odyssey* was written, and not the Late Bronze Age which nominally is being described?

Audience: Who controlled the clay pits from which the artisans got their raw materials?

Heltzer: I think the royal authorities did, but as far as I know, this was not the case in Mesopotamia, Syria-Palestine or Greece. There did not exist any monopoly or control of clay pits. Maybe one of my colleagues knows about this, but iron ore or copper ore, gold, silver and precious stones were property. Clay was not regarded as property in the ancient Near East.

Lamberg-Karlovsky: Can anybody indicate that there ever was a monopoly of metals, precious stones or clay? Is there a text to document such a fact? I would say, no.

Dandamayev: It would be strange.

Lamberg-Karlovsky: That is right, it would be strange. After all, there are alternative sources to which anyone could go.

Heltzer: Regarding Greece, I can refer you to the Laurion silver pits in Attica.

Lamberg-Karlovsky: That was just one silver source. By metallurgical analysis we know that coinage was being made from more than the Laurion source. Alternative sources were being utilized.

Mitchell: It also was monopolized well after the state had started to monopolize their activities.

Lamberg-Karlovsky: Right.

Heltzer: Well, Philip also took gold as his monopoly.

Lamberg-Karlovsky: The point is again that you are relying on a text that doesn't reflect that there is a system the texts don't record. Let me give you an example. There is a wonderful book recently written on Afghan craftsmen. It talks about specialist tribes. They specialize in certain labor like threshers, and groups who specialized in the production of certain things. They are migrant. There is a book called *The Nomadic Alternative* or something like that, discussing itinerant craftsmen, who move from place to place offering their specialized services or labor in a barter system. Now I am speaking of the ethnographic context of modern-day Afghanistan prior to the Soviet invasion. That is what the ethnography is recording. There is no reason to disbelieve it. We can't document it, but they don't record it. The system was observed ethnographically.

Mitchell: In studies of early Greek and Roman numismatics, one of the difficulties of identifying dies and die cutters has been resolved to a certain degree by looking at artisan production and concluding that certain dies were cut by the same craftsman, that is, the same person cut dies for different cities. If there is anything that is a monopoly, it is coinage. These are private individuals not associated with any one city, who were in fact simply selling their labor and expertise.

Heltzer: In the book of Kings we also hear about Solomon's copper mines. Malachite mines on the Sinai peninsula belonged to the Egyptian Pharaohs.

Lamberg-Karlovsky: There are more. There is the source of faience in Jordan. There is a multiplicity of sources. Texts tell you one reality; they don't deny multiple realities of multiple sources. You are relying on your texts as the only truth. I don't deny that, but I am suggesting that there is a multiplicity of both evidence and interpretations.

Levine: This is of course a major issue that has been moving about in the air all day long. This issue is becoming sharper now, as we come closer in the discussion to our own time.

Lamberg-Karlovsky: It already was sharp back then. If one looks at the alternative evidence, it is already there.

Levine: What we have to do is go as far as the text allows us to go.

Heltzer: There are multiple sources. A very interesting question is where the raw material for the ivory work came from, for the Syrian elephant did not exist anymore.

Mitchell: I want to put a question to the archaeologist, and to those more professionally concerned with archaeological material than I am. You touched just briefly on burials, and it seems to me if there is any area where you might be able to delineate the private from the public, it would be here, because many burials (at least in the Greek and Latin world) exist before and outside of any urban context — that is, before the existence of any public authority. They contain things like pots, arms and chariots. We have pieces of items about which we haven't the foggiest notion of why they are were buried, and many of these same items don't reappear in later burials. However, some burials, at least in Italy, include things like scarabs, which obviously were traded. In other instances items were buried a century or more after their production. Were these items owned and cherished as private property?

Levine: In my presentation I will make reference to a recent study of burial practices in Judah during the biblical period. Elizabeth Bloch-Smith shows that the tomb, the burial cave and the marker became symbols of private family ownership. It is not clear, however, whether such markers were initially utilized to establish or demonstrate ownership. There are several notations in the Bible to the effect that a person was buried on the boundary of his field.

I am intrigued by the fact that as we get closer to my area of research, biblical literature, literary problems become more focused. It is not merely a matter of the limitations of evidence. It is a basic question of how to read the text, to distinguish between the period of reference, as presented, and the real *Sitz-im-Leben* of the author.

ABBREVIATIONS

BASOR   Bulletin of the American Schools of Oriental Research

CIS   *Codex Inscriptiorum Semiticarium*

IFPCO   M.G. Guzzo-Amadasi, *Le iscrizioni Fenicie e Punice delle colonie in Occidente* (Rome 1967).

JNES   *Journal of Near Eastern Studies*

KTU   Dietrich, O. Loretz, J. Sanmartin, *Die keilalphabetische Texte aus Ugarit* (Neukirchen-Vluyn 1976).

PRU III: J. Nougayrol, *Le palais royale d'Ugarit*, III (Paris 1955). (Vol. IV, 1956; Vol. VI, 1970).

RS   Ras-Shamra

U.V.   *Ugaritica*, V (Paris 1968).

FOOTNOTES

1. M. Heltzer, *The Internal Organization of the Kingdom of Ugarit* (Wiesbaden 1982), and *The Royal Economy of Ancient Ugarit* (=Orientalia Lovaniensia Analecta 6, 1979):459-496.

2. M. Heltzer, *Goods, Prices and the Organization of Trade in Ugarit* (Wiesbaden 1978).

3. M. Heltzer, *The Rural Community in Ancient Ugarit* (Wiesbaden 1979).

4. *Ibid.*:52-57.

5. M. Heltzer, "Mortgage of Lands and Property and Freeing from it in Ugarit," *Journal of the Economic and Social History of the Orient* 19 (1976):90-93.

6. M. Heltzer, "Zum Hauskauf in Ugarit," *Ugarit Forschungen* 11 (1979):365-376.

7. Heltzer, *Private Property in Ugarit* (=SMEA, Incunabula Graeca 82 [Rome 1984]:161-194, esp. 165-170; M. Heltzer, "On the meaning of *unṯ/unuššu* in Ugarit," *Semitica* 30 (1980):5-12.

8. 170-74.

9. M. Heltzer, "Sinaranu, Son of Siginu, and the Trade Relations between Ugarit and Crete," *Minos* NS 23 (1988):7-13.

10. C. Zaccagnini, *Lo scambio dei doni nel Vicino Oriente durante i secoli XV-XIII* (Rome 1972).

11. *Goods, Prices*:127f.

12. *Private Property*:174-181.

13. M. Heltzer, "The Late Bronze Age Service System and its Decline," in M. Heltzer and E. Lipinski, ed., *Society and Economy in the Eastern Mediterranean (c. 1500-1000 BC)*, OLA 23 (1988):7-18, and M. Heltzer, *Die Organization des Handwerks im "Dunkelen Zeitalter," und im I Jahrtausend v.u.Z. im ostlichem Mittelmeergebiet* (Padua 1992):1-46.

14. *Organization des Handwerkes*, 57f., and M. Heltzer, "Die Entwickung des Handwerks vom Dienstsystem zum selbständigen Produzenten im Östlichen Mittelmeergebiet (1500-500 vu.Z)," *Altorientalische Forschungen* 15 (1985):124-132.

15. I. Mendelsohn, "Samuel's Denunciation of Kingship in the Light of the Akkadian Documents from Ugarit," BASOR 143 (1956):17-22.

16. M. Heltzer, "The Royal Economy of King David Compared with the Royal Economy of Ugarit," EI 20 (1989):175-180 (Hebrew).

17. J. B. Pritchard, *Recovering Sarepta, a Phoenician City* (Princeton 1978):111-130; S. Lancel and J. P. Thuillier, *Les niveaux d'ateliers metallurgiques, Byrsa II*, Mission archaeologique Francais à Carthage (Rome 1982):217-256.

18. R. D. Barnett, "Ancient Ivories in the Middle East," *Qedem* 14 (Jerusalem 1982), and F. W. von Hase, "Zum Östlichen Einfluss auf de Goldarbeiten des späteren 8 und fruhen 7 Jhd. v. Chr. in Mittelitalien," *Proceedings of the Xth International Congress of Classical Archaeology* (Ankara 1978):1101-1110.

19. Heltzer, *Die Organization*, 69-102, and "A Recently Discovered Phoenician Inscription and the Problem of the Guilds of Metal-Casters," ACISFP 1 (1983):119-124.

20. W. Huss, "Die Stellung des *rb* im karthagischen Staat," *Zeitschrift der Deutschen Morgenlandischen Gesellschaft*, 129 (1979):217-232.

21. J. M. Fernandez-Gomez and M. J. Fuentes-Estanol, "Una sepultura contenienda un askos con inscripcion fenicia," *Aula Orientalis* 1 (1983):178-183; and M. Heltzer, "The *gēr* in the Phoenician Society," *Studia Phoenicia* 5 (Leuven):309-314.

22. M. Sznycer, "L'inscription phenicienne sur une amphore de Nea Paphos," *Report of the Department of Antiquities of Cyprus* (1985):263-55; Heltzer, "The *gēr*," 312ff.

23. G. Coacci-Polselli, *I. MHSBM Cartaginesi, Studi Maghrebini* 12 (1980):83-85.

MICHAEL HELTZER

24. Pritchard 1978:111-130.

25. V. Tusa, *Sicily and the Phoenicians* (New York 1988):189, and P. Bartaloni, *Commerce and Industry of the Phoenicians*, 78-85 (literature, p. 575).

26. H. Frost, "La reconstruction du navire punique de Marsala," *Archaeologie* 170 (1982):42-50, and P. Bartloni, *Ships and Navigation of the Phoenicians* (New York 1988):72-77.

27. *Die Organization des Handwerkes*, 103-112.

28. J. D. Amusin and M. Heltzer, "The Inscription from Meṣad Ḥashavyahu," *Israel Exploration Journal* 14 (1964):148-157, and A. Lemaire, "L'Ostracon de Meṣad Ḥashavyahu (Yavneh-Yam) replace dans son context," *Semitica* 12 (1971):57-79.

29. D. Ussishkin, "Royal Judaean Storage Jars and Private Seal Impressions," BASOR 223 (1976):1-14; N. Na'aman, "Sennacherib's Campaign to Judah and the Date of the *lmlk* Stamps," *Vetus Testamentum* 29 (1979):61-86; and N. Na'aman, "Hezekiah's Fortified cities and the *lmlk* Stamps," BASOR 261 (1980):5-21.

30. M. Mommsen, I. Perlman and Y. Yellin, "On the Provenence of the *lmlk* Jars," *Israel Exploration Journal* 34 (1984):89-113.

31. *Die Organization des Handwerkes*, 143-150.

32. J. W. Betlyon, *The Coinage and Mints of Phoenicia: The Pre-Alexandrian Period* (Chicago 1980), and "The Provincial Government of Persian Period Judea and the Yehud Coins," *Journal of Biblical Literature* 105 (1986):433-442; L. Mildenberg, "Yehud: A Preliminary Study of the Provincial Coinage of Judea," in *Greek Numismatics and Archaeology: Essays in Honor of M. Thompson* (Wetteren 1979):183-196, and "Über das Kleingeld in der Persischen Provinz Judea," in H. Weippert, *Palastina in vorhellenistischer Zeit* (Munich 1988):721-728; and Heltzer, "The Provincial Taxation in the Achaemenidean Empire and 'Forty Shekels of Silver,' (Neh. 5.15)," *Michmanim* 6 (1992):15-26.

7.

An Age of Privatization in Ancient Mesopotamia

Muhammed Dandamayev
Institute for Oriental Studies

In the third and early second millennium, the palace ("state") economy played the leading role in Southern Mesopotamia. In the absence of a market economy, this enormous state-controlled sector was an inevitable and indeed, even a natural means of coping with "the difficulties of procurement of raw materials" (Oppenheim 1977:80). But based as it was on large bureaucratic machinery and semi-free labor, this economy proved inefficient, and was replaced by private and temple households employing mainly free labor, supplemented by slave labor.

By the Neo-Babylonian and Achaemenid periods (626-331 BC), Babylonia had developed three distinct sectors: the royal or palace economy, temple estates, and private households both large- and small-scale. The leading role belonged to the private and temple households.

The Royal Economy

The king maintained his court, official staff and army out of taxes levied on an enormous territory stretching from Mesopotamia as far west as Egypt's border. But only a relatively insignificant amount of land was actually owned by the king, and by Neo-Babylonian times he managed his estates on the pattern of private households.

A document drafted in 587 shows a "royal field" near Babylon belonging to Nebuchadnezzar II. His steward rents it out "forever" to Shulaja, head of the Egibi business firm, in order to plant date palms there (Nbk, No. 115; cf. Ries 1976:14 and 82). A contract drafted in Sippar during Nabonidus' reign shows 66 ducks belonging to the "royal property" being leased out to a bird keeper of the Ebabbar temple (CIS 2/I, No. 61).

But as far as we know, Neo-Babylonian rulers owned no handicraft workshops of their own, nor are slaves ever referred to as workmen in the palace economy during the period under consideration.

The Achaemenids considerably increased the area of royal land in Mesopotamia. The king held part of this land directly. Fields belonging to him were located mostly in the Nippur region, and were leased out (for references see Cardascia 1951:158ff. and Stolper 1985:36ff.). The Achaemenids also owned some large canals, which royal managers leased out. In the Nippur region such canals were rented by the Murashû business firm, which subleased them to groups of small landowners (Stolper 1985:37f.). In addition, members of the royal family and Persian nobility owned vast landed estates, which they put out on lease (for references see Dandamayev 1974:123ff.).

Archaeological reconnaissance shows that the expansion of population, cultivation of long-abandoned lands, construction of new canals and the founding of new settlements were typical of this region during Achaemenid times (Oppenheim 1985: 577; Stolper 1985:37; van Driel 1987:171). Written sources indicate that the Neo-Babylonian and Achaemenid kings also carried out important hydraulic efforts to improve water supplies for consumption, irrigation and navigation in the regions of Babylon, Sippar and Borsippa (Cole 1994:93ff.).

Land redistribution by the Persian kings created different types of allotments to royal soldiers, often foreigners (for literature see Cardascia 1983:547ff.). The royal administration allotted these fiefs from state land in exchange for military service obligations. (The opinion of Oppenheim (1985:574), that these persons were *glebae adscripti* "assigned permanently to the fields and gardens" cannot be correct, at least *de jure*, inasmuch as they were recruited from the king's free subjects.) Various teams of royal artisans such as carpenters, builders, etc. also were given allotments from state land (BE 10, Nos. 6, 99, etc.). Special "associations of merchants" whose members served the king were allotted fields in 5th-century Nippur, headed by "chiefs of the merchants" responsible for paying royal taxes (BE 10, No. 54).

Despite the fact that the Achaemenid kings owned large amounts of property in Mesopotamia, private and temple households continued to play the leading role. In first-millennium Babylonia an overwhelming royal economy would have been anomalous, incompatible with the development of private property and a market economy. In fact, the needs of the royal economy were partly covered by temples, which were obliged to pay considerable revenue to the government (Dandamayev 1979:594f.).

The Temple Economy

The archives of the Eanna temple in Uruk and the Ebabbar temple in Sippar provide especially abundant information on temple households. (Much less information has been preserved from archives of such sanctuaries as Esagila in Babylon, Ezida in Borsippa, Ekur in Nippur, Ekishnugal in Ur and other temples, cf. below.)

During the period under consideration, Uruk was largely a temple city and Eanna was its economic center. This temple owned most of the land in the rural environs of Uruk, although private land ownership also continued there (see Cocquerillat 1968:35ff.). To judge from archaeological surveys, the Uruk area "included only one small urban center" and "107 much smaller sites" (Adams and Nissen 1972:18). Extensive areas belonging to the Eanna temple were turned into date-palm plantations.

The following data provide an estimate of the Eanna's economy. One document shows about 7,500 hectares of temple land leased out to two persons (YOS 6, No. 11, cf. below). The Eanna temple owned 5,000-7,000 head of cattle and 100,000-150,000 head of sheep and goats (San Nicolò 1948:285; Freydank 1974:337; cf. TEBR, No. 58, according to which two persons delivered 290 talents, *i.e.* 8,700 kg. of wool to the temple during a two-month period).

Only an insignificant part of Eanna's lands was cultivated by temple slaves. The temple leased out land to free tenants, occasionally to slaves (see Dandamayev 1984:510), and often was forced to employ seasonal workers. The temple's normal practice was to lease out much of its land to so-called rent collectors, who were responsible for delivering a fixed annual amount of produce to the temple. As seen from documents dating between 529 and 520 BC, most exploitation of temple date-palm groves and grain fields was done through these officials (who could belong to middle or low classes, or even be temple slaves). Their role was to supervise the collection of rent, subleasing the land rather than cultivating it themselves (Cocquerillat 1968:37ff.). One collector, Nergal-nāsir, son of Nanaja-ibni, started out as an Eanna temple foreman overseeing ten workmen. During 558-543 BC he was a tenant, and then a rent collector from the Eanna's grain fields and date palm groves (GCCI I, No. 418; YOS 6, Nos. 35, 107, etc.).

In 553 BC, one rent collector paid the Eanna temple 10,136 *kur* (~1,824,480 liters) of barley (YOS 6, No.78). Two other rent collectors rented 6,000 *kur* (~7,500 hectares) of land belonging to the Eanna. They were to pay the temple an annual rent of 24,000 *kur* (~4.5 million liters) of top-quality barley and 10,000 *kur* (~1.8 million liters) of choice dates. The contract stipulates that half the rented land should lie fallow (YOS 6, No. 11).

The Eanna possessed several hundred slaves, including artisans, but they were in no position to supplant free labor in handicraft production. Most artisans worked voluntarily, under contract in exchange for wages in money and food ration of dates, barley, beer, etc. The Eanna's administrators hired numerous jewelers, leather workers, blacksmiths, bronzesmiths, carpenters, builders, weavers, bleachers, potters, engravers of seals, launderers and others (for more details see Dandamayev 1984:302ff.). According to an Uruk document dating from the reign of Cyrus, the supreme officials of the Eanna told thirty persons listed by name, and "all (the other) artisans of Eanna" (carpenters, blacksmiths, engravers of stones, jewelers, etc.) that they would be required to work solely for the Eanna temple and none other (YNER I, No.1). Apparently they would lose their jobs in Eanna if they concluded an analogous agreement with another temple.

Like most other temples, the Eanna provided for a substantial portion of its own economic and cultic requirements. Its operations were organized on the basis of prebends, stipulated yields by various properties. Prebendaries derived their income by working for the temple as brewers, butchers, doorkeepers, etc. for specified periods of time. Their prebend income depended on their service obligations, ranging from one to three *kur* (180-540 liters) of barley or dates a month (cf. San Nicolò 1934:179 ff.). Many citizens held temple prebends, which could be sold or assigned to other citizens.

The Eanna engaged in business operations and international trade, especially to import metals from abroad (Oppenheim 1967:237). For all these reasons, its role in the Uruk region's overall economy was enormous. To judge from extensive documentary evidence, the Ebabbar temple played a similar role in the Sippar region. It possessed extensive landholdings, engaged in moneylending, business and trade, and exchanged its surplus production for metals or other commodities that it did not itself produce. Like Eanna, it used the services of rent collectors in leasing land to tenants, including temple slaves. It employed its own artisans, free craftsmen and slaves. One weaver, Bakua, worked with his master for the Ebabbar for at least twenty-one years (from 552 through 531 BC) making or dying apparel for Shamash and other gods (CT 55, Nos. 860, 865; Nbn, Nos. 302, 465, 532, etc.). The temple also hired artisans from other cities when local workers were not available in Sippar, as evidenced by a number of documents recording the issue of provisions "to artisans who have arrived from Babylon" (Nbn, Nos. 56, 407, 409; Cyr, No. 103). The Ebabbar temple even hired seasonal laborers from Elam (for references see Dandamayev 1992:152).

Information about the estates of other temples is limited, even for Babylon's Esagila temple, the sanctuary of Marduk, the supreme state deity, but enough documents have survived to show that this and other temples held large expanses of land, on which they supported their own cattle, sheep and fowl. Their major source of revenue, however, consisted of the tithe, approximately one-tenth of the taxpayer's income. All free members of the population paid tithes to the temple nearest where they held their land or other source of income (Dandamayev 1979:593). To this extent, temples were dependent on the private economy.

The Private Economy

If temple households were a more or less homogeneous sphere throughout Mesopotamia, private households reflect a more varied range of practices. The best known examples are the large business firms: the houses of Egibi, Nur-Sîn and Murashû.

The large-scale enterprises

The activities of the Egibi can be traced in more than a thousand documents drafted between 690 and 480 BC, mostly in Babylon but also in other cities, including even some towns in Elam and West Iran. The Egibi firm sold, bought and traded houses, fields and slaves. It also engaged in banking operations, accepting money on deposit, giving and receiving promissory notes, paying debts on behalf of its clients, financing and founding commercial enterprises. It played an important role not only in internal trade, but also in long-distance commerce (at least, in Elam and Media). Some Egibis were in the king's service, including the firm's head, Nabû-ahhe-iddin, a royal judge who enjoyed good relations with Neriglissar, Nebuchadnezzar II's son-in-law and future king (van Driel 1985/86:50ff.).

Under Nebuchadnezzar II, Babylon expanded intensively and became the most important city in the world which housed perhaps about 200,000 inhabitants. This naturally created a large demand for agricultural products. About four hundred documents and letters deal with the activities of the businessman Iddin-Marduk (son of Iqîshaja, descendant of Nûr-Sîn) in Babylon and other cities between 557 and 517 BC. Working independently as well as in partnership with others, he bought large amounts of garlic, barley and dates in suburbs of Babylon and other places from farmers, large landowners and tenants, shipped them to the capital by canal and sold them in the city.

The following documents give an idea of his operations. According to Nbk, No. 406, he acquired 75,000 strings of garlic. Nbn, No. 1014 refers to him as creditor of another 90,000 strings. Cyr, No. 41 mentions 395,000 strings of garlic belonging to him. In Cyr, No. 51, his wife Ina-Esagila-ramât appears as creditor of 150,000 strings of garlic. He obviously is selling this garlic in Babylon as an intermediary between producers and consumers (Oelsner 1984:233f.; Wunsch 1993:1, 19-61). He traded also in livestock and wool. In addition, there is some evidence on his commercial activity in Uruk province (Wunsch 1993:1, 30).

Nûr-Sîn's and Egibi's families were related through the marriage of Nuptaja, the daughter of Iddin-Marduk, and Itti-Marduk-balatu, the eldest son of Nabû-ahhê-iddin. After this marriage, the Egibis actively participated in Iddin-Marduk's trade operations, using his money and well-established commercial connections. On his side, Iddin-Marduk profited from Nabû-ahhê-iddin's influence at royal court (Wunsch 1993, vol.1:78-82).

The activities of the house of Murashû, attested in about 800 documents drafted in Nippur and a few other cities between 454 and 404, reflect the changes introduced by the Achaemenid administration into property policies in the Nippur region during this half-century. Babylonia's land was divided into allotments and distributed to royal officials and collectives of soldiers (cf. above). Not being farmers themselves, both these groups turned their land over to others to cultivate, including the Murashû firm. It leased these lands, paying rentals to their holders as well as taxes to the state treasury. The Murashûs rented also crown properties and manors belonging to Persian nobility, paying rental income to the owners and taxes to the palace by selling their produce for money (unminted silver). In fact, their main function was to mediate between the system of land tenure and production by selling crops for silver to pay landholders and the royal treasury (Cardascia 1951:17f.; Stolper 1985:27f.; van Driel 1987: 169). For instance, during the first regnal year of Darius II (423 BC) the Murashûs received 20,000 *kur* (~36,000 hectoliters) of dates from their tenants, valued at 750 minas (350 kg) of silver (Cardascia 1951:18).

The Murashû firm sublet its leased lands to tenants, along with livestock, implements and seed. One contract records that ten free persons and one slave have obligated themselves to brew 5,825 vessels of beer of one *kur* each (all in all, 10,485 hectoliters) in return for wages and provisions. The customer supplied the brewers with 5,825 *kur* of dates, vessels and other necessary items (TMH 2/3, No. 216/BE 10, No. 4). Apparently the beer was to be sold (cf. van Driel 1989:226).

A number of legal documents drafted in Nippur during the Achaemenid period closely resemble the texts in the Murashû archive, without mentioning the Murashûs at all (see TEBR, Nos.1-26). It therefore can be assumed that the Murashû house was just one of numerous firms mediating between producers and consumers in the Nippur region and elsewhere.

The scale of transactions conducted by Tābija, son of Nabû-apla-iddin, descendant of Sîn-ili, was much smaller than that of the Egibis and other powerful business houses, but can be followed for forty years (585-545 BC). His permanent residence was in Babylon, but he also owned fields in the suburbs of Borsippa, Sippar, Kish, Marada and some other towns. (One of these rental fields was 2 *kur* 3 *pan* 2 *sût*, ~3.5 hectares.) Although he had a scribal education, he did not consider this activity as an essential source of his income but used his professional knowledge and skill to conduct business. He rented out his lands to freemen and slaves for an annual revenue of about ten thousand liters of barley and dates. In addition to engaging in trade, he acted as a creditor, lending money and agricultural produce (for more details see Dandamayev 1986:51ff.).

Joannès (1989:119ff.) has traced the activities of the Ea-ilûta-bâni family of Borsippa during the years 687-486 BC. This family seems to have belonged to the "middle class," often participating actively in temple affairs as functionaries, prebendaries or artisans of various trades. The lands of such families rarely exceeded a few hectares. The value of their transactions usually amounted to a few minas of silver or several *kur* (1 *kur* = ~180 liters) of dates or barley.

What is noteworthy is that some of these families did not till their lands themselves, but rented out them to tenants. They were able to maintain their properties and social status at least for two centuries, until the beginning of Xerxes' reign, after which only a small number of documents survive from Borsippa.

The small-scale private sector

Despite the fact that about twenty thousand economic and legal documents from the period under consideration have been published, next to nothing is known about the households in the areas located far from urban centers. Most documents come from large cities. But in antiquity the city dominated the countryside, and the urban population itself was chiefly engaged in agriculture, tilling the lands in adjoining rural areas. Thus, the cities were agricultural, as well as handicraft, centers.

Smallholders had holdings of about half a hectare to one hectare of land. We know little about their households except that they cultivated their fields with the help of family members. Probably most of them maintained a subsistence in-kind economy, entering the market only marginally to exchange or sell their produce (cf. below).

Some rural areas were settled by groups of *glebae adscripti* who occupied an intermediate position between free people and slaves. They lived on state or temple land, and hence were subject to royal or temple administration. Some such groups settled in the Nippur region in the second half of the 5th century, and can be traced in the Murashû documents.

Market relations in a primarily subsistence "dual economy"

Economic historians and Assyriologists have long described Ancient Mesopotamia as a self-sustaining subsistence economy, inferring by this label that a market economy did not exist. This opinion reflects the influence of Karl Polanyi's model of the ancient Near Eastern economies as being non-market in character. But documentary evidence has now called his arguments into question.

Polanyi (1957:16 and elsewhere) refers to a passage from Herodotus (I,153; see also Strabo 15,3,19) which, in his opinion, economic historians of Mesopotamia have unduly ignored. He interprets this passage to mean that the Babylonians had no marketplaces. But as Renger (1984:59) has noted, Herodotus is referring to Persia, not Babylonia. Despite the fact that the father of history never visited Persia, he knew that Persians did not have markets, and that they neither sold nor bought, as their commodity-money relations were very poorly developed. By contrast, Herodotus visited Babylon some time between 460 and 454 BC, and specifically mentions market places (*agorê*) there (see Herodotus I,97).

Some other arguments of scholars who deny the existence of a market economy in Babylonia deserve more attention. According to Renger (1984:114), Babylonia's socio-economic system was based on farming by "self-sufficient agricultural households," leaving "practically no room for a self-regulating market or market system." In the opinion of Oppenheim (1970:19), agricultural products from fields and gardens around cities provided for the inhabitants of these cities. "For those who had to live by hiring themselves out (as harvest workers *e.g.*) there was apparently enough marginal land available to raise occasional food crops instead of relying on a food market," and such a situation existed not only during the Old Babylonian period but also in the first-millennium urban economy. According to Zaccagnini (1989:423), ancient Mesopotamia had no "evaluation of any sort of commodity and labor services in terms of 'prices' expressed in 'money' units." He adds (*ibid.*:425) that "Fluctuations did not automatically (and entirely) depend upon the 'law' of demand and supply," as such "basic factors like wages and rations" were resistant to market forces.

It is true that fixed tariffs of prices, wages and services existed in first-millennium Babylonia, as in earlier periods. However, they bore more of a theoretical than real-life character. For instance, prices for local agricultural products fluctuated in response both to their quality and the season of the year. Documents accordingly refer to prices in specific months for Babylon and other cities or rural districts. The range of price variation can be demonstrated by the fact that an adult male slave cost an average of one mina of silver, but one particular slave was sold for 4 minas 10 shekels. The prices of a bull, ox or cow ranged from 7 to 37 shekels, depending on age and fatness. Prices for asses varied from 38 to 52 shekels, but in one case a donkey cost 6 minas of silver (for references see Dandamayev 1988:53ff.).

As noted above, hired labor played an important role. Both the temples and private families regularly needed the services of hired workmen, especially at harvest time. The annual wage of an adult hired worker averaged 12 silver shekels, the equivalent of about 6 liters of barley or dates per day. However, this wage fluctuated between 3 and 12 shekels per year, and not infrequently reached 30 shekels (for references see Dandamayev 1987:273f.).

A significant number of documents from temple archives attest to the payment of money wages to workers digging or cleaning irrigation canals, engaged in manufacturing, baking, painting or glazing bricks, ship carpenters, boatmen, etc. Groups of hired laborers numbering up to several hundred men are referred to in the letters of Eanna temple officials. One such letter reports that "evil rumors" against the temple officials are circulating among hired laborers. For this reason their wages, in the sum of 20 minas of silver and wool valued at 10 silver minas, should be paid immediately (Dandamayev, *loc cit.*). It sometimes was difficult to find enough workers, forcing high wages to be paid — up to 60 shekels per year (instead of the average 12-shekel rate). Workers would not agree to work for low pay, and refused to work as a sign of protest against overdue wages.

In sum, the wages of hired laborers fluctuated, reflecting the type of the work they performed, their professions and qualifications, and the dynamics of supply and demand in the labor market. Thus, if any fixed tariffs for wages existed in first-millennium Babylonia, they were not very effective. In all probability there existed no obligatory tariffs officially in the first millennium.

It also is unlikely that hired laborers had enough food from their own holdings so that they did not have to resort to any market. Many scholars believe that ancient economies were not profit-seeking (i.e., that their managers or entrepreneurs were not motivated by profit), and artisans and other people had enough land to obtain their own food. But if this was the case, it hardly is possible to explain why Neo-Babylonian free hirelings worked for other individuals and temples at all!

In the first place, the socio-economic structure of first-millennium Babylonia differed from that of the Old Babylonian period. Radical changes had occurred, especially in the system of land tenure. Abundant Neo-Babylonian documentary evidence shows that goldsmiths, silversmiths, oil pressers, carpenters, bleachers, weavers, builders, beer brewers, seal engravers and many other craftsmen concluded contracts to manufacture various items (furniture, utensils, doors, clothes, boats, bricks, etc.). These documents also show that some of these artisans possessed their own fields, but it is improbable that they had no need to buy food through the market.

It is also reasonable to assume that some of the artisans produced goods for market sale. According to one contract, the yearly wages of a slave sent for training in the shoemaker's trade consisted of ten pairs of leather shoes (Dandamayev 1984:117). Evidently, the master who taught this slave did not need all the shoes manufactured in his workshop for himself and members of his family, and therefore sold them.

A number of Neo-Babylonian texts mention retail sellers of salt, wine, beer and some other condiments and imported luxuries (Oppenheim 1970:21). Some peddlers engaged in small-scale trade, merchants (*tamkarū*) and wholesale dealers were employed by the palace or temples, but most were independent traders engaged in domestic and international commerce, operating with their own resources and at their own risk. Long-distance trade was mainly in the hands of private individuals (see for details Dandamayev 1971:71ff.). In addition to these professional merchants and their agents, private individuals could engage in trade. This was particularly true of inter-city trade as well as trade between cities and their adjoining rural regions. Also important were commercial companies (*harrânu*), in which two or more business partners conducted trade and divided profit and losses among themselves (Lanz 1976:8ff.).

It is important to note that royal taxes were paid in silver. Herodotus (3,92) describes how, beginning in the reign of Darius (522-486 BC), Baby-lonia paid an annual tribute to the Persian king amounting to 1,000 talents (30 tons) of silver. Many Babylonians had to sell their products or labor to pay their assessments. The development of monetary and commercial relations was promoted by the fact that lacking local mines, Babylonia's population had to obtain silver from foreign countries in exchange for its agricultural and craft products.

Some Babylonians mortgaged their fields to obtain the silver they needed to pay taxes. Such monetary loans led to an increase in interest rates. Documents from the Marushû archive show that in cases where the land was placed at the disposal of this firm as mortgage collateral, it paid the assessments on behalf of the landowner (Cardascia 1951:190ff.). Inevitably, not all taxpayers were able to redeem their properties once they fell into arrears. Some became hired workmen, or ended up handing over their children into debt bondage (for more details see Dandamayev 1984:178ff.).

Long before the period under consideration, much of Babylonia's land had been privatized nearly to the same degree as occurred in the classical Mediterranean realms. The land had become truly private property held by those who cultivated it, unless they were tenants or military soldiers settled on state lands. Hundreds of documents attest to the fact that land was freely sold for money (cf. Ries 1976:34-38). The Egibi and other wealthy families bought many fields, while the activities of firms such as the Murashû had a ruinous effect on the economy.

The house of Murashû began as an institution of agricultural credit, but after a few decades it began to take the landowners' place, concentrating the land in its own hands. Yet there was no concentration of landholdings for Babylonia as a whole. Moreover, the dynamic of economic development was so intensive, and the situation so unstable, that even powerful families (let alone members of the middle classes) were not safe from ruin. Abundant documentation in the form of promissory notes shows that owing to rapid expansion of commodity-money relations, a certain number of well-to-do families lost their houses, land and slaves or had to find guarantors in order to borrow even insignificant sums of money (Dandamayev 1983:137ff.). Thus, as far as first-millennium Babylonian society can be traced from city archives, it is based on the same kind of individualism as any other developed market economy. It consisted of nuclear families, in which usually three or more children survived.

Any society's surplus depends on its dynamics. The Neo-Babylonian economic surplus consisted mainly of rent collected by temples such as Eanna or Ebabbar, and by some important business houses. This rent took the form of many tens of thousands of hectoliters of barley, dates and other agricultural products annually for major public and private institutions.

Any doubts as to the existence of a market economy in first-millennium Babylonia thus are groundless. What remains to be clarified is how decisive the market system was within the overall economy. More systematic research of the large archives of economic and legal documents might provide a more comprehensive understanding of the Neo-Babylonian market system, its commodity production mechanisms and their supply response.

Certainly a developed private economic sector was typical of first-millennium Babylonia, a period of unprecedented growth and privatization (cf. van Driel 1989:226). The labor of free farmers and tenants was the basis of agriculture, even as large landowners increased their sway, for they preferred the services of free tenants, to whom they rented small parcels of land. State or royal land was also settled mostly by free tenants and soldiers. Large-scale landownership thus was accompanied by small-scale land tenure.

Temple property nominally belonged to the principal deity of the temple, and in practice was deemed to be the collective property of the citizens of the temple neighborhood. It was used as a source of income by citizens in the form of prebends and indirectly in the form of services provided by free artisans and hired laborers. During religious festivities, temples distributed meat and other food to members of the local communities, and also supported their communities in times of famine or other disastrous events.

The documentary evidence shows no concentration of property in just a few hands, no mass ruination and enslavement in first-millennium Babylonia. Individuals who were deprived of land or did not possess sufficient property had a wide range of opportunities. They could become hired laborers, or rent land and implements, draught animals and seed, or enter royal service or work for the temples.

Most of the population enjoyed a relatively high living standard for the time. The fact that there was no time limit for debt bondage (in contrast to earlier periods) suggests that the transformation of debt bondsmen into outright slaves did not present an essential danger for Babylonian society, which did not experience a mass enslavement of free persons.

To be sure, it was only natural that such a developed system of privatization would influence the institution of slavery. It was difficult to establish any effective control over slaves, because the main type of rural economy consisted of small peasant households. As noted above, most large landowners preferred to rent their lands to tenants (including their own and other people's slaves), because slave labor required constant supervision and, consequently, considerable expenditures. Slave labor likewise was not of decisive importance in the craft industries, for only very wealthy persons could afford to send their slaves to learn trades, all the while maintaining them throughout the period of their apprenticeship, which usually lasted several years.

Slave-owners therefore considered it more profitable to allow their slaves to manage property of their own, and to pay an appropriate quitrent. This practice became increasingly widespread. In a significant number of documents, slaves appear as tenants of lands; others maintained their own taverns and artisan workshops, plots of land, or capital for trading and money-lending operations (for references see Dandamayev 1984: 320ff.). Thus, a comparatively large number of slaves was involved in the process of the privatization.

To sum up, in earlier periods of Mesopotamian history the state-controlled economy was able to obtain all important resources (including essential raw materials from abroad), and to supply a considerable number of workmen and officials with food rations, wool, etc. However, the forced semi-free labor used extensively on palace estates required constant supervision, as such workmen rarely showed much interest in the results of their labor.

Even more serious was the fact that over time the elite (mostly royal functionaries) used the advantages of centralized economy for their own enrichment. Officials and workmen of the palace and temple households frequently stole royal or temple property outright. Although the laws of Hammurapi nominally called for thirty-fold compensation for stolen public property, this could not prevent from day-to-day encroachments. Neo-Babylonian archives are filled with legal proceedings from trials for the plunder of poultry and livestock, and thefts of objects belonging to the temples. As seen from documentary evidence, in first-millennium Babylonia the sections of Hammurapi's laws on thirty-fold compensation for stolen temple possessions were still valid (for references see San Nicolò 1932:327ff.), but we have no analogous Neo-Babylonian information on the theft of royal property. Perhaps this reflects the comparatively modest scale of the palace household during the period under consideration.

It goes without saying that, for behavioral reasons, private households based mainly on free labor were enterprising, competitive and efficient.

Historical experience shows that various economic systems frequently show much the same pattern throughout history. In theory, a state-controlled economy is an advantaged sector. It can concentrate large resources and carry out major projects. It can provide people with jobs or otherwise support them. The private economy for its part tends to polarize society between rich and poor. Yet human factors make state-controlled economies inefficient in comparison to the more entrepreneurial and competitive private sector. If the price of this superior efficiency is a concentration of economic gains in the hands of the well-to-do and powerful, this phenomenon is not absent from state economies either.

DISCUSSION

Heltzer: We heard here really a report about the society where privatization was on its highest level — not in Babylonia in all ages, of course, but at least in Neo-Babylonian and Persian times. Here the interesting thing is, first of all, royal taxes in silver. We know this from Herodotus, also from the Bible. The peasants say they borrowed silver for the royal tax (*mandattu*). We see this also from the other places in the Persian Empire (for example, from Judah), borrowing silver to pay taxes.

Second, for Neo-Babylonian and Persian times we have definitions of four kinds of economy in the pseudo-Aristotelean *Oeconomica*. Looking at Assyrian documents from Sargonid times as published by Larsen, and all his other publications, along with the state archives of Assyria published by Parpola, we see that private economic relations played a major role in Assyria, at least in the Assyrian heartland. The provinces were despoiled and booty was taken, but private economic activities existed in the heartland.

Dandamayev: That is right. We have clear documentary evidence that the population paid royal taxes in silver, not only from Herodotus but also from Babylonia.

von Dassow: I would suggest that to call this the age of privatization, one would have to point to what was not private *before* this age. While we cannot say much about the status of land in Babylonia immediately before the Neo-Babylonian period, what we can point to (and you alluded to it with regard to the Murashû archive) is the privatization of such things as tax collection and temple rent collection. So we have what you can call private individuals contracting with the temple to collect the temple's rents on its lands. You have the Murashû Family acting as an intermediary between a kind of system of land tenure and a system whereby the empire was remunerated.

Dandamayev: Could you repeat . . .

von Dassow: I think I basically repeated what you said. The Murashû Family, probably among others for whom we don't have documentation, served as an intermediary between the Achaemenid system of land tenure whereby land was granted to functionaries and soldiers, and the system whereby agrarian income accrued back to the government. Iddin-Marduk of the Nur-Sîn family, whom you mentioned in your paper, evidently played a role in converting into silver the tax revenue on various types of produce, in particular transport taxes (I would not say export taxes, because produce was being exported from places along the Borsippa Canal to Babylon). Some members of the Egibi family may also have played such a role. So, what was privatized was a function that we normally would expect to be governmental, as in the modern example Professor Levine mentioned yesterday: tax collection was managed by a private individual. In the Neo-Babylonian period this seems to have been a widespread practice.

Also, I think the idea of temple lands being the property of the citizen community is a little bit idealistic. I would hesitate to say that citizens received income from temple property in the form of prebends. First of all, the prebend system probably has a different basis than temple land being considered in some sense to belong to the community. Also, while many citizens were prebendaries, some individuals who were definitely citizens apparently did not hold prebends — for instance, Iddin-Markduk and his family, as well as prominent members of the Egibi Family.

Dandamayev: First of all, we do not know when this last privatization of land was made, because we don't have much evidence from the preceding period. At least in Neo-Babylonian times, beginning from the end of the 7th century, there was privatization. We can only suppose something about the preceding period, but we do not know this exactly.

As to prebends, it was not necessary that Iddin-Marduk should have enjoyed them. It seems to me that without doubt, he or any citizen could have prebends. They could sell these to other citizens, and temple officials checked and approved these transactions. If Iddin-Marduk needed any prebends, he had enough money to buy them. But we cannot be sure that he did not possess any prebend. His prebends should be mentioned in documents only in cases where he rented or sold them. Otherwise it should not be mentioned in documents. It was not necessary that all citizens had prebends, of course, but any citizen *could* have a prebend, as these could be sold among citizens.

Finally, I would not say that "tax collection was allotted to a private person." In any case, the state did not allot such prerogatives to anybody. The role of tax collectors was accepted by private individuals when they used lands belonging to other people (*e.g.*, mortgaged or rented lands) and when the real owners were not in a position to pay state taxes incumbent upon their property. Otherwise, the state could confiscate such lands.

Buccellati: You said that the temple commission adjudicated the prebend. What was this commission?

Dandamayev: A special commission of temple officials, citizens, or in some cases even *puhru* was convened to hear each case. Eventually it became an approved decision of the temple — let's say of the popular assembly of the citizens (*puhru*) of the city. The petitioner's biography was told to the people, questions were asked about his family, and so on. Afterwards, the verdict was announced: such and such petitioner is fit to have such and such prebend.

Hudson: There didn't seem to be any point in bringing up yesterday the well-known role of prebends in Old Babylonian society, because the subject is not new anymore. But for theoretical completeness I think it important to mention the Nippur temple of Inanna after 2000 BC. Charpin has shown that its prebends were consistently subdivided among heirs each generation for hundreds of years. Finally, you find sales of prebend revenues covering just a few days at a time out of each year. To me, this represents the origin of *rentier* securities. It clearly represents a privatization of temple revenues. I agree with Richard Zettler and Elizabeth Stone, who have reconstructed how the temple prebends were turned over to Amorite chieftains for their own benefit as a way of buying them off. These prebends can be bequeathed within the family, or sold.

The other point — and I think a very strong point that you made in your history of slavery in Babylonia — is that despite the sophisticated development of credit, interest, and usury in Neo-Babylonian society, this did not reduce the population to mass slavery. Creditors discovered that they could get more by leaving their debtors free, extracting money from them as rent and usury, rather than by reducing them to debt bondage.

Buccellati: Does the *babtum*, the neighborhood, play any role in Neo-Babylonia?

Dandamayev: I'm afraid we don't have clear information about it.

Buccellati: So the *puhrum* is of the whole city, or would it be the equivalent of a *babtum*?

Dandamayev: *Puhru* refers to an assembly of all citizens of a particular city, of free people, of citizens or elders. In first-millennium Babylonian documents the word *babtu* never occurs as a synonym of *puhru*, although it is attested mainly to denote a part of a city.

Maidman: Does the appearance of mercenary soldiers play a significant role in the economy's privatization?

Dandamayev: We know little about the army in the time of Nebuchadnezzar and Nabonidus. As to the Achaemenid period, we have abundant information. Apparently, soldiers were given allotments of sufficient size to support their families. So it seems it was important for privatization during the Achaemenid period.

Maidman: A fragment of one Greek poet, Archilochus, says that his brother was a mercenary. Was that Neo-Babylonian?

Dandamayev: As far as I know, it was Antimenidas, brother of the Aeolian poet Alcaeus, who served, among some other Greeks, in the army of Nebuchadnezzar II as a mercenary. But we do not have any Babylonian evidence about these Greek mercenaries, and know about them only from Greek literature.

Mitchell: Archilochus was not only a mercenary, he was an aristocrat, apparently a bastard with an aristocratic father. He is out for hire, although he supposedly would normally have had enough wherewithall to make ends meet without fighting. Consequently, we can conclude that fighting was something aristocrats did — part of their code of conduct. It was Archilochus who said, "He who throws his shield and runs away, lives to fight another day."

The British have a term for the conversion of labor to money: *scutage*. Personal military obligations were commuted to payment of money. The funds were then used to employ troops who were personally tied to those who paid them and, therefore, presumably were more loyal. The conversion thereby minimized the danger of rebellion by those who were once personally obligated to serve or to provide troops. We have examples of this process of commutation in both Greek and Roman history. Archilochus, as a mercenary, may well have been an early example. We have relatively early evidence of taxation and of tribute collection from the Greek world. In the Athenian tribute lists, for example, the evidence is earlier than Herodotus and much earlier than Aristotle. The tribute lists reflect the sums of money cities paid to Athens. Many of the cities originally supplied their own ships and troops to the common cause — the war against Persia. However, when Athenian participation in the Hellenic League turned the League into the Athenian Empire, the ships were

Athenian and they were purchased and paid for by tribute. Several cities had their military contributions commuted into a monetary payment. Is a similar phenomenon at work somewhere in the second or early first millennium?

Levine: Paying for the service instead of doing it?

Mitchell: Yes. In the first stage, you are obligated to do something yourself. Then the centralized state says, "Don't do it, just pay me and I'll employ somebody else who is loyal to me." This is clearly part of the baronial struggle in England, and it also is a feature of many earlier stages of history.

Buccellati: Hammurapi has a law against that, against people taking over or assuming someone else's obligation, although it seems this might have been possible under some exceptional circumstances. But normally the principle is disallowed.

Mitchell: I'm not talking about somebody replacing you in terms of obligation to a central authority. I'm talking about the central authority collecting money and using it to employ someone else other than the person making the payment, to perform a task once performed by the one making the payment.

von Dassow: The little documentation we have for military service in Neo-Babylonian private archives typically concerns sending substitutes or paying a certain amount of silver in place of doing service. Texts record that a person is quit if his *ilku* or *urashu* (a labor service), either by providing a man or by paying in silver. These two options are attested in different archives. Iddin-Marduk, for instance, typically pays in silver.

Dandamayev: It was possible. People could send substitutes instead of themselves to perform corvée works as well as military service.

Buccellati: You were describing what other people think about the market or non-market economy in the Old Babylonian period, but you didn't state your own opinion. Do you have one? My own inclination is to see a form of market economy in the Old Babylonian period. What is your feeling?

Dandamayev: I think this was a market economy, certainly. I am somehow unhappy that A. Leo Oppenheim considered in his *Ancient Mesopotamia* the entire history of Mesopotamia as something homogeneous. In first-millennium Babylonia we have quite a different society from the Old Babylonian and Kassite periods, but I believe that during this period a market economy existed. I don't see much difference between the market economy in 5th-century Babylonia and the same type of economy in classical Greece. I might be wrong, but I don't see much difference.

Buccellati: How about the Old Babylonian period? Do you think there was no market economy?

Dandamayev: I would abstain from any conclusion. You know there are some 20,000 Neo-Babylonian published documents, and I have enough trouble with them. For the Old Babylonian period, I must rely on other scholars.

Hallo: Regarding the difference between Old Babylonian and Neo-Babylonian Babylonia, a major factor for the state economy in the earlier period was collectivization, if you would like to call it that, reflecting the needs of irrigation. What happens differently in the Neo-Babylonian period? Did they maintain a collective effort on behalf of irrigation in Neo-Babylonian times.

Dandamayev: Some canals belong to the king. They were rented out, and I think they also were maintained out of this rent. Some canals belong to temples, which were responsible for maintaining them. Other canals, perhaps many, belonged to communities. As far as I can conclude, free citizens of local districts had to pay fees to maintain or support these canals. As far as I can conclude, there thus existed three different administrative systems.

Edzard: I want to return to the question of the market. I personally have never had the slightest doubt that there was a market in Old Babylonian times. I never understood why this became an object of mystification. When you have the karum and you have lots of trade goods and interest, what is more clear? When I wrote the article *sâmu* and *simu* for the CAD, I made an alphabetical list of objects that go with *sâmu* "to buy." It was a very long list, and for reasons I do not know the editors edited it out.

When you get a letter from Tell ed Der: go to Sippar and find a nice *sâm-tu* pearl for me. The person doesn't go to some backyard.

Maidman: The evidence for Nuzi is somewhat ambiguous in regard to the role of markets. First of all, there is the phenomenon of money conceived of as a standard of value. That is clear. When a purchase takes place, it will be said that the cost of this amount of land is so many shekels of silver, and then later in the document we are told that such-and-such an individual has delivered the barley. Consequently, the barley is conceived of in terms of its value in silver shekels. If it is not ubiquitous, it is not rare either.

Second, you do indeed have consistent examples of acquisitiveness over generations, the collection of more and more land. If there is no profit in it, I don't understand why it is being done. Likewise in terms of the archaeological evidence, there seems to be a market place within the city, although I learned to beware of equating the existence of a market place with a market economy. Price fluctuations are attested, but they seem to occur within carefully prescribed parameters. Zaccagnini (private conversation), for one, does not conceive of this in terms of supply and demand, and I am inclined to go along. Whatever fluctuation there seems to be is seasonal, within the agricultural cycle. But the jury is still out.

ABBREVIATIONS

BE   The Babylonian Expedition of the University of Pennsylvania, Series
      A: Cuneiform Texts (Philadelphia)

      vol.9 (1898): Hilprecht,H. V. and Clay, A. T., *Business Documents of
      Murashû Sons of Nippur Dated in the Reign of Artaxerxes I (464-424
      B.C.)*;

      vol.10 (1904): Clay, A.T., *Business Documents of Murashû Sons of Nippur
      Dated in the Reign of Darius II (424-404 B.C.)*.

CIS   *Corpus Inscriptionum Semiticarum*, vol.2/I, Paris,1889.

CT   Cuneiform Texts from Babylonian Tablets in the British Museum, vol.
      55 (1982): Pinches, T. G., *Neo-Babylonian and Achaemenid Tablets* (Lon-
      don).

Cyr   Strassmaier, J. N. (1890), *Inschriften von Cyrus, König von Babylon (558-
      529 v. Chr.)* (Leipzig).

GCCI Goucher College Cuneiform Inscriptions, vol.I: Dougherty, R. P., *Ar-
      chives from Erech, Time of Nebuchadrezzar and Nabonidus* (New Haven:
      1923).

Nbk   Strassmaier, J. N. (1889), *Inschriften von Nabuchodonosor, König von
      Babylon (604-561 v. Chr.)* (Leipzig).

Nbn   Strassmaier, J. N. (1889), *Inschriften von Nabonidus, König von Baby-
      lon (555-538 v. Chr.)* (Leipzig).

TEBR Joannès, F. (1982), Textes économiques de la Babylonie récente. *Etudes
      assyriologiques*, cahier 5 (Paris).

TMH   Texte und Materialien der Frau Professor Hilprecht Collection of Ba-
      bylonian Antiquities im Eigentum der Universität Jena, vol.2/3 (1933).
      Krückmann, O., *Neubabylonische Rechts-und Verwalwungstexte* Leipzig).

YNER Yale Near Eastern Researches, vol.1: Weisberg, D. B. (1967), *Guild
      Structure and Political Allegiance in Early Achaemenid Mesopotamia* (New
      Haven).

YOS   Yale Oriental Series, vol. 6: Dougherty, R. P. (1920), *Records from Erech,
      Time of Nabonidus (555-538 B.C.)*, (New Haven).

BIBLIOGRAPHY

Adams, R. McC., and H. J. Nissen (1972), *The Uruk Countryside. The Natural Setting of Urban Societies* (Chicago and London).

Cardascia, G. (1983), *Les archives des Murasû* (Paris 1951) "Lehenswesen in der Perserzeit," in *Reallexikon der Assyriologie* 6:547-550.

Cocquerillat, D. (1968), "Palmeraies et culture de l'Eanna d'Uruk (559-520)." *Ausgrabungen der deutschen Forschungsgemeinschaft in Uruk-Warka* 8 (Berlin).

Cole, S. W. (1994), "Marsh Formation in the Borsippa Region and The Course of the Lower Euphrates," *Journal of Near Eastern Studies* 53:81-109.

Dandamayev, M. (1971), "Die Rolle des tamkārum in Babylonien im 2. und 1. Jahrtausend v.u.Z." *Schriften zur Geschichte und Kultur des Alten Orients, 1. Beiträge zur sozialen Struktur des Alten Vorderasien* (Berlin):69-78,

— (1974), "The Domain-Lands of Achaemenes in Babylonia," in *Altorientalische Forschungen* 1:123-227.

— (1979), "State and Temple in Babylonia in the First Millennium B.C.E.," in E. Lipinski (ed.), *State and Temple Economy in the Ancient Near East,* (Leuven):II:589-596.

— (1983), *Vavilonskie pistsy* (Babylonian Scribes), (Moscow).

— (1986), *Slavery in Babylonia from Nabopolassar to Alexander the Great (626-331 BC),* (DeKalb: Northern Illinois University Press)

— (1986b), "Economy of Tābiya, a Babylonian of the Sixth Century B.C.," *Oikumene* 5:51-53.

— (1987), "Free Hired Labor in Babylonia during the Sixth through Fourth Centuries B.C.," Powell, M. A. (ed.), *Labor in the Ancient Near East.* (American Oriental Series 68:271-279 (New Haven).

— (1988), "Wages and Prices in Babylonia in the 6th and 5th Centuries B.C.," *Altorientalische Forschungen* 15:53-58.

— (1992), *Iranians in Achaemenid Babylonia* (Columbia Lectures on Iranian Studies 6: Costa Mesa and New York).

Freydank, H. (1974), "Wirtschaft und Gesellschaft in Uruk in der zweiten Hälfte des 6.Jahrhunderts v.u.Z," in *Asien in Vergangenheit und Gegenwart* (Berlin):335-345.

Joannès, F. (1989), *Archives de Borsippa. La famille Ea-ilûta- bâni. Etude d'un lot d'archives familiales en Babylonie du VIIIe au Ve siècle av. J. -C.* (Genéve).

Lanz, H. (1976), *Die neubabylonischen harrânu: Geschäftsunternehmen* (Münchener Universitätsschriften. Juristische Fakultät. Abhandlungen zur rechtswissenschaftlichen Grundlagenforschung 18).

Oelsner, J. (1984), "Die neu-und spätbabylonische Zeit," in A. Archi, (ed.), *Circulation of Goods in Non-Palatial Context in the Ancient Near East* (Rome):221-240.

Oppenheim, A. L. (1967),"Essay on Overland Trade in the First Millennium B.C.," *Journal of Cuneiform Studies* 21:236-254.

— (1977), "Trade in the Ancient Near East," *Fifth International Congress of Economic History* (Moscow).

— (1977), *"Ancient Mesopotamia: Portrait of a Dead Civilization"* (Revised Edition, Completed by E. Reiner), (Chicago and London).

— (1985), "The Babylonian Evidence of Achaemenian Rule in Babylonia," *Cambridge History of Iran,* 2:529-587 (Cambridge).

Polanyi, K., Arensberg, C. M. and Pearson, H. W. (ed.) (1957), *Trade and Market in the Early Empires - Economies in History and Theory* (New York).

Renger, J. (1984), "Patterns of Non-Institutional Trade and Non-Commercial Exchange in Ancient Mesopotamia at the Beginning of the Second Millennium B.C.," in A. Archi (ed.), *Circulation of Goods in Non-Palatial Context in the Ancient Near East* (Rome):31-123.

Ries, G. (1976), *Die neubabylonischen Bodenpachtformulare.* (Münchener Universitätsschriften. Juristische Fakultät. Abhandlungen zur rechtswissenschaftlichen Grundlagenforschung 16).

San Nicolò, M. (1932), "Der 7 & 8 des Gesetzbuches Hammurapis in den neubabylonischen Urkunden," *Archiv Orientální* 4:327-344.

— (1934), "Einiges über Tempelpfründen (*isqu*) und *hemerai leitourgikai* in Eanna," *Archiv Orentální* 6:179-202.

— (1948), "Materialien zur Viehwirtschaft in den neubabylonischen Tempeln," *Orientalia* 7:273-293.

Stolper, M. W. (1985), *Entrepreneurs and Empire. The Murasû Archive, the Murasû Firm, and Persian Rule in Babylonia* (Leiden)

van Driel, G. (1985-6), "The Rise of the House of Egibi. Nabû-ahhê-iddina," *Jaarbericht van het Vooraziatisch-Egyptisch Genootschap* 29 (1985/86): 50-67.

— (1987), "Continuity or Decay in the Late Achaemenid Period: Evidence from Southern Mesopotamia," in H. Sancisi-Weerdenburg (ed.), *Achaemenid History* I:159-181 (Leiden).

— (1989), "The Murasûs in Context." *Journal of the Economic and Social History of the Orient* 32:203-229.

Wunsch, C. (1993), *Die Urkunden des babylonischen Geschäftsmannes Iddin-Marduk. Zum Handel mit Naturalien im 6, Jahrhundert v. Chr.* (Styx Publications vols. 1-2, Groningen).

Zaccagnini, C. (1989), "Markt," *Reallexikon der Assyriologie* 7:421-426 (Berlin).

8.

Farewell to the Ancient Near East: Evaluating Biblical References to Ownership of Land in Comparative Perspective

Baruch A. Levine
New York University

The purpose of this study is to inquire into the relevance of biblical literature for the investigation of ancient Near Eastern economic institutions, above all those operative within the biblical societies. My particular concern is with the private ownership of land in Israel in contrast to royal lands, temple estates and other forms of ownership that we would classify as public. In which ways, and to what degree can we mine literature for historical information about private property in the Land of Israel of biblical times?

The Hebrew Bible incorporates within its codes of law, its narratives and court literature, and even in its prophecy and wisdom, extensive references to ancient Near Eastern social, legal and economic practices known to us from comparative cultures. For the most part, scholarly interest in such comparative evidence has been for the purpose of sustaining the authenticity of biblical literature and law, for validating the Bible as a reliable record of what it purports to document, namely, the early history of Israel. There can be no question that the main burden of biblical literature is to tell, in different ways, the salvific history of the Israelite people — their origins, their settlement and habitation of the land of Canaan, their exile and restoration, and the inner development of their social, economic, political and religious way of life.

There are other agenda, however, that warrant scholarly interest. We should seek to understand the Hebrew Bible as a repository of ancient Near Eastern law and lore, literature and culture, religion and myth, economy and government. A relatively late arrival on the ancient scene, the Hebrew Bible may represent (in addition to all else) one of the last major collections of ancient Near Eastern literature, a closing statement on that manifold civilization. The biblical record shows how a small nation, inhabiting a vital crossroad of the world, drew on the institutions of larger Near Eastern societies to structure its life, and to define its collective values and objectives.

The nature of the biblical evidence

Biblical literature does not preserve any actual documents of land conveyance or deeds establishing ownership of land in Israel. Nor do we possess court records, official correspondence or royal edicts from the kingdoms of northern Israel or Judah. Such original documents would have to be provided by ancient Hebrew epigraphy, or by inscriptions found in nearby areas inhabited by Israelites, such as Transjordan. Such extrabiblical evidence is, however, extremely sparse and unusually disappointing in its yield. What we have to work with are canonical law codes, which often approximate original documents in their formulation. These collections of laws, preserved in the Torah (Pentateuch), specify terms of land sale and purchase and impose restrictions on such transactions. They establish liability for damage to crops, levy taxation in various forms, provide for the use of land as security for debt, establish forfeiture procedures and the like. The major problem is that these codes of law cannot be precisely dated or their exact provenance determined. The Bible operates with traditional chronologies, so that we can only approximate the time of promulgation. Torah literature in particular lacks the historical indicators present in the historical books of the Bible and in biblical prophecy.

We also find references to the legalities of land ownership in biblical historiography, in narratives and chronicles, in prophecy and other types of biblical writings, all of which are regularly utilized by scholars to infer the operations of Israelite government and economy. As examples of inferential sources we may include the record of Jeremiah's redemption of land about to be forfeited by a clan relative because of debt (Jeremiah 32), and the record of Abraham's purchase of a field and cave as a burial site from its non-Israelite owners (Genesis 23). The latter is similar to the brief record of Jacob's purchase of a field near Schechem (Genesis 33:18f.).

The biblical evidence for reconstructing the Israelite economy is, therefore, very limited. But there are other complications even with respect to what is available. To illustrate the problem we may refer to comparable questions which persist about the realism of the Code of Hammurapi. It is still unclear whether the Code of Hammurapi was forward looking or retrospective, functional or merely for display. Nevertheless, we are in a position to evaluate it on the basis of numerous court records, royal edicts and official correspondence to and from contemporary Babylon, so that the legal realities of the period and place may be clarified. In evaluating biblical law codes we inevitably find ourselves shifting quickly to comparative evidence from other societies, which though plentiful at times and enlightening in itself, cannot be used as directly as homegrown evidence. Imagine for a moment how the picture would change if 100 court records from Jerusalem of Hezekiah's time were to be uncovered by archaeologists.

Of late, there has been a growing interest in utilizing external theoretical models for the interpretation of biblical literature, which, once again, may be enlightening, although not necessarily historical for the relevant biblical period. If at the very least, the Hebrew Bible had presented a consistent record of the conquest and settlement of Canaan and had characterized the organization of Israelite societies in a consistent way, it would have been simpler to arrive at credible definitions of public and private property, respectively. Our first task is, therefore, to come up with such definitions as the biblical evidence can reasonably sustain.

There is a network of biblical traditions in which tribal origins are projected for the Israelites, and there are intimations of nomadism. The constitution of the Israelite monarchies is said to have come about subsequent to a period of settlement and limited wars, during which a tribal confederation operated without benefit of monarchy or standing armies. Are these traditions realistic, and are they reconcilable with each other?

The archaeological enterprise in Israel and in neighboring Jordan and Lebanon, when assessed with economic concerns in mind, could potentially yield valuable information about the ancient economies of Bible lands. Although archaeologists have of late become more concerned with economic and environmental concerns, we are still far from a proper treatment of the economic ramifications of archaeological discovery, especially with respect to land ownership.

We possess a study by C. H. J. de Geus entitled "Agrarian Communities in Biblical Times: 12th to 10th Centuries B.C.E." (1983). Although it addresses important questions, de Geus' work cannot be compared for historical import with the other chapters in the same volume on agrarian communities in antiquity, precisely because of the severe limitations of biblical evidence outlined above.

De Geus is of the view that the economy of ancient Israel during the early Iron Age (1200-900 B.C.E..) was based primarily on the private ownership of land and cattle, and that many Israelites lived in cities. His evidence for this conclusion is both negative and positive. On the one hand, he shows how flawed are the accepted nomadic theories of Israelite origins. The often assumed processes of Israelite sedentarization don't accord with patterns known elsewhere and at different periods. On the other hand, de Geus (1983:218f.) shows how the introduction of iron into Canaan and advances in the technology of terracing brought about a change from a "dimorphic society" based on both pastoralism and farming, "to an agrarian, urban society with a market economy and private ownership of land."

De Geus goes on to adduce fascinating external models in support of his proposed reconstruction, but he operates with rather loose definitions of "public" and "private," and is scarcely able to document his conclusions, *e.g.* in his statement that:

> Even when a farmer was not the actual owner of his land, it was he who worked the land in the first place for the benefit of his own family. (de Geus: 1983, 207).

The principal model de Geus adduces is the "musha" of the modern Near East, a feature of Ottoman administration which, in de Geus's view, harks back to very ancient custom. It is a system of parceling land owned by the Emir to individual farmers, and, at that, is predicated on ownership of such communal lands by the ruler, the Emir. This all sounds familiar to those who have studied biblical traditions regarding the allocation of the land of Canaan to the Israelite tribes and clans by lot, a system alluded to only vaguely in Micah 2:5, Ps 16:5-6, and stipulated in the priestly code of Numbers 26:52-56. However, more study would be required to ascertain in what sense "musha" land can be classified as private.

Although de Geus uses biblical evidence that he assigns to the early period of Israelite history to argue plausibly for the agrarian character of the Israelite economy, he can argue less convincingly for the private status of agrarian property in the usual legal terms. His utilization of the biblical evidence is not systematic, nor is the source material thoroughly analyzed in its own terms.

A more systematic attempt to deal with political, social and economic organization, especially in Judea of the post-exilic Achaemenid period is by Joel Weinberg, some of whose earlier essays have been published in English translation under the title "The Citizen-Temple Community" (1992). At points, Weinberg, who is representative of the Russian school of economic history, touches on questions of land ownership and imperial administration in Judea of the Achaemenid period. Although Weinberg does little with the law codes of the Torah, except to mention a few terms of reference occurring in them, he does utilize the evidence of biblical prophecy, historiography, and identifiably post-exilic writings. Most important of all, he regards the post-exilic experience of the restored Judean community as paradigmatic for an understanding of contemporary Achaemenid societies in other regions of the Persian Empire.

He integrates biblical evidence into the structure of economic and political models drawn from other spheres, where the intent was, initially, to understand the "pre-Hellenistic" socio-political and economic units of the Near East, the antecedents of the Hellenistic polis. Weinberg's methodology is valuable in and of itself, although at times it appears that external models have taken over from the biblical sources.

For the purposes of the present study, two of Weinberg's essays are particularly enlightening. "Agricultural Relations of the Citizen-Temple Community" (Weinberg 1992:92-104) deals with the status of arable land and takes account of the changes brought about by the event of the Babylonian exile. The socioeconomic unit which interests him most is the *bêt 'ābôt* "patrilineal 'house'" of the 6th to 4th centuries B.C.E., the subject of another of his essays. His conclusion is that clan lands often were parceled out to individual families, who in a real sense owned and worked these subdivisions.

"Central and Local Administration in the Achaemenid Empire" (Weinberg 1992:105-126) makes the important point that Persian imperial administration was a stable system based on taxation; one which allowed for and even stimulated considerable local and regional autonomy throughout the empire, including of course Judea. This system, which was to influence the Hellenistic *polis*, significantly featured the temple-centered community. Weinberg correctly views the formation of this type of community as the result not of internal development alone, but principally as an outcome of Persian administrative policy. This policy in turn affected the thinking of the Jewish exiles in Babylonia as well as those Judeans who remained in their homeland.

Weinberg's contribution to the subject of the present study is, therefore, considerable. In criticism it can be said that if he had devoted attention to Torah literature he might have seized upon the priestly model of the *'ēdāh* "community" as correlating with the "citizen-temple community" of Achaemenid times more precisely than the *bêt 'ābôt*. He also would have noted that the socio-political term of reference *'āmît*, occurring in priestly law, most closely approximates the term "citizen." The failure to place the evidence of Torah law and narrative within the larger context of biblical literature deprives the scholar of valuable sources for the study of biblical economies.

Then, too, Weinberg fails to subject some of the biblical terminology to a precise analysis. As will emerge in due course, there are important legal differences between land designated *'aḥuzzāh* and that designated *naḥalāh*. These differences are crucial not only for identifying the *Sitz-im-Leben* of Torah legislation, but also for determining the status of land in reality. Yet Weinberg usually hyphenates the two terms, ignoring the diachronic factor affecting their respective definitions.

The foregoing evaluations of only two of many recent statements on the economic realities of biblical times suggest the desiderata of future research. The challenge is to fashion a methodology for reading the Bible, all of it, with the objective of deriving realistic economic knowledge from its text. In pursuit of this objective, I will begin by probing two examples illustrating the methodological problems involved in mining the Hebrew Bible for economic information: (1) The subject of royal land grants in the pre-exilic period as an instrumentality for generating private property, and (2) The economic effects of war on the ownership of family land.

After thus suggesting methods for reading biblical texts with an economic agenda in mind, I will explore the system of land ownership expressed by the Hebrew term *'aḥuzzāh,* "acquired land, domain." I have been studying this system for some years, and the occasion of this conference provides an opportunity to venture some tentative conclusions about its bearing on land ownership in biblical times. In my view, the *'aḥuzzāh* system has the greatest bearing on the period of the return to Zion and thereafter, during the Achaemenid period.

Anticipating the discussion to follow, it is here proposed that private land was most often family land in biblical Israel. There is surely nothing unusual about this status, except that we must be clear about what is meant by a "family." The term is ambiguous. It may designate a unit consisting only of parents and children, perhaps of grandparents as well. It also may refer to an extended family, or clan, which includes first cousins and certain affinal relatives extending over several generations. In biblical usage, Hebrew *mišpāḥā* is best rendered "sib" or "clan," because all indications are that it designated an extended family, if not an even larger unit. In contrast, Hebrew *baît,* literally "house, household," probably designated, in the first instance, a family sharing the same domicile.

Presumably the head of a family, limited or extended, was the owner of its property, unless he had otherwise disposed of it, which often happened. Family land thus was private in the sense that it did not belong to the tribe as a whole, or to the realm in the office of the king, or to a temple, city or nation collectively. It was not, however, entirely private inasmuch as restrictions usually were placed on its alienation at arm's length, and clan members usually bore obligations with respect to preserving its integrity. These factors will come up for discussion in the description of the 'aḥuzzāh system. There also will be more to say about God, or the gods, as landowners, and how this notion affected private ownership.

Royal land grants in biblical Israel

Biblical literature provides suggestive evidence of royal land grants, indicating that at least some privately owned, or family owned land was generated in this way. The law codes of the Torah only go so far as to envision a monarchy, and the so-called law of the king in Deuteronomy 17 says nothing about land ownership or land grants. The Torah codes where we logically would seek such information are disguised, one would say. They project the collective as a tribal federation, not a kingdom, so that we read (also in Deuteronomy 17) that the entire tribe of Levi was to be denied a naḥalāh "domain" in the projected apportionment of Canaan.

The Hebrew naḥalā, is of basic importance, because it designates property that is conquered, possessed, granted or inherited. More will be said about it as the discussion unfolds. The overall result of the given textual situation is that we must look to nonlegal, biblical sources for information on royal grants of land in pre-exilic Israel and Judah.

In 1 Samuel 22:7-8 we find a telling allusion to such grants. While pursuing David, Saul was informed that some of his fellow Benjamites had defected to his adversary:

> Saul then said to his courtiers, who were in attendance upon him: "Hear me, sons of Benjamin! Will the son of Jesse indeed grant all of you fields and vineyards; will he appoint all of you commanders of thousands and commanders of hundreds that you have all conspired against me?"

A similar allusion to royal grants appears in a tale of two brothers who fomented rebellion against Moses in the wilderness. Moses had summoned to him Dathan and Abiram, sons of Eliab, probably Reubenites, in an effort to quell their rebellion. They refused to appear, and taunted Moses as follows:

"You have not yet brought us to a land flowing with milk and sap, or granted us fields and vineyards as our domain (*naḥalāh*)."

The first point to be made is that some of the narratives of the wilderness period, preserved in the synthetic historiography of the Pentateuch known as JE (=Jahwist-Elohist) seem to have been modeled after court history, as it is called. It is entirely possible that they actually derive from the same court circles and portray Moses *in loco regis*. When we read, therefore, that Moses, like David, is taunted about granting the leading warriors of Israel fields and vineyards we are actually being told something about the emergence of private land ownership through royal grants.

As has been noted by any number of scholars, the Caleb traditions fit into this scheme. Caleb conquered the area around Hebron in the Judean hills and was granted these territories by Moses. Subsequently his daughter induced him to give some of his land to her on the occasion of her marriage to a young conqueror as a dowry (Joshua 15, Judges 1). The connection with war, and the granting of land by rulers to returning warriors is, of course, a widely known practice throughout history.

There is a series of narratives strung across 2 Samuel, chapters 9, 16 and 19, about a steward of the house of Saul named Ziba, who was the recipient of a royal land grant. In the first link of the narrative chain, 2 Samuel 9, David summons the steward and questions him about surviving scions of Saul, learning that one of the sons of Jonathan, son of Saul, a certain Mephibosheth (Meribaal), had indeed survived. Mephibosheth, who was lame, was summoned by David and told that he would be installed as a palace retainer to eat at the king's table in Jerusalem. In an effort to act kindly toward the dislodged northern, royal house of Saul and to assist the son of his beloved companion Jonathan, David granted to Mephibosheth all of Saul's lands:

"I shall restore to you all of the fields of Saul, your ancestor" (2 Samuel 9:9:7).

The details of the arrangement are interesting: Ziba and his fifteen sons and twenty servants were to work the arable land and bring forth its yield, which was to go to Mephibosheth as income. What remains unclear is the basis of David's interim ownership of the land, or jurisdiction over it. It would seem from the manner in which the story is told that David had gained ownership over Saul's paternal estate on two related accounts: He succeeded Saul as king, and since no heir to the house of Saul had been found, all heirs having been presumed dead, the former king's estate went to his successor.

The plot thickens as we proceed to 2 Samuel 16. Fleeing from his insurrectionist son, Absalom, David meets up with Ziba in Transjordan. The latter had traveled far to bring David food and drink. Ziba maligns Mephibosheth, charging that the latter had remained in Jerusalem in the hope that David would be overthrown, and the monarchy would return to the House of Saul. Hearing of Mephibosheth's betrayal, David revoked his earlier grant, saying to Ziba: "Behold, everything that is Mephibosheth's [henceforth] belongs to you."

The final phase of business comes in 2 Samuel 19, when David finally is restored to his throne in Jerusalem and Absalom's insurrection is quelled. Appearing in a disheveled state, Mesphibosheth comes to plead for his life. He claims that the steward Ziba had deceived David; that he had brought pack animals loaded with food to David only so as to spy on him in Transjordan, and that he, Mephibosheth, had always been loyal. David replied:

> Why do you continue to speak about such of your concerns? I have [already] ordered that you and Ziba should divide the fields between you (2 Samuel 19:30).

Imbedded in this narrative of court intrigue is a complex of legalities. One should not be surprised to discover the blending of more than one legality in the same episode, and a degree of imprecision in the telling. But on the whole we observe the subsequent transfer of land appropriated by David to the heir of Saul, his predecessor, who had died after his dynasty had been deposed. We read further of another transfer of royal land to a king's steward, a man of considerable wealth and status, who is rewarded for his service to the king.

A further allusion to royal land grants is found in 1 Samuel 8, in a passage that has been widely discussed for what it projects as royal prerogatives. In attempting to dissuade the Israelites from constituting a monarchy, the cult prophet, Samuel, warns of the potential cost. The king will conscript Israelites in various ways — as *corvée*, as a work force to reap his harvest and manufacture weapons, and as members of the royal bureaucracy, while daughters will be summoned to perform domestic chores in the palace. Then Samuel has the following to say:

> He will confiscate (*yiqqaḥ*) your fields, and your best vineyards and olive trees so as to grant (*wenātan*) them to his courtiers, and he will exact a tithe of your grain and vineyards and give that to his personal guards and courtiers.

A case where such expropriation was attempted is recorded in 1 Kings 21. We are told that Ahab, king of northern Israel, sought to purchase a vineyard adjacent to his own fields, but was refused by its owner, Naboth, who told him: "God forbid that I convey my ancestral *naḥalāh* to you."

Initially the king resigned himself to the refusal, which, in fact, has led most commentators to assume that one had the right in the northern Israelite kingdom of the 9th century B.C.E. to refuse to alienate ancestral land, even to the king. It was only by ruse that Ahab's Phoenician wife, Jezebel, had poor Naboth condemned to death for blasphemy and sedition. At this point Ahab simply expropriated the field.

It is likely that a customary right overrode royal authority in land ownership. The king of Israel was expected to respect the *naḥalāh* status of family property. Nevertheless, it would seem that the property of condemned Israelites legally accrued to the state, namely to the king, not to the heirs of the executed person. This process was denounced by the prophet Elijah, but only because Naboth was falsely condemned to death.

We are fortunate to have informative studies pertaining to royal land grants, and royal versus private ownership of land in biblical Israel. Zafrira Ben-Barak has dealt with the principal biblical passages cited above, and has attempted to define the legal and economic realities that inform them. Although she may be accused of supplying much that is not actually said in the text, her methods of textual analysis are carefully reasoned, and she considers every source contextually and systematically.

In the case of Ahab and Naboth it is her view that kings of Israel often purchased private lands in the normal way, without any attempt at coercion (Ben-Barak 1978-9). She cites David's purchase of the threshing floor of Araunah, the Jebusite, as the site for an altar in Jerusalem after its conquest (2 Samuel 24), and Omri's purchase of the property of Shemer for his capital, Samaria (1 Kings 16:24). This is, of course, the reverse of privatization, and reflects the aggrandizement of royal holdings, but it does attest, initially, to the rights of private landowners over their property. The fact is that Ahab, king of Israel, was compelled to circumvent these rights deceitfully; he could not simply issue an order to confiscate Naboth's property.

More to the point of the present study, Ben-Barak's discussion of the Mephibosheth incident is particularly enlightening (Ben-Barak 1981). Adducing parallels from other societies of the ancient Near East, most notably Ugarit, Ben-Barak shows a widespread pattern of royal land grants. The operative formula of conveyance in Akkadian is *našû . . . nadānu*, in Hebrew *lāqaḥ . . . wenātan* "to take [and] to give." This formula is used in the admonition on royal prerogatives in 1 Samuel 8. The king will predictably take from the populace, and give to his favorites, warriors and courtiers. Ben-Barak notes that the Philistine ruler, Achish of Gath, granted David, his mercenary commander, the town of Ziklag as his fief (1 Samuel 27:6-12).

Ben-Barak isolates three stages in the Mephibosheth transaction: (1) David restores what had been Saul's paternal estate to Saul's sole surviving heir, Mephibosheth. In Ben-Barak's view, David was more or less required to do so because his appropriation of Saul's estate was legal to start with only because there was no living heir of the former king in evidence. Once Mephibosheth was discovered, David could no longer hold on to Saul's ancestral estate. (2) David revokes the grant to Mephibosheth and transfers Saul's original estate to Ziba. Ben-Barak correctly notes ancient Near Eastern parallels, from Alalakh and Ugarit, attesting to the practice of confiscating land as punishment for treason. This is, of course, what we learn from the Naboth incident, and the same legal norms are to be seen in the present narrative. Furthermore, David in this case did just what Samuel warned that kings would do: He handed over an ancestral estate to one of his favorites! (3) David returns half of the estate to Mephibosheth, taking that half from Ziba, after Mephibosheth begged for his life. Such actions on David's part may have been motivated by political considerations, and their only legal import is to suggest that what kings gave, they could take away!

Those investigating royal land grants at Ugarit have original documents at their disposal; students of biblical law and economy have only narratives from the court histories of Judah and Northern Israel. And so, while it appears that the broad pattern of royal land grants operated under kings of Judah and Israel, we have no notion of its extent, and to what degree it actually generated private property in Canaan of biblical times. The sense is that given the dominant concerns of biblical writers, even the few references preserved in biblical literature attest to more widespread practices.

The economic effects of war on ownership of family land

A second methodological exercise pertains to the economic effects of war, especially on the status of agricultural land in the country that went to war. In a recent study of 2 Samuel 24 (Levine 1993), I attempted to explain the dynamics of census-taking in biblical Israel so as to understand why the writers of 2 Samuel 24 regarded as sinful David's insistence on taking a census after having fought many wars.

In the history of biblical exegesis, this chapter has been compared to another example of the sinfulness of census-taking, namely, the imposition of a head-tax on all adult Israelite males in support of the Tabernacle project, as recorded in Exodus 30. There it is explained that payment of a *kôper* "ransom," would avert a plague, and in 2 Samuel 24 we read that a plague was the punishment for David's census. It is my view that it was not the taking of a census *per se* that implicated David, but the particular circumstances under which it was conducted.

The use of cultic language to characterize census-taking has directed scholarly attention to another instance of the same usage in the Mari letters. Both J. R. Kupper (1950) and E. A. Speiser (1958) regarded the procedure known at Mari as *tebibtu* to be relevant to our understanding of the biblical fear of the military census. Both these scholars vacillated between the cultic and administrative interpretations of the *tebibtu* process that troops at Mari underwent before going into battle. It is obvious, as both Kupper and Speiser understood at the time, that the Akkadian verb *ebēbu*/D-stem *ubbubu* is often used legally, like other similar verbs connoting cleansing and purification, to refer to clearance from debt and obligation. The question that these scholars should have sought to answer, had their attention been squarely focused on the economic effects of war, can be formulated as follows: Which obligations were incumbent on the troops at Mari, and by comparison, on David's troops as they were mustered throughout Israel to require clearance, and why was securing clearance a hardship, one which David was so strongly advised to avoid imposing?

In 1 Samuel 17:18, where we are told that young David was sent by his father, Jesse, to bring a "care-package" to his brothers who had followed Saul to war and were encamped far from home. There was a package for the military commander, as well, and then we read:

> Inquire after the well-being of your brothers, and take their guarantee (Hebrew *'arubbāh*).

Translators of this passage have fudged on the function of the *'arubbāh* in this context, notwithstanding the fact that the meaning of this term is hardly in doubt. The Hebrew term *'arubbāh* is a cognate of Akkadian *erēbu* "to enter," a verb which often signifies entry into various legal arrangements such as indenture, slavery, and into the role of voucher. In Hebrew, a person designated *'āreb* "voucher" literally stands in for another, guaranteeing payment in case of default (Prov 20:17). Hebrew *'ērābôn*, surviving as Greek *arabôn*, "pledge," is the term used in the curious story of Judah and the harlot for hire. Out of cash at the moment, Judah left the harlot his cylinder seal and its fillet, along with his staff as *'ērābôn* (Genesis 38). Another related term is Hebrew *ma'arāb* "exchange," in Ezekiel's angry prophecy condemning the profit-hungry merchants of Tyre (Ezekiel 27). Interestingly, a cognate of the same term occurs in a Ugaritic ritual text recently studied by J. M. de Tarragon and B. A. Levine (1993), where it means "gift," literally a gift one brings into the Temple.

In ancient Israel, as elsewhere, the calling up of militias in time of war brought many hardships to the folks back home, and this is just as true today. The absence of many able-bodied men from their farms and vineyards, and from their flocks and herds, for extended periods of time, often seasonally, made it appreciably harder to till the soil, plant and harvest. Large mounts of foodstuffs and other material were used up or lost in war. Who would pay the land taxes and cover the debts of those away from home? Mobilization triggered an economic cycle that was bound to produce hardship. In the best-case scenario the spoils of war might compensate in part for this situation, but domestic production would inevitably go down in the short term. This is why David's brothers were required to pledge that their agrarian obligations had been met, or would be met.

New studies of the Mari documents are required in light of the many additional texts that have recently been published, but it would not be unreasonable to suggest, based on what is already known, that the *'ērābôn*, like the *tebibtu*, was aimed at assuring that homefront obligations would be met by soldiers going to war. This is why the only son of a family is often exempted from conscription, and why, apart from sentimental reasons, Deuteronomy 20:5-7, exempt from military service one who has just built a home, planted a vineyard, or betrothed a wife. In all three cases the fear expressed is that someone else will gain possession.

And so it is, that random references to "pledges" and a highly etiological tale about David serve as vague sources of economic information about the obligations of land ownership in time of war, although it must be conceded that even the explicit letters from Mari have produced their own enigmas!

The *'aḥuzzāh* system of land tenure

The only coherent legal code in the Torah that governs land ownership is Leviticus 25, with some corollary provisions appearing in Leviticus 27.

These texts are predicated on the *'aḥuzzāh* system, and their proper interpretation would add considerably to our knowledge about the private ownership of land in biblical Israel. Some words of introduction are necessary before outlining the *'aḥuzzāh* system.

The Hebrew Bible uses three principal terms of reference to denote land ownership; or, to put it another way, to designate the legal status of land. All three terms run the gamut from collective to private ownership. They are: 1) *yerussāh*, 2) *naḥalāh*, and 3) *'aḥuzzāh*. Of the three, *'aḥuzzāh* is in my view the latest, or youngest, and its usage is discretely confined to the priestly source of the Pentateuch, and to sources that can be traced to the influence of the priestly school.

The other two terms, *yerussāh* and *naḥalāh*, are distributed in more than one literary source, or collection of laws. In contrast to *'aḥuzzāh*, the terms yeruvah and naoalah share a semantic range that extends from conquest, to settlement, to legal possession, to inheritance. Although it was undoubtedly true that land owned as *'aḥuzzāh* would normally be inherited by the next generation, inheritance is not connoted by the term 'aouzzah, itself, which focuses attention on the initial basis of land acquisition and tenure.

1) The term *yerussāh* derives from a verb whose primary sense is physical possession by conquest or seizure, and which has the extended meaning of inheritance (Jer 32:8). Cognates of this verb are attested in Ugaritic, where the connotation of inheritance appears to dominate usage. However, one would not use this verb to designate land that was purchased in the first instance, and this is an important point. In the collective dimension, other nations have a *yerussāh* in God's plan for the world, just as Israel does, because God granted them lands and territories as their *yerussāh*. Israel therefore must respect their territorial integrity. As for the Israelites, they are commanded to conquer Canaan, a mandate expressed in statements which employ the verb yarav. See Deuteronomy 1:21:

> Behold, the LORD, your God, has placed this land at your disposal; ascend! seize! (*'alēh rēš*) just as the LORD, God of your ancestors has commanded you; have no fear nor be dismayed.

The point is that translating *yerussāh* as "inheritance" masks other realities of land ownership in the first instance. Similarly, the causative stem, *hôrîš*, describes the Israelite takeover of Canaan and the dispossession of its inhabitants; in effect, their reduction to serfdom, sometimes deportation, but consistently their disenfranchisement. By designating family land, tribal lands or national territory as *yerussāh* the text is defining it as a possession taken, or received, or even redeemed by a clan relative, but not as one purchased or sold.

2) The Hebrew term *naḥalāh* is anticipated by Ugaritic *nḥlt*, which designates the domain of a god in myth. We have such constructions as *ǵr nḥlt* "mountain domain" (cf. Hebrew *har naḥalāh*), and *arṣ nḥlt* "sovereign territory." In Ugaritic personnel lists we find what is apparently a participial form, *naḥilu* "heir," although this meaning is uncertain.[1] The basic sense of Hebrew *naḥalāh* is hard to pin down. In Mari usage, studied by D. O. Edzard (1964) the verb *naḥālu* means "to hand over, convey," sometimes by way of inheritance, but not necessarily so. It yielded the denominative *niḥlatu*. In Hebrew the cognate verb more often connotes receipt of a possession, not the conveyance of property to another. But this is not always the case. Thus, Zechariah 2:16:

> The LORD shall grant to Judah (*wenāḥal 'et Yehûdāh*) his portion (*'et ḥelqô*) on the sacred soil, and shall again select Jerusalem. (Also Exodus 34:9).

In any event, I doubt if in biblical usage (apparently in contrast to Mari usage) land classified as *naḥalāh* could have been purchased in the first instance; it can only be granted by some authority, human or divine, and consequently received or inherited, as within a family; or, it can be physically possessed as through conquest. The term *naḥalāh* is used extensively, and has many predications.

3) This brings us to the priestly term *'aḥuzzāh*. What is the status of arable land designated in this way?

From the very beginnings of modern biblical scholarship it has been accepted as a methodological principle that priestly law on the one hand, and priestly narrative and historiography on the other hand, reflect each other and must be correlated. I am far from comprehending the *'aḥuzzāh* system to my satisfaction, but there is some progress to report.

Let us begin with the priestly recasting of the patriarchal period and the Egyptian sojourn as told in the book of Genesis. This literary tradition comes on the heels of earlier historiographic and narrative sources, and characterizes the habitation of Canaan by the patriarchs and their clan in a distinctive way. I understand this retrojection to be the product of post-exilic literary creativity of the early Achaemenid period. In effect, it creates a pre-history of Israel aimed at legitimating the policies of the exilic leadership during the waves of return to Zion subsequent to the Cyrus edict. This is also the *Sitz-im-Leben* of the priestly legislation found in Leviticus 25 and 27, which is retrojected into the wilderness period and the lifetime of Moses and thereby attached to the earlier versions of the Sinaitic theophany.

How does this retrojection work in Genesis? Abraham sets out to purchase a burial site near Hebron for Sarah from the so-called Hittites (Genesis 23). He presents himself as *gēr wetôšāb*, "a resident alien," asking to be sold *'aḥuzzāh qeber*, "a grave site as an *'aḥuzzāh*."

The status *gēr wetôšāb* usually is taken to indicate a legal disadvantage, as if to imply that Abraham was seeking an exceptional favor. I take it differently: By identifying himself as *gēr wetôšāb*, Abraham was invoking an acknowledged right to negotiate the purchase of land in Canaan. Once he gained ownership of land, his status would be confirmed as a permanent resident. This analysis will receive a degree of confirmation in Genesis 34, the Schechemite episode, as we shall see. The so-called Hittite responded favorably, with honor and respect, and pledged that no person of their community would deny Abraham this right. I dispute the interpretation that this indicates the offer of a gift to Abraham, but that issue is not essential to the present discussion.

The narrative is not entirely consistent in designating the object of purchase. Most of the time, Ephron, the Hittite, is said to be ready to sell Abraham the cave at the edge of his field, but as the negotiations proceed we read of both the cave and the field as having been purchased by Abraham, and this would seem to be more realistic.

Actually, burial practices in biblical Israel bear a relationship to land ownership. In several instances, the Bible records that a leader, such as Joshua, was buried on the border of his *naḥalāh* (Joshua 24:30, Judges 2:9), and Rachel was buried on the border of the territory of the tribe of Benjamin, according to 1 Samuel 10:2. A recent archaeological study of Judahite burial practices by Elizabeth Bloch Smith (1992) deals briefly with burial sites and land ownership by extended families, showing that the grave or burial cave could often be taken as evidence of ownership by a family, perhaps even as evidence of title.

The terms of reference used in connection with Abraham's purchase of a burial site and a field are also discrete, and fill out the system. Two such terms are found in Genesis 23. Thus, we read hat the field and cave and all of its trees "became the property of" Abraham. The Hebrew verb for legal acquisition is *qûm*, "to arise, stand." I have shown, as have others, that this is Aramaistic usage. In Aramaic "to stand" (*qûm*) connotes established ownership, and the binding force of a contract. Its use indicates that the sale has, as we would say, "gone through has been finalized." The second term, *miqnāh*, from the verb *qānāh*, means "purchase." It defines the status of the *'aḥuzzāh*: It has been acquired. Now both these terms, or forms of them, occur in the laws of Leviticus 25 (Levine 1981).

To continue the references to the *'aḥuzzāh* system in the priestly recasting of the patriarchal narratives, we turn now to Genesis 34, where we read about the rape of Dinah, Jacob's daughter, by the son of the local ruler of Schechem, a Canaanite. The violent young man told his father that he actually loved Dinah, and so, a delegation approached Jacob to negotiate a marriage, but also to form a new relationship between Jacob's clan and the Canaanite city-state. The proposed terms are spelled out in the following way:

> Become related to us through marriage. Give us your daughters and take our daughters for yourselves. Settle down with us, and the land shall be at your disposal. Settle, and trade it (*ûseḥārûhā*), and acquire land in it (*weḥē'āḥazû bāh*).

Hebrew *heʾāḥazû* is a denominative verbal form based on the noun *'aḥuzzāh*, namely, "to exercise the right of *'aḥuzzāh*." What we learn from this tale is that the right to acquire land could be part of an arrangement that included trading rights and exogamous marriage. As the story is set, the clan of Jacob are resident aliens, granted the right to buy land in Canaan from its rightful owners. This right is to be provided for in a treaty, or contract. It is not coincidental that in Genesis 23 the Hittites refer to Abraham as *neśî' 'elôhîm,* which probably means "a headman favored by God," whereas the ruler of Schechem is referred to in Genesis 34 as *neśî' hāʾāreṣ,* "the headman of the district."

The final chapter in the Genesis projection of the *'aḥuzzāh* system in priestly literature comes in the narrative of the Egyptian sojourn, in chapter 47. There we read that Joseph had brought his father's clan to Egypt, and had presented his father, Jacob, before Pharaoh together with several representatives of his family. This detail is not to be overlooked because it suggests that members of the clan other than the patriarch himself had a voice in its decisions.

Then the following:

> Then Joseph settled his father and his kinsmen, and granted them *'aḥuzzāh* in the land of Egypt, in the choice section of the land, in the district of Ramses, as Pharaoh had ordered.

Further in the same chapter we read:

> The Israelites dwelled in the land of Egypt, in the district of Goshen, and they acquired *'aḥuzzāh* land in it, and they greatly multiplied.

Bearing the discrete terminology and provisions of the priestly narratives in mind, let us now take up the provisions of Leviticus 25, remembering that they quite possibly reflect conditions in post-exilic Jerusalem and Judah, under Persian administration. I conclude this from Nehemiah 5, where similar economic conditions are reflected. In a sense, Nehemiah 5 may be utilized as an inner-biblical commentary on Leviticus 25, whose provisions may be outlined as follows:

1) **The Jubilee year.** Every fiftieth year (seven rounds of Sabbaticals) *derôr* (traditionally rendered "liberty," as in the Liberty Bell) shall be proclaimed throughout the land and to all its inhabitants, at which time each person who had lost his *'ahuzzāh* due to debt shall be restored to it and rejoin his clan. That year shall be a fallow year.

There is an extensive literature on the putative relevance of Syro-Mesopotamian *andurāru*, usually a royal edict of debt remission as known from the Old Babylonian and Old Assyrian periods, as well as from Neo-Assyrian and Neo-Babylonian documents, to this biblical law (Levine: 1989). Although some have been too eager, perhaps, to adduce extra-biblical parallels, and with questions remaining as to the realism of Jubilees precisely scheduled every fifty years, there is little doubt that the two terms *andurāru* and *derôr*, derive from cognates of the same verb, meaning "to turn, revert," and that they refer to similar legalities. The first biblical reference to *derôr* outside of Torah literature is Jeremiah 34. It correlates with Neo-Babylonian usage in that it refers to the manumission of slaves. With the Chaldeans at the gates of Jerusalem, Judean slave owners are commanded to enact a *derôr*, thereby freeing their slaves who would presumably be conscripted into the army. Deutero (Trito)-Isaiah 61:1 refers to the year of the end of the exile as *šenat derôr*, "the year of release," namely, the year of return from exile and repatriation. In Ezek. 46:17 *šenat hadderôr* refers to "the Jubilee Year," in a late excursus outlining the powers of the *nāśî'*, "elected leader," who replaces the king in the prophet's program for the restored community. The passage is interesting in that it limits the prerogatives of the *nāśî'*. He may not expropriate the *'ahuzzāh* of the people, though he may bequeath his own *'ahuzzāh*, delimited in Ezekiel to his own sons. Of particular interest is the provision that if the *nāśî'* grants a part of his *'ahuzzāh* to any of his courtiers, it is subject to the law of Jubilee, and reverts to the *nāśî'* at that time.

A general statement in the opening section of Lev. 25 guarantees the restoration of land forfeited by debt to its owners at the Jubilee. This is followed by a specific law prohibiting alienation of arable land held as *'aḥuzzāh*. An Israelite who sold (the verb *makar*) or purchased (the verb *qānāh*) arable land to or from his *'āmît*, "fellow citizen" must calculate its purchase price on the basis of crop years remaining until the next Jubilee, because at that time the field would revert to its original owner. It is to be assumed from what follows in Lev. 25 that such sales were normally compelled by debt. They were more like long-term leases, assuming the law was implemented in practice. Title was not transferred, with only an arrangement resembling usufruct rights coming under contract.

A second term of reference after *derôr*, and which further defines the limitations of ownership, is adverbial *liṣemîtût*, "irretrievably, finally handed over." Land may not be sold under terms that do not allow for its redemption or retrieval. Now, as is known, the stative form *ṣāmit* is attested in the Akkadian documents from Ugarit, where it means "transferred, finally handed over." The terms of sale described in the Akkadian documents from Ugarit refer to real estate, in one case a house, that changed hands, with verbs such as *leqû*, and *nadānu* used to connote purchase and conveyance. It also characterizes royal land grants, by the way. Occurrence of stative *ṣāmit* is always followed by the clause: *a-di da-ri-ti ur₅-ra še-ra LÚ ma-am-ma-an la i-la-qi-šu* "forever, day and night, no person may take it away." The stative verbal form *ṣāmit* may be West Semitic to start with, as has been suggested.[2]

Now, this is precisely what is prohibited in Leviticus 25: Arable, Israelite land may not be sold in this way. A theological basis is adduced for the restriction on alienations: All land belongs to God, and even the Israelites, themselves, do not have title to it! They are like Abraham, *gerîm wetôšābîm* "resident aliens," the God of Israel having granted them the land of Israel as an *'aḥuzzāh*. In the priestly covenant promise to Abraham after his circumcision, the land of Canaan is granted to his descendents as *'aḥuzzāt 'ôlām* "an *'aḥuzzāh* forever" (Gen 17:8). In Jacob's blessing to Joseph in Egypt (Gen 48:4), the Patriarch states that the God of Israel has granted their descendents the land of Canaan as *'aḥuzzāt 'ôlām*. We observe, once again, the correlation of priestly law with priestly narrative.

Exceptions to such restrictions are forfeited urban dwellings, which may be redeemed within a year of sale, and Levitical property, which may always be redeemed and is not subject to the Jubilee.

2) Land forfeited because of debt. The provisions of Lev. 25 reflect a substantial breakdown of the clan system in favor of private owners, whose rights are being protected at the expense of fellow Israelites, including clan relatives. Revoking the laws of Exodus 21 and of Deuteronomy 15, Israelites no longer will have their debts waived every seventh year. The precise provisions of the *'aḥuzzāh* system thus detract somewhat from the heuristic rhetoric surrounding its legislation.

Indenture continues until the Jubilee, although usury is disallowed. Israelites are entitled to redeem forfeited arable land, and the purchaser must comply. But one unable to redeem forfeited land, or whose clan relative won't do it for him, has no alternative but to await the Jubilee. The only exception is in the case where forfeiture was to a non-Israelite resident of the land, a *gēr* or his descendant. In such an event, clan relatives were required by law to come to the aid of the disenfranchised promptly so as to prevent the loss of arable land to non-Israelites (Leviticus 25:47). One senses that this particular provision points to a mixed population under foreign domination rather than to the pre-exilic situation under the Judean monarchy.

There are two curious provisions of the *'aḥuzzāh* system stated in Lev. 27:16-24. First is the distinction between one's original *'aḥuzzāh* and land one had acquired by purchase, most likely through foreclosure, and which is termed *miqnāh*. This is the same term used in Genesis 23 to define Abraham's acquisition of land. The distinction relates to land that one may devote to the temple, as the text has it "to the LORD (leYHWH)."

Original *'aḥuzzāh* land may be permanently devoted as temple property, and becomes subject to various obligations. Such land, unless it is bought back by the original owner with a 20% surcharge, remains temple property and is unaffected by the Jubilee. Its value is assessed according to crop years. It is of interest to note how the status of such land is defined in Leviticus 27: Its status is that of condemned land, *śedēh haḥērem*, such as would be expropriated by the state, or, in this case, the temple from a condemned murderer. In other words, we can now confirm our reading of the tale of Naboth of Jezreel (1 Kings 21) from a different biblical source.

So much for original *'aḥuzzāh* property. But what if a man had devoted to the temple land he acquired from a debtor or otherwise, and which had not been part of his original *'aḥuzzāh*? The assessment of value is the same, by crop years, but such property remains in the possession of the temple only until the Jubilee; at that time it will revert to its original owner, not to its subsequent purchaser.

We are required to clarify what is meant by original ownership. In all Torah traditions, including the priestly source, the entry of the Israelites in Canaan *en masse* after forty years of wilderness migration is projected as Year One. Very often, legislation is introduced by the formula: "When you enter the land," or variations of the same. In other words, the given laws are presented in terms of what is projected as an original, one-time apportionment of Canaan.

This is the *mis en scène*, unhistorical, to be sure, but important to factor into our reading of Torah legislation. As a result, Deut 19:14 states:

> Do not overreach your neighbor's boundary, which the first [settlers] (Hebrew *ri'šônîm*) delimited in your *naḥalāh* that you will receive in the land which the LORD your God is granting you, to take possession of it.

In summary, Leviticus 25 and 27 describe a system of limited, private ownership of arable land in the land of Israel. The Israelite landowner is treated as a firm legal entity in his own right, rather than merely as a clan, or tribal member. The Temple administers dealings in the real estate of the Israelite community. There is an overriding concern with retaining arable land in Israelite hands, so that the clan obligation to act on behalf of a fellow Israelite is stronger in the case of land forfeited to non-Israelites than it would be in the case of foreclosure by another Israelite.

Nehemiah 5: A Biblical Chronicle from the Mid-Achaemenid Period

Another biblical source relevant to our understanding of land ownership as legislated in Leviticus 25 and 27 is Nehemiah 5. In fact, the striking similarities between the two sources argue in favor of assigning Leviticus 25 also to the Achaemenid period.

Early in the second half of the 5th century B.C.E. Nehemiah, a Jew who served as the Persian *peḥāh* in Jerusalem and Judah, was engaged in severe conflict with the Jewish leadership and populace. Nehemiah 5 lists a succession of economic complaints.

> And there are some who say: "We are indenturing our sons and daughters so that we may buy grain and have food to eat and survive."

> And there are those who say: "Our fields, vineyards and houses we are mortgaging (the participle *'ôrebîm*) to be able to buy grain during a famine."

> And there are those who say: "We borrowed silver to pay the royal land tax (*middat hammelek*) [mortgaging] our fields and vineyards."

"And now, our flesh is as good as that of our brothers, and our children as good as theirs, and yet we are reducing our sons and daughters to slavery — some of our daughters are already subjected — but we are powerless. Our fields and vineyards belong to others."

What is Nehemiah's response? He censures the *ḥôrîm* and *segānîm*. Between the two of them, these terms of reference have much to tell us about Persian administration. Without entering into great detail, Hebrew *ḥôrîm*, in its cognate, Aramaic form *ḥāre*, corresponds to Akkadian *mār bāne*, most often Old Persian *fratama martiya*, "foremost men," or *fratama amisiya*, "foremost followers" in the trilingual Bisitun inscription of Darius I, as I recently learned from Muhammad Dandamayev by oral communication. As for Hebrew *segān* it is cognate with Akkadian *šaknu* "governor," a term having many meanings. Here it is used with reference to Judeans who may have held official positions or served as land managers. Nehemiah has the following to say to these personages:

"You are foreclosing on debts against one another. We have bought back our Judean kinsmen who had been sold to gentiles, to the extent possible for us, and yet you continue to sell your kinsmen so that they are sold away from us? Even I and my kinsmen have foreclosed against them for silver and grain. Let us abandon this indebtedness. Restore to them as of this day their fields and vineyards, their olive groves and houses, and the hundred [shekels] of silver, and the grain, wine and oil which you are expropriating from them."

The leading Judeans promised to comply, and to dramatize this commitment, Nehemiah shook his sash loose. The ironic reference to buying back fellow Israelites who had suffered foreclosure because of debt incurred to gentiles correlates with Lev 25:47, which requires one's clan relatives to come to his aid in such circumstances. This is one of the telling links between Leviticus 25 and Nehemiah 5.

What is missing in Torah legislation, for reasons already explained, is any reference to royally imposed taxes, or state taxes. All taxes are "to the LORD." The only clue to royally imposed taxation earlier in Scripture is in that old statement on royal prerogatives in 1 Samuel 8, where the intended king would have the authority to impose a tithe on the yield of farm and vineyard. In Nehemiah 5 we find a more realistic reference to the *mandattu* "land tax," (Aramaic *mindāh*, in Ezra 4:13), payable to the

Persian authorities. This detail is significant, because it helps to explain the 'aḥuzzāh system.

From Nehemiah 5 it would seem that the 'aḥuzzāh system was not working well. There were undoubtedly external reasons for this situation, having to do with the changing fortunes and policies of the Persian empire. An internal reason was that Judeans were foreclosing on each other right and left, reducing one another to virtual serfdom, and probably charging usurious interest to boot. In other words, they weren't keeping the commandments of Leviticus 25 and 27. As a result, what the 'aḥuzzāh system had sought to achieve, to protect the rights of individual landowners, was not achieved. This objective also involved retaining Jewish land in the possession of Jews, a theme which resonates loudly in Nehemiah 5. Judeans are losing their land to local creditors, including agents of the Persian rulers. On the basis of such comparisons between Leviticus 25 and 27 and Nehemiah 5 we see preliminary grounds for assigning the former, like the latter, to the Persian period, perhaps to different phases of it.

Determining the Sitz-im-Leben of the 'aḥuzzāh System: The Comparative Agenda

The preceding discussion illustrates the methodological problems we face in mining the Hebrew Bible for economic information. Referring to the discussion of the 'aḥuzzāh system, the principal subject of this study, and the suggestion that it may reflect the realities of Persian administration in Palestine of Achaemenid times, it must be emphasized that we are still far from any valid understanding of Leviticus 25 and 27 in economic terms. Thus far, it has been possible to describe their provisions as the Hebrew Bible presents them, to place them in biblical context, and to adduce some preliminary comparative references. The only advantage held by Nehemiah 5 over Leviticus 25 and 27 is its discernible historical setting; the economic and administrative realities it reflects need much further investigation.

The hypothesis that Leviticus 25 and 27, and the priestly narratives derive from the Achaemenid period cannot be demonstrated from within. To know what Leviticus 25 and 27 are referring to historically requires knowing when their provisions were instituted and operative, and under which circumstances. In turn, this necessitates the integration of contemporary, comparative evidence that correlates with their provisions and makes sense out of them.

Our task and our method is to study patterns of Persian imperial policy and administration in those regions of the empire which have yielded extensive documentation, especially Babylonia and Egypt. We may learn how land was owned and managed in Judea by learning how it was owned and managed in Babylonia and Egypt during the same historical period, under the same empire.

It is fortunate that this area of inquiry is presently attracting intensive scholarly interest, especially with respect to Mesopotamia. The works of Muhammed Dandamayev, a pioneer in the elucidation of economic systems operative during the Achaemenid period, and of M. W. Stolper, whose study of the Murašû archive deals methodically with economic issues, are prime examples of the kinds of investigations most likely to be of assistance to biblical scholars.[3] Indeed, the biblical period most inviting to comparative investigation in the economic sphere may turn out to be the Achaemenid period after all. Before this harvest can be fully reaped, certain schools of biblical scholars must liberate themselves from theological and other concerns impeding the proper, critical study of Torah literature in all its parts. Attitudes toward Torah literature must change. The Torah must be seen as a collection of sources compiled over many centuries. reaching from the early monarchic period to the late phases of Achaemenid rule in the Land of Israel. It is part and parcel of the grand farewell to the ancient Near East announced by the Hebrew Bible.

DISCUSSION

Mitchell: You really got my attention when you started on the census. It has long been thought that societies evolved from those based on kinship to those based on status. This assumption has been reinforced, it is argued, by the evidence of societies very early in their development undertaking censuses on which the obligations to the state are based on property or wealth – the latter presumably having replaced birth as the basis for the obligation or service. It is now fairly clear that the first census in Rome was, in fact, a review of all those drawn up for military service. The census was simply a gathering of all those who were obligated to show up and thus to serve or fight. Piéri's study makes this absolutely clear. The ancient Roman practice has a parallel in the origin and evolution of the British Parliament. Both the Roman *comitia* and the British Parliament began as bodies of men obligated to serve, who were drawn up and reviewed by their leaders before battle. Gradually, these men obtained the right or power to vote on various measures and, in the case of the Roman *comitia*, they obtained the right to elect those who commanded them.

Going from there to records (you mentioned on page 17: "from the beginning of modern Biblical scholarship . . ."): Some time ago I wrote an article for the Illinois Law Journal titled "Roman History, Roman Law, and Roman Priests," because all three had a common ground. Priests maintained the records of the law. Until the very end of Roman history, priests continued to be trained in the law. Cicero was trained by the Scaevola brothers, one was a pontiff and the other an auger, and the civil law was very much part of their expertise.

I was curious when you were talking about whether or not God owned the land. Since it is difficult for those of us who are not well connected to have a direct pipeline to God, we usually have to go through some intermediary. Is it the case that priests are so in charge of the formulae of transfer, of sale or whatever, that they are God's representatives? While the land may belong to God, the priests can dole it out.

Levine: I think so. If this textual material belongs to the Achaemenid period, then it reflects that Judea was a temple-run province. The temple would have been the agency that collected taxes due the Persians as well, or at least, that funneled the taxes to those authorities. The temple administration worked with the Persian *Pehah*. Nehemiah himself held that office, and he said that there had always been a resident *Pehah* in Judea.

Most historians agree. In Leviticus you find, once or twice, that tithes and other in-fact taxes were to be remitted: *leYHWH lakkôhēn*, "to the Lord, to the priest," as if the two designations were apposite. The one reference to a royal tithe is in I Sam 8, the admonitions on the prerogatives of the king. There, we are told, *inter alia*, that the king will impose a tithe on livestock and produce. So, when a king is in office, as in the pre-exilic period of Biblical society, the tithe is a donation, albeit compulsory to God! Just how the temple administration handled such matters I don't know.

Heltzer: I can agree with everything you said, but while we have these elements of private economy, the overwhelming context may still be the traditional economy. You have invaded a field where nobody has worked, and therefore I think it is very interesting to ask about the period until the destruction of the first Temple. Is it a private or traditional economy? There was a term *śākîr*, "a hired man." I know of only one work about the *śākîrs*, J. D. Amusin's *Śakîr: On the Problem of Hired Labour in the Ancient Near East* (Peredneaziatski Sbornik, III (Moscow 1979):4-14 (Russian, English summary). Even in the Biblical Encyclopedia you don't have *śākîr*.

Levine: You are saying it is pre-exilic?

Heltzer: Of course, it is. According to the Book of Judith, chapter 4, we see free-born people, metics *(gērîm)*, hired people and slaves. So the *śākîr* is second from the bottom. From the beginning of the fourth century we have the coinage. The Judean coin was very small, weighing just 0,1 or even 0,08 grams. If I take forty shekels, using a shekel of 11½ grams, I would need some 4,500 such coins to make forty shekels.

I choose this sum because Nehemiah says that forty shekels is one of the elements of *leḥem happenḥāh*, "the bread of the governor," and thus a provincial tax. The satrapial tax was separate. So it can be that this coinage enabled the Judean people to have a means to pay their tax obligations.

The peasants needed money. They had to get it by selling their products. The only products that could be sold abroad were olives and olive oil, the only natural advantage of Judea. In Persian times we also see the beginning of private relations in Judea's commercial life, which was much less developed than that of the coastal cities, Ashdod and the Phoenician cities. But the details will have to await the expanded version of my published papers, "Again on Some Problems of the Achaemenid Taxation in the Province of Judah," *Archaeologische Mitteilungen aus Iran,* 25 (1992 [1994]):173-175, and "The Provincial Taxation in the Achaemenian Empire and 'Forty Shekels of Silver' (Neh. 5.15)," *Michmanim,* 6 (Haifa 1992):15-25.

Maidman: You are saying that being a *gēr* doesn't refer to a state of real disadvantage. But doesn't the mere contrast of Israelite vs. *gēr* imply disadvantage?

Levine: It does, but the answer to the problem is that the Torah projects a self-sufficient and restricted legal system. It only legislates for the Israelite community, however that polity is defined. If you are dealing with foreign merchants, foreign craftsmen or the like, a special statement is required precisely because the body of Israelite law did not provide for non-Israelites.

In Leviticus we find the lovely statement: "Love your neighbor as yourself," which is to say, your fellow Israelite, for that is what *rēʾā* means, in this context. Read further, and you'll find: "You must love the *gēr* as much as he," namely, as much as a fellow Israelite.

Certainly the *gēr* is disadvantaged relative to the native, but the priestly recasting of the patriarchal stories makes the point that, when the shoe is on the other foot, the *gēr* has some right. Abraham flashes his Green Card when he refers to himself as a resident *gēr.* He is saying that initially, he has the right to make contracts, and to negotiate for purchase of land. Of course, the natives can refuse him. But they don't, and treat him as a *nāśîʾ,* a "headman."

Maidman: In response to the question which closed your presentation, you have correctly emphasized the importance of *Sitz-im-Leben* throughout; the function and time of authorship and its implication for historical evaluation. It behooves all of us, no matter what documents we use, to recognize and practice that same sensitivity.

Buccellati: Along these lines you did bring out a connection with the earlier periods with the *tebibtu.* Another pertinent and interesting parallel is the *liṣemîtût,* which corresponds to the notion of what is called in the Khana texts a *naṣbu* field, and in the Babylonian texts as a field which is defined as *malā libbi mašû,* which I would understand as being at the full discretionary power of the owner (as different from the *ekil muškēnim,* which I would consider as a homestead that cannot be alienated). There presumably were fields which could be alienated, and which did not matter for the religious law. Those would have been *lisemîtût,* and would have been "irretrievably handed over," and the equivalent then in the Old Babylonian then would have been either *naṣbu* or *malā libbi mašû.*

Lamberg-Karlovsky: You are deriving an understanding of land tenure from Biblical scholarship, and in the course of the talk you were indicating that it may be based on an Achaemenid situation. This in turn may be based on things like the Avesta, Zoroastrian sacred literature. My understanding of the Avesta is that the charge being made by the priest is to redistribute the land. Is there any scholarship comparing the aspects of Zoroastrian literature and the Avesta with Biblical scholarship?

Levine: Morton Smith in the new *Cambridge History of Judaism* made some comparisons with Deutero-Isaiah along these lines. It is all very embryonic as far as I understand it, but he does touch vaguely on it. There always was a school of Biblical scholarship that pointed to early Persian literature, but nobody has spelled it out the way you have suggested.

NOTES

1. See R. Whittaker, *A Concordance of Ugaritic Literature* (Cambridge, Mass.: Harvard University Press), 1972:445f. s.v. *nol, nolt.*

2. CAD (*The Assyrian Dictionary*), University of Chicago, S, 93ff, s.v. *samatu.*

3. See Stolper 1985, and Dandamayev 1983, 1987, 1988, for only a few of his recent studies. The *Jahrbuch für Wirtschaftsgeschichte* for 1987, entitled *Das Grundeigentum in Mesopotamien* (Berlin: Akademie Verlag, 1988) contains important studies by J. N. Postgate, M. Dandamayev and Joachim Oelsner on subjects related to the present discussion.

BIBLIOGRAPHY

Amusin, J. D. (1979), *Šakîr: On the Problem of Hired Labour in the Ancient Near East* (Peredneaziatski Sbornik, III (Moscow):4-14 (in Russian, English summary).

Ben-Barak, Z. (1978-9) "The Confiscation of Land in Israel and the Ancient Near East," (Hebrew) *SHNATON - An Annual for Biblical and Ancient Near Eastern Studies* (Jerusalem: Israel Bible Society), Volumes V-VI, 101-117.

— (1981), "Meribaal and the System of Land Grants in Ancient Israel," *Biblica* 62:73-91.

Bloch-Smith, E. (1992), *Judahite Burial Practices and Beliefs about the Dead* (JSOT/ASOR Monograph Series 7), Sheffield: JSOT Press.

Dandamayev, M. (1983), "Aliens and the Community in Babylonia," Rural Communities, Second Part, Antiquity (*Receuils Jean Bodin*, IV), (Paris: Dessain et Tolra):133-145.

— (1987), "Free Hired Labor in Babylonia During the Sixth through Fourth Centuries B.C.E.," *Labor in the Ancient Near East*, ed. M.A.Powell, (New Haven: American Oriental Society: AOS Series 68):221-27

— (1988), "Wages and Prices in Babylonia in the 6th and 5th Centuries B.C.E.," *Altorientalische Forschungen* 15:53-58.

de Geus, C. J. (1983), "Agrarian Communities in Biblical Times: 12th to 10th Centuries B.C.E.," *Rural Communities, Second Part, Antiquity = Receuils Jean Bodin*, IV, (Paris: Dessain et Tolra):207-237.

Edzard, D. O. (1964), "Mari und Aramäer," *Zeitschrift für Assyriologie* 56:142-149.

Kupper, J. R. (1950), "Le Recensement dans les Lettres de Mari," *Studia Marianat*, (Paris):99-110.

Levine, B. A. (1983), "Late Language in the Priestly Source: Some Literary and Historical Observations," *Proceedings of the Eighth World Congress of Jewish Studies*, Panel Sessions: Bible Studies and Hebrew Language (Jerusalem: World Union of Jewish Studies):69-82.

— (1989), *Leviticus*, JPS Torah Commentary (Philadelphia: Jewish Publication Society):171, 172, 270-274.

— (1993), "'The Lord your God Accept You'(2 Samuel 24:23): The Altar Erected by David on the Threshing Floor of Araunah," *Eretz-Israel*, 24 (Avraham Malamat Volume):Jerusalem:122-129.

Levine,B. A., and J. M. de Tarragon (1993), "The King Proclaims the Day: Ugaritic Rites for the Vintage (KIV 1.41/1.87)," *Revue Biblique, Centieme Annee*, Tome C:76-115.

Speiser, E. A. (1958), "Census and Expiation in Mari and Israel," *Bulletin of the American Schools of Oriental Research* 149:17-25.

Stolper, M. W. (1985), *Entrepreneurs and Empire, The Murašû Archive, The Murašû Firm, and Persian Rule in Babylonia* (Nederlands Historisch-Archaeologisch Instituut Te Istanbul), (Leiden: Nederlands Instituut voor het Nabije Oosten).

Weinberg, J. (1992), *The Citizen-Temple Community* (Sheffield: JSOT Press).

9.

Ager Publicus: Public Property and Private Wealth During the Roman Republic

Richard E. Mitchell
University of Illinois

The romantic past

The origin of private property in archaic Italy is shrouded in the mist created by the guesswork of our sources about the early development of Rome. Penetration of that mist is further complicated by the debate among modern historical and legal scholars. One school of thought piously defends their orthodox position that private property developed only gradually from what had been communal ownership of land, and that private ownership was once limited to movable goods. A schism exists between this school and those who maintain that private ownership of land always existed, however limited in scope and however defined by law or custom.

Although we all know that history is the one topic where we cannot begin at the beginning, let us nevertheless make an attempt. "Before Jove," said Virgil in his romantic *Georgics*, "no farmer tamed the fields, nor was it proper (*fas*) to mark off or partition the land with boundary stones. The farmers sought everything in common, and the earth itself produced everything without anyone asking"(*Geor.*1.121-129; *cf.* Cicero, *de off.* 1.21).[1] Virgil did not stop with this fanciful depiction. In the *Aeneid*, when Aeneas and Turnus are about to fight, Turnus hesitates, saying he is not afraid of Aeneas but of Jupiter, who has not shown him much favor of late. Turnus nevertheless looked around for a weapon or for something to hurl, and sees a large ancient stone used to mark off the fields in order to avoid disputes about ownership (*Aen.* 12.897).[2]

Of course, for all we know the stone may have marked off the communal lands of one clan (*gens*) from the territory of another, but we should not demand too much precision from the poet. Besides, there is a strong er tradition crediting King Numa Pompilius, good religious king that he was, with establishing the primitive rule that forbade the removal of boundary stones (*termeni*). Dionysius of Halicarnassus did not know if Numa's laws had been written down or existed merely as custom, but he stated that the king's purpose was to inspire frugality and moderation, by encouraging individuals not to covet more than they had. Consequently, the king decreed that stones be placed on the boundaries, that these stones be consecrated to Jupiter Terminalis, and that anyone who removed them was *sacra* and could be killed with impunity. It is stated that Numa also created boundaries between Rome and neighboring territory and between Roman private and public lands. Dionysius (2.74.2f.) lamented the decline in the religious importance of the stones in his day and said currently some people recognized no boundaries, there was no check on greed or on the desire to possess everything.[3]

I am aware that removal of boundary stones was a heinous crime also in classical Greece and the ancient Near East.[4] My point is not to stress the commonplace nature of such rules, but to highlight the fact that the existence of communal property was placed nearly in a Garden of Eden context while boundary stones and private property make their first appearance in the earliest period of Rome's legendary and romanticized prehistory.

Without giving much thought to consistency, traditional accounts also insisted that private property started with Romulus. He built Rome by *vi et armis* (Livy 1.19.1; *cf.* 1.21.1). Citizens alone fought and they alone worked the land they conquered.[5] Furthermore, the tradition told how. Romulus gave out to each Roman only a modest parcel of conquered land consisting of two *iugera* as an *heredium*. Emilio Gabba (1991: 172) points out that this is an "egalitarian division of land . . . totally neglected" in the historical tradition because of "the insoluble problem of having to explain the subsequent change."[6]

Moreover, as early as Romulus's reign variations in wealth were assumed, because the king also had selected the first *patres*, the ancestors of the patricians, as his senatorial advisers. Senators were called *patres* because they were the most prominent and wealthy men in the city. The poor — that is, the plebeians — were assigned as clients to wealthy patrician patrons. Some sources also believed that land originally was distributed to *patres* alone, and that they in turn parceled it out to plebeians, thereby making them clients and thus treating the poor like children.[7]

Another pervasive tradition asserted that noble aristocrats migrating to Rome during the course of the monarchy received large parcels of land for themselves, and smaller parcels for their followers. Plutarch mentioned that those who accompanied Appius Claudius each received two *iugera* from the state, while Appius was given twenty-five *iugera* and Senate membership.[8] Implicit in these tales is the equation of followers with clients, and their identification as those who received lands from those who were, or who became, *patres*/senators.[9]

Dionysius insisted that some landless plebeians who became citizens too late to receive land or booty from Romulus complained, and Numa gave them small plots from Romulus's own property and from public land. This made the peaceful arts of agriculture equal in importance to the military arts taught by Romulus.[10] Moreover, Romulus had militarily extended Roman territory, and was unwilling to recognize boundaries. As noted above, it was Numa who created boundaries to guarantee peace and promote justice.[11]

The royal estates of Romulus were the first — presumably public — lands distributed among the poor. Some parcels apparently were reserved as sacred, cult, or temple lands. Still other tracts once used by Numa were subsequently given *viritim*, individually, to the poor by Rome's third king, Tullius Hostilius.[12] The fourth king of Rome, Ancus Marcius, also divided conquered territory among the citizens, and made the coastal forest public property (Cicero *de rep.* 2.18.33).

King Servius Tullius, in turn, declared that public lands acquired by the military success of the poor should not be monopolized by the wealthiest citizens. Instead, *ager publicus* was to be divided into lots and given to propertiless debtors so that they, as freemen, could cultivate their own lands and not have to work the lands of others as slaves. A list of debtors was compiled and tables set up in forum, from which creditors were paid. An edict was issued demanding that those currently enjoying the use of public lands should give up possession, and that citizens without allotments of land should make their names known. The public lands were then divided among those who had previously worked for others.[13]

However, Gabba (1991:178f.) suggests, "the distribution of public land to the more needy citizens is, in any event, a preliminary step in the timocratic system created by the king." He goes on to point out that when King Servius introduced the census classes and the centuriate system he thereby "stabilized social and economic inequality" and thus "rationalized the social system that had been introduced by Romulus." Livy (1.42.2-43.1) said that Servius's introduction of the census was most beneficial to the state because now the obligations, both in war and peace, were not fixed on all individual citizens equally but were based on the amount of wealth each possessed. On this basis the classes and centuries were drawn up.

Over the course of two centuries, in a very inconsistent tradition, our sources have portrayed Roman development going from a legendary period of communal property to parity in private property among citizens under Romulus, culminating in Servius Tullius's recognition of different classes of citizens based upon wealth, which presumably was calculated in terms of land.[14]

Of course, none of the aforementioned can be regarded as reliable information about Rome during the regal period. As is well known, the complaints voiced about indebtedness and the cries for land redistribution in this period have their origin in the socio-economic crises of the later Roman Republic. However, our sources made several assumptions about the past that must be highlighted. They assumed that all citizens originally possessed a minimum amount of land, and also that discrepancies in landed wealth existed as early as human history. Finally, it was assumed that rich and powerful citizens received the lion's share of the lands and wealth resulting from Rome's military success. In many instances these assumptions are at variance with the idealized depiction of the simple and modest life of the earliest Romans. This idea owed its existence to late Republican and early Imperial authors who contrasted the greed and moral bankruptcy of their own day with the society of the founding fathers. Yet these assumptions do not appear implausible when examined in light of what is known about more reliable periods of late Republican history.

Two-iugera heredium *estates*

It is more credible to believe that the countless stories about the small size of earlier holdings are designed to evoke an uncorrupted and simple past, but some scholars find in such stories an echo of the modest size farms they believed were normal before the late Republic. Whatever we make of the stories about the seven-*iugera* estates of L. Quinctius Cincinnatus, M. Curius Dentatus and C. Fabricius Luscinus, we would be wise to remember that a farm of that size assigned to M. Atilius Regulus, consul in 257 BC, was in the hands of a *vilicus*, or steward, probably a slave, and that a hired hand ran off with the livestock. It is also important to note the difference between a seven-*iugera* farm near Rome in the time before *ager Romanus* extended very far, and a farm of a similar size in a later period. As William Harris (1979:66, 264f.) points out a modest size farm was not necessarily the only property owned. This was particularly true for aristocrats as the Republic wore on.[15] Romulus granted only two *iugera* as a *heredium* to each citizen. This naturally made them modest and virtuous, but according to Pliny the Elder (*NH* 19.4.50), *heredium* was the word used only for gardens at the time of Twelve Table laws, traditionally dated to 450 BC.[16] Consequently, some authorities insist that the two-*iugera* garden was the only private land, and hence the only land that could be inherited (White 1970:336; *cf.* Mommsen 1952:23ff.). Inasmuch as two *iugera* were insufficient to meet the needs of an individual, let alone a family, it followed that access to common lands was needed by one and all. This fits with another theory, that cultivation of land on a larger scale than a household garden came about only gradually, as tilling replaced animal husbandry and as common lands used for grazing gave way to the plow. As proof for this hypothesis, the legal confusion between *familia* and *pecunia* is frequently cited.

Familia *and* Pecunia

We find in the so-called Twelve Table laws the earliest reliable traces of private property, but both *familia* and *pecunia* are employed to describe it. That is where the debate begins, because both words suggest that inheritable private property was originally limited to movables. Although the two terms are used interchangeably in the laws, it is widely believed that the words originally had different meanings. Festus said *familia* derived from *famuli*, from the Oscan *famel*, the word for slave (Festus 76-7L: *s.v. familia*: from *famuli* and the latter *origo ab Oscis dependit, apud quos servus famel nominabatur, unde et familia vocata*). Since *famuli* denoted only persons, it was argued that *familia* originally did not include house or land, but only those under the control (*potestas*) of a single male (*paterfamilias*). Moreover, since *familia* encompassed all members of the household including slaves, the latter were not originally considered chattel but were more like helots and hence on the order of servants, clients, or even dependent neighbors.[17]

Obviously, the origin of *familia* lies in the darkest days of Roman prehistory, in the distant past when free and slave were not very distinct in status. The distinction began to emerge later, as Roman conquests extended beyond Italy. Individuals captured in war were not from Italian peoples, and hence were less easily incorporated into the Roman population. Before these conquests began in the 3rd century BC, both free and slave were within the *familia*. This is documented by the ease with which

Romans extended freedom to slaves and made them citizens with particular close ties to their ex-master, now patron. The Romans even
permitted slaves to be included in the private family burial plot.[18]

The origin of *pecunia*, money or wealth, is not controversial. It derives from *pecus*, a herd of domesticated animals, because — we are told
— domesticated animals were the first form of wealth. Consequently,
fines were once levied in animals, and early coins had animal types.[19]

There also was a popular explanation for the origin of the peninsula's
name. It came from a magnificent bull named "Italos," brought by Her-
cules. Since the peninsula was rich in cattle it was appropriately called
Italia. As in the case of *familia*, *pecunia* likewise initially must have consisted of movables, and did not include houses or land (Varro, Festus,
Gellius, Livy etc.; *Cf.* Jolowicz 1972:137f. for discussion).

Since both *familia* and *pecunia* were subject to the laws of inheritance and family control, but neither seems to cover land, some scholars
have concluded that manpower and cattle were once the core of private
property. Land was unimportant, because tillage was limited. Therefore,
the argument continues, originally private property was limited to movable goods. Land was held in common, not inherited, except perhaps for
the *heredium*. In addition to arguing that *familia* was originally distinct
from *pecunia* because the former consists of humans and the latter of
animals, it further is that *familia* should be identified with *res mancipi*,
and *pecunia* with *res nec mancipi*.

Res mancipi *and* res nec mancipi

Mancipatio was a kind of sale particularly appropriate to objects which,
in the distant past, were considered fundamentally important to an agricultural society: slaves, large draft animals, family members, and rustic
praedial servitudes. Only eventually, it is believed, did *mancipatio* become
applicable to land. These objects could only be conveyed, bought, sold,
or freed from authority or ownership by *mancipatio*, a procedure that
involved a considerable amount of publicity and ritual activity: five witnesses, scales held by another person, and a piece of bronze used
symbolically to mark the exchange and conclude the conveyance or change
in status. *Res nec mancipi*, on the other hand, were items that could be
transferred by simple delivery (*traditio*). Theodor Mommsen (1952:22ff.)
emphasized that *mancipatio* once applied only to movable property, because the object had to be grasped or taken by hand — *mancipatio*, from
manus capere — and thus applied to persons and animals, not land.[20]

Furthermore, it was argued that the distinction accorded *res mancipi* shows that originally a *paterfamilias* was not completely free to dispose of such property if he had *sui heredes* — that is automatic heirs. *Pecunia*, on the other hand, is sometimes considered more in the nature of personal property, and thus presumably could be freely alienated from the heirs. However, it is neither possible to limit legacies to *pecunia* and *res nec mancipi,* nor to consider all animals as *res nec mancipi.* Large domesticated animals, for instance, were *res mancipi* because of their obvious agricultural importance. The original meaning of *pecunia*, a flock, does not suggest anything about animals other than their probable domestication.[21]

To add to our confusion, there is general agreement that *familia* and *pecunia* are both used in the Twelve Tables to refer to private property generally — including land — and do not refer exclusively to slaves and animals. There is, moreover, specific proof in the laws that land was included among *res mancipi.* Many laws in the Tables govern the use and obligations of land ownership. One law mandates a two-year period for the usucapion of land, in contrast with a single year for movables (Table VII contains most of the land law; *cf.* Jolowicz 1972:137-140, and Kaser 1968:7.1 and 18.1).

There is no reliable evidence from the Twelve Tables that land was ever owned in common. True, one law dictates that if a person dies intestate, his automatic heirs (that is sons or *suos heredes*) inherit. If no son exists, then the nearest agnate kinsmen inherits; if there is no agnate, the *gentiles* take the *familia.* However, the rights of agnates were not an innovation of the Tables designed to place agnates ahead of clansmen (*gentiles*). Agnates were, by extension, simply a natural interpretation and expansion of *sui heredes,* just as *gentiles* were the final heirs, thanks to their common *nomen.*[22] Consequently, it is not possible to argue that *gentiles* originally inherited after sons and before agnates because property initially belonged to the clan in common, not to private families. The *gentiles* in question must have been those in agnatic succession.

The demographic evidence, so-called, for the Roman world suggests that a large percentage of fathers could not count on having a living son inherit the property. Those who did inherit were most likely to do so before they reached legal adulthood. To my mind, intestate succession must have been common, particularly below the aristocratic class. Guardianship of minors also must have been common throughout Roman society. It was essential to have pools of potential heirs available who would take control of the property and also assume the responsibility mandated by the state (and incumbent upon the owner). Among the original *gentiles* were the dependent and related companions on whom the military obligation ultimately devolved, and also the witnesses before whom soldiers made unwritten wills (*in procinctu*) in order to fix inheritance and responsibility, at a time before writing became common.[23] In the late 3rd century, when military obligations ultimately were placed on members of the thirty-five tribes, wills *in procinctu* disappeared. But their disappearance had nothing to do with that of communal property rights.[24] Only the nostalgia expressed for a simpler and nobler time controverts these facts. We cannot accept the argument that by the time of the Twelve Tables, private land ownership had become so central that the original role of common property was obfuscated (as Diosdi 1970 assumes). There is no evidence of communal property in early Rome for the simple reason it was never a feature of Roman society. There certainly is no vestige of it in Roman law.

There is a more compelling explanation for the confusing use of several interchangeable words to encompass all forms of private property, without resorting to conjectures about the romantic period of communal ownership of land. The key to our understanding lies in the Twelve Table laws themselves. Scholars once commonly doubted the existence of the Twelve Table codification, but in doing so they denied the survival of any rules from the 5th century. This was too extreme. Faith in the existence of authentic legal evidence that can be dated to the 5th century is stronger than ever, but none of the details concerning the Code's creation (nor any of the hypotheses about its subsequent preservation) inspires much confidence. For example, even scholars who believe that a 5th-century Code existed cannot accept the circumstances of its creation or explain the anomaly of publication. There certainly were collections of legal materials, but the next — that is the first — codification of Roman law was not undertaken until the end of the 3rd century AD. Moreover, Romans were not accustomed to publishing all public documents — even laws — and did not even routinely consult existing records, much less organize them in collections.[25]

There is a good reason why no historical record of the Twelve Tables exists in any form, and why no ancient author presents a detailed description or analysis of the Code. Neither the content of the Tables nor the historical process of publication was known to them. Neither Livy nor any major historical source dealt with the Twelve Tables in detail, and there is no agreement even on the specific title or name of the Code. There is no reliable record of a legal code known as the Twelve Tables being publicly displayed in Rome on bronze or wood.[26] No standard text of the law ever existed. Before 200 BC, Romans were not concerned with the historical value or usefulness of earlier materials. Consequently, materials were not routinely preserved as part of a record of chronological development.

By the time Romans began to reconstruct their past, the "evidence" they had was neither chronologically nor historically reliable, and in any event it was extremely limited in quantity (Crook 1994). Even the historical narrative recorded that the Twelve Tables were destroyed when the Gauls sacked the city in 390 BC. Of course, we are told that the laws were soon after reconstructed and republished from memory, although some material was now kept secret by the *pontifex maximus*.[27] Finally, as the story continued to unfold, it was only in the late 4th century that the legal secrets of the pontiffs were published for the first time — the material included the civil law, the *legis actiones*, the *fasti* and the calendar.[28]

Of course, much of the aforementioned presumably had been published by the decemvirs. But the Romans turned even reliable evidence from the earlier period into evidence for the struggle between patricians and plebeians, without worrying about inconsistencies and contradictions. Moreover, only a few of the laws are placed by our sources in any particular table. Even the organization of the laws into tables is a modern creation, by and large. This organization owes more to modern assumptions about archaic Roman legal practices and the growth of secularization than to anything found in the sources (see Rawson 1991:339 n. 52).[29]

As a matter of fact, our sources knew that later laws obscured, updated, replaced or destroyed earlier measures and often were erroneously considered part of the original codification (Macrobius, *Sat.* 3.17.7-8). Most scholars have lost sight of the fact that one provision of the Twelve Tables permitted additions and changes in the original laws: whatever was passed last was binding (Riccobono, *FIRA* I, 73; Livy 7.17.12). Consequently, much of the extant material attributed to the Twelve Tables cannot possibly emanate from the 5th century. Individual measures were merely the only and/or the last known legal pronouncements preserved, and thereby erroneously assigned to the "fountainhead of all private and public law" (Livy 3.34.6: *fons omnis publici pirvateque est iuris*).[30]

Doubtless some extant laws, procedures, and other materials preserved evidence from the 5th century, but earlier laws and procedures were simply not recorded. Over the decades, laws were actively applied and changed by interpretation. This was easier than one might suppose, because extant materials were in the private collections, not part of the "public" record preserved in archives. In fact, collections of laws included private interpretations and opinions, and grew organically through several redactions as generations of aristocratic legal experts added to the body of material. This is why the modernized wording found in Cicero does not square with "archaic" features of laws from other sources. The praetor's edict was nothing more than this type of legal redaction. Presumably, several editions of (and commentaries on) such collections existed, and it was unquestionably difficult to distinguish law from commentary or interpretation, since the Romans showed so much respect for aristocratic status and legal experts were aristocrats. For instance, Cicero indicated that if one studied the peculiar areas examined by Aelius — probably Sextus Aelius, the 2nd century author of the *tripartita* — it was possible to find a complete picture of the "good old days" in the *ius civile*, *pontificum libri*, and in *duodecim tabulis*. Cicero believed his little volume on the Twelve Tables (*duodecim tabularum libellus*) surpassed all other books in importance, but he certainly exaggerated its contents.[31] His legal training was primarily under the supervision of the legal experts of his day, the aristocratic priests, Mucius Scaevola the pontiff and Mucius Scaevola the augur (Mitchell 1979:1-92 presents the early years). It is not fully appreciated how much the documentary record of Roman legal development known to Cicero was the private creation and property of the aristocrats with whom he was working.[32]

In sum, there is little reason to believe that an authentic code known as the Twelve Tables ever existed other than in the form of individualized copies of laws, procedures, and interpretations meant to serve as instructions for parties, mainly students, interested in Roman legal development. Sextus Aelius's *tripartita* consisted of laws, their interpretations, and the appropriate formula (*legis actio*). The *tripartita* remained the standard antiquarian legal text at least until the time of Pomponius, but few Romans appear to have been personally familiar with its material.[33] The *tripartita* was little more than the most respected private collection of standard legal information, a college outline of Roman law with the most widespread name recognition — surprisingly, a work more referred to than read or cited.[34] The material contained in the various individual copies of collections was inconsistent and at times contradictory. Consequently, the confusion over *familia* and *pecunia* did not exist because the law was codified in the mid-5th century, well after the disappearance of communal property and the eclipse of the clan (*gens*) as the most important social unit. It existed because the various pieces of legal material identified as part of the so-called Twelve Table codification actually date from many periods. They do not derive from a single source, and were not transmitted by a single authority.[35] Nevertheless, understanding the Roman family and *gens* can aid our understanding of the origins and importance of private property in Rome's historical evolution.

Property, the family and the gens

The debate over the origin of private property pales in comparison to the debate over the *gens* or clan in Roman history. Unfortunately, we must enter that controversy, because the origin of the *gens* and the origin of private property are related.

Gens does not always mean the same thing in our sources. Families, kinsmen broadly interpreted, clients, and even ethnic units, tribes or entire populations are sometimes called *gentes*. Modern scholars commonly assume that a group of extended families once lived in the same area, possessed some private property but also worked other lands in common, and that collectively these families constituted a *gens*. It is also assumed that each *gens* was characterized by common religious beliefs and practices, and possessed a common burial ground.[36] All the members of a particular *gens* within the territory were organized on the basis of real or quasi-kinship into bands for mutual benefit, assistance, protection and expansion. Presumably, the natural progression was from this gentilic period of communal activity to the city-state. This took place, by and large, in the classical Mediterranean world in the 8th century.

The rise of the city-state generally resulted in the incorporation of more land, which increasingly was used for agricultural purposes. The rise also coincided with a series of social and political changes which, it is argued, transformed the earlier private gentilic kinship organizations into public urban institutions. The aristocrats who emerged with sufficient private property to support larger families and more clients were able to acquire position, privilege and power in the new state system. In the city-state, private wealth was the hallmark of aristocratic status. It often had its origins in the pre-urban period, but the distinctions often drawn between the two periods are not as stark as some have suggested.[37]

It once was universally accepted that societies evolved from groups based upon birth to those based upon status, or from kinship to territorial principles of social and political organization. This was the accepted view of the change that occurred in the Graeco-Roman world. Urban societies and the public state systems were viewed as extensions of the earlier archaic period of family or clan dominance. It was believed that the archaic aristocracies obtained superiority by their hereditary domination of kinship-based institutions, but lost this advantage once the organization of citizens changed from kinship to territoriality and status. However, it is now clear that these assumptions about the emergence of urban societies no longer can be supported. As E. H. Winter (1966:173) notes: "In its day" the distinction between kinship and status societies based upon the evolution from one to the other "was a useful dichotomy, but that day has passed, even though some . . . appear to be unaware of the fact." Recent studies of pre-urban societies show what Max Weber long ago pointed out: clans, brotherhoods and tribes were characteristic of later urban communities alone and were not found in the "tribal" communities that preceded them. "We are left to believe," observes Moses Finley (1986:91), "the improbability that the evolutionary path proceeded from a kinship basis to a territorial basis, but that in those communities which failed to take the step the subordinate kinship-based units somehow disappeared"(cf. Donlan 1985:293-308. Watson 1975:67-70 discusses Rome before the Twelve Tables).

Individual families, not clans or *gentes,* are the key to understanding the origins of the aristocracy. Kinship, succession and inheritable private wealth were concerns first and foremost of individuals within families, not of groups of families, *e.g.* clans or *gentes.* Not all *gentiles* shared in hereditary claims, for as Antony Andrewes (1961:137) points out: "Kinship . . . is always a relationship to a particular person. It is not a principle of organization, either in the army or in civil life."

Roman *gentes* consisted of individuals bound by personal ties to a particular chief for economic and, I would offer, military interests. Although all members might share the gentilic nomenclature, it was based on a fictional kinship. Actual kinsmen constituted only one, perhaps small but important, element of the entire group. The first phalanx consisted of bands of men under an aristocratic chief. To the extent that larger numbers of non-aristocratic hoplites were employed, they consisted of clients, retainers, dependents — even slaves, and tenants of the aristocrats, many of whom did not necessarily possess sufficient wealth or independence to arm themselves. They were "recruited" along with kinsmen, neighbors, friends, and even mercenaries (cf. Scullard 1967:238).[38]

I have argued elsewhere that the archaic state lacked the information and ability to recruit and mobilize troops quickly in any quantity. It thus assigned responsibility to prominent individuals with their own private forces who had knowledge of particular regions and populations (Mitchell 1990:49-53). We cannot place too much faith in the stories of how specific individuals and populations were incorporated into the Roman state, but local aristocrats did migrate to Rome, as many Latins later did, following acceptance of the *foedus Cassianum* in 493 BC. This increased the number of senators, just as their warrior clans increased the city's military force. The addition of various Alban clans resulted in several of their leaders becoming senators, and a decimal increase in the Roman infantry and cavalry when the Alban *populus* was incorporated into the state. Earlier, Tarquin Priscus presumably encouraged several *gentes* to migrate to Rome. The Senate and the military were correspondingly enlarged. The Claudii also came to Rome with an extensive *clientela*. The Claudian "entourage" consisted of one or several military clans (*gentiles*), and presumably constituted the *vetus Claudia tribus* (*cf.* Livy 1.30, 35-38, 2.16.4-5; and Dion. Hal. 3.29-31, 48, 67-68; see Ogilvie 1965:147-52, 273-75, and Palmer 1970:140).

Servius Tullius

Most modern scholars believe Servius Tullius restrained these private clan leaders by introducing the centuriate system, thereby checking private kinship-based military units. Theoretically, by introducing the census, he imposed the obligation to arm and fight upon reluctant individual wealthy *assidui*, landowners whose sudden military prominence supposedly contributed to the political decline of the archaic aristocracy. Different ranks of the Roman legion were filled by recruits required to equip themselves with arms and armor commensurate with their census classification. But the original Servian system disappeared long before the appearance of our earliest sources. I want to emphasize that the system attributed to Servius is a product of the 3rd century, when ancient authors began researching Rome's past and as a result assigned an antiquarian version of the contemporary system they knew to Servius Tullius (Mitchell 1990:53-62 has details and bibliography).

The original census was only a review of the *classes* drawn-up for battle. It was not — I repeat, was not — a procedure to determine the relative military responsibility of individuals based on a census of their private wealth, presumably mainly in land. Servius Tullius mobilized the individual hoplite units consisting of the private escorts (*i.e., gentiles*) brought by prominent local leaders summoned to Rome, who were required to provide fixed quotas of manpower (*i.e.,* centuries). These soldiers armed, marching and fighting as hoplites, were not necessarily independent, wealthy, landholding hoplites. Many were part of the personal retinue of prominent individuals. Their presumed private wealth is a modern conjecture that needs revision.[39]

Servius Tullius was the first to require hoplites from prominent local leaders. He thus mobilized the first public military force. Actually, he created the state. His "reform" is described more accurately as the initial incorporation and organization of the *ager*, the Latin countryside, from which local leaders and their entourages came. When he imposed an organization and created a centuriate system for a particular purpose — to unite the private and regional forces in a common public effort (*cf.* Snodgrass 1991:18f.) — there was no older hereditary aristocratic system based on communal property for him to replace. When hoplites gathered in formation outside the city, they constituted the *populus* — from *populare* "to lay waste." These soldiers were the first citizens.[40] Individual *populi* first gathered on the Aventine, predecessor of the Campus Martius. Situated outside the *pomerium*, the Aventine was the hill where most of the agitation by plebeian soldiers for reform took place from 494 to 449 BC protesting against serving in the military and bearing the greatest hardship and burden for Rome's territorial expansion. It thus became the stage on which soldiers expanded the meaning of citizenship. The Aventine was where plebeian soldiers registered their complaints about not sharing in the rewards of territorial expansion (Livy 2.28.1, 32.2-3; 3.32.7, 50-2). But we are getting a little ahead of our story.

By institutionalizing the status of the various local leaders as aristocrats, Servius legitimized their existing control (dare it be called ownership at this time?) of land and other resources in their respective districts. It is clear that urbanization occurred simultaneously with the introduction of public institutions and the emergence of Rome's aristocracy.[41] Consequently, we ought to assume that the change was not from communal to private owership of land but from the private property claims of local strongmen (reinforced simply by their bands of followers) to the public recognition of those claims. Rights of ownership that once grew out of the point of a sword now could be voiced in a public forum.

This conclusion is reinforced by the archaeological record of Rome under the kings, a record that becomes more voluminous and unambiguous daily. In the course of the 6th century BC, both the city of Rome specifically, and Latium generally, were greatly enriched.[42] Presumably, smaller regional communities disappeared as independent entities, as they and their populations were incorporated into larger centers. There is no reason to believe that drastic changes occurred in either the use or ownership of incorporated lands,[43] but ownership became increasingly a question of the "public" record and less the product of force. This public record was Roman in origin.

The rich private tombs of the "princes" also disappeared during the 6th century, the period of Servius Tullius's reign, and the hoplite armor so characteristic of these graves was no longer entombed, although we know that it continued to be employed by the military forces at the time. (Thomsen 1980:33-36 summarizes the debate over the urbanization of Rome.) Mark Toher (1986:325) observes that "It is probably not simple coincidence that at the same time that the burials in Latium become less elaborate, public sanctuaries appeared in the region." In other words, nothing much changed except public institutions replacing private practices. It follows that just as the state now employed the "princes," making use of their armor as well. Although family members may have been buried together, bones and ashes do not tell us whether they belonged to aristocrats or dependents. There is no evidence that the tombs belonged to clans instead of families, or that the *gens* heretofore had maintained its dominance through inheritance (as argued by Cornell:1979-1980:80 and 1986:66). The armor remained in fashion, but it was so important and costly that public policy prohibited its burial. Even when buried in the earlier period, it does not tell us whether it was the private property — *familia* or *pecunia* — of the deceased or of aristocrats or dependents.[44]

It is not easy to date the transition from the system Servius imposed on local strongmen to the one that imposed obligations upon individuals. Changes in the system certainly occurred during the course of several centuries, most dramatically in the 3rd century. It cannot be denied that 6th-century Rome was large and prosperous, but soon after 500 BC the city fell on hard times. It has been estimated that the *ager romanus* under the first kings consisted of approximately 150 square kilometers, and that soon after the Republic began, it had grown to more than 900 square kilometers. Such estimates are far too generous. They are based on the assumption that Rome controlled much of territory associated with seventeen rural tribes.[45]

I do not want to debate here the question of the Servian origin of Rome's archaic rural tribes (or the four urban tribes, for that matter). I simply want to point out that there was not much territory under Roman control before the conquest of Veii in 396 BC, and most of what there was was contested. Rome was constantly at war in the 5th century, and even when it was victorious the gains were modest. In fact, "much of the recorded warlike activity of this period involved mysterious bands of warriors who accompanied individual leaders as clients or 'companions,' and functioned as private armies" (Momigliano 1988:7.2, 97f.; *cf.* 292). Obviously, Servius Tullius's organization of private aristocratic forces broke down in the aftermath of the collapse of Etruscan rule at Rome.

Rome controlled only the left (south) bank of the Tiber before Veii fell. Judging from the references to constant conflict over the same territory within 15 or 20 kilometers of the city, Rome was not even completely dominant in its own backyard. The Roman aristocracy must have been increasingly hard pressed to protect what it had and to satisfy its desire for more land. Warfare was always the aristocracy's primary endeavor and the most profitable (Harris 1979, esp. 54-67).

In any conflict, the main "objective was always the acquisition of booty"(Cornell 1988:293), and this of course included land and slaves. Momigliano (1988:99) observes that during the 5th century the "existence of private land ownership and instability of the upper classes must have been connected," because "the band chiefs and their followers gained or lost land held as private property." Aristocratic warfare meant that property was constantly changing hands. This property included land, persons and animals (*familia et pecunia*). In other words, during the 5th century the pressure for centralized control was nearly matched by the independent behavior of aristocrats supported by their private armies. However, the fact that the land changed hands apparently did not disrupt production over the long term.

In contrast with this picture, it is claimed that the *foedus Cassianum* of 493 BC shows Roman dominance over members of the Latin League. However, Servius may have successfully organized the Latins, for they were still on king Tarquin's side against Rome at the battle of Lake Regillus (496 BC). Regardless, after the treaty Latins and Romans were equal partners in a military alliance. Inasmuch as the league's primary purpose was military, each of the original signatories must have agreed to supply their own fixed quota of manpower, according to what eventually was known as the *formula togatorum* (Brunt 1971:57f., 545-48). Latins and Romans were to share command as well as all booty. The latter included land on which Latin, not Roman colonies were established. Moreover, in a kind of *isopolitia*, Romans and Latins shared private and public rights (*iura*), including *commercium, conubium* and *ius migrandi* (Livy 2.33.4,9; and Dion. Hal. 6.95.1-3; *cf.* Ogilvie 1965:280-85, 316-17, and Sherwin-White 1973:11-37).

Disputes were dealt with in the city of their origin. This doubtless gave impetus to the development of general rules governing land, property, inheritance and, perhaps, obligations. The development of Roman property rights thus cannot be disentangled from the complex problem surrounding Latin rights just as the growth of the Roman aristocracy and Republican institutions cannot be separated from the assimilation of Latin peoples and territories. Nevertheless, it is tempting to date the Twelve Table provision about selling a citizen enslaved for debt across the Tiber to the 5th century, for at that time the other side was foreign territory.[46]

The situation started to change in the late 5th century with a series of Roman successes that culminated in Rome's defeat of Veii. Both sides of the Tiber started to fall under Roman control, which also extended farther north, west, and south. Doubtless it must have been the destruction of Veii that brought the Romans into contact with the Gauls at the Allia River. On the other hand, Veii may have been so concerned with the Gauls that the threat from Rome was underestimated. After defeating Veii, Rome created four rural tribal districts from the territory taken from the Etruscan city and other lands which previously had been contested. The increase in *ager romanus* began a veritable explosion in the amount of territory that came under Roman control over the course of the next century. Between 358 and 299 BC, in what has been described as a "drive to acquire land" (Harris 1979:60, *cf.* 264), Rome created eight more rural tribes, established dozens of colonies, and added thousands of acres to the *ager romanus*, most of which must have been *ager publicus*.[47] On the eve of the First Punic War it is estimated that Roman territory consisted of 26,850 square kilometers, with a population of 900,000 (Cornell 1988: 7.2, 367, 382, 403 with references).

Perhaps as much as a third of the added land resulted from colonial foundations and direct Roman possession, with a similar amount of *ager publicus* having been sold off or rented. Neither practice, of course, prevented wealthy Romans from taking direct advantage of Roman conquests to obtain greater land holdings (*cf.* Harris 1979:60f.).

It also has been noted that during this same period (366-291 BC) of rapid incorporation of territory into the *ager romanus* "a handful of talented and charismatic individuals" dominated the political scene. Conclusive evidence is lacking, but it is tempting to attribute their importance to their ability to profit from the socio-economic changes that accrued from the territorial expansion — an expansion they not only helped engineer, but which they took advantage of, by obtaining political influence in the new tribal districts.[48] However, the Roman aristocracy always consisted of a narrow group of families. Virtually all of the most important families, or groups of families (*gentes*) came into existence before the war with Pyrrhus (283-272 BC) (Mitchell 1974:32-4).

The influence of these families had grown with Rome's systematic 4th century territorial expansion. They took full advantage of that territorial growth to institutionalize their own political standing in Rome's governmental tribal system. By the 3rd century, Roman aristocrats had successfully established their wealth by occupying countless tracts of land, including *ager publicus*, in various tribal districts.[49] The pattern of occupation is much like what we find later, when our information is better. Aristocrats had several estates, of various kinds, in many districts.

We can only guess that the occupation pattern matched the pattern of Roman conquests, for it is a well-established fact that aristocrats who conquered particular towns, peoples, or regions became their patrons, as did Roman officials sent out to parcel out the lands to settlers or colonists. In other words, those with direct contact with the peoples and places that Rome defeated and enslaved were frequently the ones who benefited the most from the seizure of lands subsequently turned into *ager publicus*. Over time, their descendants benefited from the hereditary support of clients who emerged from the ashes of the defeated.

The pages of our narrative sources also are filled with the constant complaints of those who did not benefit from Roman expansion. For instance, there is the portrait of the small farmer called upon to help extend Roman rule and increase Roman territory, who loses his farm because of his absence or because of enemy raids. He fell into debt, was imprisoned or enslaved, and threatened with execution or sale *trans Tiberim*. The poor — nearly always identified as urban, plebeian, and as soldiers or veterans — cried out for debt relief and land redistribution. The land in question was *ager publicus*, public land, taken as a direct result of Roman conquests. These cries were heard from the day the city was founded. So were complaints that rich, creditor, patrician commanders oppressed the poor and took the fruits of Rome's military success, including the *ager publicus*, for themselves. They contrived to still the complaints of the poor by constantly waging war, thereby keeping those demanding reform occupied outside the city (see Mitchell 1995:199-214).

Debt relief and demands for land are said to have been behind the first plebeian *secessio* (494 BC), a military strike that resulted in the election of the first plebeian tribunes.[50] For more than a century afterwards, tribunes unsuccessfully introduced plebiscites to reduce debt and redistribute the land. Finally, in 367 BC, the Licinian-Sextian laws prohibited occupation of more than 500 *iugera* of *ager publicus* by an individual, and provided that the interest already paid on a loan should be subtracted from the principal (Livy 6.34, 39). Debt remained a problem, but agrarian proposal disappeared from our narrative until the end of the next century, and the problem of redistribution is not an issue until well into the 2nd century.

Clearly, the various reports of agrarian reform attempted between the proposal of Spurius Cassius and that of Licinius and Sextius owe more to the 1st-century crisis than to reliable complaints made by poor soldiers in the 5th century. Poor soldiers may have remonstrated about being cheated out of booty (land), but land could not have been much of an issue before the fall of Veii, unless it was a question of small parcels taken in conquest and not given to soldiers. Furthermore, the fall of Veii had more to do with the Licinian-Sextian law than did plebeian demands for land redistribution. After the defeat of her chief rival, Rome had a great deal of *ager publicus*. Placing a limit of 500 *iugera* on the occupation by individuals is more in the nature of a simple statutory limitation than it is an attempt to curb the greed of the patricians — or Latins for that matter, since they shared in the land according to the terms of the *foedus Cassianum*.

Colonies are the reason we do not hear demands for land redistribution in the 4th century. From the fall of Veii to the First Punic War (396-264 BC), except for the setback caused by the Gauls, Roman conquest of the peninsula was rapid and remarkably successful. Success was punctuated by the foundation of nearly two dozen Latin colonies. The evidence suggests that veterans were rewarded with lands in these colonies as their share of the booty, although complaints about not receiving their share continued (see Mitchell 1995:205f., 211 n.10).

I want to draw a distinction between allotments made to veterans from conquered territory and the demands for reform and redistribution of *ager publicus* made by the urban poor in the 2nd century. Earlier land grants to soldiers were routine, but after the conquest of Veii, demands for land made by soldiers stopped. This suggests that earlier demands were fabricated on the basis of the 2nd-century conditions (*cf.* Brunt 1971:639-644).

Let us return briefly to the question of the two-*iugera* grants, or *heredium*. Land allotments to colonists are occasionally said to have been two *iugera*. Complaints were voiced about these two-*iugera* grants when aristocrats received 500 (Livy 6.36.11; 4.47.7; 8.21.11). Land for colonization or settlement came from conquered territory. The process can best be understood from evidence from a more historically reliable period. On the eve of the 2nd Macedonian War, Livy reported that *ager publicus* consisting of confiscated land in Samnium and Apulia was assigned to Scipio

Africanus's African veterans. Each man was to receive two *iugera* for each year he served in Spain and Africa. There is no reason to believe that this was an unusual allotment, or that it was the first time the state awarded land to veterans (as Briscoe 1973:62 claims). From the beginning, demands for land were voiced by soldiers, which I take to mean that from the outset land was the primary reward given to the successful soldiers.[51] Moreover, when Livy mentioned that *Castrum Frentinum* (near Thurium) was settled, the colonists consisted of 3,000 infantry and 300 equestrian veterans. This was a legion, if we subtract the 1,200 to 1,800 supernumerary troops recruited from the poor. Infantry and cavalry were to receive thirty and sixty *iugera* respectively, although that figure was lowered to twenty and forty in order to reserve some land for other colonists, perhaps for the aforementioned supernumerary soldiers.[52] A colony at Vibo similarly consisted of 3,700 foot and 300 equestrians colonists who received fifteen and thirty *iugera* respectively (Livy 35.9.7-8 193 BC; 35.40.6 192 BC). Other examples exist, but we do not know how long these troops served. The grants may have been calculated on the formula of two *iugera* for every year of service, except for the poor. They obtained only two *iugera* and then only as an afterthought (Livy 40.34.2-3; 41.13.4-5).

In this regard there is a distinct group of colonies that merit attention: the *coloniae maritimae*, or maritime colonies. All were established along the Italian coast between 334 and 241 BC. The usual explanation for their creation is that they were garrisons guarding against marauders. The colonists were unique for this period: They remained Roman citizens, yet the evidence suggests neither the colonies nor the colonists were held in high repute. Apparently each settlement consisted of 300 colonists. Each colonist received two *iugera* of land, and was exempt from military service, for each was already on garrison duty it is argued (Salmon 1969:70ff., 81, 97 is standard; Sherwin-White 1973:77; see Livy 8.21.11: Anxur in 327 BC).

I want to suggest another explanation for the status of these colonists. They were 300 low-born Romans, recruited as rowers and sailors to man a single ship stationed in the new coastal colony. Such ships served as part of an early warning system, or played a communication role. Sailors were of low status, but these colonists remained Roman citizens because they were active over a wide area and often might have to seek a safe harbor where their Roman status would protect them. Their naval service would explain their low status despite Roman citizenship, and also their exemption from the army. The two-*iugera* allotment, on the other hand, established their continuing obligation to serve.[53]

It is important to note that colonists might well avail themselves of other lands, including unoccupied *ager publicus*. However, occupation of additional public lands did not matter in terms of the obligation to serve militarily. When each colonists received his two *iugera,* this in itself established that responsibility. Also, it must be stressed that maritime colonists were not veterans. They were recruited from the urban poor. As such, they were forerunners of those who demanded land redistribution in the 2nd century.[54]

I cannot develop the argument fully here, but my point is that two *iugera* was the amount of land that a foot soldier received as booty for each year of successful military service. It also was the minimum amount of land necessary to establish the military obligation for each colonist. This was the *heredium,* and it has nothing to do with the limited amount of private property (garden) recognized during the period of communal ownership of lands. It is possible that the two-*iugera* grants go back to the distant past when campaigns were seasonal and annual, and to the time when all acquisitions lay within a short distance of Rome. The *heredium* obligated those who received it (and those who inherited it) to serve. In fact, a colony was a military outpost. Although farmers (*coloni*) were sent out, they went out with all the pomp and circumstance of a military force and there can be little doubt about their future obligation to serve (Salmon 1969:24f.).[55] The timocratic classification of the so-called Servian system was part of a political reform that meant little in terms of military responsibility. A minimum classification was all that was necessary to establish the obligation.

It cannot even be argued that the *proletarii* were below the minimum census required for military service, for no reliable census data existed until the end of the 3rd century at the earliest (Brunt 1971:33). Moreover, in the Pyrrhic War *proletarii* were armed by the state, perhaps for the first time. It was not the first time they served (Skutsch 1986:338; see Mitchell 1995:206f.).[56] In an emergency, Rome even conscripted slaves, accepted slave volunteers in the army, and required the wealthy to contribute both slaves and their maintenance (Livy 22.57; 24.11).[57]

Early Roman law drew a distinction between citizens who were *assidui* and those who were *proletarii* (Gellius, 16.10.5). Another military distinction was drawn between the *classes* and the *infra classem* (Festus, 100L: s.v. *infra classem*). In my view, the *proletarii* were once *infra classem*. This did not mean they were outside the military, but that they were below the three ranks (*classes*) of the legion. The *infra classem* numbered between 1,200 and 1,800 per legion. They are the veterans of Scipio's army not mentioned as recipients of colonial allotments. Perhaps they received smaller parcels as a result of reducing those allotted to other veterans, or maybe they obtained lands elsewhere later. Or, perhaps, they were left to swell the ranks of the urban poor. Land was given veterans who possessed a slightly grander status, but not because only farmers of modest wealth fought for Rome. More work must be done on the military obligation of the lower classes in order to fully appreciate the pieces of "evidence" we have about the military obligations of the poor.[58] When colonization stopped in 173 BC it contributed greatly to the changes taking place in the cities and countryside — changes that ultimately resulted in the Roman Revolution (Brunt 1988:70, 74 for the end of colonization).

Everything we know about the rewards for military success shows that aristocratic commanders, their companions and higher military personnel obtained a disproportionate percentage of all forms of booty (*cf.* Gelzer 1969:21f., Brunt 1971 *passim*, and Cornell 1988:7.2, 1989:125f., 312f., 331-34, esp. 389). The evidence also clearly indicates that in the 2nd century BC many individuals possessed large tracts of *ager publicus* in excess of the legal limit. These large estates were increasingly given over to specialized agriculture production and grazing, and their labor force increasingly consisted of chattel slaves. Little or no tax was paid for the use of the *ager publicus,* because records were poorly kept. Consequently, the land tended to be treated as private property, and gradually merged with other parcels purchased in the area or occupied after being abandoned by tenants who were unable to make a go of it — or who were forced out — and consequently moved to the city (see Livy 42.1.6).

It is equally clear that before the 2nd century there was no dearth of *ager publicus* available for settlement and no surplus of individuals demanding the right to occupy it.[59] Thus, excessive and illegal occupation was ignored. Individuals made use of as much *ager publicus* as "patrimonial resources would permit," and in this respect aristocratic occupants had superior resources (Cornell 1988:7.2, 326). They used their extensive clientele and slave labor to occupy more and more land (Appian *BC* 1.7-9). By the 2nd century, slaves increasingly came from outside Italy, but for several centuries before they came from Italy.

In other words, very early in Rome's territorial expansion slaves came from ethnically similar peoples. This explains the ease with which they were manumitted and identified as part of the *familia.* Slaves, of course, were part of the booty shared by soldiers and here again commanders obtained the largest number. These slaves worked the confiscated lands — sometimes lands that had been their own. Even after manumission they remained legally tied to their owner/patron. Frequently they worked lands held from the patron under precarious tenure, whereby occupation was protected from action by a third party, but not from the owner (Brunt 1988:410f.).

Finally — a word that every audience eagerly awaits — a few observations about debt-bondage, or *nexum*. The status is not unknown in other parts of the ancient world. Their plight is often interpreted as the direct result of inalienability of land. Hence, land's original communal nature meant that an individual pledged himself or members of his family as security. The problem for the Roman legal historian has been to understand how an individual who fell into debt came subsequently to be "enslaved" for still more indebtedness. Individuals were condemned for debt throughout Roman history, but a strong tradition pointed to the legal prohibition of *nexum* in the late 4th century BC. Most often, *nexum* is seen as a labor contract whereby the rich acquired the labor of the poor. It was this voluntary debt bondage that was outlawed in the 4th century. However, defaulting debtors continued to exist, and were still subject to prosecution and bondage. It is suggested that Rome's territorial expansion, particularly during the Second Samnite War (327-304 BC), resulted in so many slaves that poor Roman debt bondsmen no longer were needed, and the practice was outlawed.

What has been forgotten in this solution is that the debtors are always characterized as soldiers or veterans. They sometimes are called upon to serve despite their indebtedness. I have argued at greater length elsewhere that *nexi* were ransomed soldiers who worked off their indebtedness (see Mitchell 1995:209ff. with notes and references). It appears that the redeemer's loan was worked off over a period of five years. The soldier then regained his freedom, and perhaps even obtained Roman citizenship. Perhaps we therefore should identify the mysterious class of *nexi* with the thousands of *captivi* taken from the Italian peoples before the end of the 4th century. Many of them must have been forced to work for a period of time because they could not pay their ransom. These slaves (*famuli*) were frequently manumitted, and many must have swollen the ranks of the plebeian poor.

As a parting observation, intended to be more provocative than anything else, I want to point out that one method of manumission was by *censu*, which occurred every five years (Gaius *Inst.* 1.17, 44,138-40). New citizens were enrolled in the territorial tribes of their patrons, thereby increasing their patron's influence within the tribe. They subsequently were enlisted as part of the military unit supplied by the tribal district.

Finally, after a successful military campaign, they were rewarded with a parcel of land in a different tribal district. This added still more to their patron's political clout, at the same time the ex-slave's or captive's family entered into the Roman political system, by the very same means their ancestors had lost their independence. What goes around comes around.

DISCUSSION

Heltzer: In July 1993, some of the participants at the Society of Biblical Literature meeting at Münster insisted that there was no "house of David" in Judah. Then the Tel Dan inscription was found, where the "house (dynasty) of David" is mentioned, and A. Lemaire discovered mention of the "House of David" in the Mesha inscription. Can it not be that one day we will find the Twelve Tables, or is it really as impossible as you say? We know of such things as the city law of Gortyn on Crete, and we can go see the inscription if we go there. So this is news to me that the Twelve Tables didn't exist.

Mitchell: It's new to a great many scholars. But there isn't a chance that the Twelve Tables will be found, because they never existed in the form of a public monument. Our only reference is to an obscure document found in Carthage in the 4th century AD which might be associated with the Twelve Tables. If reliable, it is certainly a fabrication designed to win favor.

I think the telling fact is Cicero's own reference to his little book, and also the fact that various parts of the Twelve Table laws are mutually exclusive. If you have a single document that everybody is using, you expect some kind of agreement as to what it says. If we all have to learn the Declaration of Independence by heart, we are not going to have different versions of it. But if there are different family traditions, and different private traditions are being handed down, these will tend to differ. Once they start to be incorporated into the official canon, you are going to have conflicts between *familia, pecunia* and many others as well. The ancient authors were as involved in scholarship in the same way we are. There are layers and layers and layers of interpretation that must be considered — or removed — before we can hope to discover "original" details.

Edzard: You say that because the *ager publicus* records were poorly kept, the land tended to be treated as private property. This I thought extremely interesting, because that never comes to our mind, we are so impressed by the neatness and efficiency of cuneiform record-keeping bureaucracies. Paul Koschaker once said that the Babylonians were not just bureaucrats, but "*bureaucratissimi.*" Of course, in periods of upheaval, natural catastrophies or other irregular turbulence it would have been natural for some archives to get lost. And some things just get forgotten in these situations.

RICHARD E. MITCHELL   277

Mitchell: Regarding the problem with the Gracchi, Tiberius creates a commission to adjudicate disputes concerning the *ager publicus*. One of the complaints about the commission is that its three-man committee would have too much power over, and would receive too much credit for, resolving all the controversy surrounding the occupation of *ager publicus*.

The reason why a three-man commission with judicial power was needed was that there were so many disputes about what was and what was not private property. Records were poorly kept. The state did not need (and had not been collecting) the rents and taxes on the public lands. In 167 BC the state even relieved all citizens of the burden of paying the war tax or *tributum*. Until late in the 2nd century it was just too profitable to go out and beat up people. The Roman government did not need to collect taxes from its own citizens, and did not see the necessity to maintain the records of occupied *ager publicus*. By 133 BC, times and conditions had changed.

Buccellati: Richard has already preempted the opportunity of saying thank you, but there is never an end to how often and how well we can say thank you. Besides we couldn't let a mere Roman outdo an ancient Mesopotamian. We shall have the last word to thank you for all the organizing, proposing the topic and being such a marvelous host.

I thought along the lines of the talk and of the Mesopotamian background, we started out as individual, private scribes, and we have aimed to achieve a collegiality as the children of a scribal house, trying to achieve some sort of common ideas, not so much because we all have to share them, but because we try to gain from each other. You have led us on this path very well. I am very grateful for that aspect, and I am looking forward to continuing with the work of publication. So, thank you very much personally, Baruch and Michael, and to the institutions you represent.

Hudson: Thank you, Giorgio. I have been called upon to say a word on behalf of our sponsors, and to reassure them of the relevance of what we have said for the timelessness of rent and land-tenure issues throughout history. What would Henry George have said if he had sat through this whole conference? There are two things I want to say. First, land tenure, its rent and fiscal yield form the most important economic phenomena of ancient societies, which is why we have been concentrating on land above all other areas of privatization. Second, the dynamic that George found to be the most disturbing in his century was monopolization of the land. If anything that dynamic grew even stronger throughout the course of antiquity, culminating in Rome.

What I haven't learned from this conference (we'll have to have another one, I can see) is whether this monopolization occurred because the ancient safeguards against privatization broke down. Is it because there was less and less tradition of clean slates, or were they ineffective from the beginning? Is it because armies depended more and more on mercenaries rather than their own free peasantry, and thus no longer needed to protect them?

Progress indeed led to poverty in antiquity. It was in response to this poverty that the Biblical legislation was framed, wrapped in the stories that became the foundation myths for this core body of Biblical law. Biblical stories such as Naboth and his vineyard had a lasting relevance for the privatizations found in much more naked form in European feudal history.

In the middle of the sixteenth century, in 1552, Bernard Gilpin preached a sermon before Edward V describing how

> the rich people are able to find six or seven counselors to use subtleties and sophisms to cloak the evil of taking their land. Poor men are being expropriated from their land by the enclosures. The rich have such quick-smelling hounds, they can lie in London, and turn men out of their farms and tenements, an hundred, sometimes two hundred miles off. When wicked Ahab hunted after Naboth's vineyard, he could not, though he were a King, obtain that prey until cursed Jezebel took the matter in hand, so hard a thing it was then to wring a poor man from his father's inheritance, which now a mean man will take in hand.

Now *that's* privatization, to a degree not reached in the periods we have been discussing here. This colloquium stopped, appropriately, with classical Rome, for it was Roman law that protected the debt polarization leading to the monopolization of land, causing unprecedented poverty. It hardened to such an extent that the Romans did something no earlier civilization had done: They banned usury, debt bondage and, ultimately, slavery in general.

You can look at our subsequent civilization as being shaped by the way in which the Roman economy fell apart from the crises caused by this privatization and monopolization of the land. It was the legacy of Roman civil law that overshadowed Judaic law in shaping the emerging Christianity. The upshot was the final outcome of the long dynamic of privatization that we have been discussing for the last two days.

I want to thank you all for going into new areas and putting so much effort into your contributions.

RICHARD E. MITCHELL

NOTES

1. Virgil *Geor.* 1.121-129: I give only a rough translation of *nec quidem erat fas signare aut partiri campum limite. Querrebant in medium, que tellus ipsa ferebat omnia, liberius nullo poscente. Cf.* Cicero *de off.* 1. 21, who believed individuals eventually held their own share of what had been common.

2. Virgil *Aen.*12.897: *ingens saxum, antiquum saxum, ingens, quod forte iacebat campo, positus limes argro, ut discerneret litem arvis.*

3. Gabba 1991:170-177 is especially important for the early part of the paper.

4. Gaius, *Dig.* 10.1.3 (on Solon and the Twelve Tables); Deut. 19.14; 27.17; Ruth 4.3-8; Numbers 26.7; Kings 21.3.

5. Livy 1.19.1, 21.1. Gabba 1991:171 points to the the Aristotelian parallel of citizen/farmer/soldier (*Pol.* 1329a3-18).

6. *Cf.* Mommsen 1952:23-25 n.1. Note Pliny *NH* 18.2.7: *bina tunc iugera populo Romano satis erant, nulloque maiorem modum adtribuit; cf.* Varro RR 23.n.3, 25 n.1; Gabba, *Dionysius* 172 is quoted.

7. *Cf.* Festus 289L: *patres senatores ideo appellati sunt, quia agrorum partes adtribuerant tenuioribus ac si liberis propriis.* Livy 1.9-10. Gabba, *Dionysius* 171f. Brunt, *(Fall* 410f.), in a particularly valuable discussion, notes that Paul's version confirms Festus: *patres* were considered both senators and fathers, because they "had assigned parts of their lands to humbler persons as to their children." Brunt objects to the equation of those who obtained land grants in this fashion with clients, for the practice would certainly never be confined to them. However, it must be admitted that those in such a relationship might well take on some of the most recognizable features of the client/patron relationship. It must also be noted how unlikely a father of any stripe was to be succeeded by his own biological son. On which, see Saller 1994.

8. Plut. *Publ.* 21.6. On the migration of Attius Clausus (Appius Claudius) also see Livy 2.16.3-4; Dion. Hal. 5.40.5; but the dating of the migration is not consistently given. *Cf.* Ogilvie 1965:273f.

9. *Cf.* Brunt 1988:410.

10. Dion. Hal. 2.62.3-4; according to Cicero (*de rep.* 2 (14). 26) lands conquered by Romulus were distributed *viritim* by Numa, who thereby displayed how it was possible to live *sine depopulatione atque praeda.*

11. Plut. *Numa* 16 contrasted Romulus's unwillingness to fix boundaries to his military conquests. *Cf.* Festus 505L; and Ogilvie 1965:211, who says it was necessary to protect the early idea of private property, the antiquity of which Ogilvie avers is established by the ancient cippus c. 500 BC

(CIL 1.2.1) found near the Lapis Niger with an opening clause: *quoi hoi... sakros essed* and restored to give the meaning of the Numa law — a very doubtful interpretation.

12. Dion. Hal. 3.1.4-5.

13. Dion. Hal. 4.8-13, has the most complete, but needless to say, the most suspect account. Cicero, *de rep.* 2.21 (37-38) and Livy 1.41-48 supply other details incorporated into this summary. Galba 1991:172-189 is an excellent survey of the regal tradition. All translations, unless noted, are from the Loeb editions.

14. Monetary classifications are given and presumed to have existed even as early Servius, but this is impossible even if we accept the king's reforms as historical. In general, see Mitchell 1969:41-71, 1973:89-110 and 1985: 314-17 with bibliography.

15. For additional discussion of these "Tales about the modest means of the old aristocrats," see White 1970:345-48. See Broughton 1951: I, 207f. n.1, for the existence of a fabricated story that depicted Regulus being called from the plow like Cincinnatus.

16. *Cf.* Festus 89L: *heredium praedium parvalum.* Also called *ager* in Cic. *re pub.* 2.14.26.

17. Isidorus *Diff.* 1.525; *inter servum et famulum, servi sunt bello capti, famuli autem ex propriis familiis orti.*

18. ILS 8283; *Dig* 50.16.195. 1-5 (*cf.* 21.1.25.2). Material is conveniently collected in Wiedemann 1981:3, 54. It is impossible to quantify the practice of intermarriage between Romans and freed slaves but it was not an uncommon occurrence even among those in the higher classes. (See Andrew Wallace-Hadrell's review of Saller 1994, in *Times Literary Supplement,* April 14, 1995:12.)

19. Thomsen 1957:20-3, collects the ancient testimony and has depictions of the animal coin types.

20. Possibly a provision permitted a clump of earth from the land in question to be carried into the court, hence land too could be grasped at least symbolically (*cf.* Gaius *Inst.*4.17). Jolowicz (1972:138), thinks this "an impossible, or at least an undignified gesture."

21. The Romans of course made a distinction between ownership and responsibility over and for domesticated and wild animals.

22. See Crook 1994, and most recently Saller 1994:163.

23. Harris 1989 *passim,* establishes that writing was never very common and the literacy rate was never high. On the commonplace nature of wills see the conflicting views of Crook 1973:38-44, and Daube 1965:253-62.

24. See Gellius 15.27.3, on *procinctus*; *cf.* 1.11.3; Cicero, *De nat. deor.* 2.3.9; Gaius, *Inst.* 2.101; and Plutarch, *Cor.* 9. *Cf.* Mommsen 1952: III, 307f.; Watson 1975:66, esp. n.38; the will was a military version of the testament before the *comitia calata.* Florentinus (*Dig.* 29.1.24) gives evidence for the soldier's will, done even without writing with oral declarations alone.

25. I do not believe in the laws of the kings, but Republican plebiscites were certainly known and preserved after a fashion, as were *senatus consulta.* From the mid-Republic on, of course, there were magisterial decisions, praetor's edicts, and even juristic interpretations. However, one of the reasons for codification in the Empire was that the legal record — history — was such a mess for those who deal with the archival records and public documents, or the lack of them. *Cf.* Culham 1989:100-15 and Williamson 1987:159-183.

26. Greenidge 1905:13: "we have no evidence for their exhibition either in Rome or in any other place until a chance reference in Cyprian reveals the surprising fact of their presence in the Forum at Carthage in the third century AD." *Cf.* St. Cyprian, *Epist* 2.4; *Ad Donat.* 10; and Salvianus, *De Gub. Dei* 8.5. Jolowicz 1972:108, says such references amount to "no more than rhetorical flourish." Schulz 1967:61: "no jurist troubled to establish a correct version of even the Twelve Tables." For samples of the problem surrounding publication, see Livy 3.34.2-6, 37.4, 51.3, and 57.10. Ogilvie 1965:507; and Ungern-Sternberg 1986:81, offer solutions.

27. Scholars do not seem to be bothered by the contradiction that some of what had presumably once been public was the private secret keep by the pontiffs after the sack.

28. Livy 3.9. Codification dominates Livy Book 3 (see esp. 3.33-57). *Cf.* Cicero, de rep. 2.37 (63); and Dion. Hal. 10.60.5. Watson 1975:20, 177-86; Rotondi 1922:201f.; and Riccobono 1968: I. 23-25, are excellent summaries. Cicero, *Pro Murena* 11.25, even is confused about the floruit of Cn. Flavius and the predominance and nature of his publication. He thought pontiffs created legis actiones to ensure their monopoly of the law after Flavius published their secrets. Pais 1913-20: I.1, 558-604, I.2, 546-72, offers a strong argument for compilation around 300 BC.

29. Rawson says "There is little evidence for the organization of the Twelve Tables." Nineteenth-century scholars have probably introduced too much Greek logic into the arrangement we have in *e.g.* Riccobono 1968:1.21ff.

30. Among others, Jolowicz (1972:109) does not note that Livy's reference is to the first ten tables only as the *fons.*

31. Cicero, *de orat.* 1.43.193: the civil law, *pontificum libris, et in duodecim tabulis, antiquitatis effigies, quod et verborum prisca vetustas cognoscitur . . .*;

1.44.195: *usus mihi videtur duodecim tablularum libellus ; totam hanc, descriptis omnibus civitatis utilitatibus ac partibus.*

32. *Cf. Dion. Hal.* 1.74.5, where the censorial records are also said to have been preserved by families and the information passed from father to son.

33. Cicero, *de orat.* 1.56. 240, referred to the material in Sext. Aelii *commnetariis scriptum protulisse.* See Pomponius, Dig. 1.2.2.4. An excellent bibliography and provocative discussion of the *tripartita* and other legal materials and legal experts are found in Bauman 1983:129-48. *Cf.* Watson 1974:112-20, 135f.

34. *Cf.* Cicero, *de inven* 2.50.148, with other versions cited by Riccobono 1968, I, 37-40. Cicero's comment on the study of *ius civile* is appropriate: *neque ita multis litteris aut voluminibus magnis continentur: eadem enim sunt elata primum a pluribus; deinde, paucis verbis commutatis, etiam ab eisdem scriptoribus, scripta sunt saepius (de orat.* 1.43.193-94). Watson 1974:122, briefly discusses modernizing. Daube (1956) contributes important observations on archaic linguistic aspects of the law.

35. I borrowed shamelessly from my own work (1990:122-132, 169-176, 229-233), for this section on the Twelve Tables.

36. Numa Denis Fustel du Coulange, *The Ancient City* (Baltimore, The Johns Hopkins University Press, 1980), is of course the "classic" attempt to show the parallel development of private property emerging from the communal sacred burial plot.

37. Morris 1987:57ff., *passim*, for example, convincingly questions the standard dramatic interpretations that frequently accompany descriptions of the transformation to urban communities based primarily on analysis of burials.

38. Cristofani (1979) argues that the traditional dual nomenclature (praenomen, nomen) had its origins in the late 7th century, but the gentilic was not solely determined by blood.

39. Scholars persist in asserting that the military force consisted of those "citizens" who were prosperous enough to arm themselves, hence the assumption they were all landowners. Cornell (1995) and Snodgrass (1991:18-20), present the unproven thesis for the Roman and Greek worlds respectively. Thus Census records were part of the private records of individual families and were transmitted, originally, from father to son: *cf.* Dion. Hal. 1.74.5.

40. They were the early Latin peoples around Rome, who Sherwin-White (1973:8) says "were originally organized in small village communities, each a tiny *populus*, grouped together in religious leagues, each of which had its own cult-centre." Temples, cults, sanctuaries, and shrines were

focal points for bringing together the rapidly expanding population, they were centers of economic, political, and judicial organization and administration which enabled the developing city-state to recruit manpower for its own defense and expansion. See Livy 2.44.8; 4.23.5, 25.7, 61.2; 5.1.5, 17.6, 33.9; 6.2.2; *cf.* Ogilvie 1965:353, 571 and 705.

41. See the many articles in Cornell and Lomus 1995, where this fact stands out.

42. Cornell (1986:66). *Cf.* 1979-1980:71-89; 1988:7.2. *passim*, with the extensive bibliography.

43. As was the case when Romans took over vast tracts of Tuscan territory following the defeat of Veii. No disruption of agricultural settlement, apparently, occurred (Ward-Perkins, Kahane, and Murray-Threpland 1968:132-79; and Potter 1991:197-99.

44. Comparable medieval evidence is cited by Mitchell 1989:37, 45-48. See Pritchett 1985:7-44, who successfully defends the view that Greek military tactics changed very little from Homer to the historical period and that they display similarities with much earlier Near Eastern tactics.

45. Beloch (1926:620) has figures. Beloch's often repeated estimate of the size of Roman territory at the end of the 5th century is moved back to the beginning of the century by associating it with the generally accepted, without good reason, creation of Clustuminian and the Claudian tribes in 495 BC. Consequently, we have the unlikely existence of twenty-one territorial tribes entirely too early in the city's development. See Cornell 1988:7.2, 254 fig. 43; *cf.* 281. Note the criticism by Badian (1962:201) of Taylor's 1960 work whose reconstruction Cornell generally follows.

46. The problem is, of course, that later in the Republic captives were also sold across the Tiber which suggest a possible connection between debtors and captives. (Livy 8.20, etc on Velitri and Privernium). *Cf.* Cicero *de off* 1.12.37; *cf.* Sherwin-White 1973:6f, 48.

47. My view is that Rome created the four urban tribes late in the 4th century and after the creation of two rural tribes in 299 only two more were added in 241 BC, after which a complete "reform" of the system was mandated; or should we say that the system known to the Romans was at that time introduced?

48. *Cf.* Cornell 1988:7.2, 347 is quoted: In 72 years, between 366 and 291, there were 14 men who held 54 coss., 38 by only 8, each of whom was cos. 4 times or more. They included the patricians: C. Sulpicius Peticus, L. Papirius Cursor, M. Valerius Corvus, Q. Fabius Maximus Rullianus; and the plebeians M. Popillius Laenas, C. Marcius Rutilus, Q. Publilius Philo, and P. Decius Mus. Ruled with associates, by virtue of power held,

positions obtained, tenure dep. on popular appeal, electoral success. Thus, this system had substantial democratic element that was absent from later period when senate control govt. and the outcome of elections had little effect on general direction of policy. Patterson 1990:150-2, presents several later examples of aristocrats who benefited their regions and doubtless obtained the commensurate political rewards.

49. This runs somewhat counter to the usual interpretation offered by L. R. Taylor (1960:35-45), who identifies individual gentes with particular tribes because of an unproven assumption that their prominence depended upon their importance in specific incorporated tribal districts. My assumption is that the territorial tribal units were a later creation and that from the beginning many gentes had members in several tribes and that was the basis of their political strength.

50. For discussion of the military origins of plebeian tribunes see Mitchell (1990:139-50).

51. I combine Livy 31.4.1-2 with 31.49.5 because Spanish veterans also served in Africa (see Livy 32.1.6, lands for veterans from Spain, Sicily, Sardinia). *Cf.* Briscoe (1973:62f.).

52. If 36,000 *iugera* were saved by reducing alotments to *pedites* and *equites*, then two *iugera* could be allotted each one of the 1,800 supernumerary soldiers. Thus the legion would number 5,000, a figure often encountered.

53. For example, in 207 BC the Antiates complained they were exempt from military service as maritime colonists and should not be asked to serve as regular soldiers (*Cf.* Livy 27.38; 36.3).

54. Elsewhere, in a longer essay, I will spell out the difference between *ager publicus* and *privatus* as distinct parts of the *ager Romanus*. Also, a distinction will be drawn between occupation and possession.

55. Colonists must have been bound by oath to follow their leader and in this were very like soldiers under oath to follow their commander. I see a possible connection between the *ver sacrum* (*cf.* Livy 22.10.1; 33.44.1; 34.44.3), the "primitive pattern of initiation by which young men who had reached a certain age were segregated from the rest of the tribe and sent away to fend for themselves by raiding and pillaging" (Cornell 1988:294), and the later practice of sending out colonists. Both groups were meant to remain within the orbit of the metropolis and to supply assistance whenever called upon.

56. Livy 8.20.3-5 (329 BC) mentioned a military levy without a single exemption, which included the least qualified for military service. We are also told that nexi were recruited: *cf.* Mitchell 1995:209f.

57. There are many instances of earlier use of slaves and servile attendants for military purposes, but the last word has not been said on the topic. However, Rouland 1977:25-75 is a convenient collection.

58. How can one overlook the romantic story of Spurius Ligustinus, a veteran of 22 campaigns, who still lives in the house on the one iugera estate left to him by his father. Furthermore, Spurius has four sons currently in service and two more to follow. Our sources did not find it inconsistent to believe that such a humble family could produce so many soldiers. None of whom, we must assume, could afford their armor. See Livy 42.34.

59. The question of Latin or Italian occupation of public land cannot be dealt with here. In general, see the discussion in Bernstein 1978; esp. chapters 3-5.

BIBLIOGRAPHY

Andrewes, A. (1961), "Phratres in Homer," *Hermes* 89:129-40.

Badian, E. (1962), *JRS* 52:200-210.

Bauman, R. A. (1983), *Lawyers in Roman Republican Politics. MBPAR* 75 (Munich).

Berstein, A. (1978), *Tiberius Sempronius Gracchus. Tradition and Apostasy* (Ithaca and London: Cornell University Press).

Briscoe, John (1973), *A Commentary on Livy: Books XXXI-XXXIII* (Oxford: Clarendon Press).

Broughton, T. R. S. (1951), *The Magistrates of the Roman Republic*, I-II (New York: American Philological Association).

Brunt, P. A. (1962), "The Army and the Land in the Roman Revolution," *JRS* 52:69-86.

— (1965), "Italian Aims at the Time of the Social War," *JRS* 55:90-109.

— (1971), *Italian Manpower 225 B.C.-A.D. 14* (Oxford: Oxford University Press).

— (1988), *The Fall of the Roman Republic* (Oxford: Oxford University Press).

Cornell, T. J. (1980), "Rome and Latium Vetus, 1974-1979," *Archaeological Reports, 1979-1980*:71-89.

— (1986), "The value of the literary tradition in archaic Rome." In *Social Struggles in Archaic Rome* (Berkeley: University of California Press):52-76.

— (1988), "Rome and Latium to 390 B.C."; "The recovery of Rome"; "The conquest of Italy." In the *Cambridge Ancient History*, Vol. VII. Part 2 (1989), eds. F. W. Walbank, A.E. Astin, M. W. Frederiksen, R. M. Ogilvie (Cambridge: Cambridge University Press):243-419.

Crawford, M. H. (1976), "The early Roman economy," *Melanges J. Heurgon, Collection de l'Ecole Francaise de Rome 27*, I, Rome, 197-207.

Cristofani, M. (1979), *The Etruscans: A New Investigation* (London).

Crook, J.A. (1967), *Law and Life of Rome* (Ithaca and London: Cornell University Press).

Culham, P. (1989), "Archives and alternatives in Republican Rome." *CP* 84:100-115.

Daube, D. (1956), *Forms of Roman Legislation* (Oxford: Oxford University Press).

Diosdi, Gyorgy (1970), *Ownership in Ancient and Preclassical Roman Law* (Budapest: Akademiai Kiado).

Finley, M. (1982), in *Economy and Society Ancient Greece*, eds. B. D. Shaw and R.P. Saller (New York: The Viking Press):150-166.

Gabba, E. (1991), *Dionysius and The History of Archaic Rome* (Berkeley: University of California Press).

Garland, Y. (1988), *Slavery in Ancient Greece*, trs. Janet Lloyd (Ithaca and London: Cornell University Press).

Gelzer, M. (1969), *The Roman Nobility*, trs. Robin Seager (Oxford: Blackwell,1979).

Harris, W. V. (1979), *War and Imperialism in the Roman Republic 327-70 B.C.* (Oxford: Oxford University Press).

Jhering, Rudolph von (1891), *Geist des romischen Rechts auf den verschiendenen Stufen seiner Entwicklung*, 3 vols. 5th ed. (Leipzig).

Levy, E. (1943), "Captivus redemptus," *Classical Philology* 39:159-76.

Mitchell, R.E. (1969), "The 4th century origin of Roman didrachms," *Museum Notes* 15:41-71.

— (1973), "Hoard evidence and early Roman coinage," *Rivista Italiana di Numismatica* 21:89-110

— (1974), "The Aristocracy of the Roman Republic," in *The Rich, The Wellborn, and the Powerful: Elites and Upper Classes in History*. C. Jaher ed. (Urbana: University of Illinois Press):27-63.

— (1985), "The historical and historiographical prominence of the Pyrrhic War," in *The Craft of the Ancient Historian: Essays in Honor of Chester G. Starr*, eds. John W. Eadie and Josiah Ober (Lanham Md.: University Press of America):303-330.

— (1990), *Patricians and Plebeians. The Origins of the Roman State* (Ithaca and London: Cornell University Press).

— (1995), "Demands for land redistribution and debt reduction in the Roman Replublc." In *Social Justice in the Ancient World*. K. D. Irani and Morris Silver eds. (Westport: Greenwood Press):199-214.

— (1979), *Cicero: the Senior Statesman* (New Haven: Yale University Press).

— (1991), *Cicero: The Ascending Years* (New Haven: Yale University Press).

Momigliano, A. (1963), "An interim report on the origins of Rome," *JRS* 53:93-121.

— (1986), "The rise of the plebs in the Archaic Age of Rome," *In Social Struggles in Archaic Rome*, ed. K. Raaflaub (Berkeley: University of California Press):175-197.

— (1988), "The origins of Rome," *Cambridge Ancient History*, Vol. VII. Part 2 (1989)

Mommsen, Theodor (1875), *The History of Rome*. 4th ed. trs by W. Dickson (New York).

— (1952), *Romisches Staatrecht*, 3 vols in 5. 3rd ed. (Reprint, Basel).

Morris, I. (1987), *Burial in Ancient Society* (Cambridge: Cambridge University Press).

Ogilvie, R.M. (1960), *A Commentary on Livy. Books 1-5* (Oxford: Clarendon Press).

Pais, E. (1913-20), *Storia critica di Roma durante I primi cinque secoli*. 5 vols. (Rome).

Patterson, John R. (1991), "Settlement, city and elite in Samnium and Lycia," *City and Country in the Ancient Word*, eds. John Rich and Andrew Wallace-Hadrill (London):150-2.

Potter, T.W. (1991), "Towns and territories in southern Etruria," in *City and Country in the Ancient World* (London: Routledge):191-209.

Pritchett, M.K. (1985), *The Greek States at War*. Part IV. (Berkeley: University of California Press).

Riccobono, S., *et al.* (1968), *Fontes iuris Romani anteiustiniani*, 3 vols. 2nd ed. (Florence).

Rickman, G. (1980), *The Corn Supply of Ancient Rome* (Oxford: Oxford University Press).

Rotondi, G. (1922), *Leges Publicae populi romani* (Milan).

Rouland, N. (1977), "Les esclaves romains en temps de guerre," *Collection Latomus* 151:1-106.

Saller, Richard P. (1994), *Patriarchy, Property and Death in the Roman Family* (Cambridge: Cambridge University Press).

Salmon, E. T. (1969), *Roman Colonization under the Republic* (Ithaca and London: Cornell University Press).

Schulz, F. (1967), *History of Roman Legal Science* (Oxford: Oxford University Press).

Scullard, H.H. (1967), *The Etruscan Cities and Rome* (Ithaca: Cornell University Press).

Shatzman, I. (1972), "The Roman general's authority over booty," *Historia* 21:177-205.

Shelton, Jo-Ann (1988), *As the Romans Did* (Oxford: Oxford University Press).

Sherwin-White, A.N., *The Roman Citizenship* (Oxford: Oxford University Press).

Skutsch, Otto (1986), *The Annals of Q. Ennius* (Oxford: Clarendon Press).

Thomsen, Rudi (1957-61), *Early Roman Coinage*. 3 vols. (Copenhagen).

— (1980), *King Servius Tullius: A Historical Synthesis* (Copenhagen).

Toher, Mark (1986), "The tenth table and the conflicts of the orders," in *Social Struggles in Archaic Rome*. K. Raaflaub ed. (Berkeley: University of California Press).

Ward-Perkins, J. B., A. Kahane, and L. Murray-Threpland (1968), "The *Ager Veientanus* north and east of Veii," *PBSR* 36.

Watson, A. (1970), *The Law of the Ancient Romans* (Dallas).

— (1972), "Roman private law and the *leges regiae*," *JRS* 62:100-105.

— (1974), *Roman Law Making in the Later Roman Republic* (Oxford, Oxford University Press).

— (1975), *Rome of the XII Tables: Persons and Property* (Princeton: Princeton University Press).

Westbrook, R. (1988), "The Nature and Origins of the Twelve Tables," *Zeitschrift der Savigny-Stiftung für Rechtsgeschichte, Romanistische Abteilung* 105:73-121.

— (1989), "Restrictions on Alienation of Property in Early Roman Law," in *New Perspectives in the Roman Law of Property* ed. Peter Birks (Oxford: Clarendon Press):207-213.

White, K. D. (1970), *Roman Farming* (Ithaca: Cornell University Press).

— (1977), *Country Life in Classical Times* (Ithaca, Cornell University Press).

Williamson, C. (1987), "Monuments of bronze: Roman legal documents on bronze tablets." *CA* 6:159-183.

Winter, E. H. (1966), "Territorial groupings and religion among the Iraqis," *Anthropological Approaches to the Study of Religion*, ed. M. Banton (New York).

Zulueta, F. de (1946-53). *The Institutes of Gaius*, I-II (Oxford: Oxford University Press).

Early Privatization and its Consequences

Michael Hudson

This colloquium has focused on the growing private control of the land, workshops and credit system over the course of antiquity. The discussions have brought out how this shifting balance occurred informally and indeed, often by stealth secured simply by force of arms. An essential characteristic of privatization is thus its surreptitiousness, above all in periods of weakening palace rule and social breakdown, and in peripheral regions that had not developed traditions to keep large-scale commercial and financial self-seeking from unduly polarizing economies. Record-keeping weakens as a check, and royal power itself is overthrown.

Prof. Mitchell accordingly contrasts the unsanctioned *occupation* of Rome's public lands with the more formal, legal *possession* that in time came to legitimize these occupations. But not even Rome developed an ethical or economic rationale for privatization. It is rather seen emerging via "loopholes" in the matrix of traditional sanctions designed to prevent its widespread alienation on more than a temporary basis. Profs. Maidman, Hallo and Heltzer discuss the stratagem of "fictitious adoptions" used in Nuzi and Ugarit to cloak what in essence were debt foreclosures and sales under economic duress.

Over the course of antiquity the trend was to weaken sanctions against the overgrowth of debt, debt bondage and land forfeitures. Private law suits, and Ammisaduqa's elaborate *mišarum* edict, reflect the powerful drives to evade Babylonian Clean Slates, especially as well-placed families operated within Babylonia's temple or palace bureaucracies to obtain the land's crop yield and interest on their own account. Their economic assertiveness represents an almost timeless phenomenon, akin to the drive by Europe's feudal barons seeking to keep the land's rent for themselves, and to "privatize" what hitherto had been royal privilege or traditional communal rights. It is the dynamic that led England's barons to wring the

Magna Carta from King John. Likewise for Nuzi, Prof. Maidman emphasizes that royal *šudutu* edicts seem not to have led to a return of the land from the large land-acquiring families to its former smallholders. By the late Bronze Age, when royal power was unseated in Babylonia and Mycenaean Greece, properties were left in the hands of the local *apparatchiks* in charge.

Noting that the term privatization today connotes a deliberate policy — and indeed, a market-oriented ideology — Prof. Buccellati asks whether it really is appropriate to speak of privatization that occurred by such surreptitious encroachment rather than by countering government control by exposing it as inefficient, wasteful, and often corrupt.

It certainly is true that nobody in antiquity advanced the idea that private property and personal self-seeking would bring about a more efficient social system than communal property or private property managed unselfishly. Just the opposite: The Stoics disparaged private self-seeking. Antiquity produced no Milton Friedman or Margaret Thatcher, nor did an Adam Smith emerge to suggest that an Invisible Hand would guide personal self-seeking to increase the nation's wealth. The policy objective was not efficiency, but "straight order" in Babylonia, social equity for the Biblical prophets, and an appeal to the "constitution of the fathers" (*patrios politeia*) by the Athenian oligarchs and by Cicero's upholding of patrician Roman values. Creditors were not euphemized as savers performing a public service; they were condemned throughout antiquity as usurers preying on the poor. Nobody suggested that debt-ridden economies might work their way out of debt by saving and investing more. In these respects there indeed was no *doctrine* of privatization in antiquity.

The *phenomenon* of privatization did exist, however. Although it represented an *ad hoc* dissolution of centralized royal power, it brought about new types of centralization as economic polarization resulted from the unchecked dynamics of interest-bearing debt and monopolization of the land.

This privatization did not have an economic rationale; indeed, it elicited a growing protest. Babylonia's *mišarum* acts became more elaborate in countering the stratagems of land appropriators trying to evade royal annulment of their debt foreclosures. Wisdom literature from Babylonia down through the Bible's Old and New Testaments to the works of Livy and Plutarch (his *Moralia* as well as his *Parallel Lives*) reflect the moral condemnation of debt and the monopolization of land that were the consequences of antiquity's privatizations.

These widespread protests are what make antiquity's privatizations so striking. By classical antiquity, members of each society's ruling families — the Biblical prophets, Sparta's "Lycurgus" and its kings Agis IV and Cleomenes III, Solon and Plato in Athens, the Gracchi in Rome, and the Hellenistic epoch's Stoic philosophers — perceived privatization to involve the impoverishment of so many families as to threaten economic instability, flight or widespread exodus, or a defection to enemies as was threatened under Zedekiah in Judah and Coriolanus in Rome. The result was seen to be either civil war or a depopulation impairing the ability of communities to field a landed and self-supporting infantry.

In view of these excesses, why was privatization permitted to occur in the way it did, to so extreme a degree? What made its dynamics so inexorable? That is the ultimate question opened up by this conference.

The "mixed" character of most economies, and the symbiosis between public and private

In one sense, this colloquium picks up the story "in the middle," at the point where there already were public assets to privatize, for how can assets be spoken of as being privatized, after all, until they have come into being in a non-private form? Taking the long perspective, Prof. von Dassow accordingly asks what (if anything) went "before" privatization — and indeed, we all may ask, before public institutions as such?

Prof. Lamberg-Karlovsky points out that before temples are found in the archaeological record, large T-shaped complexes were developing, apparently as extended households. These seem to have formed the model from which Sumer's temples evolved.

No doubt he is correct that extended families supplied the basic idea for temple hierarchies headed by a "father" or "shepherd" administrator. A rhetoric of public-spirited impersonality developed, but royal records from Lagash's Ur-Nanshe dynasty through Urukagina and Lugalanda, from Sargonid Akkad to Babylonia, show rulers using their control over the temples to promote their own family interests. In the face of their protestations about being "sons of the city," they developed personal power bases by the time the palaces began to emerge out of the temples c. 2700 BC. But by the same token, these public institutions became something more than family households — something more "cosmopolitan" in the sense of spanning family units.

Above all, they were more formalized. Prof. Dandamayev points out that before price-setting markets developed, public institutions were the major vehicle for distributing output at standardized prices. For these large institutions it was natural for prices to be administered, if only as an internal control to check abuses and as a means of keeping accounts in common denominators such as silver and barley. Common prices, once established in this way, helped catalyze the development of market exchange, and ultimately price-setting markets for goods and services that did *not* pass from the public institutions to the rest of the economy.

Of course, most output was for self-use, and hence either was unpriced or exchanged at prices which, under normal conditions, followed the lead of the large institutions whose transactions tended to dominate the market. However, there was room for prices to vary for goods sold by private households. This occurred most notoriously when barley prices soared in times of famine at the end of the Ur III period (late third millennium). In the end, as more goods were produced by and for private households than by temple or royal households, unregulated market pricing became a major characteristic of privatization.

Karl Polanyi's idea of a "redistributive stage of development" preceding that of market pricing therefore must be superseded by recognition that public distribution took place largely *via* the pricing mechanism. Setting such prices was part of the public administration of measures, weights and interest rates (which were among the last prices to be deregulated, precisely because of the visible role of coercion between strong creditors and dependent debtors falling below the break-even level). Such prices accordingly were announced at the outset of many early royal laws, and appear throughout Hammurapi's laws.

The important point is that prices did not settle at what modern economists would call "equilibrium" in the sense of reflecting costs and normal profit rates. Powerful landowners and creditors are found gouging wherever they could, or simply ignoring public laws.

Land-rent and interest charges that originally accrued mainly to public institutions shifted to private owners, especially in periods of distress conditions. This was particularly the case with land pricing. Strictures against subsistence lands being sold or forfeited at "less than the full price" are familiar throughout Mesopotamia. Prof. Edzard points out that various kinds of *ilkum* subsistence-land allotments could be sold, but under conditions in which royal service obligations remain linked to it — and even so, these alienations were subject to reversal by royal Clean Slates.

What terminology should be used to describe this situation? If public administrators are found mixing personal self-seeking with their public position, how reasonable is it to idealize the "public" as opposed to private? Was the rhetoric of higher civic ideals of carefully measured equity (administrative and more broadly social) merely hypocritical? Prof. Lamberg-Karlovsky warns that it is futile to idealize any one structure as representing a pristine or originally "good" way of doing things, from which subsequent society fell away. What is at work is a dynamic whose symbiotic strands interact differently in every region and epoch.

Because Sumer's temple innovations operated initially in the context of a *rasa tabla* as far as formal economic institutions were concerned, they took root wherever traders conveyed them, starting at least as early as the Uruk expansion in the mid-fourth millennium. My own paper lists among the commercial innovations which I believe originated in the public sphere the practice of charging interest on debts. In time this became a major endogenous lever of privatization, but we first pick up its documentation (and that of large-scale enterprise generally) in public contexts.

Prof. Edzard suggests that this is only to be expected, for it is mainly in the public institutions that tracking and accounting for production inputs and output was a necessary part of the system of accumulating large surpluses and savings that were not one's own. It was part of the system of checks and balances designed to prevent abuses. Pointing out that this public record-keeping constitutes a bias in our sources, Prof. Edzard points out that enterprise and interest-bearing debt may well have flourished in undocumented private contexts. The point cannot be answered empirically, of course. All that can be said is that a hyperdevelopment of public-sector production was centered in southern Mesopotamia.

Examining possessive personal pronouns applied to alienable objects, Prof. Edzard notes that *responsibility* for goods, such as is signified by sealing by public officials, may indicate subordination as well as ownership. This idea of responsibility attached to ownership suggests something conditional, accountable and fiduciary about archaic ownership.

If privatization is nearly synonymous with "ownership," it turns on the right to freely alienate the assets owned. In this sense the right of alienability emerges as the main characteristic of privatization. In practice it represents a loosening of responsibility of the holder (*e.g.* for providing labor services, or paying taxes or fees). At the same time, the alienability of land (and of personal freedom) *on a permanent and irrevocable basis* represents a dissolution of communal overrides (such as Clean Slates). The removal of such checks and balances tends to lead in time to monopolization of the land and other natural resources, even of water.

Prof. Dandamayev points out how striking it is that extreme polarization is not found in the Neo-Babylonian economy. Was this because strong rulers countered the emergence of strong economic powers outside of the palace (as he describes the large tax farmers)? Or because creditors found their own interest in leaving their debtors free, so as to extract yet more of a return? What was the secret here, in comparison to that of Greece and Italy?

Mesopotamia's need to generate export commodities, dependent as it was on an import trade to obtain metals and stone, and not initially marked by large inequalities of wealth among families, may suggest a motive for centering commercial handicraft enterprise in public institutions rather than in more visibly private households. It is a universal characteristic of public bureaucracies to create checks on personal gain-seeking. Privatization may be defined as a shifting of the balance in such a way as to dismantle these public checks.

If Mesopotamia's public institutions were administered by leading family heads, then it was these individuals, or new rivals (including warlords pressing in from outside the core) who became the dominant figures in a privatization dynamic that probably took as long to unfold as the preceding development of public or pan-familial enterprise. It is logical to surmise that both the elaboration of temples and their subsequent privatization were alternative strategies for ambitious family heads. Inasmuch as ambition is a constant human trait, we may view the kinds of land-acquiring and entrepreneurial structures that the colloquium's members have discussed as representing variations on the theme of how to organize large numbers of people to create a surplus that the most powerful individuals will control in one way or another, at first by administering the means of production and finally by owning it in various degrees of personal autonomy.

What we see in antiquity is thus a "first version" of institutional administrators acting on their own behalf while sanctimoniously cloaking their gains as being public spirited. Checks and balances were developed to keep the balance within bounds, but in the end private self-seeking emerged dominant, having historical momentum on its side. Still, the symbiosis between public and private persists even today. Social costs are financed by public taxes to provide benefits taken by individual wealth-holders.

Royal families, head-men and other public officials as the primordial privatizers

If control of public institutions starts at the top of the social pyramid, then it may be said that privatization also occurs first at the top, by individuals in the palace regime or otherwise well connected: the ruler himself, then royal collectors foreclosing on hitherto communal land (and by the Middle Bronze Age, tribal chieftains taking over temples for their own families).

Colloquium members who addressed the topic agreed that the key criterion making land and other property "private" was its alienability. The right to sell land or pledge it as collateral can be viewed not only as opening up opportunities for gain by the well-to-do, but as a stripping away of protection against the loss of self-support for families living on the edge of poverty. The wealthy person's gain is achieved at the expense of the poor, not necessarily in a *quid pro quo*, especially where debt foreclosure or forceful occupation of public lands are concerned. Privatization thus tended from the outset to go hand in hand with economic polarization as communal overrides were dissolved against undue alienation of the land, and its concentration in the hands of the rich and powerful (including kings).

Individuals at the top of the social pyramid broke "free" of the traditional obligations of tribal chieftains to support their clients and supporters. The tendency was to act for their own families, with fewer social checks, balances and responsibilities attached to their wealth. But it also was from the top of the social pyramid that many reformers emerged, including kings such as Josiah of Judah and Sparta's Agis and Cleomenes, as well as Solon of Athens as *archon*, followed by the Peisistratids and Cleisthenes after a series of well-born reformer-tyrants had emerged in other Greek cities to cancel debts and redistribute the land.

To be sure, rulers had a self-interest in alleviating poverty quite apart from how deeply they may have felt a conviction to promote social equity. To have permitted cultivators to lose their lands to creditor-merchants would have meant giving up the obligations of these small-holders to provide corvée labor and serve in the army, while permitting an oligarchy to build up its economic power at the expense of the palace.

Prof. Edzard's paper shows that the ruler's public and private *personae* were so closely intertwined that "private" ownership, in the sense of personal autonomy from communal checks, emerged first and foremost within the palace. Of course, rulers sought to override self-seeking by *other* families. Their success no doubt varied between strong and weak rulers, and from one time and region to another. What is ironic is that it was the imperial ambitions of Hammurapi that led him to delegate authority to local leaders in exchange for their military support. This was the inception of "feudalism." Inevitably, headmen sought to hold onto the local economic surplus for themselves rather than pass it on to the palace.

As local headmen (*lugals* in a smaller-scale "privatized" capacity) became creditors, they appropriated the lands of royal soldiers, typically by lending money or seizing the land for various types of debt arrears. Rulers countered by "restoring order" with Clean Slates: Babylonia's *mišarum* acts, Sumerian *amargi*, Akkadian *andurārum*, and probably also Hurrian *šudutu* and the Biblical Jubilee Year as a principle that passed out of the hands of kings into those of religious leaders.

If rulers constrained private self-seeking, the force of tradition is likewise seen limiting royal economic power. The story of the Israelite king Ahab coveting Naboth's vineyard represents one of the best-known examples of rulers appropriating the land of their subjects. Colloquium participants also noted the appropriate complementary passages of Saul's warnings about the dangers of kingship as exemplifying this kind of abuse. The important point of such stories is that rulers were constrained to operate within the bounds of popular tradition, which dictated that kings could obtain property only by voluntary sale or by confiscating it as punishment for a capital crime (*viz.* Prof. Levine's paper).

More than a thousand years earlier, Sargon and his Akkadian successors took over southern Mesopotamia. The first land transactions on record are those bought by these rulers, probably using tribute money for their initial acquisitions. No doubt royal appropriation of land within the ruler's own community was circumscribed by traditional norms of behavior, leaving the conquest of foreign lands as the major "state" acquisition that rulers could keep for their own account or delegate to their companions. This association between foreign conquest and royal land ownership is seen down through imperial Roman times. Should it be called "privatization," or a transfer of property within the public sphere?

The discussions following each paper have brought out the extent to which ancient terminology and iconography remain a kind of intellectual Rorschach test reflecting the interpreter's preconceptions. Even the ostensible symbols of "rule" remain controversial. Was the attribute of a ruler his ruling-stock to measure out his city's sacred precincts as a model of a straight and well-ordered *kosmos*, or was it merely a club? Was the "ring" a measuring rope to complement the ruler, or a nose-ring to lead the people like cattle? Modern interpretations tend to polarize among these two extremes: measured public images signifying the ruler's role in sponsoring equity on the one hand, or force and unregulated *hubris* on the other.

This iconographic problem is not merely one of art-historical interest. It reflects the guiding spirit that shaped society's economic structures, particularly in the "restorations of order" as one of equity. Inasmuch as royal gifts seem also to have reverted to their former status after such proclamations, it was these acts that represented early antiquity's response to privatization's tendency to result in what was perceived to be undue concentration of wealth, above all by monopolizing the land.

Differing degrees of royal overrides to economic polarization

Each region examined at this colloquium exhibits a common economic phenomenon, although not all members thought that it should be called privatization. As creditors and merchants appropriated the land, they did not take responsibility for providing the corvée labor, military or tax obligations of its former holders. Indeed, such service would have been impossible for large land-acquirers such as Tehip-Tilla of Nuzi. His archive shows him to have acquired hundreds of subsistence-land parcels, typically by getting himself adopted as heir by cultivators in exchange for a money payment or loan. If rulers were to maintain their fiscal revenue on lands transferred in such a manner, the gap would have to be made up by more intense levies on the remaining sectors of local landed communities.

Was this merely a case of large owners appropriating the lands of smaller ones *within* the "private" sector, or an extension of the privatization dynamic by absentee owners, often basing their status in the public institutions, stripping "communal" subsistence land — or royal land designated for the support of soldiers — away from its customary holders and breaking free of royal checks? The latter formulation views privatization essentially as absentee ownership in contrast with the tradition of owner-occupancy.

Prof. Maidman finds that the model which Igor Diakonoff developed for Sumer and Babylonia is not applicable to Nuzi, and that Jankowska's application of this model is generally perceived to be anachronistic. He thus finds in Nuzi a sharp contrast to Babylonia's property structures and traditions, and points out that only the palace and the "private" sector appear in Nuzi's records. "Communal" property as such is not involved, for all property already is held privately. The debt dynamics that appear in Babylonia, characteristically as appropriations by royal officials taking subsistence lands assigned to infantrymen owing *ilku* and *biltu* obligations, appear in Nuzi partly as royal gifts, but mainly as a debt polarization between smallholders and large absentee creditors such as Tehip-Tilla.

But Prof. Hallo's question remains open. If there was not what Prof. Buccellati calls "tensional force" of communal traditions, then why was there a need to use the loophole of "fictive adoptions" to convey land titles? Prof. Maidman sees this simply as a vestigial anachronism, an archaic literary *topos* that has lost whatever meaning it may originally have had. But such a stratagem suggests the need to circumvent some constraint on alienating subsistence land out of one's own family. If such a constraint existed, it would imply the prior existence of kinship-based landholding bodies. The land being alienated to Tehip-Tilla and other large landowners would be passing out of these landed family groupings.

Who then *is* Tehip-Tilla, and how did he get his power? What is his public status? Did he have his own army of supporters, perhaps as clients? If Jankowska is incorrect in identifying him as a military commander, is he simply a wealthy person? How did he get his money in the first place? What is his relation to the palace, or for that matter, to the men who adopted him and bequeathed their land to him and his own heirs? Most important of all, on what basis did they sue Tehip-Tilla or his heirs to recover their land?

These questions touch on the very character of Nuzi society. It seems to have been a unique character, a military regime overlayering a local populace and its own institutions, but whose rulers emulated the more public-spirited formalities found in the Babylonian core. In any case, it exemplifies the axiom that all economies are "mixed economies," each in their own way.

One may ask whether Nuzi's *šudutu* proclamations may be akin to those in, say, Byzantium, where some emperors announced pro-debtor legislation largely to undercut the rising power of local warlords? Prof. Maidman's paper throws down the gauntlet, so to speak, by finding no evidence that Nuzi's real estate *šudutu* acts actually were obeyed in practice. Examining property records by Nuzi's large landholders, he finds that although rulers proclaimed Clean Slates (*šudutu*) in the 16th and 15th centuries BC, they seem to have been unable to obtain compliance by the large absentee owners. At least, large private holdings composed of parcels obtained from diverse groups of cultivators survived intact for time periods which span such proclamations. The inference is that royal authority was too weak to enforce itself, so that Tehip-Tilla and other large land appropriators were able to act independently of the palace. Yet at a point these grandees disappear from the record. What happened? The dynamic seems to have been highly unstable.

Is the idea of communal equity an anachronistic modernism? Or does the practice of false adoptions hint at an originally communal state of affairs? Prof. Maidman concludes that Nuzian traditions were essentially private, and that Mesopotamian-type Clean Slates were adopted merely as royal formalities that had lost the substance of legally enforceable practices. Yet we find lawsuits over them similar to those documented in Babylonia. At the very least it appears that Nuzi was an economy in a state of flux. The question is, from what to what?

How broadly should "privatization" be defined?

The discussions reflect how the colloquium's participants are more able to agree on the details that constitute a phenomenon (such as the *ilku* and *biltum* obligations found in Babylonia and Nuzi giving way in the face of absentee ownership) than on just what to call it. At issue is the extent to which "public" or "private" property and obligations are being referred to. Repeatedly in the papers and their discussion, the terminological problem has arisen as to whether Bronze Age property holders/occupiers "possessed" their lands as modern owners, or merely "occupied" them.

Looking back from today's vantage point, privatization connotes not only an appropriation of land, enterprise and credit in the hands of individual families, but a *concentration* of ownership. Privatized modes of centralization find their counterpart in a general economic *polarization*, with dependency and loss of self-sufficiency on the land for a substantial part of the population. Much of the land appropriated by absentee owners, for instance, was royal land designated for the support of soldiers. Royal collectors and other mercantile individuals extended credit (or established other interest-bearing claims) on these individuals, and collateralized these obligations by the debtor's land-rights and even his personal freedom. In this respect privatization was antithetical to royal interests, especially as local officials, merchants, war chiefs or other powerful men used their economic power to form a political base against the ruler.

This early absentee ownership occurred long before the idea of self-adjusting, freely price-setting markets. Privatization dynamics produced symbiotic, mixed systems, if only because they were an adaptation of structures that went before. Privatization thus represents not only a step forward, but also a breaking away. Nearly every participant in these discussions has alluded to the role of general breakdown in the privatization process. Profs. Edzard and Mitchell, for instance, note how the destruction of records (mirroring the parallel collapse of public authority) facilitated personal encroachments on the communal or public domain, culminating in the seizure of Rome's *ager publicus* by armed bands, only later sanctified by laws legitimizing *occupatio* as *possessio*. (Does this mean that "privatization" emerges only at the point where formal "possession" is legalized? Mitchell points to Rome's legendary King Servius as changing the land's legal status, just as he created the oligarchic Roman constitution by giving electoral weight to the wealthiest classes.)

If record-keeping is a characteristic of public undertakings, the loss (or absence) of property records opens the way for a free-for-all. It is characteristic of economies lacking public sectors, especially in Dark Age periods of economic and military breakdown. Stated another way, if one of the innovations of public institutions was record keeping, then the destruction of records and cessation of record-keeping certainly tended to facilitate the crudest form of "primitive privatization" (if this term can be suggested as an analogue to Marx's "primitive accumulation"). This is much what happened in Babylonia after 1595 BC and Mycenaean Greece after 1200 BC. It is in such periods that local administrators find no strong power above them, and break away. Military force often becomes the major shaping influence in such situations.

How broadly, then, should the term "privatization" be conceptualized? Should it include as a natural corollary the monopolization of the land by absentee owners, attested throughout the course of antiquity in nearly every region? Is this economic polarization an inherent part of the privatization phenomenon, or merely part of the private sector's own internal dynamics? And what of the privatization of credit, breaking free from royal oversight and its Clean Slates?

It may be relevant to note that antiquity experienced a fiscal crisis not unlike those of modern-day America and Britain, Latin America and the former Soviet sphere. Today's fiscal crisis is forcing further privatization in the form of a sell-off of publically owned assets. A similar phenomenon is seen in Rome after the Punic Wars at the end of the 3rd century BC. It seems to me (but not to all colloquium members) that this kind of debt and fiscal dynamic is part of a larger, overarching privatization dynamic — one which, in the end, included a transition from public reliance on self-armed citizen infantrymen to the hiring of mercenaries.

"Privatization" historically has been associated with absentee landlordship. A natural upshot has been that large land acquirers manage to shed the social obligations hitherto attached to their property by custom. This starves the public sector of revenue. The fiscal problem was aggravated by the fact that public sectors no longer were self-supporting, especially as industrial enterprise passed out of the large institutions (the Sumerian temples, emulated by palace workshops in northern Mesopotamia and the Levant) into private hands in the emerging oligarchies.

The social costs and benefits of privatization

Privatization brought in its train a lessened public responsibility to guarantee the means of self-support to the citizenry at large. It meant a loss of the customary freedom of citizen-cultivators and infantrymen from the threat of losing their land and their personal liberty on more than a temporary basis, that is, until the next Clean Slate was proclaimed. But Clean Slates became vestigial as the economic and military center moved northwest, up the Euphrates. By the late second millennium, as the economic innovations developed in the Mesopotamian core took root and flourished on the Phoenician shore of the Mediterranean, Clean Slates either are lacking in the commercial center of Ugarit (which Prof. Heltzer points out, to be sure, restricted the "freedom" of citizens to forfeit their land to foreclosing creditors, especially foreign merchants). But they are found in Israel, whose Jubilee Year redistributing the lands and cancelling consumer debts may represent an archaism used to counter privatization's tendency to lead to undue monopolization of landholding. This monopolization is denounced by biblical prophets such as Isaiah, and by Pliny complaining that *latifundia* had ruined Italy.

The irony is that although the Torah made the Jubilee Year a focal point of the Mosaic laws of Leviticus and Deuteronomy, and despite the fact that Jesus's initial sermon inaugurating his program at Nazareth's synagogue announced that he was bringing news of the Year of the Lord (that is, the Jubilee Year referred to in Isaiah 61, as related in Luke 4:16-30), modern Judeo-Christian religion has all but ignored the Bible's economic program as lacking relevance to the modern era. Yet on the verge of the transition from feudalism to modernity, Bernard Gilpin's 1552 sermon, quoted in my closing remarks, shows the force that such biblical traditions retained in the midst of Europe's peasant wars that followed discovery of the New World.

The monetary inflation that resulted from the influx of silver and gold during the course of the 16th century transformed traditional systems of land tenure, and hence the rural/urban and royal/aristocratic balance. Rising crop prices provided a powerful motive to appropriate land, whose revenue had languished since the plague depopulated much of Europe in the 14th century. In this new empire-building context the major form of privatization took the form of enclosing hitherto common lands, rack-renting its former customary tenants. Henry VIII seized England's monasteries, and was emulated not only by wealthy nobles seizing common land, but by economically aggressive middling families. And as the enclosure movement gained momentum during the course of the 16th century, Roman legal traditions were drawn upon to rewrite common law into a more modern, property-based law. Once again, *occupation* was legitimized as *possession*, in the New World as in the Old.

Still, the spirit of the Israelite laws found an echo in the highest ranks of European religion and royalty. Such men as Bernard Gilpin were not radicals criticizing from outside England's social center. The official prayer from Edward VI's prayer book recalls the spirit of the great Old Testament prophets:

> We heartily pray thee to send thy holy Spirit into the hearts of them that possess the grounds and dwelling places of the earth, that they, remembering themselves to be thy tenants, may not rack and stretch out the rents of their houses and lands, nor yet take unreasonable fines and incomes after the manner of covetous worldlings but let them out to other, that the inhabitants thereof may both be able to pay the rents, and also honestly to live, to nourish their families, and to relieve the poor. . . .

These ideas reflected the Mosaic laws enjoining the Israelites not to dispossess their brethren or charge them usury, "For remember, ye are all tenants in the land." The critique of usury would play a major role in the theology of Martin Luther and his contemporaries who identified usury and foreclosure with theft, and hence with breaking the Eighth Commandment: "Thou shalt not steal."

But we all know how matters worked out. Medieval Europe's royal appropriations occurred much as in antiquity, by military seizure. Kings granted huge tracts of land in the conquered European and New World territories to their companions, often for a pittance. The new democracies would follow suit with their own land grants, capped by those to the railroad robber barons in the 19th century. Meanwhile, summarizes Francis Nielson (1944:306), already by the reign of Charles II, "the landlords succeeded in shifting their burdens from their shoulders and began the process of placing them upon those of the poor. Indirect taxation in the form of excise duties was introduced . . ." This shift of taxation away from landlords and creditors to sales taxes, excise taxes and import duties (and finally, modern income taxes, which typically exempt real-estate rent and capital gains) is simply a continuation of the historical drive towards privatization, whose first three thousand years are described in this colloquium's papers.

By reviewing the dynamics set in motion by privatization of the land, industry and credit in early societies, this colloquium has focused on the single most important dynamic of ancient civilization, and indeed of its decline as well. The economic imbalances associated with privatization shaped each society's ideological and even religious responses. In this broad sense, the colloquium has laid a foundation for placing privatization at the center of history's cultural as well as economic laws of motion. It has shown that the particular way in which the land and other resources are privatized — and the checks and balances to which this privatization is subject (or not subject) — has shaped the balance between freedom or slavery, the distribution of wealth and income, the pattern of urbanization, and ultimately the economic destiny of civilization.

Privatization thus represents more than just a shift in ownership from public to individual absentee holders; it connotes a shift of social burdens away from land onto the shoulders of the population at large, in the form of excise taxes, poll taxes or monopoly pricing and other burdensome levies which find their counterpart in spending to strengthen the social position of absentee landlords and creditors, intensifying the rate of economic polarization.

If this is an inexorable law of history, is it all to the good, or not? This colloquium has established that economic rationalizations of privatization came much later than the surreptitious appropriation and seizure by force that represent the first forms of privatization. An obvious reason why no ideological rationale appeared was that society at large did not in fact benefit. We therefore may ask in whose interest privatization *was*. When land passed into private hands, what were the consequences?

Dispossession was one result. Debtors and other impoverished families were uprooted from the land by the well-to-do. Many of the dis- possessed had owed corvée labor and military services to the palace. When royal collectors or other creditors claimed this labor (along with the land's crop usufruct) as owed to themselves as interest on debt, the palace suffered — unless other community members made up the shortfall. This was one reason why, "in the beginning," private absentee ownership (that is, dispossession of customary tenants) was limited to only temporary duration, being subject to reversal by royal "economic order" proclamations restoring the *status quo ante*. However, as privatization became irreversible, it undercut social solidarity by hollowing out communities' traditional self-support system.

Regarding the impact of privatization on productivity, when absentee landlords removed the former tenants and invested capital in olive trees and grape vines, were the increased revenues taxed, or did taxes lag behind output on these wealthy plantations? Was the land appropriated by the best-placed families removed from its traditional role of providing subsistence to citizens who contributed corvée labor services to the palace and were subject to the military draft? What were the economic consequences of displacing the former cultivators from the land, and changing the character of rural labor from free to slave status by Roman times? Was this not part and parcel of ancient privatization? In posing these questions, this colloquium has defined a new research agenda.

These questions go beyond the scope of the present conference, to be sure, but the dynamics that have been described provide an object lesson for today's world. At issue is the idea of economic efficiency on the broadest level. The immediate consequence of England's enclosures replacing men and their families with sheep from the 16th to 18th centuries, for instance, was a rural exodus to the cities, creating a pool of pauperized potential wage-labor. This poverty became an important factor contributing to the Industrial Revolution. But nothing like this occurred in antiquity. If there was scant wage-labor, it was because mody families were self-supporting on the land. Dispossessed families had little option but to join roving bands or become mercenaries. Temple labor forces were composed mainly of individuals that could not support themselves on the land for physical reasons — infirmity, or having lost their husbands or fathers through war or natural causes such as disease — not because they belonged to a dispossessed class of wage labor as such. As for the urban poor, they were more a mob than a productive labor force. Productivity was still centered on the land, mainly in the great-family households.

Will today's resource owners and lenders act much differently from those of antiquity? Are landlords and creditors inherently more efficient than public agencies in overseeing society's land, natural resources and other means of production? Will they invest their revenue productively to bring new productive powers into being? Or will they merely strip assets in foreclosure proceedings and distress sell-offs, while manoeuvering to shed their tax obligations and thereby create a fiscal crisis, as has occurred so often over the millennia?

As a legacy of the conquest by feudal European powers, many third world countries now find themselves plunged into a chronic debt crisis largely as a result of having created great export-oriented *latifundia* in the hands of a relatively few owners. The result is that these lands are not used to grow domestic food crops and provide the widespread land tenure that characterized the most successful economic upsweeps of the periods this colloquium has discussed. As third world countries have become food-dependent, their balance-of-payments deficits have widened, and been financed by running deeply into foreign debt. They now are being forced to pay these debts by selling to private buyers their remaining public lands and resources, public utilities and transport systems. This colloquium has begun to show the extent to which such consequences of privatization represent invariants throughout history.